17th International Conference Information Systems 2024

Held at MCCSIS 2024

Porto, Portugal
9-11 March 2024

Editors:

Miguel B. Nunes
Pedro Isaías
Philip Powell
Luís Rodrigues

ISBN: 979-8-3313-0140-8

Printed from e-media with permission by:

Curran Associates, Inc.
57 Morehouse Lane
Red Hook, NY 12571

Some format issues inherent in the e-media version may also appear in this print version.

International Association for Development of the Information Society (IADIS)
Rua Sao Sebastiao Da Pedreira
No. 100, 30, 1050-209
Lisbon, Portugal

Phone: 351 21 3151373
Fax: 351 21 3151244

secretariat@iadis.org

Additional copies of this publication are available from:

Curran Associates, Inc.
57 Morehouse Lane
Red Hook, NY 12571 USA
Phone: 845-758-0400
Fax: 845-758-2633
Email: curran@proceedings.com
Web: www.proceedings.com

17th IADIS INTERNATIONAL CONFERENCE

INFORMATION SYSTEMS 2024

PROCEEDINGS OF THE 17th IADIS INTERNATIONAL CONFERENCE

INFORMATION SYSTEMS 2024

9 - 11 MARCH, 2024

Organised by

iadis

international association for development of the information society

As a member of Crossref (a non-profit membership organization for scholarly publishing working with the purpose to make content easy to find, link, cite and assess) each published paper in this book of proceedings will be allocated a DOI (Digital Object Identifier) number for its fast and easy citation and indexation.

Edited by Miguel Baptista Nunes, Pedro Isaías and Philip Powell

Associate Editor: Luís Rodrigues

TABLE OF CONTENTS

FOREWORD ix

PROGRAM COMMITTEE xi

KEYNOTE LECTURE xiii

KEYNOTE PAPER

DECODING DECISION MAKING: AI SENSEMAKING AND THE AUTHENTICITY DILEMMA IN IS STRATEGY xv
Ashok Jashapara

FULL PAPERS

ANALYSIS OF INDUSTRY 4.0 TECHNOLOGIES' ADOPTION USING INTERPRETIVE STRUCTURAL MODELLING 3
Sevgi Özkan Yıldırım and Omer Ozturk

CRITICAL SUCCESS FACTORS OF BUSINESS MODEL INNOVATION TO TAKE ADVANTAGE OF DISRUPTIVE TECHNOLOGIES: A STRUCTURED LITERATURE REVIEW 11
Mikhail David Edwards and Hanlie Smuts

CONTEXT-AWARE SHIPBUILDING KNOWLEDGE RECOMMENDATION: EXPLOITING KNOWLEDGE GRAPHS WITH DIFFERENT STRUCTURE 21
Bo Song, Qiao Zhou and Zuhua Jiang

DESIGN REQUIREMENTS FOR HYBRID COLLABORATION IN THE REALM OF CREATIVE GROUP WORK 29
Pia Gebbing and Christoph Lattemann

WELL-BEING AND LIFE STAGES IN DIGITAL WORK ENVIRONMENTS 37
Maximilian Helms, Julia Bosbach, Pia Gebbing, Audris Umel and Christoph Lattemann

BEHAVIOURAL RESEARCH IN MANAGING INFORMATION TECHNOLOGY: A SYSTEMATIC LITERATURE REVIEW 45
Mark van der Pas, Jannika Leckebusch and Max Schrijen

ON THE APPLICATION OF STATIC CODE ANALYSIS TOOLS IN THE SERBIAN IT INDUSTRY: AN EMPIRICAL STUDY 53
Aleksa Komosar, Sara Kijanovic, Vladimir Mandic, Danilo Nikolic and Teodora Vuckovic

A GREY WOLF ALGORITHM FOR INDEX OPTIMIZATION IN RELATIONAL DATABASES 61
Fernando Verástegui, Rony Cueva and Manuel Tupia

A CAPABILITY SYSTEM PERSPECTIVE TO CONCEPTUALIZE A BUSINESS MODEL 69
Mikko H. Hirvonen

INSTANTIATION OF ONTOUML MODELS IN MULTI-LABELED GRAPH DATABASES 78
Jaroslav Pokorný, Zdeněk Rybola, Michal Valenta, Jiří Zikán and Robert Pergl

TOWARDS AN ARTIFICIAL INTELLIGENCE PROJECT METHODOLOGY WITH AN INTEGRATIVE APPROACH TO DELIVER INNOVATIVE SOLUTIONS 87
Nilo Sergio Maziero Petrin, Henrique Cordeiro Mariano and João Carlos Néto

ATTAINING SCIENTIFIC RIGOUR IN SOCIO-TECHNICAL RESEARCH WITH HUSSERL'S DESCRIPTIVE PHENOMENOLOGY 95
Gianni Jacucci

UTILIZING STRATIFIED SYSTEMS THEORY TO OPTIMIZE WORKFORCE ALLOCATION FOR SUSTAINABLE QUALITY DELIVERY IN DEVOPS TEAMS: A CASE STUDY 106
Hanlie Smuts, Paul Louw, Danie Smit, Ingo Waechter and Vanessa Sardinha-da Silva

INCREASING TIME REGISTRATION IN AN AGILE ENVIRONMENT THROUGH NUDGING IN HUMAN-COMPUTER INTERACTION 116
Max Schrijen, Mark van der Pas and Ksenia Podoynitsyna

SHORT PAPERS

INVESTIGATING SOFTWARE DEVELOPMENT BUSINESS PROCESSES USING SOFT SYSTEMS METHODOLOGY 131
Gökçe Günaydın and Sevgi Özkan Yıldırım

SUSTAINABILITY TRACING FOR COMPANIES: GOVERNANCE, REGULATION, ECONOMICAL AND ETHICAL CONSIDERATIONS 136
Galena Pisoni, Bálint Molnár, Szabolcs Korba and Maria Moloney

TOWARD INTEGRATED DISASTER PREVENTION AND MITIGATION SYSTEM LINKING DISASTER INFORMATION COLLECTION AND PROPERTY DAMAGE SIMULATION 141
Toshihiro Osaragi, Noriaki Hirokawa and Maki Kishimoto

RETHINKING THE CENTRALIZATION OF IT GOVERNANCE: VOICES OF SENIORS FROM A LARGE TECHNOLOGY ORGANIZATION 147
Burcin Sari and Sevgi Özkan Yıldırım

IMPACTS OF DIGITAL–HEALTH LITERACY AND HELPING BEHAVIORS ON SPORTS AND RECREATION-RELATED INJURY PREVENTION IN SENIOR CITIZENS 153
Terence Kam-Ho Chau, Ron Chi-Wai Kwok and Jessica Choi-Fung Cheung

ORGANIZATIONAL CULTURE AND DIGITAL RESILIENCE: COMPETING VALUES PERSPECTIVE 158
Anita Neumannova

AGILE IT MANAGEMENT: DEVOPS ADOPTION IN THE FINANCE INDUSTRY 163
Lars Günthardt, Rehmil Sabani, Simon Bärtschi and Mike Krey

DATA LITERACY MEASUREMENTS: A SYSTEMATIC LITERATURE REVIEW 169
Aleksa Komosar, Sara Koprivica, Davide Taibi, Aleksandar Ivic, Darko Stefanovic and Sara Kijanovic

REDUCING COMPLEXITY BY USING LINGUISTIC SUMMARIES FOR BUSINESS INTELLIGENCE REPORTING 174
Galena Pisoni, Erika Mináriková, Miroslav Hudec, Hanna Kristin Skaftadottir, Bálint Molnár, Miljan Vučetić and Denisa Sedláková

OVERVIEW OF USAGE OF OPEN GOVERNMENT DATA IN BUILDING MACHINE LEARNING AND AI SOLUTIONS: A SYSTEMATIC LITERATURE REVIEW 179
Sara Kijanovic, Sara Koprivica, Davide Taibi, Aleksandar Ivic, Darko Stefanovic and Aleksa Komosar

IS CAPABILITY DRIVEN BUSINESS VALUE FOR SOUTH AFRICAN FINANCIAL SERVICE PROVIDERS FROM DIGITAL TRANSFORMATION PERSPECTIVE IN EMERGING ECONOMIES 184
Michael Makgale Modiba and Raymond Mompoloki Kekwaletswe

REFLECTION PAPERS

DEBUNKING THE MYTH OF CRYPTO ASSETS AS FINANCIAL INNOVATION: UNPACKING THE FALLOUT FROM THE CRYPTO WINTER 193
Wendy L. Currie and Jonathan J. M. Seddon

WHAT ARE WE TALKING ABOUT WHEN WE TALK ABOUT DIGITAL RESILIENCE? 197
Everist Limaj

INTEGRATING CHATGPT DEVELOPMENT WITH JSON IN INFORMATION SYSTEMS EDUCATION 201
Ming Wang

AUTHOR INDEX

FOREWORD

These proceedings contain the papers of the 17th IADIS International Conference Information Systems 2024, which was organised by the International Association for Development of the Information Society in Porto, Portugal, during 9 – 11 March 2024.

The IADIS Information Systems Conference 2024 aims to provide a forum for the discussion of IS taking a socio-technological perspective. It aims to address the issues related to design, development and use of IS in organisations from a socio-technological perspective, as well as to discuss IS professional practice, research and teaching. A set of key areas has been identified. However, these do not aim at being prescriptive, or set in stone, and any innovative contributions that do not fit into these areas have also been considered.

The following main tracks have been object of paper submissions:

- IS in Practice, Technology Infrastructures and Organisational Processes
- IS Design, Development and Management Issues and Methodologies
- IS Professional Issues
- IS Research
- IS Learning and Teaching

The IADIS Information Systems Conference 2024 had 94 submissions from more than 20 countries. Each submission has been anonymously reviewed by an average of 4 independent reviewers, to ensure the final high standard of the accepted submissions. Out of the papers submitted, 14 got blind referee ratings that published them as full papers, which means that the acceptance rate was 15%. Some other submissions were published as short and reflection papers. Extended versions of the best papers will be selected to be published in the IADIS Journal on Computer Science and Information Systems (ISSN: 1646-3692) indexed by Emerging Sources Citation Index by Thomson Reuters and also in the Journal of Electronic Commerce in Organizations (JECO) (ISSN: 1539-2937).

The conference, besides the papers' presentations, also includes a keynote presentation from an internationally distinguished researcher. We wish to thank Professor Ashok Jashapara, Royal Holloway – University of London, School of Business & Management, Egham, United Kingdom, for accepting our invitation as keynote speaker.

As we all know, a conference requires the effort of many individuals and this year we faced a new challenge that brought us more together. We would like to thank all members of the Program Committee for their hard work in reviewing and selecting the papers that appear in the book of the proceedings. We would also like to thank all the authors who have submitted their papers to this conference. We wish to thank all members of our organizing committee.

Last but not the least, we hope that everybody enjoyed the presentations and we invite all participants for the next year edition of the IADIS International Conference on Information Systems.

Philip Powell, University of London, UK
Conference Chair

Miguel Baptista Nunes, Xi'an Jiaotong-Liverpool University, China
Pedro Isaias, Information Systems & Technology Management School, The University of New South Wales, Australia
Program Co-Chairs

March 2024

PROGRAM COMMITTEE

CONFERENCE CHAIR

Professor Philip Powell, University of London, UK

PROGRAM CO-CHAIRS

Miguel Baptista Nunes, Xi'an Jiaotong-Liverpool University, China
Pedro Isaias, Information Systems & Technology Management School, The University of New South Wales, Australia

COMMITTEE MEMBERS

Ali-Reza Montazemi, Mcmaster University, Canada
Amelia Badica, University of Craiova, Romania
Betim Cico, Epoka University, Tirana, Albania
Binshan Lin, Louisiana State University Shreveport (LSUS), USA
Brian Thoms, California State University, USA
Carlos Medina, Technological University of Panama, Panama
Christos Kalloniatis, University of the Aegean, Greece
David G. Rosado, University of Castilla-la Mancha, Spain
Demetrios Sarantis, United Nations University, Portugal
Dimitar Trajanov, Ss Cyril and Methodius University, Macedonia
Dimitrios Buhalis, Bournemouth University, United Kingdom
Dimitris Kardaras, Athens University of Economics and Business, Greece
Eddie Soulier, Université de Technologie de Troyes, France
Efthimios Tambouris, University of Macedonia, Greece
Fernando Arias, Technological University of Panama, Panama
Gabriele De Vito, University of Salerno, Italy
Giacomo Vella, Politecnico Di Milano School of Management, Italy
Hans-Peter Steinbacher, University of Applied Sciences, Austria
Hisham Al-Mubaid, University of Houston, USA
Hussein Al-Yaseen, Al-Ahliyya Amman University, Jordan
Ina Kayser, IST-Hochschule, University of Applied Sciences, Germany
Iyad Zoukar, Higher Institute of Applied Sciences and Technology, Syria
James Thong, HKUST Business School, Hong Kong
Jeffrey Parsons, Memorial University of Newfoundland, Canada
Kamel Rouibah, Kuwait University, Kuwait
Karsten Boehm, University of Applied Sciences, Austria
Kevin Grant, University of Stirling, United Kingdom
Khalid EL KHADIRI, Chouaib Doukkali University, Morocco
Leandro Antonelli, Lifia, Universidad Nacional de la Plata, Argentina
Lorna Uden, Staffordshire University, United Kingdom
Luis Mendoza Pittí, Universidad Tecnológica de Panamá, Panama
Luis Enrique Sánchez Crespo, University of Castilla-la Mancha, Spain
Majid Alsubaie, University of Canberra, Saudi Arabia

KEYNOTE LECTURE

DECODING DECISION MAKING: AI SENSEMAKING AND THE AUTHENTICITY DILEMMA IN IS STRATEGY

by Professor Ashok Jashapara
Royal Holloway – University of London
School of Business & Management, United Kingdom

Abstract

The paper explores the strategic implications of generative AI in organizations. It starts with an overview of AI's evolution, highlighting the rise of machine learning, deep learning, and General Adversarial Networks. The paper emphasizes generative AI's transformative role across various sectors while noting the challenges of biases and fake content generation.

The paper introduces the 'Authenticity Dilemma' framework, advocating a knowledge-based approach for strategic AI integration. This framework focuses on AI capabilities in decision-making and sensemaking, distinguishing between authentic and fake processes. The paper presents four levels of strategic positioning – Smoke Screen, Echo Chamber, Chameleon, and Greenhouse – illustrating different organizational approaches to AI application.

In summary, the paper provides a framework for understanding and navigating the complexities of AI in organizational strategy. While offering valuable insights, the paper also acknowledges potential limitations in oversimplifying decision-making complexities and defining 'authentic' versus 'fake' AI applications.

Keynote Paper

DECODING DECISION MAKING: AI SENSEMAKING AND THE AUTHENTICITY DILEMMA IN IS STRATEGY

Ashok Jashapara
Royal Holloway – University of London
School of Business & Management, Egham, Surrey TW20 0EX, United Kingdom

ABSTRACT

The paper explores the strategic implications of generative AI in organizations. It starts with an overview of AI's evolution, highlighting the rise of machine learning, deep learning, and General Adversarial Networks. The paper emphasizes generative AI's transformative role across various sectors while noting the challenges of biases and fake content generation.

The paper introduces the 'Authenticity Dilemma' framework, advocating a knowledge-based approach for strategic AI integration. This framework focuses on AI capabilities in decision-making and sensemaking, distinguishing between authentic and fake processes. The paper presents four levels of strategic positioning - Smoke Screen, Echo Chamber, Chameleon, and Greenhouse - illustrating different organizational approaches to AI application.

In summary, the paper provides a framework for understanding and navigating the complexities of AI in organizational strategy. While offering valuable insights, the paper also acknowledges potential limitations in oversimplifying decision-making complexities and defining 'authentic' versus 'fake' AI applications.

KEYWORDS

Generative AI, IS Strategy, Sensemaking, Decision Making, ChatGPT

1. INTRODUCTION

The concept of artificial intelligence began in the 1950s with the work of pioneers such as Alan Turing and John McCarthy. This developed into the emergence of machine learning where algorithms learnt from data. Increased computational power and data availability led to breakthrough in deep learning in 2010s particularly through deep neural networks that propelled AI forward. In 2014, the development of General Adversarial Networks (GANs) by Ian Goodfellow and his colleagues (2014) was a landmark. GANs involved two neural networks contesting each other to generate new instances of data. Subsequently, the introduction of models such as Transformers improved natural language processing that led to development of more sophisticated generative models. Such models have had a transformative effect on organizations.

Generative AI is being used to create personalized content from marketing emails to targeted ads. AI models can generate new product designs, simulate performance and optimize manufacturing processes. Similarly, drug discovery and development has been expedited using such models. Chatbots and virtual assistants have gained greater prominence providing more natural and context aware interactions. Financial advice has been tailored to experiences of individual users (Dowling and Lucey 2023). Strategically, AI models have generated scenarios and forecasts to aid the strategic planning process.

Despite the significant benefits accrued by generative AI, it has been strategically problematic in organizations. AI systems perpetuate and amplify biases in the training data. This can lead to discriminatory outcomes in recruitment, lending and customer service. More problematic is the ability of AI models to create realistic fake content such as deepfakes raising concerns about misinformation, fraud, and an erosion of trust on how organizations can use such digital content. There are privacy concerns as many generative AI models rely on large training datasets that include sensitive personal information in potential violation of GDPR regulations. Similarly, questions arise around ownership as the models may have been trained on copyrighted materials.

While generative AI offers transformative potential for businesses, it is accompanied by a host of challenges that need careful strategic consideration. No previous studies has analyzed the strategic dimension of generative AI or its impact on organizational effectiveness and innovation (Korzynski et al. 2023).

Strategically, we adopt the knowledge-based view in this paper arguing that knowledge is the most important asset in any firm. We build on historical advances in information systems strategy from data processing to management information systems, strategic information systems and IS capabilities (Ferlie et al. 2015). We further develop this trajectory to mobilize knowledge by developing the 'Authenticity Dilemma' framework that advances the importance of two principal AI capabilities needed in the changing global environment; organizational decision making (authentic and fake) and AI sensemaking.

2. KNOWLEDGE BASED VIEW OF FIRM

The Industrial Organization (IO) perspective of strategy, rooted in the structure-conduct-performance paradigm, emphasizes the importance of industry structure in determining firm strategy and performance. It posits that competitive advantage is primarily derived from the external environment. However, this view is often criticized for its overemphasis on external factors, neglecting the internal capabilities and unique resources of firms. It assumes a relatively static environment and often fails to account for rapid changes and innovations in the market such as generative AI.

In contrast, the Resource Based View (RBV) focuses on the internal resources and capabilities of a firm as the primary sources of competitive advantage. This perspective argues that firms are heterogeneous in terms of the resources they control, and these differences can lead to sustainable competitive advantages. The RBV's emphasis on unique resources - tangible and intangible - allows firms to develop strategies that are more tailored to their specific strengths and weaknesses. This internal focus provides a more dynamic approach to strategy, enabling firms to adapt and evolve in response to changes in the business environment (Pereira and Bamel 2021).

The Knowledge Based View (KBV) further extends the RBV by emphasizing knowledge as the most strategically significant resource of a firm. In today's information-driven economy, the ability to create, acquire, and leverage knowledge is crucial for maintaining competitive advantage. The KBV highlights the role of organizational learning, knowledge management, and innovation as key drivers of strategic success. Unlike the IO perspective, which is more static and externally focused, the KBV allows for a more adaptive, agile approach to strategy, reflecting the rapidly changing and knowledge-intensive nature of modern business environments (Singh et al. 2021).

Both the RBV and KBV offer significant advantages over the IO perspective by focusing on the internal strengths of a firm, advocating for a more dynamic and proactive approach to strategy. While the IO perspective provides valuable insights into the impact of industry structure and external forces, the RBV and KBV encourage firms to look inward and leverage their unique resources and knowledge. This internal focus is particularly relevant in today's fast-paced, innovation-driven business world, where adaptability and unique capabilities are key to sustaining competitive advantage.

While KBV emphasizes the strategic importance of knowledge within organizations, Artificial Intelligence (AI) sensemaking involves the use of advanced algorithms to interpret and derive meaningful insights from complex data sets. AI sensemaking, on the other hand, involves the application of AI technologies to analyze large and complex data sets, extracting patterns, trends, and insights that are not immediately apparent. This process enhances decision-making by providing a deeper, data-driven understanding of various aspects of the business environment. AI sensemaking tools can process information at a scale and speed far beyond human capabilities, leading to more informed and strategic decisions. It is this intersection of AI Sensemaking and organizational decision making that forms the basis of our proposed AI strategic framework as shown in Figure 1.

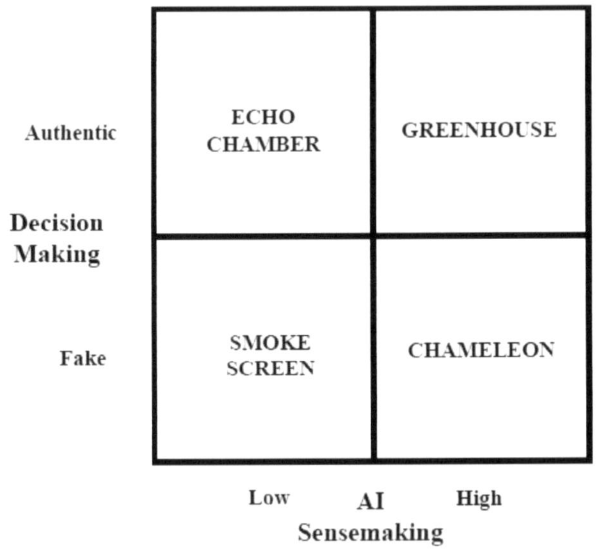

Figure 1. Authenticity Dilemma IS Strategy Framework

3. AI SENSEMAKING

Sensemaking is a process by which individuals or organizations interpret and create an understanding of the events, situations, or data they encounter. It involves constructing a narrative to make sense of the ambiguous, complex, or uncertain aspects of their environment. This process is inherently human and relies heavily on cognitive abilities like perception, interpretation, and the synthesis of information. In an organizational context, sensemaking is crucial for decision-making, strategy formulation, and adapting to change. It involves the collective pooling of insights, experiences, and knowledge of organizational members to navigate complex situations (Aguinis and Glavas 2019).

This includes understanding the significance of information within the context of past experiences, organizational culture and current circumstances. Stories provide a bridge to explain and give meaning to various events and data points. Social interaction becomes central through dialogue and discussion to shape a collective understanding (Christianson and Barton 2021).

AI sensemaking, in contrast, refers to the use of artificial intelligence technologies to analyze and interpret large volumes of data. Unlike human sensemaking, which is subjective and influenced by personal experiences and biases, AI sensemaking is based on algorithms and computational processes. It involves machine learning, data mining, and pattern recognition to identify trends, anomalies, and correlations in data sets that might not be apparent to human observers (Verganti, Vendraminelli, and Iansiti 2020).

This involves data processing vast amounts of data at volumes and speeds beyond human capability. Algorithms are used to detect patterns, trends and relationships within the data. Predictive analysis adopts statistical techniques and machine learning to make forecasts based on large volumes of data.

The primary difference between human and AI sensemaking lies in their approaches and capabilities. Human sensemaking is qualitative, context-rich, and narrative-driven, relying on cognitive and social processes. It excels in understanding the nuances of context, emotional undercurrents, and complex social dynamics. AI sensemaking, on the other hand, is quantitative, data-driven, and pattern-oriented. It excels in processing large data sets, identifying patterns, and making predictions based on statistical analysis.

Our conception of AI sensemaking does not see these two forms of sensemaking as mutually exclusive. They complement each other. AI can augment human decision making by providing comprehensive data analysis, while human sensemaking can add context, ethical considerations, and creative problem-solving to AI insights. Combining human and AI sensemaking bear significant synergies leading to more informed, nuanced and strategic decision making, leveraging the strengths of human insights and AI's analytical power (Schildt, Mantere, and Cornelissen 2020).

4. AI DECISION MAKING

The advent of generative AI has revolutionized the landscape of decision-making in organizations. This technology, capable of synthesizing and analyzing vast amounts of data, presents new opportunities and challenges in distinguishing between authentic and fake decision-making processes.

Authentic decision-making in the realm of generative AI is characterized by a genuine intent to leverage technology for insightful, ethical, and responsible outcomes (Newman, Fast, and Harmon 2020). It involves using AI to enhance human judgment, not replace it. In this paradigm, decisions are made with a clear understanding of the AI's capabilities and limitations, ensuring that the technology serves as a tool for augmenting human expertise and intuition. Authentic decision-making also prioritizes transparency, both in how AI algorithms function and in how decisions are derived from AI-generated insights. This transparency is crucial for maintaining trust among stakeholders and for the ethical use of AI (Vrontis et al. 2022).

Conversely, fake decision-making in the context of generative AI refers to the use of technology in a way that is deceptive, unethical, or solely for the sake of appearances. This might involve using AI as a facade to justify predetermined decisions or to give an illusion of innovation and modernity without a genuine commitment to these values. In fake decision-making, there is often a lack of transparency about how AI insights are generated and used, leading to decisions that may be biased, uninformed, or ethically questionable. This approach can erode trust and lead to strategic missteps, as the decisions are not grounded in a true understanding of AI's potential and limitations (Awan et al. 2021).

The distinction between authentic and fake decision-making in the context of generative AI has significant implications for organizations. Authentic decision-making can lead to more innovative, effective, and ethically sound strategies, enhancing the organization's competitiveness and reputation. It fosters a culture of trust and accountability, where AI is used as a force for good. On the other hand, fake decision-making can undermine an organization's integrity and lead to poor strategic outcomes. It can damage stakeholder trust and result in a misuse of AI capabilities, potentially causing harm or perpetuating biases (Abubakar et al. 2019).

5. INFORMATION SYSTEMS STRATEGY FRAMEWORK IN THE ERA OF GENERATIVE AI

As generative AI continues to transform the business landscape, the distinction between authentic and fake decision-making becomes increasingly critical. Organizations can choose either to understand and embrace the true potential of AI, using it to complement human decision-making processes or to act as a substitute or a smokescreen. By prioritizing authenticity, transparency, and ethical considerations in their use of AI, organizations can harness this powerful technology to drive genuine innovation and sustainable success. In the context of generative AI, we offer four strategic choices for organizations based on their emphasis on AI sensemaking and the nature of their decision making as shown in Figure 1.

5.1 Smoke Screen Strategy

An organization that engages in fake decision-making combined with low levels of AI sensemaking is likely to face significant challenges. Such an approach can lead to suboptimal strategic decisions, loss of trust among key stakeholders, and an inability to compete effectively in the modern business environment. We have adopted the metaphor of a 'Smoke Screen Strategy' to describe an organization that struggles to stay afloat due to lack of strategic direction and leadership where decisions obscure the true state of affairs creating a false sense of security and progress.

Fake decision-making in an organization refers to a superficial or deceptive approach where decisions are either a facade for hidden agendas or are made to give an illusion of sound management without genuine commitment to those decisions. This approach often involves bypassing thorough analysis and critical thinking in favor of decisions that are more performative than substantive. In such settings, decisions are not necessarily aimed at addressing real issues or leveraging opportunities but are more about maintaining appearances or satisfying short-term goals (Smith and Besharov 2019).

Coupled with this is the aspect of low levels of AI sensemaking, where an organization either underutilizes AI technology or uses it ineffectively. This could be due to a lack of expertise, inadequate investment in AI infrastructure, or a superficial application of AI tools without a deep understanding of their potential or limitations. As a result, the organization fails to harness the power of AI for data-driven insights, predictive analytics, and strategic decision-making.

Such organizations are likely to face unique and detrimental challenges. Decisions not grounded in reality or data-driven insights are likely to lead to ineffective strategies, missed opportunities, and operational inefficiencies. Stakeholders, including employees, customers, and investors, may lose trust in the organization's leadership and its ability to make informed decisions, leading to a decline in employee morale, customer satisfaction, and investor confidence. The perception of inauthenticity and technological ineptitude can harm the organization's reputation, making it harder to attract talent, partners, and customers. Without proper AI sensemaking, there is a risk of relying on biased algorithms or unethical use of data, leading to further legal and reputational risks. Ultimately, such organizations are likely to lag competitively behind their rivals in the long term.

5.2 Echo Chamber Strategy

In the contemporary business landscape, the integration of Artificial Intelligence (AI) in decision-making processes is increasingly seen as a cornerstone of strategic management. However, not all organizations are equally equipped to leverage AI for sensemaking - the process of interpreting and understanding complex data sets.

Authentic decision-making refers to a process where choices are made based on genuine understanding, ethical considerations, and a commitment to the organization's values and goals. In such an organization, decisions are transparent, involve stakeholder input, and are driven by a true desire to achieve the best outcomes. This approach fosters trust, boosts morale, and often leads to ethical and sustainable business practices. However, the absence of advanced AI sensemaking capabilities can present unique challenges. We have adopted the metaphor of 'Echo Chamber Strategy' for such organizations to describe the same ineffective decisions and strategies being adopted without gaining new insights or understanding.

Low levels of AI sensemaking imply that the organization either lacks the technological infrastructure, the expertise, or both, to effectively analyze and interpret large data sets. In the age of big data, this limitation can be significant. AI sensemaking tools offer the ability to process information at a scale and speed that human cognition cannot match, uncovering insights that can inform and enhance decision-making processes (Fernandez and Shaw 2020).

The organization may struggle to fully harness the wealth of data available in today's digital world. This can lead to missed opportunities, as data-driven insights often reveal trends and patterns not immediately apparent through traditional analysis methods. Without AI's rapid data processing capabilities, the organization might be slower in responding to market changes, customer needs, or emerging trends, potentially losing competitive advantage. While human insight is invaluable, over-reliance on it in the absence of AI support can lead to biases or errors in judgment, especially in complex or ambiguous situations. Leadership decisions are made without the full backing of AI-driven insights.

5.3 Chameleon Strategy

In an era where artificial intelligence (AI) is revolutionizing business operations, the juxtaposition of high AI sensemaking capabilities with fake decision-making presents a unique and paradoxical scenario.

High levels of AI sensemaking imply that the organization has robust capabilities in analyzing and interpreting vast amounts of data. This includes predictive analytics, trend spotting, and generating deep insights into customer behavior, market dynamics, and operational efficiencies. Such capabilities should, in theory, empower the organization to make informed, strategic decisions that are aligned with its goals and market realities. We have adopted the metaphor of a 'Chameleon Strategy' to describe how such organizations adapt and blend into their various environments with skill, while hiding their true nature.

Despite the advanced AI capabilities, if the organization's decision-making is characterized as 'fake', it indicates a disconnect between the insights generated and the actions taken. Fake decision-making can manifest as decisions made for appearances, to conceal real motives, or to maintain the status quo. It might involve ignoring AI-generated insights in favor of personal agendas, political maneuvering within the organization, or decisions that prioritize short-term gains over long-term sustainability.

While having access to high-quality data and insights, such organizations fails to leverage them effectively. This underutilization of resources can lead to missed opportunities and poor strategic choices. Externally, the organization might gain a reputation for being data-rich but insight-poor, which can affect its brand image and customer trust. Ignoring AI insights can lead to operational inefficiencies, financial losses, and a failure to adapt to market changes, putting the organization at a competitive disadvantage. There may be ethical implications if AI insights are used to manipulate or mislead stakeholders, customers, or the market, leading to potential legal and compliance risks (Raisch and Krakowski 2021).

5.4 Greenhouse Strategy

The synergy of authentic decision-making and high AI sensemaking in organizations offers a blueprint for success in the rapidly changing external environment. This approach allows organizations to make decisions that are not only smart and data-driven but also ethical and aligned with their core values. As AI continues to evolve, the organizations that will thrive are those that manage to balance the power of technology with a deep commitment to authenticity and ethical responsibility. We use the metaphor of 'Greenhouse Strategy' to describe a nurturing environment where informed decisions allow for growth and flourishing of innovative ideas. This presents a powerful paradigm for organizational success.

Authentic decision-making is characterized by transparency, ethical considerations, and a genuine commitment to the organization's values and goals. It involves making choices that are not only beneficial in the short term but also sustainable and responsible in the long run. In an organization that prioritizes authenticity, decisions are made with stakeholder interests in mind, fostering trust and credibility.

When this authentic approach is combined with high levels of AI sensemaking, the organization is equipped to make decisions that are not only ethically sound but also deeply informed by data and advanced analytics. AI sensemaking involves using sophisticated algorithms to analyze large datasets, uncovering patterns and insights that might be invisible to the human eye. This capability allows organizations to anticipate market trends, understand customer needs more deeply, and identify potential risks and opportunities with greater precision (Ma and Sun 2020).

The integration of AI sensemaking into authentic decision-making processes enhances the organization's ability to make strategic, data-driven decisions. This combination ensures that decisions are not just based on human judgment and experience but are also backed by empirical evidence and predictive analytics. As a result, the organization can navigate complex business environments more effectively, making decisions that are both morally sound and strategically astute. Such organizations are likely to be at the forefront of innovation and generate significant competitive advantage.

Perhaps one of the most significant impacts of this combination is the reinforcement of ethical integrity and stakeholder trust. In an age where consumers and employees are increasingly concerned about ethical business practices, organizations that demonstrate a commitment to authenticity, bolstered by the responsible use of AI, can build stronger relationships with their stakeholders. This trust is invaluable, translating into customer loyalty, employee engagement, and a positive brand reputation.

6. CONCLUSION

The framework of authentic vs. fake decision-making and AI sensemaking is a valuable tool for researchers, managers, and organizational leaders. It provides a comprehensive approach to understanding and navigating the complex interplay between human decision-making and AI technologies in modern organizations.

This framework offers researchers a rich analytical tool to study organizational behavior and decision-making. It allows for a more nuanced understanding of how decisions are made, and the role technology plays in these processes. Researchers can use this framework to identify emerging trends and patterns in organizational decision-making, particularly in relation to the adoption and impact of AI technologies. The framework encourages cross-disciplinary research, combining insights from management science, information technology, ethics, and psychology (Desouza, Dawson, and Chenok 2020).

Managers can use this framework to assess their own decision-making processes and the extent to which they are leveraging AI for sensemaking. It helps in aligning decision-making strategies with organizational goals and values. Understanding the pitfalls of fake decision-making and the benefits of AI sensemaking can aid managers in risk assessment and mitigation strategies. The framework can guide managers on how to effectively integrate AI into their decision-making processes, ensuring that technology is used ethically and effectively.

Leaders can use this framework to foster a culture of authenticity and ethical use of AI in their organizations. It serves as a guide for developing policies and practices that support ethical decision-making and responsible AI use. This framework aids leaders in understanding the long-term implications of their decision-making strategies and the role of AI, helping them to plan for sustainable growth and innovation. By emphasizing authentic decision-making and responsible AI use, leaders can build and maintain trust with stakeholders, which is crucial for reputation management and customer loyalty (Fernandez and Shaw 2020).

The limitations of this framework are an over-simplification of the complexities and nuances inherent in organizational decision-making processes. Determining what constitutes 'authentic' versus 'fake' decision-making can be highly subjective and context dependent. Different stakeholders may have varying perceptions of authenticity, making it challenging to apply a uniform standard across diverse organizational contexts. There is a risk of technological determinism, where the role of AI in decision-making is overemphasized. The framework does not explicitly address the ethical implications and potential biases inherent in AI systems. AI sensemaking is only as good as the data and algorithms it relies on, which can perpetuate existing biases if not carefully managed. This framework primarily focuses on internal organizational processes and may underestimate the impact of external environmental factors on decision-making and AI implementation. Market dynamics, regulatory changes, and socio-economic factors play a significant role in shaping organizational strategies. The framework does not explicitly consider the skill gaps that might exist in organizations, particularly in understanding and leveraging AI technologies. The effectiveness of AI sensemaking is contingent upon the capabilities of the workforce which underlies the knowledge-based view of the firm.

REFERENCES

Abubakar, A. M., H. Elrehail, M. A. Alatailat, and A. Elçi. (2019). 'Knowledge management, decision-making style and organizational performance', *Journal of Innovation & Knowledge*, 4: 104-14.

Aguinis, H., and A. Glavas. (2019). 'On Corporate Social Responsibility, Sensemaking, and the Search for Meaningfulness Through Work', *Journal of Management*, 45: 1057-86.

Awan, U., S. Shamim, Z. Khan, N. U. Zia, S. M. Shariq, and M. N. Khan. (2021). 'Big data analytics capability and decision-making: The role of data-driven insight on circular economy performance', *Technological Forecasting and Social Change*, 168: 12.

Christianson, M. K., and M. A. Barton. (2021). 'Sensemaking in the Time of COVID-19', *Journal of Management Studies*, 58: 572-76.

Desouza, K. C., G. S. Dawson, and D. Chenok. (2020). 'Designing, developing, and deploying artificial intelligence systems: Lessons from and for the public sector', *Business Horizons*, 63: 205-13.

Dowling, M., and B. Lucey. (2023). 'ChatGPT for (Finance) research: The Bananarama Conjecture', *Finance Research Letters*, 53: 6.

Ferlie, Ewan, Tessa Crilly, Ashok Jashapara, Susan Trenholm, Anna Peckham, and Graeme Currie. (2015). 'Knowledge mobilization in healthcare organizations: a view from the resource-based view of the firm', *International Journal of Health Policy and Management*, 4: 127.

Fernandez, A. A., and G. P. Shaw. (2020). 'Academic Leadership in a Time of Crisis: The Coronavirus and COVID-19', *Journal of Leadership Studies*, 14: 39-45.

Goodfellow, Ian, Jean Pouget-Abadie, Mehdi Mirza, Bing Xu, David Warde-Farley, Sherjil Ozair, Aaron Courville, and Yoshua Bengio. (2014). 'Generative adversarial nets', *Advances in neural information processing systems*, 27.

Korzynski, P., G. Mazurek, A. Altmann, J. Ejdys, R. Kazlauskaite, J. Paliszkiewicz, K. Wach, and E. Ziemba. (2023). 'Generative artificial intelligence as a new context for management theories: analysis of ChatGPT', *Central European Management Journal*, 31: 3-13.

Ma, L. Y., and B. H. Sun. (2020). 'Machine learning and AI in marketing - Connecting computing power to human insights', *International Journal of Research in Marketing*, 37: 481-504.

Newman, D. T., N. J. Fast, and D. J. Harmon. (2020). 'When eliminating bias isn't fair: Algorithmic reductionism and procedural justice in human resource decisions', *Organizational Behavior and Human Decision Processes*, 160: 149-67.

Pereira, V., and U. Bamel. (2021). 'Extending the resource and knowledge based view: A critical analysis into its theoretical evolution and future research directions', *Journal of Business Research*, 132: 557-70.

Raisch, S., and S. Krakowski. (2021). 'Artificial Intelligence and Management: The Automation-Augmentation Paradox', *Academy of Management Review*, 46: 192-210.

Schildt, H., S. Mantere, and J. Cornelissen. (2020). 'Power in Sensemaking Processes', *Organization Studies*, 41: 241-65.

Singh, S. K., S. Gupta, D. Busso, and S. Kamboj. (2021). 'Top management knowledge value, knowledge sharing practices, open innovation and organizational performance', *Journal of Business Research*, 128: 788-98.

Smith, W. K., and M. L. Besharov. (2019). 'Bowing before Dual Gods: How Structured Flexibility Sustains Organizational Hybridity*', *Administrative Science Quarterly*, 64: 1-44.

Verganti, R., L. Vendraminelli, and M. Iansiti. (2020). 'Innovation and Design in the Age of Artificial Intelligence', *Journal of Product Innovation Management*, 37: 212-27.

Vrontis, D., M. Christofi, V. Pereira, S. Tarba, A. Makrides, and E. Trichina. (2022). 'Artificial intelligence, robotics, advanced technologies and human resource management: a systematic review', *International Journal of Human Resource Management*, 33: 1237-66.

PROCEEDINGS OF THE
17TH IADIS INTERNATIONAL CONFERENCE

Information Systems 2024

9 - 11 MARCH
PORTO, PORTUGAL

EDITED BY

MIGUEL BAPTISTA NUNES
PEDRO ISAÍAS
PHILIP POWELL

iadis
international association for development of the information society

Full Papers

ANALYSIS OF INDUSTRY 4.0 TECHNOLOGIES' ADOPTION USING INTERPRETIVE STRUCTURAL MODELLING

Sevgi Özkan Yıldırım[1] and Omer Ozturk
Department of Information Systems, Middle East Technical University, 06800 Ankara, Turkey

ABSTRACT

Emerging disruptive technologies, especially big data, Internet of Things (IoT), cloud, cyber physical systems, and 3D printing technologies, have led to the emergence of a new industry era called Industry 4.0. The concept of Industry 4.0, which emerged at the technology fair held in Germany in 2011, has established its foundations on increasing productivity in the industry and the digitalization of systems. Although Industry 4.0 technologies have various benefits to the manufacturing sector, various difficulties may arise during the adaptation of these technologies. The aim of this research paper is to conduct a detailed study on the Industry 4.0 revolution to reveal the obstacles that may arise during the application of Industry 4.0 technologies to the manufacturing sector, and to guide the managers who want to implement Industry 4.0 applications in this direction, thanks to the roadmap obtained after the findings. Interpretive Structural Modelling (ISM) technique has been used to determine barriers and barrier levels to the implementation of Industry 4.0. This study will support managers to produce solutions that will reduce the impact of barriers to industry 4.0 adaptation.

KEYWORDS

Industry 4.0 Adoption, Barrier, Adaptation, Interpretive Structural Modelling (ISM)

1. INTRODUCTION

The scope of the concept of Industry 4.0 may vary depending on the sector in which it is evaluated or the geography in which it is addressed. It can be broadly defined as: "integration of information technologies into traditional industry; digitization and flexible structure of the process in the manufacturing system; digital tracking of manufactured products; active communication between sub-materials, products and machines where production takes place; ensuring optimization in production with high technology; Increasing productivity by obtaining a living smart production system, continuation of processes with environmentally friendly methods (Shafiq et al., 2016).

In the Industry 4.0 revolution, it is aimed to create a technology ecosystem by properly integrating cloud computing, autonomous robots, system integration, internet of things, cyber security, additive manufacturing, big data, augmented reality, digital twins, virtual reality, 3d printing technologies.

In order for Industry 4.0 to be implemented in organizations that continue traditional processes, traditional organizations need to be convinced of the value that digital transformation will bring here. In addition, while organizations understand Industry 4.0, the challenges that will arise in the application should also be evaluated. Being aware of the barriers to Industry 4.0 adaptation will be critical in producing solutions to these barriers or reducing the impact of barriers. Industry 4.0 is socio-technical systems. For this reason, it is necessary to be aware of the criticality of social factors during the industry 4.0 adaptation (Moghaddam et al., 2018). In addition to knowing the content of Industry 4.0 in Industry 4.0 applications, it is very critical to know the dynamics of the institution or factory where the application will take place. Depending on the size of the organization, manufacturing processes, and end-user criteria reached by the manufactured product, the application methods of technologies will be different. In the manufacturing sector, products are tangible, in the service sector they are not. Different measurement methods should be used when

[1] Corresponding author email: sevgiozk@metu.edu.tr

examining the adaptation in these two sectors and the success of industry 4.0 (Bibby & Dehe, 2018). Considering the size of the organization, different studies have been carried out for small-medium enterprises. Considering that 90 percent of the companies in the European Union continue their processes as Small Medium Enterprises, the work for these organizations is very valuable (Masood & Sonntag, 2020).

It is known that the implementation of these technologies in the IT sector is very fast. However, when the manufacturing sector is examined, it is seen that the implementation phase is slower and various difficulties are encountered. Adaptation to the new revolution in the manufacturing sector should be considered as a step-by-step process. Bosch, one of the leading companies in the adaptation of Industry 4.0 technologies, states that the following factors are important in the adaptation process: First of all, it is a facilitated process as the effect of lean production; secondly, a factory with an information technology architecture and finally the integration of internet of things (IoT), cloud and CPS systems is critical (Buer et al., 2020). Thanks to the Industry 4.0 application, it has been determined that services and products can be customized in line with user demands, supply times are shortened, product quality increases, long-term operating costs are reduced for the company, and production costs can be analyzed more comprehensively (Peukert et al., 2015).

The aim of this study is to examine the adaptation process of industry 4.0 technologies to the manufacturing sector. The criticality of the barriers to the adaptation process varies according to the geography and the sector studied. In the study, critical barriers have been identified and the relationship between them have been revealed. The driving power in the industry 4.0 adaptation obtained from the literature research and the barriers in front of the adaptation in other geographies and in other sectors have been examined with literature research. In the methodology part of the study, the opinions of the people working in the manufacturing sector were collected through a questionnaire. Based on the collected information, critical barriers to adaptation were identified. Using the Interpretive Structural Modelling (ISM) method, the relationship between the barriers have been placed in the ISM framework in a hierarchical structure. The practical implication of this study is to create a roadmap and guide the managers in the industry 4.0 adaptation process.

2. METHODOLOGY

This study utilizes quantitative experimental research methodology. In that, Interpretive Structural Modelling (ISM) method has been used. By using this method, it is aimed to model the relationship between the barriers in the adaptation process to industry 4.0 technologies. The ISM methodology helps to simplify the relationships between parts of the system being studied from a complex situation. The reason for using the ISM methodology during this study is that there is more than one variable in front of the adaptation of Industry 4.0 technologies to the production sector and the aim of the study is to determine the relationship between these variables. Singh and Deshmukh (2007) define the ISM methodology as an interactive learning process (Singh et al., 2007). The ISM methodology applied in the study will be a resource for managers to re-evaluate the priorities of the barriers identified in the study.

Thanks to the ISM methodology, the interconnections and mutual influences between the barriers to IE 4.0 adaptation will be examined. These barriers will be systematically analyzed using the ISM methodology and presented in a more understandable format. The framework to be obtained as a result of the study will reveal the hierarchical structure between the barriers. In addition, the ISM methodology reveals the relationship between criteria (Singh et al., 2007).

The general steps of the ISM methodology to be followed during the study are given below. These steps are customized for the subject of interest during the study.

i. Researching the literature, asking expert groups or determining the variable items about the research as a result of a survey.

ii. Deciding on the contextual relations of the determined variables by examining them in pairs.

iii. Generating the Structural Self-Interaction Matrix (SSIM) in which the binary relationships of the variables are shown.

iv. Creating an initial reachability matrix based on the SSIM table obtained in the previous step. In the ISM methodology, transitivity between variables is assumed. For example, if the X variable has an effect on the Y variable and the Y variable has an effect on the Z variable, it is assumed that the X variable has an effect on the Z variable.

v. Developing the reachability matrix at different levels starting from the initial reachability matrix, creating the final reachability matrix
vi. Creating a Directed graph (Digraph) and Creating the final ISM structure
vii. Evaluation of ISM model results, implementation of changes if needed.

2.1 Data Collection

One of the key elements in this study is the evaluation of the barriers that affect the adaptation of industry 4.0 technologies to the production sector. At this point, deciding on the barriers to which the ISM method will be applied is one of the critical stages of the research. During the literature search, the active variables in the articles developed in the similar field were brought together by taking note of their sources. After creating the table in which 62 factors are specified, the explanation of each item is detailed. The variable table was narrowed down to 25 items by leaving one of the similar items from the literature. For example, there were articles with the "Cybersecurity issues" barrier (Kamble et al., 2018), (Orzes & Sarkis, 2019). There were studies that included the "Data security and data protection" barrier (M. Sharma et al., 2021) Only "Data security and data protection" was chosen because the two barriers have similar meanings. The same was true for the "Enhanced skill requirement for employees" (Kamble et al., 2018) barrier and the "Need for enhanced skills" (Majumdar et al., 2021) barriers. The 25 barriers identified are shown in Table 1.

Table 1. Barriers for IE 4.0

No	Barrier and Description	Source (Rajput & Singh, 2019)
1	**Workers'resistance**: Industry 4.0 technologies will cause changes in job description and processes. Each change will mean that employees give up their habits. This may cause resistance to IE 4.0 by workers.	(Jadhav et al., 2014)
2	**Lack of digital culture**: It is critical to have a digitalization culture in the production sector in order to adapt to Industry 4.0 technologies. Without a culture of digitization, IE 4.0 will be difficult to maintain.	(Rajput & Singh, 2019)
3	**Lack of trained staff**: Personnel working in the current situation may be ignorant and untrained on how to use new technologies to be adapted. Trained employees are needed for the implementation of IE 4.0 technologies.	(Orzes et al., 2019)
4	**Employment disruption**: Some of the tasks can be done without the need for human intervention. This may result in the loss of workers.	(Raj et al., 2020)
5	**High implementation cost**: Developing infrastructure for Industry 4.0 technologies can result in high implementation costs. This requires high capital.	(Raj et al., 2020)
6	**Seamless integration and compatibility issues**: With new technologies, seamless integration between equipment and network systems is one of the critical issues.	(Raj et al., 2020)
7	**Poor R&D on Industry 4.0 adoption**: As Industry 4.0 is a relatively new field, it is a missing field in research and development. The number of studies evaluating concrete results is limited.	(Ajmera & Jain, 2019)
8	**Inadequate maintenance support system**: There is a scarcity of expert maintenance and repair teams in this field.	(Ajmera & Jain, 2019)
9	**Lack of methodical approach for implementation**: There are not sufficient number of reference architectures and standards to follow for perfect implementation.	(Orzes et al., 2019)
10	**Problem of coordination and collaboration**: There is a high risk of hardware and software compatibility issues. Adaptation requires the coordinated work of each stakeholder in the process.	(Luthra & Mangla, 2018)
11	**Time constraint**: The transition to the new application may cause pauses and delays in production processes. Factories that have very high time constraints in their production may find it difficult to afford it.	(Rajput & Singh, 2019)
12	**Lack of experience in project management and budgeting**: It is very difficult for project management to manage cost analysis, budgeting, resource allocation, predicting possible risks during the transition to Industry 4.0 technologies.	(Müller, 2019)
13	**Lack of risk management tools for investments**: Since there are not many application examples, there is no risk management tool to decide the risk amount of investments.	(Ajmera & Jain, 2019)
14	**Lack of clear apprehension of benefits**: There is a lack of data on the benefits of Industry 4.0.	(Orzes et al., 2019)

15	**Fear of failure**: Since there is not enough concrete data on the success of Industry 4.0, entrepreneurs may have the thought of failure.	(Kamble et al., 2018)
16	**Lack of government support and policies**: The fact that the government has not announced a specific policy method on Industry 4.0 is one of the obstacles. Having a law restricting IE 4.0 technologies that the government can disclose is a risk.	(Luthra & Mangla, 2018)
17	**Compatibility issues between existing and new systems**: It is difficult to manage the transition between the current operating system and the new system to be installed.	(Luthra & Mangla, 2018)
18	**Lack of infrastructure and internet- based networks**: New technologies require strong internet connection and infrastructure. Their lack is one of the barriers to adaptation.	(Yadav et al., 2020)
19	**Data security and data protection**: Information about the process in the factory is stored as data along with the digitized process. If the necessary security measures are not taken, this data may fall into the hands of malicious people.	(Ivanov et al., 2021)
20	**Lack of standards and reference architectures**: The absence of global standards such as data sharing protocols in this area is an obstacle.	(Yadav et al., 2020)
21	**Lack of management dedication, commitment, and leadership**: The senior management's belief in industry 4.0, their encouragement and dedication to this change are critical factors during adaptation. Its absence is a barrier.	(Luthra & Mangla, 2018)
22	**Lack of futuristic outlook**: Companies should be aware that they are making a move for the future, not the moment. Otherwise, if they do not develop their vision in this direction, it is an obstacle.	(Govindan et al., 2014)
23	**Managing employee anxiety**: Change can cause anxiety and restlessness in employees. The inability to manage this environment is one of the obstacles.	(Kamble et al., 2018)
24	**Undevelopment of social infrastructure**: If no contribution is made to the development of the social infrastructure of the team working in the factory in this respect, this will be an obstacle.	(Kamble et al., 2018)
25	**Regulatory compliance concerning social requirements**: The new order will require new social guidelines. One of the obstacles is the immaturity of yet functioning instructions.	(Kamble et al., 2018)

Before the 25 items in Table 1 were presented as inputs to the ISM method, they were presented to individuals working in the manufacturing sector through a questionnaire to identify the most critical items. The questionnaire consists of two different parts. In the first part, the participants scored 25 items in front of adaptation in the production sector using a 5-point- Likert scale. In the second part, the participants were asked to rank these 25 items from the most critical to the least critical via a questionnaire. Age information, years of experience in working life and gender information were collected.

2.1.1 The Self-Structural Interaction Matrix (SSIM), Reachability Matrix and Level Partitioning

The 25 barriers presented in the questionnaire are ranked in the order of 5 points according to the answers given by the participants. 11 barriers with a score of 3 and above were used in the matrix while developing the SSIM. Barriers selected as a result of this ranking Workers' resistance (B1), Lack of digital culture (B2), Lack of trained staff (B3), High implementation cost (B4), Seamless integration and compatibility issues (B5), Poor R&D on Industry 4.0 adoption (B6), Lack of methodical approach for implementation (B7), Problem of coordination and collaboration stakeholder (B8), Lack of clear apprehension of benefits (B9), Lack of infrastructure and internet- based networks (B10), Lack of management dedication , commitment, and leadership (B11). In order to facilitate the naming of the barriers during the study, the symbols starting with the barriers B are given. The meanings of the expressions V, A, X and O to be used in the matrix are as below:

V: There is a forward relationship from Bi to Bj. The Bi barrier acts on the Bj barrier.
A: There is a reverse relationship from Bj to Bi. The Bj barrier acts on the Bi barrier.
X: There is a reciprocal relationship between the Bi and Bj barriers. Both affect each other.
O: There is no relationship between the Bi and Bj barriers.

While creating the SSIM, the bilateral relations between the barriers were decided by working with five experts working in the manufacturing sector. Next, SSIM is converted into a binary matrix. V, A, X, and O expressions in SSIM take the values 1 or 0 depending on their meaning. The initial and final reachability matrix was obtained by converting the values in the SSIM matrix into binary values by considering the conversion method.

After the iterations are completed, the barriers according to their levels are shown in Table 2.

Table 2. Levels of barriers

Level 1	B1 (Workers 'resistance) B4 (High implementation cost) B5 (Seamless integration and compatibility issues) B8 (Problem of coordination and collaboration stakeholder)
Level 2	B7 (Lack of methodical approach for implementation) B9 (Lack of clear apprehension of benefits) B10 (Lack of infrastructure and internet- based networks)
Level 3	B2 (Lack of digital culture) B6 (Poor R&D on Industry 4.0 adoption) B11(Lack of management dedication, commitment, and leadership)
Level 4	B3 (Lack of trained staff)

2.1.2 The Classification of the Barriers and the Final ISM Framework

According to the driver power and dependency scores in Table 3, barriers can be evaluated in 4 different categories. These categories are Drivers, Linkage, Autonomous and Dependent. The characteristics of each category are summarized in Table 3. The purpose of this classification of barriers is to analyze the dependency and driving power characteristics of the barriers. In this analysis, the barriers are placed on the coordinate plane according to the driving power and dependency information. Figure 1 was created as a result of this step. Figure 2 depicts the final ISM Framework.

Table 3. Characteristics of categories

Category	Autonomous	Dependent	Linkage	Drivers
Properties	Weak driving power	Weak driving power	Strong driving power	Strong driving power
	Weak dependence	Strong dependency	Strong dependency	Weak dependence

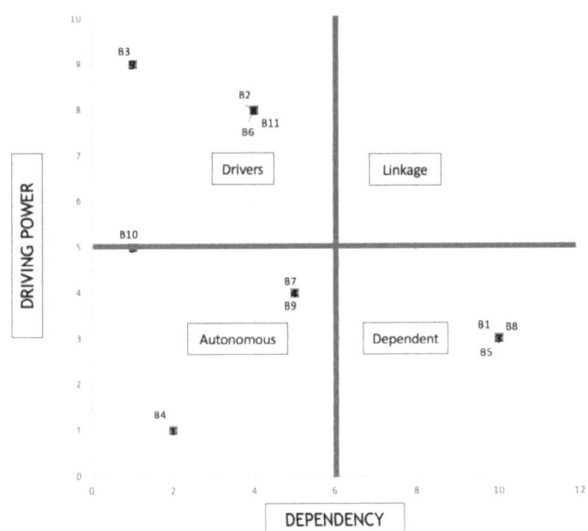

Figure 1. MICMAC analysis of barriers

Barriers in the quadrant named as *Autonomous* are relatively unrelated to other barriers in the system. In this respect, "B4-High implementation cost" has a low score in terms of both driving power and dependency. While the barriers of "B1-Workers' resistance", "B5-Seamless integration and compatibility issues" and "B8-Problem of coordination and collaboration stakeholder" in the quadrant named as *Dependent* are high in terms of dependency, they are low in terms of driving power. These barriers are equal in this analysis in terms of both dependency and driving power score. In this study, there is no barrier that has the characteristics of the quadrant named as *Linkage*. In the quadrant named as *Drivers*, the "B2-Lack of digital culture", "B6-Poor R&D on Industry 4.0 adoption", "B11-Lack of management dedication, commitment, and leadership" barriers are at the same point. The driving power and dependency scores of the B2, B6 and B11 barriers are the same. The "B3-Lack of trained staff" barrier in the *Drivers* quadrant has relatively lower dependency and higher driving power. The "B10-Lack of infrastructure and internet-based networks" barrier is located between the *Autonomous* and *Drivers* quadrants, while the driving power is at medium level, the dependency score is relatively low.

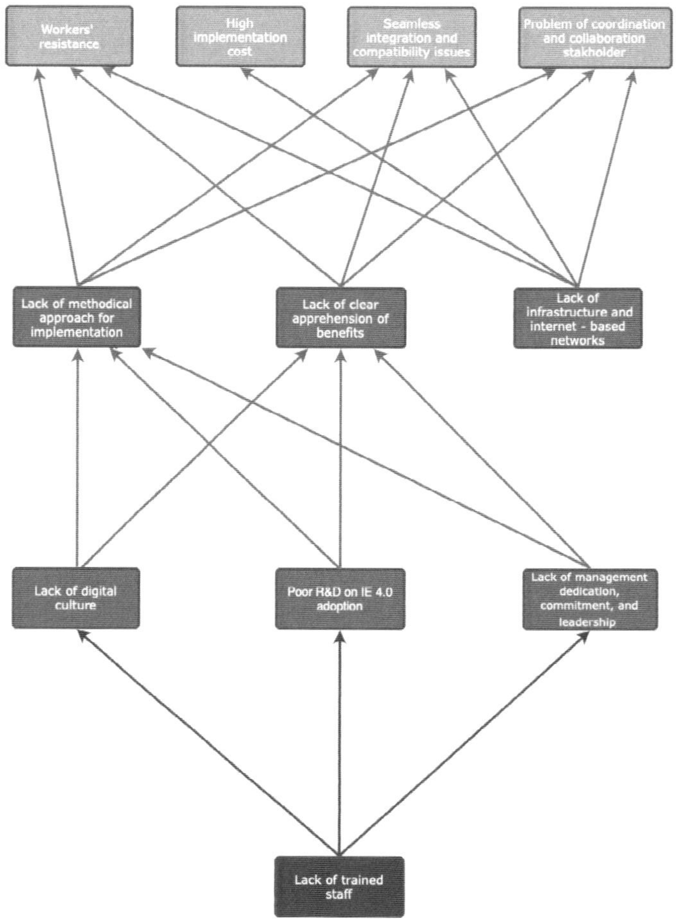

Figure 2. ISM Framework

The resulting ISM framework is shown in Figure 2. The "Lack of trained staff" barrier is located at the bottom of the framework. Other barriers are placed above this barrier. This means that the "Lack of trained staff" barrier affects all other barriers. It can also be stated that "lack of trained staff" is the most basic barrier in this working group. The barriers to "Lack of digital culture", "Poor R&D on industry 4.0 adoption" and "Lack of management dedication, commitment, and leadership" are at the next level. These barriers also affect each other. "Lack of methodical approach for implementation", "Lack of clear apprehension of benefits" and "Lack of infrastructure and internet-based networks" barriers are at a higher level. At the top of the ISM framework are the "Workers' resistance", "High implementation cost, "Seamless integration and compatibility issues" and "Problem of coordination and collaboration stakeholder" barriers. In the resulting model, these barriers, which are at the top, have relatively less effect on other barriers.

3. CONCLUSION

The use of the Industry 4.0 revolution in the manufacturing sector increases the added value of the processes for the company, increases their productivity, provides an advantage in market competition, opens new business opportunities and at the same time ensures the optimized use of energy. These mentioned advantages are just some of the Industry 4.0 advantages detailed throughout this paper. Manufacturing methodologies change as they adapt to this revolution; infrastructure works are carried out; Technologies such as big data, cloud, IoT are integrated into the system; Technologically skilled workers are needed.

The purpose of this article can be listed as follows: ,

- To explain the Industry 4.0 revolution in detail.
- Identify critical barriers that emerged during the industry 4.0 adoption in the manufacturing sector.
- Evaluating the relationship between the barriers obtained as a result of the study, based on expert opinions, and creating a hierarchical structure if possible.
- To perform the analysis of the resulting hierarchical structure.

Having identified the driving forces and barriers for IE 4.0 from the literature, Interpretive Structural Modelling (ISM) method was used to realize the purpose of this study. The ISM method is used to establish relationships between different components that affect a system and to create a hierarchical framework. The 62 barriers obtained in the literature search section were reduced to 25 barriers by removing similar expressions. These 25 barriers are available to people working in the manufacturing industry. According to the survey results, 11 barriers above the mean were moved to the self-structural interaction matrix. With the study carried out with 3 experts with different working experience in the manufacturing sector, bilateral relations between these barriers were determined. The final reachability matrix was obtained from SSIM by proceeding with the transitivity assumption of the ISM method. Level partitioning is done by using the final reachability matrix. In this way, 11 barriers were revealed at 4 different levels. The developed model reveals the hierarchical relationship between barriers. Figure 11 shows the developed model.

According to the results of the study, "Lack of trained staff (B3)" is the main obstacle during the adaptation of the industry 4.0 revolution to the manufacturing sector. It can be considered as a root barrier that has an effect on other barriers. It is located at the 1st level of the developed model and affects the barriers at other levels as it is located at the bottom of the model. "Workers' resistance (B1)", "high implementation cost (B4)", "seamless integration and compatibility issues (B5)", "problem of coordination and collaboration stakeholder (B8)" emerged as directed barriers most affected by other barriers. The effect of these obstacles on other obstacles is limited and is not reflected in the model. According to the model, the lack of infrastructure and internet-based networks (B10) barrier is not affected by other barriers.

During the adaptation of Industry 4.0 technologies, it is very critical that employees are trained in this regard. The cultural structure of a company consisting of untrained personnel will be far from digital culture. Untrained personnel will see that they bring industry 4.0 technologies as a risk and will be able to resist. As the education level rises, both the skills of the employees will increase and the adaptation to industry 4.0 will be easier. In this respect, managers who want to benefit from the advantages of the industry 4.0 revolution should choose people who have been trained as their employee profile and train their existing staff. The payoff from government and manufacturing collaboration for education will be huge in a positive way (Majumdar et al., 2021). The beginning of education before business life, the inclusion of industry 4.0 innovations in the curricula will play a role in the adoption of the IE 4.0 revolution by the society in general.

In this context, managers who want to implement industry 4.0 should try to remove the obstacles starting from the most effective one, starting from the framework in the model. The barriers or the effects of the barriers in each sector may be different. In this context, this study is specific to the manufacturing sector. The studies here can guide factories in the manufacturing sector around the world. Especially in the adaptation of IE 4.0 technologies, the culture of the region where the applications will be carried out together with the sector is also very critical. When evaluated in terms of culture, it is seen that the studies in this field in the Turkish manufacturing sector are limited. This study is unique in that it sheds light on the IE 4.0 adaptation to the manufacturing sector in Turkey.

REFERENCES

Ajmera, P., & Jain, V. (2019). Modelling the barriers of Health 4.0–the fourth healthcare industrial revolution in India by TISM. Operations Management Research, 12(3–4), 129–145. https://doi.org/10.1007/S12063-019-00143-X

Bibby, L., & Dehe, B. (2018). Defining and assessing industry 4.0 maturity levels – case of the defense sector. https://doi.org/10.1080/09537287.2018.1503355, 29(12), 1030–1043.

Buer, S.-V., Semini, M., Strandhagen, J. O., & Sgarbossa, F. (2020). International Journal of Production Research The complementary effect of lean manufacturing and digitalisation on operational performance The complementary effect of lean manufacturing and digitalisation on operational performance. https://doi.org/10.1080/00207543.2020.1790684

Govindan, K., Azevedo, S. G., Carvalho, H., & Cruz-Machado, V. (2014). Impact of supply chain management practices on sustainability. Journal of Cleaner Production, 85, 212–225. https://doi.org/10.1016/J.JCLEPRO.2014.05.068

Ivanov, D., Tang, C. S., Dolgui, A., Battini, D., & Das, A. (2021). Researchers' perspectives on Industry 4.0: multi-disciplinary analysis and opportunities for operations management. International Journal of Production Research, 59(7), 2055–2078. https://doi.org/10.1080/00207543.2020.1798035

Jadhav, J. R., Mantha, S. S., & Rane, S. B. (2014). Exploring barriers in lean implementation. International Journal of Lean Six Sigma, 5(2), 122–148. https://doi.org/10.1108/IJLSS-12-2012-0014

Kamble, S. S., Gunasekaran, A., & Gawankar, S. A. (2018). Sustainable Industry 4.0 framework: A systematic literature review identifying the current trends and future perspectives. Process Safety and Environmental Protection, 117, 408–425. https://doi.org/10.1016/J.PSEP.2018.05.009

Luthra, S., & Mangla, S. K. (2018). Evaluating challenges to Industry 4.0 initiatives for supply chain sustainability in emerging economies. Process Safety and Environmental Protection, 117, 168–179. https://doi.org/10.1016/J.PSEP.2018.04.018

Majumdar, A., Garg, H., & Jain, R. (2021). Managing the barriers of Industry 4.0 adoption and implementation in textile and clothing industry: Interpretive structural model and triple helix framework. Computers in Industry, 125, 103372. https://doi.org/10.1016/J.COMPIND.2020.103372

Masood, T., & Sonntag, P. (2020). Industry 4.0: Adoption challenges and benefits for SMEs. Computers in Industry, 121, 103261. https://doi.org/10.1016/J.COMPIND.2020.103261

Moghaddam, M., Cadavid, M. N., Kenley, C. R., & Deshmukh, A. v. (2018). Reference architectures for smart manufacturing: A critical review. Journal of Manufacturing Systems, 49, 215–225. https://doi.org/10.1016/J.JMSY.2018.10.006

Müller, J. M. (2019). Assessing the barriers to Industry 4.0 implementation from a workers' perspective. IFAC-PapersOnLine, 52(13), 2189–2194. https://doi.org/10.1016/J.IFACOL.2019.11.530

Orzes, G., & Sarkis, J. (2019). Reshoring and environmental sustainability: An unexplored relationship? Resources, Conservation and Recycling, 141, 481–482. https://doi.org/10.1016/J.RESCONREC.2018.11.004

Orzes, G., Rauch, E., Bednar, S., & Poklemba, R. (2019). Industry 4.0 Implementation Barriers in Small and Medium Sized Enterprises: A Focus Group Study. IEEE International Conference on Industrial Engineering and Engineering Management, 2019-December, 1348–1352. https://doi.org/10.1109/IEEM.2018.8607477

Peukert, B., Benecke, S., Clavell, J., Neugebauer, S., Nissen, N. F., Uhlmann, E., Lang, K. D., & Finkbeiner, M. (2015). Addressing Sustainability and Flexibility in Manufacturing Via Smart Modular Machine Tool Frames to Support Sustainable Value Creation. Procedia CIRP, 29, 514–519. https://doi.org/10.1016/J.PROCIR.2015.02.181

Raj, A., Dwivedi, G., Sharma, A., Lopes de Sousa Jabbour, A. B., & Rajak, S. (2020). Barriers to the adoption of industry 4.0 technologies in the manufacturing sector: An inter-country comparative perspective. International Journal of Production Economics, 224, 107546. https://doi.org/10.1016/J.IJPE.2019.107546

Rajput, S., & Singh, S. P. (2019). Connecting circular economy and industry 4.0. International Journal of Information Management, 49, 98–113. https://doi.org/10.1016/J.IJINFOMGT.2019.03.002

Shafiq, S. I., Sanin, C., Szczerbicki, E., & Toro, C. (2016). Virtual Engineering Factory: Creating Experience Base for Industry 4.0. https://doi.org/10.1080/01969722.2016.1128762, 47(1–2), 32–47.

Yadav, G., Kumar, A., Luthra, S., Garza-Reyes, J. A., Kumar, V., & Batista, L. (2020). A framework to achieve sustainability in manufacturing organisations of developing economies using industry 4.0 technologies' enablers. Computers in Industry, 122, 103280. https://doi.org/10.1016/J.COMPIND.2020.103280

CRITICAL SUCCESS FACTORS OF BUSINESS MODEL INNOVATION TO TAKE ADVANTAGE OF DISRUPTIVE TECHNOLOGIES: A STRUCTURED LITERATURE REVIEW

Mikhail David Edwards and Hanlie Smuts
University of Pretoria, Pretoria, South Africa

ABSTRACT

Business model innovation (BMI) plays a crucial role in the digital era, enabling enterprises to utilise disruptive technology to generate value and attain a competitive edge. Nevertheless, the expeditious advancement of these technologies poses various obstacles such as uncertain environmental conditions, potential financial risks in the initial stages, reluctance to accept from employees, and the possibility of diverting attention away from essential duties at work. This study aimed to identify the key characteristics that contribute to the success of business model innovation (BMI) in effectively utilising disruptive technologies. This was achieved by a comprehensive analysis of existing literature in a methodical manner. The study's results highlighted the significance of trust, efficiency, and adaptability in many components of BMI. Technologies such as Artificial Intelligence contribute to the improvement of objective alignment and client personalisation, whilst blockchain technology facilitates the establishment of trust and transparency. In the realm of technology, cloud computing serves to augment the accessibility and flexibility of resources. In order to achieve optimal BMI in the current digital age, it is imperative for enterprises to proactively incorporate these technologies into their operations, all the while promoting adaptability and engaging stakeholders.

KEYWORDS

Critical Success Factors, Business Model Innovation, Disruptive Technologies

1. INTRODUCTION

Business models indicate how enterprises are related to different stakeholders (Wang & Chebo, 2021). Employees, customers, investors, and the community greatly impact the value of disruptive technology. They shape technical breakthroughs by their ideas and input, benefit from such advancements, and play an important role in the acceptance and implementation of modern technologies. Their participation and acceptance are critical drivers of the value that disruptive technologies can provide (Garmulewicz et al., 2018).

The business landscape is being transformed by disruptive technology (ref). Enterprises that fail to adapt to the risks associated with obsolescence are faced with a pressing need to comprehend the key success factors (CSFs) of business model innovation. Critical Success Factors (CSFs) are essential elements that determine the success or failure of a company in attaining its objectives (ref). Ensuring a competitive edge is achieved by aligning tactics with these Critical Success Factors (CSFs). This research study investigates the impact of critical success factors (CSFs) on enterprise's performance, with a particular focus on disruptive technology. From the research problem presented, the following research question is identified: *What are the key determinants of success for business model innovation within the framework of disruptive technologies?* The purpose of this study is to analyse and examine the essential elements of effective business model innovation in the face of disruptive technological environments. The significance of this phenomenon resides in its ability to provide guidance to businesses as they navigate technological transformations and contribute to the academic literature on the subject. The paper is organised in a manner that encompasses several key components, including an introductory section that provides contextual information, a section that outlines the motivation for the study, a comprehensive description of the methodology employed, a presentation of the findings, an in-depth exploration of the implications and interpretations of the results, and a concluding section.

2. BACKGROUND

2.1 Business Model Innovation Amidst Disruptive Tech

Business model innovation focuses on new methods of creating and extracting value; innovative business models try to develop new market propositions by altering how businesses and customers interact (Spyropoulos, 2018a). The use of disruptive technologies promotes the development of flexible and linked enterprise systems. Disruptive technologies have the potential to radically disrupt a sector or a segment of the market, determining the digital revolution of enterprises and transforming their processes and business models. Disruptive technologies have encouraged businesses to make innovative decisions and attract high-technology-skilled employees to ensure that the business succeeds (Scuotto et al., 2022). Enterprises can gain a competitive advantage through business model innovation driven by disruptive technologies. Understanding client demands, adapting to changing market conditions, and establishing a continual learning and experimentation culture are all critical success elements (Budler et al., 2021). Enterprises can discover new revenue streams andprovide unparalleled value by leveraging these technologies, establishing themselves as industry leaders and fortifying themselves against future difficulties (Wang, 2022).

Despite the numerous benefits, enterprises transforming frequently need help in digitally innovating their business model. This is because digital innovation varies from traditional forms of strategic change in that digital technologies accelerate the rate of change, resulting in much greater environmental complexity, volatility, and unpredictability (ref). Business Model Innovation (BMI) is a challenging topic due to the high technological, product, and market uncertainty levels. The focus of enterprises has shifted to business model innovation due to competitive pressure, digital transformation, adverse economic conditions, and resource scarcity (Spyropoulos, 2018a). The risk of misjudging client readiness, which can lead to early investments and market misalignment, is one of the most critical concerns. Internal resistance is also risky, as employees may be apprehensive of changes that disrupt established workflows or jeopardise job security. Furthermore, a hyper-focus on innovation can often lead to an enterprise neglecting its core business, diluting its brand and losing loyal customers. These problems, if not managed with forethought, might outweigh the benefits of innovation, resulting in financial failures and loss of market position (Chen et al., 2022). Poor management can result in enterprise resistance, misaligned corporate processes, squandered resources, and potential failure to meet customer expectations. As a result, for successful integration of disruptive technologies, the deployment process must be methodically planned and implemented, and risks must be proactively addressed (Wang, 2022).

To ensure the continued successful administration of people, the business model should be aligned with strategy, taking into account changes in the external environment and business processes (Spyropoulos & Varsakelis, 2023). A business model defines how an enterprise creates and delivers value to its customers (Spyropoulos, 2018a). Business Model innovation is crucial, particularly for radical and disruptive innovation. Agility, stakeholder engagement, an innovative culture, and strategic foresight are critical success elements for business model innovation to exploit disruptive technologies. Successful implementation can lead to market leadership, better profitability, and a competitive advantage owing to improved customer experience and operational efficiency (Chen et al., 2022).

2.2 Business Model Canvas

The Business Model Canvas, first conceptualized by Alexander Osterwalder and Yves Pigneur, provides a comprehensive perspective of an enterprise's business model, which is systematically divided into nine fundamental components. The components encompassed inside the business model are Customer Segments, which serve the purpose of identifying the diverse groups that the enterprise endeavors to cater to. Value propositions refer to the distinctive value that is provided to customers. Channels refer to the various channels via which a enterprise delivers value to its customers. client relationships refer to the manner in which a enterprise engages with its various client segments. Revenue streams refer to the specific sources from which a business generates its income. Key Resources refer to the essential assets that are fundamental to the business model, whereas Key Activities encompass the vital processes that are necessary for the successful functioning of the model. The Key Partnerships component of the business model emphasizes the external enterprises or allies that provide complementary support to the enterprise. Additionally, the Cost Structure element outlines the primary expenses and costs connected with the operation of the business. Collectively, these blocks offer a comprehensive overview, facilitating enterprises in the visualisation, analysis, and innovation of their strategies with efficiency (Osterwalder & Pigneur, 2010).

3. RESEARCH METHOD

The research method applied in this study, is a systematic literature review (SLR) through which the critical success factors of business model innovation in disruptive technologies, were investigated. A SLR is a methodically prepared review that employs a rigorous and explicit approach to recognise, choose, and critically analyse the outcomes of the research studies included in the literature review (Rother, 2007). The SLR method entailed searching relevant databases using targeted keywords and filtering results to obtain a suitable sample of articles. Each article was then assessed based on inclusion and exclusion criteria, and their abstracts were examined to ensure alignment with the research question (Rother, 2007). The following keywords were used to find results in google scholar: disruptive technologies, business model innovation and critical success factors.

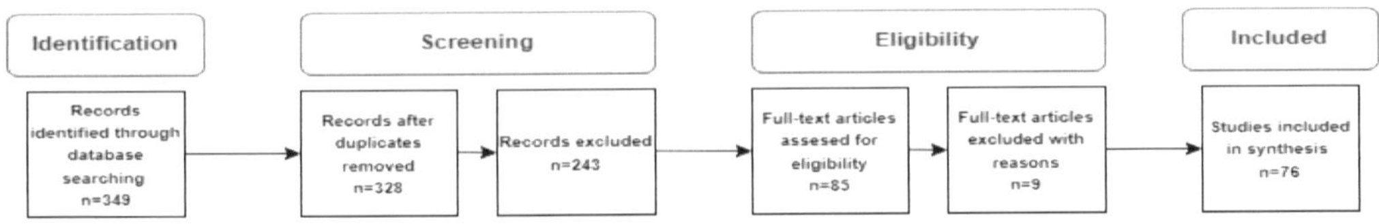

Figure 1. Total papers identified and analysed

Following screening, a dataset of 349 papers was obtained, and 76 papers were subjected to a comprehensive examination. The initial phase started with 349 articles and two more records from library catalogues, accumulating 351 articles. In the second step, 23 duplicate articles were eliminated, resulting in a total of 328 items. During the third phase, the abstracts of the 328 articles were scrutinized to assess their relevance to the research question. This led to the exclusion of 252 papers, narrowing down the dataset for analysis to 76 articles. These 76 articles underwent a thorough reading and quality evaluation in the final stage. Figure 1 depicts the procedure for this selection process.

4. DATA FINDING AND ANALYSIS

The objective of this study was to investigate and categorise the critical success factors of business model innovation that are required for harnessing disruptive technology. A comprehensive investigation yielded 44 key success criteria (sub-themes), each with its own sub-factor related to disruptive technology (Success Criteria Technology). These were subdivided into 9 overarching themes related to business model features (Osterwalder & Pigneur, 2010). This can be found in Table 1.

The Business Model Canvas, developed by Osterwalder and Pigneur, presents a comprehensive framework that delineates the nine fundamental components crucial for formulating an effective business plan. Firstly, Key Partners consist of 7 sub-themes and refer to the strategic alliances and collaborativerelationships that an enterprise forms with the objective of optimizing operational efficiency, mitigating risks, and acquiring essential resources. Next, the business model encompasses Key Activities, which serve as the fundamental processes ranging from production to problem-solving. Key resources are essential assets and instruments that are necessary for a enterprise to operate and deliver its products or services. At the core of theconcept lies the Value Proposition, which encompasses the distinctive features that set a company apart from its competitors, so providing customers with unique value (Osterwalder & Pigneur, 2010)

The Customer Relationships main theme relates to the manner in which enterprises establish and maintain connections with their consumers, encompassing considerations such as the level of engagement, customization, and approach to customer support. Channels, however, serve as the means by which a enterprise conveys its value proposition to clients, encompassing various sales outlets and online platforms. Customer segments are utilised to categorise and delineate the many groups that a enterprise caters to, with the aim of comprehending their distinct demands and preferences (Osterwalder & Pigneur, 2010).

Table 1. CSFs and the impact of disruptive technologies on key business model components

Main - The me	Sub-Theme (Critical Success Factors)	Success Criteria Technology (Disruptive Technology Aspects)	References
Key Partners	Alignment of objectives	Artificial Intelligence	(Rashed, 2021, Coulson-Thomas, 2018, Chen et al., 2022, Mariani & Borghi, 2019, Chowdhury etal., 2022, Trkman et al., Gómez & Vargas)
	Trust and transparency	Blockchain	(Turienzo et al., 2023, Koch, 2022, Nwaiwu et al., 2019, Kamers, 2018, Khan et al., 2023, Tawaststjerna, 2020, Timmer, 2019)
	Regular Communication	Augmented Reality	(Spyropoulos, 2019, Mokoena et al., 2023, Da Silva et al., Martínez-Olvera, 2022, Murmura etal., 2021, van der Meer & Track, 2019)
	Flexibility	Cloud Computing	(Koch, 2022, Coulson-Thomas, 2018, Athanasopoulou et al., 2019, Oluleye et al., 2023, Hämäläinen, 2014)
	Clear Contractual Agreements	Smart Contracts	(Allahar, 2019, Mokoena et al., 2023, Timmer, 2019)
	Mutual Benefits	Big Data and Analytics	(Koch, 2022, Coulson-Thomas, 2018, Allahar, 2019, Chen et al., 2022, Gómez & Vargas)
	Identification and Selection	Artificial Intelligence	(Rashed, 2021, Kafando, 2020, Savastano et al., 2019, Di Vaio et al., 2022, Chowdhury et al., 2022, Tawaststjerna, 2020)
Key Activiti es	Prioritisation	AI-Driven Project Management Tools	(Kafando, 2020, Bouwer, 2017, Chowdhury et al., 2022)
	Efficiency	Robotic Process Automation	(Velu, 2016, Kafando, 2020, Koch, 2022, Jabbour et al., 2019, HARBO, 2023, Kraus et al.,2022)
	Adaptability	Cloud Computing	(Allahar, 2019, Bouwer, 2017, Mariani & Borghi, 2019);(Hämäläinen, 2014)
	Skill and Expertise	Augmented Reality Training	(Spyropoulos, 2019, Di Vaio et al., 2022); (Murmura et al., 2021, Tawaststjerna, 2020)
	Technology Integration	API Management Platforms	(Budler et al., 2021, Spyropoulos & Varsakelis, 2023, Jabbour et al., 2019, HARBO, 2023, Floerecke & Lehner, 2018)
	Continuous Improvement	Machine Learning	(Rashed, 2021, Spyropoulos, 2019, Spyropoulos& Varsakelis, 2023, Wang & Chebo, 2021)
Key Resourc es	Resource Allocation	AI-powered resource management systems	(Rashed, 2021, Zubizarreta et al., 2020, Tawaststjerna, 2020, Bartoloni et al., 2022, Malik et al., 2022)
	Maintenance and upgrades	Predictive Maintenance Technologies	(Allahar, 2019, Tawaststjerna, 2020, Byers, 2011)
	Accessibility	Cloud Computing	(Pereira et al., 2020, Rashed, 2021, Budler et al., 2021, Bouwer, 2017, Manfreda, 2018)
	Protection and security	Blockchain	(Turienzo et al., 2023, Barichello, Kamers, 2018, Khan et al., 2023)
	Efficient Utilisation	Edge Computing	(de Reuver & Haaker, HARBO, 2023, Floerecke& Lehner, 2018, Tran-Dang & Kim, 2021)
	Sustainability	Smart Grid Technology	(Spyropoulos, 2019, Kafando, 2020)
Customer Relationships	Personalisation	Machine learning	(Rashed, 2021, Spyropoulos & Varsakelis, 2023, (Byers, 2011)
	Engagement	Augmented Reality	(Brailey & Bunduchi, 2017, Wang & Chebo,

			2021, Murmura et al., 2021)
	Feedback Mechanism	Blockchain	(Kafando, 2020, Murmura et al., 2021, Qin & van der Rhee, 2021)
	Customer Support	Chatbots	(Brailey & Bunduchi, 2017, Mokoena et al., 2023, Badrinas Ardèvol, 2016)
	Trust Building	Blockchain	(Turienzo et al., 2023, Spyropoulos, 2018aBartoloni et al., 2022, Özkanlısoy & Bulutlar, 2022)
Value Proposition	Relevance	Big Data Analytics	(Pereira et al., 2020, Coulson-Thomas, 2018, Nwaiwu et al., 2019, Kamers, 2018, Barichello)
	Differentiation	Blockchain	(Turienzo et al., 2023, Pereira et al., 2020); (Kafando, 2020, Jabbour et al., 2019, Guranda, 2021)
	Perceived Value	Internet of Things	(Pereira et al., 2020, von Rosing et al., 2015, Kafando, 2020, Koch, 2022, Barichello, Athanasopoulou et al., 2019, van der Meer & Track, 2019)
	Clarity	Natural Language Processing	(Rashed, 2021, Kafando, 2020, Vorholzer & Meyer, 2021)
	Consistency	Cloud computing	(Pereira et al., 2020, Rashed, 2021, Scuotto et al., 2022, Manfreda, 2018, Guranda, 2021)
Channels	Accessibility	Cloud Computing	(Pereira et al., 2020, Shang et al., Rashed, 2021, Scuotto et al., 2022, Ahmad & Van Looy, 2020, Hehle);
	Efficiency	Artificial Intelligence	(Rashed, 2021, Zubizarreta et al., 2020, Ahmad & Van Looy, 2020, Savastano et al., 2019)
	Cost-effectiveness	3D Printing	(Garmulewicz et al., 2018, Holzmann et al., 2018, Özkanlısoy & Bulutlar, 2022, Caviggioli &Ughetto, 2019)
	Integration	Blockchain	(Turienzo et al., 2023, Nwaiwu et al., 2019, Khanet al., 2023, Shakhour et al., 2021)
	Adaptability	Digital Twin	(Athanasopoulou et al., 2019); (Spyropoulos, 2018b); (Ziegler & Abdelkafi, 2022, Trapani, 2018)
Cost Structure	Cost Control	Robotic Process Automation	(Kafando, 2020, Koch, 2022, Mokgohloa, 2023);(Muraro, 2019)
	Alignment with business strategy	Business Intelligence tools	(Rashed, 2021, Brailey & Bunduchi, 2017, Wang, 2022, Weisshuhn, 2019, Shakhour et al., 2021)
	Scalability	Serverless Computing	(de Reuver & Haaker, (Spyropoulos, 2018b, Hehle, CHIK, 2016)
	Flexibility	Cloud Solutions	(Velu, 2016, Dulal & Binkele, 2021, Scuotto et al., 2022, Oluleye et al., 2023, Hehle, Trapani, 2018, Samuel, 2017)
	Investment in key areas	Machine Learning	(Rashed, 2021, Dulal & Binkele, 2021, Spyropoulos & Varsakelis, 2023)
Revenue Stream	Diversification	Blockchain	(Turienzo et al., 2023, Da Silva et al., Khan et al., 2023)
	Alignment with Value Proposition	Internet of Things	(Kafando, 2020, Wang, 2022, Weisshuhn, 2019, Müller et al., 2018, CHIK, 2016)
	Pricing Strategy	Big Data Analytics	(Pereira et al., 2020, Koch, 2022, Coulson-Thomas, 2018, Scuotto et al., 2022)
	Sustainability	Internet of Things	(Kafando, 2020, Koch, 2022); (Barichello, Wang,2022, Scuotto et al., 2022, Oluleye et al., 2023, Müller et al., 2018)
Customer Segments	Segment Identification and	Artificial Intelligence	(von Rosing et al., 2015, Dulal & Binkele, 2021, Zubizarreta et al., 2020, Tawaststjerna, 2020,

Specification		Byers, 2011)
Alignment with Other Elements	APIs	(von Rosing et al., 2015, Rashed, 2021, Mokgohloa, 2023)
Measurement and Analysis	Business Intelligence Tools	(Rashed, 2021, Brailey & Bunduchi, 2017, Weisshuhn, 2019, Shakhour et al., 2021)
Inclusivity	Natural Language Processing	(Rashed, 2021, Kafando, 2020, Wang & Chebo, 2021, Vorholzer & Meyer, 2021)

5. OPERATIONALISING DISRUPTIVE TECHNOLOGIES AND CSFs

The Business Model Canvas (BMC) is a useful tool that provides a comprehensive view of the business model of an enterprise. In order to operationalize the findings from this study, the Bussiness Model Canvass was applied to categorise the findings. At its foundation, an enterprise's operational and strategic structure is shaped by fundamental components. This begins with "Key Partners," which denotes external entities or peoplevital to the operation of a business. This is supplemented by "Key Activities," which are the primary duties anenterprise performs to develop and deliver its product or service. Similarly, "Key Resources" highlights the essential physical, intellectual, and human assets required to operate the business (Osterwalder & Pigneur, 2010).

On the customer front, "Customer Segments" define the various groups of individuals or entities that the business services. There are "Channels" – the methods used to convey the value proposition – and "Customer Relationships" that define how the enterprise interacts with its customers in order to serve them. The "Value Proposition" is central to the BMC, signifying the unique value a product or service provides to customers. All of these elements have financial ramifications, which are outlined in "Cost Structure" and "Revenue Streams" respectively. These components, collectively, offer a comprehensive overview of a enterprise's business model (Osterwalder & Pigneur, 2010). The essential success factors and the role of disruptive technologies extracted from the SLR (Table 1), were applied to each aspect of the Business Model Canvas by categorising the findings according to the Business Model Canvas integral components. The categorisation of findings is presented in detail in the next sections.

The critical success factors and disruptive technologies pertinent to business models identified in the thematic analysis of the referenced papers (refer to Table 1) were integrated with the proposed business model framework to synergise disruptive technologies and critical success factors visualised in Figure 2. Figure 2 depicts the critical success factors and disruptive technologies affiliated with each business model component. This visualization equips enterprises with a comprehensive road map that facilitates the incorporation of these success factors and technologies into their operations. This not only facilitates a more nuanced comprehension of where and how disruptive technologies can be harnessed, but also pinpoints areas crucial for achieving business objectives (von Rosing et al., 2015). With this knowledge, enterprises can improve their strategic planning processes, ensuring that their projects and initiatives are aligned with critical success factors and capitalize on relevant disruptive technologies. This targeted approach ensures that resources are effectively utilised, risks associated with technological disruptions are minimised, and the company remains agile and adaptable in a constantly changing business environment.

Key Partners	Key Activities	Value Proposition	Customer Relationships	Customer Segments	Key Resources	Cost Structure	Channels:	Revenue Streams
Critical Success Factors: Alignment of objectives Trust and transparency Regular communication Flexibility Clear Contractual Agreements Mutual Benefits Identification and selection **Disruptive Technologies:** Artificial Intelligence Blockchain Augmented reality Cloud Computing Smart Contracts Big Data and analytics	**Critical Success Factors:** Prioritisation Efficiency Adaptability Skill And Expertise Technology Integration Continuous Improvement **Disruptive Technologies:** AI-driven project Management Tools RPA Cloud Computing Augmented Reality Training API management platforms Machine Learning	**Critical success factors:** Relevance Differentiation Perceived Value Clarity Consistency **Disruptive Technologies:** Big Data Analytics Blockchain Internet of Things Natural Language Processing Cloud computing	**Critical success factors:** Personalisation Engagement Feedback Mechanism Customer Support Trust Building **Disruptive Technologies:** Machine learning Augmented Reality Blockchain Chatbots	**Critical success factors:** Segment Identification and Specification Alignment with Other Elements Measurement and Analysis Inclusivity **Disruptive Technologies:** Artificial Intelligence APIs Business Intelligence Tools Natural Language Processing	**Critical success factors:** Resource Allocation Maintenance and upgrades Accessibility Protection and security Efficient Utilization Sustainability **Disruptive Technologies:** AI-powered resource management systems Predictive Maintenance Technologies Cloud Computing Blockchain Edge Computing Smart Grid Technology	**Critical success factors:** Cost Control Alignment with business strategy Scalability Flexibility Investment in key areas **Disruptive Technologies:** Robotic Process Automation Business Intelligence tools Serverless Computing Cloud Solutions Machine Learning	**Critical success factors:** Accessibility Efficiency Cost-effectiveness Integration Adaptability **Disruptive Technologies:** Cloud Computing Artificial Intelligence 3D Printing Blockchain	**Critical success factors:** Diversification Alignment with Value Proposition Pricing Strategy Sustainability **Disruptive Technologies:** Blockchain Internet of Things Big Data Analytics

Figure 2. Operationalising disruptive technologies and CSFs: a framework for Business Model Innovation (adapted from (Osterwalder & Pigneur, 2010))

6. CONCLUSION

This study's primary objective was to investigate into the complexities of BMI and determine the crucial role disruptive technologies play in enhancing and optimising it. The research endeavoured to map the relationship between key BMI components and technological advancements such as Artificial Intelligence, Blockchain, and Cloud Computing by conducting a systematic literature review and a meticulous thematic analysis. The aim is to provide an exhaustive guide for businesses navigating the digital transformation, highlighting both the challenges and opportunities inherent to this journey. By illuminating the critical successfactors and their technological counterparts, the study hopes to equip businesses with a strategic road map formaximizing the potential of BMI in the current volatile technological environment.

The study investigated the complex relationship between Business Model Innovation (BMI) and its capacity to capitalize on disruptive technologies' dynamism. By systematically examining a vast body of scholarly literature, the aim is not only to comprehend but also to map the foundational pillars supporting successful BMI integrations. Through the rigorous examination, the goal was to identify recurrent methodologies and nuances central to BMI's success, particularly when juxtaposed with rapid technological shifts. Using the power of thematic analysis, these findings have been condensed into a structured frameworkthat provides businesses with a strategic compass for navigating the treacherous waters of digital transformation. In addition to providing theoretical insights, the research sheds light on real-world case studiesthat illustrate the tangible effects and potential pitfalls of BMI. Ultimately, this investigation serves as a beaconfor enterprises ensuring that they remain adaptable, knowledgeable, and ahead of the curve in a digital era thatis perpetually transforming.

7. RECOMMENDED FUTURE RESEARCH

The practical implementation of the business model canvas infused with the critical success factors identified in this study represents a promising avenue for future research. While the research has established the theoretical groundwork, there is an urgent need to test and validate this improved business model canvas in actual industry settings. This would entail collaborating with diverse businesses, ranging from startups to established enterprises, across various sectors to assess the applicability, robustness, and adaptability of the canvas. These empirical studies can provide invaluable insights into potential refinements and nuances that are tailored to the requirements of a particular industry. In addition, investigating the canvas's scalability and efficacy under varying market conditions and technological landscapes can strengthen its practical utility. Future research can transform the business model canvas from a conceptual tool to an indispensable instrument for industry-wide innovation and success by bridging the distance between theory and practice.

REFERENCES

Ahmad, T., & Van Looy, A. (2020). Business process management and digital innovations: A systematic literature review. *Sustainability*, *12*(17), 6827.

Allahar, H. (2019). Innovation management and Value Chain Design: Case of a Small Professional Services Firm. *International Journal of Innovation*, *7*(2), 192-209. https://doi.org/10.5585/iji.v7i2.380

Athanasopoulou, A., De Reuver, M., Nikou, S., & Bouwman, H. (2019). What technology enabled services impact business models in the automotive industry? An exploratory study. *Futures*, *109*, 73-83. https://doi.org/10.1016/j.futures.2019.04.001

Badrinas Ardèvol, J. (2016). Innovation key succes drivers of industrial companies in mature technology segments. Barichello, A. KIBS, Knowledge Management and Digital Product Service Systems: an explorative investigation.

Bartoloni, S., Calo, E., Marinelli, L., Pascucci, F., Dezi, L., Carayannis, E., Revel, G. M., & Gregori, G. L. (2022). Towards designing society 5.0 solutions: The new Quintuple Helix-Design Thinking approach to technology. *Technovation*, *113*, 102413.

Bouwer, L. (2017). Innovation Management Theory Evolution Map. *Available at SSRN 3222848*.

Brailey, J. N., & Bunduchi, R. (2017). Incumbents' response to potentially disruptive innovation in low tech service industries: The case of wearable technologies in the health and fitness industry1. 24th Innovation and Product Development Management Conference,

Budler, M., Župič, I., & Trkman, P. (2021). The development of business model research: A bibliometric review. *Journal of Business Research*, *135*, 480-495. https://doi.org/10.1016/j.jbusres.2021.06.045

Byers, T. H. (2011). *Technology ventures from idea to enterprise*.

Caviggioli, F., & Ughetto, E. (2019). A bibliometric analysis of the research dealing with the impact of additive manufacturing on industry, business and society. *International journal of production economics*, *208*, 254-268.

Chen, Y., Zhou, R., & Zhou, Y. (2022). Analysis of critical factors for the entrepreneurship in industries of the future based on DEMATEL-ISM approach. *Sustainability*, *14*(24), 16812.

CHIK, K. O. (2016). *THE UNIVERSITY OF NEWCASTLE* Newcastle Business School].

Chowdhury, S., Budhwar, P., Dey, P. K., Joel-Edgar, S., & Abadie, A. (2022). AI-employee collaboration and business performance: Integrating knowledge-based view, socio-technical systems and organisational socialisation framework. *Journal of Business Research*, *144*, 31-49.

Coulson-Thomas, C. (2018). Organisational leadership for challenging and changing times. *Effective Executive*, *21*(3), 14-37.

Da Silva, C. R., Vilela, T. B., De Faria, R. R. B., Da Silva, L. B. P., Pontes, J., De Resende, L. M. M., Yoshino, R. T., & Treinta, F. T. (2022). Systematic Literature Review on Corporate Accelerator: Benefits, Challenges and Critical Success Factors.

de Reuver, A. A. M., & Haaker, T. Designing digital tooling for business model exploration for the Internet-of-Things.

Di Vaio, A., Hassan, R., Chhabra, M., Arrigo, E., & Palladino, R. (2022). Sustainable entrepreneurship impact and entrepreneurial venture life cycle: A systematic literature review. *Journal of Cleaner Production*, 134469.

Dulal, K., & Binkele, C. (2021). Disruptive Business Model Innovation: Incumbent's perspectives and approaches to competitive advantage generation.

Floerecke, S., & Lehner, F. (2018). Success-driving business model characteristics of IaaS and PaaS providers. *International Journal on Cloud Computing: Services and Architecture (IJCCSA)*, *8*(6), 1-22.

Garmulewicz, A., Holweg, M., Veldhuis, H., & Yang, A. (2018). Disruptive technology as an enabler of the circular economy: what potential does 3D printing hold? *California Management Review*, *60*(3), 112-132.

Gómez, J. S. P., & Vargas, C. A. Digital Transformation in Quality Management Systems in Technology Companies, Link Wireless Case.

Guranda, V. (2021). Impact of Autonomous Vehicles on Automotive OEMs Business Models.

Hämäläinen, M. (2014). Customer centric and value-based business model design: impacts of the additive manufacturing technology on firm's business model.

HARBO, H. N. (2023). HOW TO SUCCEED WITH DIGITAL PLATFORM BUSINES MODELS.

Hehle, D. *Success factors of Start-up companies in the digital industry: An empirical investigation of success factors in an international context within Spain* FH Vorarlberg (Fachhochschule Vorarlberg)].

Holzmann, P., Hartlieb, E., & Roth, M. (2018). From engineer to entrepreneur-entrepreneurship education for engineering students: the case of the entrepreneurial campus Villach. *International Journal of Engineering Pedagogy (iJEP)*, *8*(3), 28-39.

Jabbour, C. J. C., Sarkis, J., de Sousa Jabbour, A. B. L., Renwick, D. W. S., Singh, S. K., Grebinevych, O., Kruglianskas, I., & Godinho Filho, M. (2019). Who is in charge? A review and a research agenda on the 'human side'of the circular economy. *Journal of Cleaner Production*, *222*, 793-801.

Kafando, I. (2020). How can Customs better leverage emerging AI technologies for more sustainable and smarter operations? *World Customs Journal*, *14*(2).

Kamers, R. (2018). *Using the scenario planning method in a systematic way to develop a new business model and reduce future uncertainty within the construction industry* University of Twente].

Khan, I. S., Ahmad, M. O., & Majava, J. (2023). Industry 4.0 innovations and their implications: An evaluation from sustainable development perspective. *Journal of Cleaner Production*, *405*, 137006.

Koch, C. M. (2022). *Digital technologies catalyzing business model innovation in supply chain management-a comprehensive overview of digitalization and emerging technologies with its implications on business process performance*

Kraus, N., Kraus, K., & Shtepa, O. (2022). Teaching notes for Casebook "How to do business in digital era?".

Malik, A., Sharma, P., Vinu, A., Karakoti, A., Kaur, K., Gujral, H. S., Munjal, S., & Laker, B. (2022). Circular economy adoption by SMEs in emerging markets: Towards a multilevel conceptual framework. *Journal of Business Research*, *142*, 605-619.

Manfreda, A. (2018). NEW BUSINESS MODELS–FROM BUSINESS PROCESS REDESIGN TO THE DIGITAL TRANSFORMATION. *CroDiM: International Journal of Marketing Science*, *1*(1), 69-79.

Mariani, M., & Borghi, M. (2019). Industry 4.0: A bibliometric review of its managerial intellectual structure and potential evolution in the service industries. *Technological Forecasting and Social Change*, *149*, 119752.

Martínez-Olvera, C. (2022). Towards the development of a digital twin for a sustainable mass customization 4.0 environment: a literature review of relevant concepts. *Automation*, *3*(1), 197-222.

Mokgohloa, K. (2023). *System dynamics approach for digital transformation and complex policy design for the postal sector in Southern Africa*

Mokoena, A., Prinsloo, J. J., Gawlik, R., & Pelser, T. (2023). A framework for the sustainability of advertising agencies in an emerging economy: the case of South Africa. *Journal of Marketing Communications*, *29*(1), 46-66. https://doi.org/10.1080/13527266.2021.1989613

Müller, J. M., Kiel, D., & Voigt, K.-I. (2018). What drives the implementation of Industry 4.0? The role of opportunities and challenges in the context of sustainability. *Sustainability*, *10*(1), 247.

Muraro, A. (2019). New business models enabled by the technological disruption of Industry 4.0.

Murmura, F., Bravi, L., & Santos, G. (2021). Sustainable process and product innovation in the eyewear sector: The role of industry 4.0 enabling technologies. *Sustainability*, *13*(1), 365.

Nwaiwu, F., Duduci, M., & Chromjakova, F. (2019). Assessment of the critical success factors that enable implementation of industry 4.0 concepts in manufacturing companies within the SME sector in the Czech Republic. International Scientific Conference „Contemporary Issues in Business, Management and Economics Engineering",

Oluleye, B. I., Chan, D. W., Antwi-Afari, P., & Olawumi, T. O. (2023). Modeling the principal success factors for attaining systemic circularity in the building construction industry: An international survey of circular economy experts. *Sustainable Production and Consumption*, *37*, 268-283.

Osterwalder, A., & Pigneur, Y. (2010). *Business model generation: a handbook for visionaries, game changers, and challengers* (Vol. 1). John Wiley & Sons.

Özkanlısoy, Ö., & Bulutlar, F. (2022). Measuring Using Disruptive Technology in the Supply Chain Context: Scale Development and Validation. *Journal of Theoretical and Applied Electronic Commerce Research*, *17*(4), 1336- 1360.

Pereira, C. S., Durão, N., Fonseca, D., Ferreira, M. J., & Moreira, F. (2020). An educational approach for present and future of digital transformation in portuguese organizations. *Applied Sciences*, *10*(3), 757.

Qin, J., & van der Rhee, B. (2021). From trash to treasure: A checklist to identify high-potential NPD projects from previously rejected projects. *Technovation*, *104*, 102259.

Rashed, F. (2021). *Leveraging enterprise architecture for data-driven business model innovation* Leuphana Universität Lüneburg].

Rother, E. T. (2007). Systematic literature review X narrative review. *Acta paulista de enfermagem*, *20*, v-vi. Samuel, P. (2017). *Strategies for integrating technological innovations in small businesses* Walden University].

Savastano, M., Amendola, C., Bellini, F., & D'Ascenzo, F. (2019). Contextual impacts on industrial processes brought by the digital transformation of manufacturing: A systematic review. *Sustainability*, *11*(3), 891.

Scuotto, V., Magni, D., Palladino, R., & Nicotra, M. (2022). Triggering disruptive technology absorptive capacity by CIOs. Explorative research on a micro-foundation lens. *Technological Forecasting and Social Change*, *174*, 121234.

Shakhour, N. H. T., Obeidat, B. Y., Jaradat, M. O., & Alshurideh, M. (2021). Agile-minded organizational excellence: Empirical investigation. *Academy of Strategic Management Journal*, *20*, 1-25.

Shang, T., Miao, X., & Abdul, W. International Journal of Innovation Science.

Spyropoulos, T. S. (2018a). Innovation mapping and business choices. In *Innovation mapping and business choices: Spyropoulos, Theocharis Stylianos*.

Spyropoulos, T. S. (2018b). Innovation mapping and business choises: a model for innovation management & marketing. *MIBES Transactions International Journal*.

Spyropoulos, T. S. (2019). Greek IT start-ups: an analysis of founder's perceptions. *Scientific Bulletin-Economic Sciences journal*.

Spyropoulos, T. S., & Varsakelis, N. (2023). Business opportunity ontology. *Economies of the Balkan and Eastern European Countries journal, Volume 2023*.

Tawaststjerna, T. (2020). Digital business ecosystems contexts for digital transformation: the point of view of an intermediary organization.

Timmer, P. (2019). Disruptive Coopetition: How Start-Ups Disrupt Industries in Coopetitive Partnerships with Incumbent Firms.

Tran-Dang, H., & Kim, D.-S. (2021). The physical internet in the era of digital transformation: perspectives and open issues. *IEEE Access*, *9*, 164613-164631.

Trapani, M. (2018). Success Factors in a Saturated Market. Is there Room for Creativity?

Trkman, P., Budler, M., & Groznik, A. 20th Anniversary special issue: A business model approach to supply chain management.

Turienzo, J., Blanco, A., F. Lampón, J., & del Pilar Muñoz-Dueñas, M. (2023). Logistics business model evolution: digital platforms and connected and autonomous vehicles as disruptors. *Review of Managerial Science*, 1-24.

van der Meer, R. J., & Track, M. (2019). MASTER THESIS REPORT.

Velu, C. (2016). Evolutionary or revolutionary business model innovation through coopetition? The role of dominance in network markets. *Industrial Marketing Management*, *53*, 124-135. https://doi.org/10.1016/j.indmarman.2015.11.007

von Rosing, M., von Scheel, H., & Rosenberg, A. (2015). 1 The Importance of a Business Model. *The Complete Business Process Handbook*, *2*.

Vorholzer, M., & Meyer, R. (2021). Open Innovation and Disruptive Capacity-An Empirical Study on the Impact of Open Innovation Practices on Disruptive Capacity within the Alternative Food Industry.

Wang, R. (2022). Business Model Innovation in Swedish FinTech Industry: A case Study of Klarna. In.

Wang, R., & Chebo, A. K. (2021). The Dynamics of Business Model Innovation for Technology Entrepreneurship: A Systematic Review and Future Avenue. *SAGE Open*, *11*(3), 21582440211029917.

Weisshuhn, O. (2019). *Platform Business Modelling for Enhancing the Efficiency of Freight Logistics in the Maritime Supply Chain*

Ziegler, D., & Abdelkafi, N. (2022). Business models for electric vehicles: Literature review and key insights. *Journal of Cleaner Production*, *330*, 129803.

Zubizarreta, M., Ganzarain, J., Cuadrado, J., & Lizarralde, R. (2020). Evaluating disruptive innovation project management capabilities. *Sustainability*, *13*(1), 1.

CONTEXT-AWARE SHIPBUILDING KNOWLEDGE RECOMMENDATION: EXPLOITING KNOWLEDGE GRAPHS WITH DIFFERENT STRUCTURE

Bo Song[1], Qiao Zhou[1] and Zuhua Jiang[2]
[1]*China Institute of FTZ Supply Chain, Shanghai Maritime University, Shanghai, China*
[2]*Department of Industrial Engineering and Management, Shanghai Jiao Tong University, Shanghai, China*

ABSTRACT

Knowledge recommendation faces unique challenges in high-tech organizations such as shipbuilding companies. Inactive interactions between users and knowledge items hinder the application of collaborative filtering, while the complexity of knowledge items makes content-based filtering challenging. In this paper, we propose a knowledge recommendation method using knowledge graphs, neural networks, and a context-aware mechanism. Utilizing two types of knowledge graphs: a sparse knowledge graph modelling the categorical relationships between knowledge items and a dense knowledge graph modelling the term-level semantic relatedness between knowledge items, we propagate shipbuilding task context and user-item interactions through the graph to assign interest scores to the knowledge items in order to determine recommendation prioritization. Experiments show that with some surprise, the sparse knowledge graph combined with RippleNet is the best model in terms of knowledge recommendation accuracy. This research points out a new direction of combinatorial optimization of knowledge recommendation and knowledge graph structures, which has a good application prospect in knowledge-intensive industry.

KEYWORDS

Knowledge Recommendation, Context-Aware, Knowledge Graph, RippleNet

1. INTRODUCTION

Knowledge supporting creative tasks is rarely systematically narrated and ready for use. People processing creative tasks must seek knowledge from various sources and properly organize them for retrieving and reasoning. To save the time and effort consumed in knowledge seeking, knowledge recommendation is proposed for proactively providing people with useful knowledge (Ji et al., 2023). The research on knowledge recommendation can benefit from the development of general recommendation techniques such as collaborative filtering and content-based filtering, nevertheless, it has unique traits that are determined by the nature of knowledge-intensive tasks and application domains. A common agreement on applying information item recommendation in a complex environment is that the context of user interests is of great importance, and context-aware recommendation has become a trend (Zammali & Yahia, 2021; Sun et al., 2021). Although context awareness has been well studied in recommending items such as movies and restaurants, the context information used in these daily life recommendation situations mainly consists of time and location (Baltrunas, 2012), which is much simpler than the knowledge context used for recommending task-relevant knowledge (Song et al., 2016).

Nowadays a lot of recommender systems are based on collaborative filtering or its variants, as these techniques have high accuracy and diversity in recommendation performance. However, there are two well-known problems perplexing this kind of recommender systems: the sparsity of user-item interaction data and the cold start problem (Guo et al., 2020). The two problems become even more serious when considering context, as the user-item interaction in a certain context is much scarcer than that in a general situation. In order to establish some relations between users and items which are not connected in the beginning, knowledge graph (KG) comes into play. KG extents the concept of semantic network and is capable of modelling large-scale relational data with easy-to-use databases and software. When used in recommender systems, KG is usually designed in such a way that the nodes representing users are connected to the nodes representing items to be recommended via the "interact with" relation, and the user/item nodes are interconnected with each other via shared properties (Kaur et al., 2023). Leveraging graph-based machine learning algorithms, a recommender system can tactfully propagate user interests to the items that have not been browsed by the user yet, so as to solve the aforementioned data sparsity and cold start problems and improve the recommendation performance (Wang et al., 2018).

Recent research in recommendation systems has seen a surge in incorporating KGs to enhance performance and explainability. For example, Ma et al. (2023) propose a novel method that integrates KGs with graph convolution networks (GCN) to alleviate error propagation and improve recommendation diversity and relevance. Chang et al. (2023) introduce MKCGN, a meta-relation-assisted graph neural network to address data sparsity issues and optimize user/item representation quality for better recommendation performance. The AGRE recommendation algorithm codes the paths between users and items with a specified RNN to accurately learn the user's preferences (Zhao et al., 2023). On the other hand, Cai et al. (2022) explore explainable recommendation using a knowledge graph and evolutionary algorithm, achieving a balance between precision, diversity, novelty, and explainability. The KGIN model learns the intents behind user-item interactions with KG, offering interpretable recommendation and significant performance improvements (Wang et al., 2021).

Based on current research findings, achieving knowledge recommendation that better meets user needs entails two primary considerations. First, a finer granularity of user interests must be mined from task information, typically achieved through context awareness. Second, establishing more connections between users and knowledge items is necessary to address data sparsity and cold start issues. However, in engineering domains, a significant challenge lies in the costs associated with establishing these data connections. Within enterprises, directly accessible user/item relations are often sparse and established via mature business processes in necessary scenarios, whose expansion requires manual intervention of domain experts. To establish rich connections between users and items at low cost, one can use concept mining and relation mining techniques to automatically construct a knowledge graph encompassing arbitrary granularity of concepts and relations. To the best of our knowledge, there has been no research evaluating the impact of different knowledge graph structures on knowledge recommendation performances. This paper proposes the Context-aware Knowledge Graph-based Recommendation Network (CKGRN), which is tested in a shipbuilding enterprise with two types of KGs: one derived from enterprise resource associations and the other obtained via information extraction algorithms. By leveraging user browsing records as input, CKGRN can propagate user interests in the KG and provide personalized knowledge recommendations. Comparative experiments will show which is the better way of building a KG for inner enterprise knowledge recommendation.

2. METHOD

In this paper, we propose CKGRN, a context-aware knowledge graph-based recommendation model. CKGRN is composed of three parts. The first is a KG relating different knowledge items, users and concepts, which is the foundation of a KG-based recommendation engine. In this part, we will explore KGs with different structures to find the type of KG that is more suitable for knowledge recommendation. Second, an interest model is incorporated into CKGRN by assigning interest scores to items and letting the scores decay with time. This will enable CKGRN to track a user's task processing steps and keep the right information to reason with. Third, CKGRN has a context-aware recommendation engine, which is instantiated through adding a context-aware mechanism to an existing KG-based recommender. The context-aware mechanism works in such a way that it actively links entities in a user's working environment to the concepts defined in the KG, and then treats the linked concepts as browsed items. The overall framework of CKGRN is shown in Figure 1, and we will introduce each part in detail.

2.1 Knowledge Graphs with Different Structures

Previous recommendation studies based on KG usually adopt publicly available KGs or build a single domain-specific KG for use. Due to the cost of building a KG from the beginning, few researchers would construct several KGs with the same topic to test their performances, thus leaving a research gap about how

KGs with different structures affect recommendation outcomes. In this paper, we will construct KGs using two representative approaches, and obtain two KGs with different structures. The most significant difference between the two KGs is the number of nodes and relations representing the same quantity of knowledge items, which can differ more than 10 times. We refer to the KG with fewer nodes and relations as the sparse KG and the one with more nodes and relations as the dense KG.

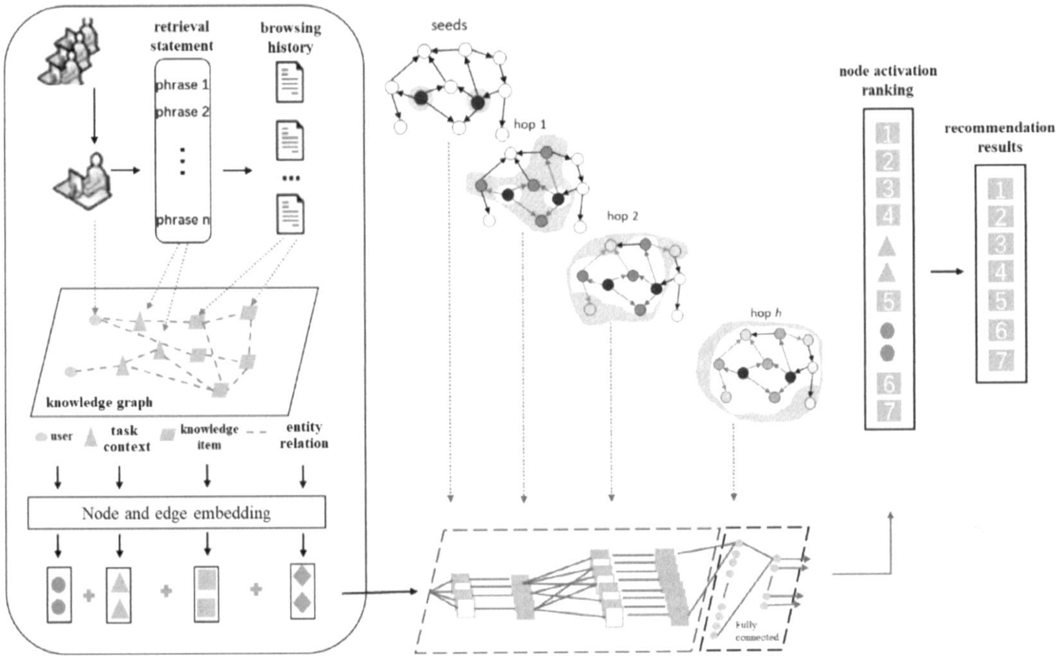

Figure 1. The Overall framework of CKGRN

2.1.1 Sparse Knowledge Graph

The sparse KG is constructed from the meta information associated with each of the knowledge items in the studied shipbuilding enterprise. An example of a knowledge item is shown in Table 1. There are 7 types of information comprising a knowledge item: *ship type, ship part, keyword, case type, case name, analysis* and *solution*. While *case name, analysis* and *solution* are the main content of a knowledge item, *ship type, ship part, keyword* and *case type* are the meta information used for classifying, managing and retrieving knowledge items. A sparse KG can be constructed by adding *hasShipType, hasShipPart, hasKeyword* and *hasCaseType* relations between each knowledge item and its four meta information, as shown in Figure 2. It can be seen that the smallest knowledge unit in the sparse KG is a knowledge item. One cannot know the detail of a knowledge item by looking at the KG and reasoning with attributes of a knowledge item is not applicable. Despite the coarse granularity of knowledge represented in the sparse KG, all the nodes and relations in the sparse KG are in fact created by experts in the enterprise, and no noise information has been introduced into the sparse KG during its construction process.

Table 1. A knowledge item

Ship type	400K VLOC	Ship part	Hull
Keyword	Web length	Case type	Drawing
Case name	Layout T-row web length error		
Analysis	Ship H1XXX in section 124 layout T-row web length is not correct, 20mm short. Some designers lack experience. A T-row is embedded on site, waste production hours.		
Solution	For T-rows with truncated ends, attentions should be paid to the concept of length correction, and each group leader needs to do spot check more in the process of drawing and proofreading.		

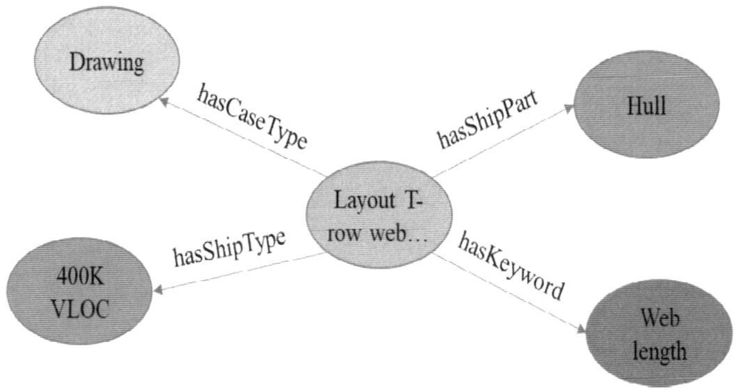

Figure 2. A knowledge item in the sparse KG

2.1.2 Dense Knowledge Graph

The dense KG is constructed based on term-level semantic relations between knowledge items and inside a knowledge item. The primary goal of constructing such a dense KG is to make knowledge items reasonable. For example, if we extract a series of (*Object, Attribute, Value, Unit*) tuples such as "web thickness xxx mm" and "deck length xxx m" from the knowledge items, then it will be possible to compare these features across the knowledge items and enable retrieval statements like "find web problems in ship hull with deck longer than 150m". In this paper the dense KG is used for knowledge recommendation instead of knowledge reasoning, as the dense relations among knowledge items provide a lot of paths for the user interest to spread.

The dense KG is constructed in the following way. First, we annotate some knowledge items with the entity types and relation types listed in Table 2, then we use the annotated data to train a BERT-CRF model for named entity recognition and a BERT-LSTM model for relation extraction, at last, the trained models are used to annotate the remaining knowledge items automatically. While in the sparse KG a knowledge item usually has 4 relations with other concepts, the number of concepts related with a knowledge item in the dense KG is determined by how many *Objects* are mined from the item and thus can reach a large value. Figure 3 is a visual comparison of the sparse KG and the dense KG, from which we can see that for the same number of knowledge items, the dense KG has far more nodes and relations than the sparse KG.

Table 2. Entities and relations defined for mining a dense KG

Entity	Examples	Relation	Explanation
Object	deck, web	RL-of-O	Object O is the first parameter of relation RL
Property	length, thickness	O-of-RL	Object O is the second parameter of relation RL
Value	200, 9.5	P-of-O	P is the property of object O
Unit	m, mm	V-of-P	V is the value of property P
Action	truncate, embed	U-of-V	U is the unit of value V
Relation	contain, larger than	RF-of-O	RF is the reference of object O
Reference	section 4	A-of-O	O is the actor of action A
		O-of-A	O is the subject of action A
		O-of-O	Object O is related to another object O

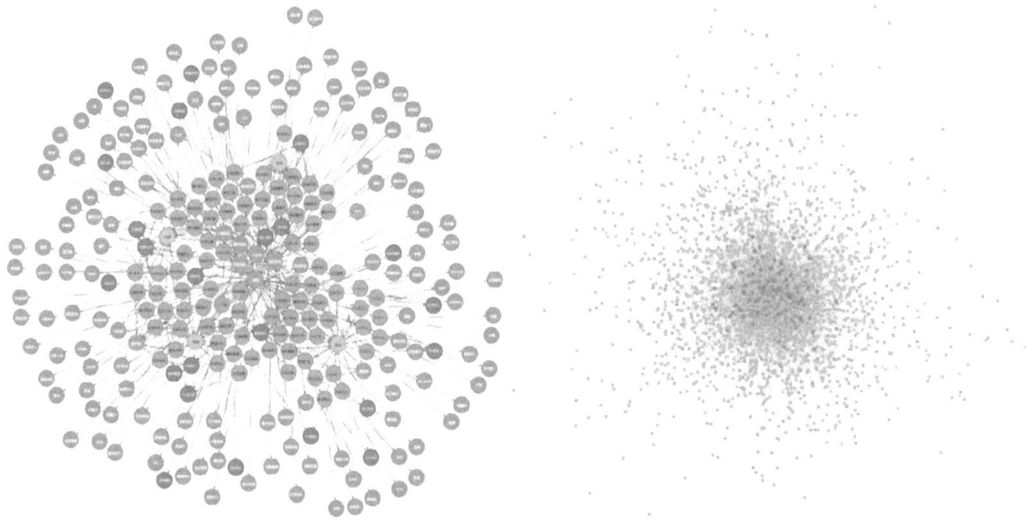

Figure 3. Sparse KG (left) and dense KG (right)

2.2 Interest Model

Generally speaking, a user's interest in a knowledge item is positively related with the number of clicks and time spent on the knowledge item. Besides, in a task-focused environment such as shipbuilding, people's knowledge needs are driven by the task context more than their interests. In order to reflect the influence of dynamic task context on knowledge needs, we apply a decay factor to each interest score considering the time passed since the click/browse takes place. Specifically, we adopt the interest model proposed by Wang et al. (2021) to calculate the interest score that a knowledge item or KG node receives.

$$F(U,I)=\begin{cases} 0 & count\left(R_L(U),I\right)=0 \\ 0 & count\left(R_L(U),I\right)=1, \Delta T \leq 30\text{s} \\ \sum_{k=1}^{L} \frac{1}{n-k+1} \cdot \frac{\Delta T^k}{\mid I^k \mid} \cdot \delta\left(I^k, I\right) & \text{other} \end{cases}$$

$$\delta\left(I^k, I\right)=\begin{cases} 1 & I^k = I \\ 0 & I^k \neq I \end{cases} \tag{1}$$

In Equation 1, $F(U, I)$ denotes the interest of user U in knowledge item I, $R_L(U) = \{(I^1, \Delta T^1), (I^2, \Delta T^2), \ldots, (I^L, \Delta T^L)\}$ is the sequence of browsed knowledge items and their browse time, $1/(n-k+1)$ is the interest decay factor, $|I^k|$ is the text length of the kth browsed knowledge item, and $count(R_L(U), I)$ is the number of times that knowledge item I has been repeatedly browsed by user U. Knowledge items that have not been browsed are irrelevant to the user and have an interest score of 0. Knowledge items that have been browsed once but for a period shorter than 30 seconds also have an interest score of 0. The remaining knowledge items have an associated interest score calculated from the accumulated browse time coordinated with the text length and decay factor.

2.3 Context-Aware Recommendation Engine

CKGRN has a context-aware recommendation engine, which is built upon an existing KG-based recommender such as RippleNet. Three modifications are made to the existing recommender, including context capturing, entity linking and user interest input. Following is the detailed explanation.

(1) Context capturing. In a task-focused environment, if a user clicks on a knowledge item and starts browsing, it means the user has already figured out what knowledge he/she needs. A helpful knowledge recommender in this situation should act in advance, by capturing signals from the user's task context and inferring the user's knowledge need. To do so, we monitor a user's desktop browser and capture the title of the active page as a context message every second. If a context message is the same as the previous one, then the knowledge item or KG nodes corresponding to the message will have duration time +1.

(2) Entity linking. We use a simple entity linking method to map the words in a context message to the nodes in KGs. First, we check for each KG node whether the Chinese character sequence of node name is contained in the context message. If we get yes for a node representing a knowledge item, then the knowledge item is linked to the context message. If we get yes for a node representing a concept, e.g., ship type, ship part, keyword, case type and object, then we check whether at least one neighbor of the node appears in the context message, and if yes, the node is linked to the context message.

(3) User interest input. The original RippleNet uses a 0-1 rating matrix as input and does not consider the decay of user interest over time. In this paper we have the interest model described in section 2.2. The interest model does not affect the training phase of RippleNet, but during the predicting phase, the heads of KG triples in the hop 1 ripple set are multiplied by their according interest score before going to the softmax operation. In doing so the influence of interest scores is passed to the tails of KG triples in the hop 1 ripple set as well as the following ripple sets.

3. EXPERIMENT

The experiment with CKGRN is conducted in a shipbuilding enterprise in Shanghai. We collected 90 knowledge items from the production design department of the shipbuilding enterprise. While the sparse KG constructed from the knowledge items has 270 nodes and 499 relations, the dense KG has 3017 nodes and 6038 relations. The personal attributes, retrieval statements, and browsing records of 5 users from the production design department are collected for training and testing CKGRN. In order to avoid possible bias of RippleNet on sparse and dense KGs, we use another KG-based recommender, MKR (Wang et al., 2019) to evaluate CKGRN. The hyper-parameters of the two recommenders are set as Table 3 in the experiment.

Table 3. Hyper-parameters of RippleNet and MKR

Recommender	Parameter	Explanation	Value
RippleNet	dim	KG embedding dimension	16
	n_hop	max hop	3
	kge_weight	weight of KG embedding loss	0.01
	12_weight	weight of l2 regularization in loss	1e-7
	lr	learning rate	0.02
	n_memory	ripple set size for each hop	32
	batch_size	batch size	24
	n_epoch	epoch number	10
MKR	dim	KG embedding dimension	8
	L	number of low layers	1
	H	number of high layers	1
	12_weight	weight of l2 regularization in loss	1e-6
	lr_rs	learning rate of recommendation task	0.02
	lr_kge	learning rate of KG embedding task	0.01
	kge_interval	interval of KG embedding training	3
	batch_size	batch size	24
	n_epoch	epoch number	20

The experimental scenario is click-through rate (CTR) prediction, and we use AUC and ACC to evaluate the performance of different models. ACC reflects the overall recommendation accuracy. Given that the experiment dataset comprises well-curated, typical cases with high-quality features, we assume there is a positive correlation between AUC and recall. This allows AUC to measure both the model's ranking capability and the diversity of its recommendations. The performances of RippleNet and MKR with and without the context-aware mechanism and the interest model are assessed respectively. The experiment results are presented in Table 4. It can be seen that RippleNet outperforms MKR in recommendation effectiveness, and the results obtained with context awareness and interest model are better than those without the two settings. To summarize, in the studied shipbuilding case, the proposed CKGRN model achieves 11.78% increase in recommendation accuracy and 34.38% increase in recommendation diversity compared with the original RippleNet when using the sparse KG. When using the dense KG, both RippleNet and MKR perform worse but the utilization of context and interest can still improve the results.

Table 4. RippleNet and MKR performance comparison

Model	Context and interest utilization	Sparse KG		Dense KG	
		AUC	ACC	AUC	ACC
RippleNet	without context and interest	0.6128	0.6071	0.5055	0.5391
MKR		0.5590	0.5741	0.4616	0.4648
RippleNet	with context and interest	0.8235	0.6786	0.5545	0.6428
MKR		0.6524	0.6073	0.4706	0.4779

To show more clearly how the sparse and dense KGs perform in knowledge recommendation, we select different parts of training data and test the RippleNet-based CKGRN with context awareness and interest model for multiple times. The results are shown in Figure 4. The average AUC was 0.82 for the sparse KG and 0.55 for the dense KG. The average ACC was 0.72 for the sparse KG and 0.66 for the dense KG. It is evident that while the dense KG modeling fine-grained semantic relations between knowledge items can better support knowledge inference and retrieval, it is less effective in supporting knowledge recommendation compared with the sparse KG. This may be due to that in a dense knowledge graph, the embeddings of nodes and relations are not sufficiently learnt with limited data samples, and the propagation of user interest is not complete at each hop due to the limitation on ripple set size.

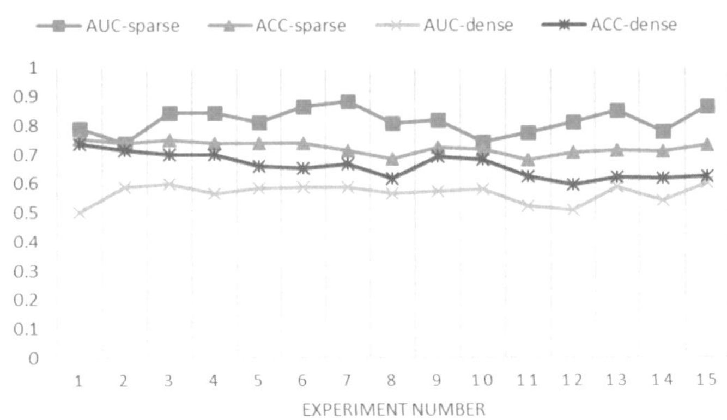

Figure 4. Performance comparison of the sparse and dense KGs

4. CONCLUSION

Due to the sparsity of user - knowledge item interactions inside a task-focused group with different user roles, the recommendation of knowledge should exploit the relation between knowledge items in addition to the user-item interactions. KG-based recommendation models become potent solutions to this problem since a KG can describe the relations between knowledge items clearly. However, among the established models, few have discussed how to build a KG facilitating accurate knowledge recommendation. In this paper, we show two ways of building KGs for a shipbuilding enterprise, and use two advanced recommendation algorithms, RippleNet and MKR, to do KG-based knowledge recommendation. Context awareness and a user interest model are also used to improve the performance of knowledge recommendation.

Through carrying out comparative experiments with differently structured KGs and recommendation algorithms, we identify a combination of the two aspects which can achieve better knowledge recommendation in the shipbuilding scenario. An important discovery is that a dense KG modeling fine-grained semantic relatedness between knowledge items is not so effective in knowledge recommendation compared with a relatively sparse KG constructed from the knowledge taxonomy manually compiled by experts in the shipbuilding enterprise. This may be caused by underfitting of KG embeddings given limited training samples. It can also be caused by the incompleteness in user interest propagation given the limitation on ripple set size. In all, we have proved that by combining context awareness, RippleNet and a KG constructed with domain expertise, a knowledge recommender with satisfactory performance can be built inside a high-tech shipbuilding enterprise.

REFERENCES

Baltrunas, L., Ludwig, B., Peer, S., & Ricci, F. (2012). Context relevance assessment and exploitation in mobile recommender systems. Personal and Ubiquitous Computing, 16, 507-526.

Cai, X., Xie, L., Tian, R., & Cui, Z. (2022). Explicable recommendation based on knowledge graph. Expert Systems with Applications, 200, 117035.

Chang, Y., Zhou, W., Cai, H., Fan, W., Hu, L., & Wen, J. (2023). Meta-relation assisted knowledge-aware coupled graph neural network for recommendation. Information Processing & Management, 60(3), 103353.

Guo, Q., Zhuang, F., Qin, C., Zhu, H., Xie, X., Xiong, H., & He, Q. (2020). A survey on knowledge graph-based recommender systems. IEEE Transactions on Knowledge and Data Engineering, 34(8), 3549-3568.

Ji, Y., Jiang, Z., Li, X., Huang, Y., & Wang, F. (2023). A multitask context-aware approach for design lesson-learned knowledge recommendation in collaborative product design. Journal of Intelligent Manufacturing, 34(4), 1615-1637.

Kaur, G., Liu, F., & Chen, Y. P. P. (2023). A deep learning knowledge graph neural network for recommender systems. Machine Learning with Applications, 14, 100507.

Ma, T., Huang, L., Lu, Q., & Hu, S. (2023). Kr-gcn: Knowledge-aware reasoning with graph convolution network for explainable recommendation. ACM Transactions on Information Systems, 41(1), 1-27.

Song, B., Jiang, Z., & Liu, L. (2016). Automated experiential engineering knowledge acquisition through Q&A contextualization and transformation. Advanced Engineering Informatics, 30(3), 467-480.

Sun, K., Qian, T., Chen, X., & Zhong, M. (2021). Context-aware seq2seq translation model for sequential recommendation. Information Sciences, 581, 60-72.

Wang, H., Zhang, F., Wang, J., Zhao, M., Li, W., Xie, X., & Guo, M. (2018). Ripplenet: Propagating user preferences on the knowledge graph for recommender systems. In Proceedings of the 27th ACM international conference on information and knowledge management (pp. 417-426).

Wang, H., Zhang, F., Zhao, M., Li, W., Xie, X., & Guo, M. (2019). Multi-task feature learning for knowledge graph enhanced recommendation. In The world wide web conference (pp. 2000-2010).

Wang, L. K., Jiang, Z. H., & Li, X. Y. (2021). Context-aware GAN-based knowledge recommendation method in engineering field. Computer Integrated Manufacturing Systems, 1-21.

Wang, X., Huang, T., Wang, D., Yuan, Y., Liu, Z., He, X., & Chua, T. S. (2021). Learning intents behind interactions with knowledge graph for recommendation. In Proceedings of the web conference 2021 (pp. 878-887).

Zammali, S., & Yahia, S. B. (2021). How to select and weight context dimensions conditions for context-aware recommendation?. Expert Systems with Applications, 182, 115176.

Zhao, N., Long, Z., Wang, J., & Zhao, Z. D. (2023). AGRE: A knowledge graph recommendation algorithm based on multiple paths embeddings RNN encoder. Knowledge-Based Systems, 259, 110078.

DESIGN REQUIREMENTS FOR HYBRID COLLABORATION IN THE REALM OF CREATIVE GROUP WORK

Pia Gebbing and Christoph Lattemann
Constructor University Bremen
Campus Ring 1, 28759 Bremen, Germany

ABSTRACT

Hybrid work provides the potential to facilitate creative collaboration and the development of innovative ideas through greater flexibility in terms of time, space, and tools used for collaboration. However, fostering creativity in hybrid teams has proven challenging in practice due to the absence of established guidelines, design principles, and tools. This paper addresses the ongoing challenges that practitioners face in implementing hybrid group work and presents requirements for designing a work environment that fosters creativity. Utilizing focus groups, the study investigates strategies to mitigate technostress effects, promote co-presence, and enhance psychological safety in hybrid meetings. The findings offer practical insights into preparing, facilitating, and integrating online participants in hybrid meetings, contributing to a deeper understanding of effective strategies for fostering creativity in hybrid group work.

KEYWORDS

Hybrid Teams, Creativity, Co-Presence, Psychological Safety, Technostress

1. INTRODUCTION

In the rapidly evolving landscape of work environments, hybrid collaboration has emerged as a pivotal trend, indispensable for fostering creativity and innovation in the digital age. The fusion of remote and in-person collaboration in digital work environments facilitates networking without location constraints, connecting a diverse pool of creative individuals and providing opportunities for co-creating ideas and problem-solving with increased stakeholder involvement (Lattemann et al., 2017; Nemiro, 2007). Additionally, computer-supported group collaboration facilitates collecting, storing, and managing ideas and information, enabling recall and access to untapped innovations (Inie and Dalsgaard, 2020; Nemiro, 2007).

Research on creative collaboration, spanning back to the early 2000s, initially showcased the capability of virtual teams to outperform face-to-face groups in idea generation and electronic brainstorming (Maaravi et al., 2021; Yang et al., 2023). Companies anticipate that embracing remote collaboration will yield significant benefits, including enhanced flexibility (e.g., through mobility, location, and time independence) and outreach (e.g., through networking and reduced travel expenses) (Aroles et al., 2021). Despite these advantages, remote work is often perceived to undermine efficient group collaboration (Gebbing et al., 2022; Weritz et al., 2022), and practitioners of creative collaboration strongly prefer a hybrid approach that combines physical and digital meetings. However, in practical application, employees and managers often encounter challenges and adverse effects in effectively establishing and coordinating virtual or hybrid teams (Nemiro, 2007), and a research gap persists regarding the optimal blend of online and offline collaboration. To address this research gap, this study seeks to answer the following research question: How can hybrid group work be designed to foster creativity?

Many companies fail to harness the potential of the new work forms due to a lack of guidelines and a deficiency in suitable tools and mindsets for successful implementation (Gebbing et al., 2022; Tønnessen et al., 2021). Therefore, the transition to hybrid collaboration needs to address three primary challenges: establishing spatial and technical infrastructures, ensuring team effectiveness, and fostering team cohesion and commitment (Hardwig and Boos, 2023). Recognizing these challenges, the study highlights three pivotal aspects of hybrid creative collaboration: (1) minimizing the impact of technostress on hybrid teams caused by increased use of technology, (2) establishing psychological safety for an adequate flow of ideas and information sharing, and (3) fostering co-presence and interaction among participants in online and offline realms.

Utilizing focus groups, this study delves into the dynamics of hybrid collaboration, focusing on the requirements of creative group endeavors. The results offer valuable insights and practical recommendations, assisting practitioners in improving hybrid collaboration and contributing to the scientific development of design theories in computer-supported creativity.

2. THEORETICAL BACKGROUND AND LITERATURE REVIEW

Virtual teams encompass a group of individuals collaborating remotely to achieve a shared objective, utilizing information and communication technology (ICT) for collaboration and information sharing (Meluso et al., 2020). Members of virtual teams do not meet in a single physical location; instead, they work independently using ICT tools such as video calls, chats, digital whiteboards, and cloud solutions. On the other hand, hybrid collaboration involves a mode of working that combines both remote and in-person collaboration (Neumayr et al., 2021). This primarily manifests in two ways: some team members convene on-site while others connect digitally, or the entire team alternates between physical in-person and virtual sessions. Hybrid collaboration is gaining relevance as businesses strive to foster creativity in innovation management.

Creativity involves generating original and novel ideas or solutions appropriate to the task at hand (Runco and Jaeger, 2012). Innovation approaches like Design Thinking integrate specific mindsets, methods, and processes to spur creativity (Brenner et al., 2016). To enhance creativity in hybrid work, it is central to consider the distinct needs of divergent (generative) and convergent (condensing, evaluative) thinking processes (Furmanek and Daurer, 2019) and select the appropriate work mode (entirely virtual, face-to-face, or hybrid) for each task (Dennis et al., 1998). Co-presence, psychological safety, and the avoidance of technostress are vital aspects of establishing a collaborative and positive atmosphere that encourages creativity through convergent thinking, information sharing, and constructive feedback. They must be considered when designing a creative environment for virtual teamwork.

2.1 Technostress

Being in a positive mood has been consistently linked to enhanced creative performance (Baas et al., 2008; Dul, 2019). However, technical failures, malfunctioning features, or prolonged wait times can easily trigger frustration and stress (Nimrod, 2018; Tarafdar et al., 2019). Coined in the 1980s, "technostress" denotes the adverse effects on individuals resulting from increased computerization (Brod, 1984) and characterizes an adjustment disorder stemming from the inability to adapt healthily to technologies. Typical stress reactions are anxiety, mental fatigue, skepticism, and feelings of inefficiency (Bailenson, 2021; Nimrod, 2018). However, technostress can also lead to positive outcomes, such as greater alertness, mental flexibility, and innovation (Tarafdar et al., 2019). The effects of technostress are thus highly individual and disclose a research gap in formal design knowledge, especially for hybrid meetings. Meeting moderation should support a mindful use of technology, which promotes positive re-appraisal of the situation and activates positive coping mechanisms, like social support and breaks (Bailenson, 2021; Tarafdar et al., 2019). Diligent planning focused on minimizing errors and complexity, for instance, through familiar technology and additional training, can further alleviate the adverse impacts of technostress (Pilcicki et al., 2022).

2.2 Psychological Safety

Creative work necessitates voicing novel and unconventional ideas, active engagement, information sharing, a willingness to trust and challenge one another, and overcoming the fear of being judged (Nemiro, 2007; Newman et al., 2017). Convergent thinking, linked to problem-solving, requires transparency, flexibility, information-sharing, and decision-making to evaluate and combine diverse information, ultimately uncovering the most valuable, novel, and useful idea (Cropley, 2006). Successful creative collaboration, therefore, depends on a high degree of psychological safety, defined as the shared belief within a group that it is safe to take interpersonal risks (Amabile et al., 1996; Edmondson and Daley, 2020; Newman et al., 2017), which fosters open communication, idea sharing, and constructive feedback. A lack of psychological safety makes the group susceptible to groupthink and adopting less unconventional and creative ideas (Brodbeck et al., 2007).

However, virtual and hybrid collaboration poses challenges to psychological safety, making it harder to convey emotions, build trust, and inhibit free expression and spontaneous reactions (Dennis et al., 1998). Rich and synchronous communication channels should support psychological safety (Edmondson and Daley, 2020). Groups should take specific measures before, during, and after virtual meetings, such as familiarizing the team with tools, appointing a facilitator, and engaging participants in advance (Edmondson and Daley, 2020). The use of video and audio is debated due to potential distractions and technostress and its inefficiency in conveying social cues like mimics and gestures (Bailenson, 2021). Utilizing features like hand-raise, polls, and chats can create less intimidating engagement opportunities (Maaravi et al., 2021). Dividing extensive meetings into smaller breakout rooms promotes organic discussions, and explicit involvement and feedback from quiet participants may further enrich the exchange (Edmondson and Daley, 2020).

2.3 Co-Presence

Co-presence refers to a sense of community that encourages participants to engage with one another in meaningful ways (Bulu, 2012). Co-presence in virtual or hybrid collaboration does not necessitate physical togetherness but signifies a psychological connection between individuals. The richness of media, encompassing visual and verbal cues like body language, facial expressions, eye contact, and vocal tone, significantly influences the sense of co-presence (Bulu, 2012). Some media, such as video conferencing, exhibit a higher degree of co-presence compared to other communication channels like email or chat, making them more effective for interpersonal connections and collaborative decision-making (Dennis et al., 1998). While co-presence can emerge across all communication modes when group members are acquainted, in-person interaction is most effective for building new relationships, followed by video, audio, and instant messaging (Sherman et al., 2013). It can be concluded that it is advisable to favor a physical gathering at the onset of hybrid collaboration.

Further, individuals often feel anonymous or unseen in virtual collaboration (Gebbing et al., 2021; Hite et al., 2014). Studies on electronic brainstorming highlight that group creativity benefits from these communication constraints and anonymity on virtual platforms in divergent tasks, as group members do not influence each other, leading to a larger number of ideas (Maaravi et al., 2021; Pilcicki et al., 2022). In contrast, co-presence is particularly valuable in convergent thinking of creative collaboration to convey social cues, spontaneous reactions, and emotions more easily when presenting ideas, giving feedback, and evaluating and selecting ideas (Bulu, 2012). Anonymity further confounds the accountability of group members and hinders the identification of the authorship or destination of a contribution (Gebbing et al., 2021). Collaboration tools aim to reduce anonymity, making the virtual environment more immersive and intensifying interactions.

Web-conferencing systems aim to facilitate virtual togetherness, offering access to remote activities and contacts (Sherman et al., 2013). However, creating co-presence in hybrid collaboration poses challenges, especially when some participants are present and others are virtual. Virtual participants receive fewer social cues, leading to potential sub-group formation and inequalities among those physically present (Brewer, 1999). To mitigate negative group dynamics, it is essential to integrate online attendees and develop a shared mental model representing a common goal, purpose, or task (Redlich et al., 2017).

The presented findings show a research gap on how to design a suitable environment for hybrid creative group work by minimizing technostress, fostering co-presence, and creating a sense of psychological safety.

3. METHODOLOGY

The objective of this research is to address challenges faced by practitioners in implementing hybrid work modes by gathering design requirements for enhancing techno-stress, psychological safety, and co-presence — three critical factors influencing creativity in hybrid collaboration. Design requirements, defined as fundamental prerequisites to achieve a specific objective (Möller et al., 2020), were identified through insights from expert focus groups. The data collection took place during a 90-minute online workshop on creative hybrid collaboration at an international Design Thinking conference in September 2022. In three focus groups, 22 experts from the creative industry, comprising 13 females and 8 males, participated. Their expertise spanned various fields, such as Design Thinking (14) and related creative consulting or coaching activities (8), including UX design, marketing, and innovation management. All participants had prior experience in online creative workshops and rated their expertise on average at 7.21 on a scale of 1-10 (10 being the highest).

The workshop began with an overview of hybrid collaboration and the three focal points of technostress, psychological safety, and co-presence. Focus groups were organized into three breakout rooms equipped with a digital whiteboard (Miro), each assigned to discuss one of the topics. Instructed by experienced coaches, participants brainstormed first individually and then exchanged ideas in the group. The participants were instructed to build on each other's ideas without criticism to create unique and innovative solutions. The results yielded numerous practical suggestions for improving hybrid creative workshop experiences.

For the analysis of group outcomes, ideas were compared and thematically grouped around the three core theories (technostress, co-presence, and psychological safety). This thematic analysis led to a collection of practically relevant design requirements and features for enhancing hybrid creative collaboration.

4. RESULTS

This study presents the findings from three focus groups comprising 22 experts from the creativity industry who explored the requirements for creative hybrid collaboration to address techno-stress, psychological safety, and co-presence (Figure 1). After the workshop, the results of the focus groups were compared, analyzed, and clustered according to similarities. The five resulting design requirements address meeting preparation, handling disruptions and focus, team bonding and warm-up exercises, valuing online participants, and raising awareness for offline participants.

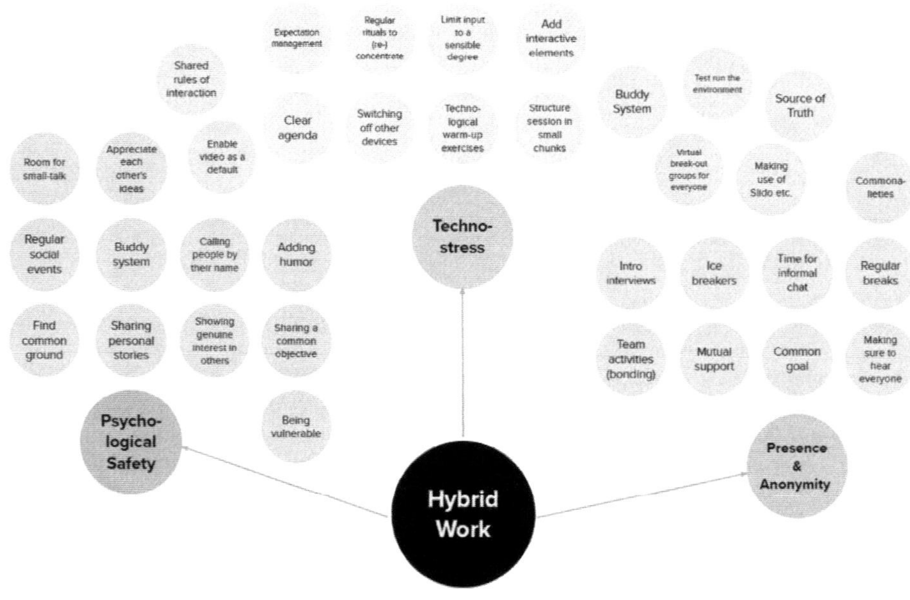

Figure 1. Requirements of creative professionals for hybrid work environments

Meeting Preparation. The focus groups stressed the importance of choosing the appropriate technology and conducting a trial run for successful hybrid collaboration. Before the meeting, it is recommended to estimate realistic workloads, manage expectations, and set a comprehensive agenda. This includes planning time for technology setups, breaks and informal socializing, task completion, and flexibility for unexpected changes.

Managing Disruptions and Focus during the Meeting. The experts agreed that staying attentive during hybrid sessions is a challenge, especially for those joining online. To ensure focus and engagement, team members should be instructed to turn off unnecessary technology and minimize distractions and complexity by using preselected tools. It is important to be mindful of the needs of both virtual and physical audiences. The group should establish relaxing routines, like breaks, breakout rooms, and informal conversations.

Team Bonding and Warm-up Exercises. The focus groups discussed creating a safe environment where people dare to speak up. Especially when teams consist of intercultural members at different hierarchical levels, anonymity and not knowing each other can be intimidating. It is necessary to open up, show genuine interest in others, and admit vulnerabilities. Team bonding refers to specific activities that help people connect and sympathize with each other informally. Therefore, creative hybrid sessions should be designed to be particularly interactive. The goal is to create space for informal conversations similar to those naturally occurring in face-to-face situations. On a personal level, team members should elicit sympathy, identify common ground, support each other, and ensure everyone is heard. The group emphasized the importance of teams coming together and getting acquainted at the beginning of a hybrid session. Many warmup exercises were suggested, including icebreakers, roundtable discussions, pen pals, and treasure hunts. Further, they suggested implementing a "buddy system," where each online person has an offline contact to capture everything in the meeting. The activities should be adapted to the group's preferences.

Attention and Appreciation for Online Participants. There is a distinct difference in the way individuals experience creative group work in online versus in-person settings. According to the experts, online participants may feel disconnected from the people in the room and perceive the situation as artificial and "robotic." They may be disadvantaged and unable to hear and see what is discussed in the room. Online participants require special attention and engagement because they are "more than just pictures on a wall." Encouragement to speak up is necessary for online participants who may feel pressured to perform and believe they cannot contribute to the conversation, especially if they feel "on the spot" and disruptive when drawing attention to the screen. To make it easier for the online participants, the volume, size, and position of the video display should be adjusted to be visible but not domineering. The requirement deducted from these observations is that people online need visibility, appreciation, and positive feedback that their ideas are received and valued. This can be facilitated by a moderator who fosters the inclusion of the online audience and encourages active participation.

Raising awareness amongst on-site participants. There is a risk that the on-site audience will "forget" about the people working remotely and engage in discussions that are difficult to follow for the online audience. The focus groups, therefore, required specific rules for conversation, such as a code of conduct. Further design features include the buddy system described above, explicitly moderating and addressing people online and offline, and creating space for small talks and discussions online and offline.

5. DISCUSSION

In the following, the findings are discussed in the context of existing literature and the overarching research question: how to design the conditions for hybrid creative group work, minimize technostress, foster co-presence, and create a sense of psychological safety.

The first finding suggests addressing technostress by reconsidering meeting preparation and moderation, as a positive mood is most beneficial to creative work (Baas et al., 2008; Dul, 2019). Studies suggest technology stimulates positive mood and innovation when used correctly but can also cause negative technostress if misused (Tarafdar et al., 2019). Due to the complexity and mental load that technology adds to hybrid meetings, special attention must be given to the preparation process, which now involves a technical layer in addition to the traditional content preparation. The findings indicate that adequate meeting preparation depends on the users' technical aptitude, prior exposure to tools, and the extent to which they are familiar with each other or collaborated before. Future research should investigate the role of each factor in minimizing technostress. Secondly, hybrid meetings require more careful and elaborate moderation than purely physical or virtual collaboration to ensure that online and offline participants are equally engaged. Previous research suggested that the technologies used should be carefully adapted to the task at hand, e.g., the creative process (Dennis et al., 1998; Furmanek and Daurer, 2019). Divergent thinking and idea generation are better facilitated in anonymous virtual settings (Frich et al., 2021). In contrast, convergent tasks such as information sharing and decision-making benefit from increased presence and trust, which can be achieved in face-to-face settings (Frich et al., 2021). In a hybrid setting, however, the moderator must balance the challenges and issues that arise with physical and virtual meetings to provide an equitable level of participation for everyone involved.

The issues concerning virtual settings encompass the absence of social cues that would facilitate more co-presence, trust, and psychological safety (Bulu, 2012; Dennis et al., 1998; Edmondson and Daley, 2020). In creative processes, these social cues are a valuable source of feedback that allows for assessing whether an idea is liked. Physical participants may unintentionally form two distinct subgroups, whereas virtual participants are viewed as an outgroup, leaving them disconnected from the stronger connections built between the physical participants (Brewer, 1999). This can lead to uneven team dynamics that influence conversations, psychological safety, and information sharing. Meeting organizers must take extra steps to ensure that virtual participants are included, engaged, and have the same access to information as in-person participants.

The third design principle expands on this reasoning, emphasizing that team-building activities play an important role in the success of hybrid meetings by helping to foster collaboration, increase psychological safety and trust, and create a shared understanding of the team's goals and objectives (Redlich et al., 2017). It also allows informal conversations between peers to occur as they would in a face-to-face setting (e.g., during pauses and short talks). The result is two different realities, online and offline, which might inhibit the integration of virtual members into on-site groups (Brewer, 1999). The aim should be to create a sensation of co-presence across the settings (Bulu, 2012). Team building activities can significantly help unfamiliar team members and newly formed groups identify and address potential challenges that may arise due to different work styles, cultures, and backgrounds.

The study's findings are limited by the small sample size and the rather specific application context of Design Thinking. Further, the question arises of how far the results are specific to the creative collaboration or can be generalized to other application contexts. During the focus groups, specific requirements were identified that seem to be universally true in any type of team collaboration, such as the need to organize meetings, handle distractions, maintain concentration, and promote team cohesion. However, during the formulation of the design principles, it became apparent that the solutions to address these requirements must be tailored to the specific context of hybrid collaboration, making them considerably unique. This involves setting up advanced audiovisual equipment and moderating social interactions between online and offline participants.

New work modes prioritize flexibility, mobility, and the use of technology to enhance collaboration, communication, and productivity, summarized in the concept of "New Work" (Aroles et al., 2021). The emergence of hybrid work has brought the potential to benefit from both virtual and physical work environments. Despite this, the concept is still in its nascent stages and lacks the necessary design principles, instructions, and resources to integrate the two work styles effectively.

The research findings may be limited since the resulting concepts, meeting preparation, moderation, and team building, are not novel and have been studied in the past. However, the application context of hybrid work brings novel, unprecedented challenges that require every element to be re-evaluated. Hybrid collaboration is not a universal approach; it might be limited to certain contexts and may not be effective in all situations. Additionally, the efficacy of hybrid collaboration may depend on the particular combination of virtual and in-person elements used (Dennis et al., 1998). Our study provides an overview of relevant design requirements that must be addressed. Further research of each requirement is necessary to gain a comprehensive understanding of the implications of hybrid work.

6. CONCLUSION

Creative hybrid collaboration is rising as organizations utilize hybrid teams for creative collaborations, expanding their capacity and reach, developing new products, services, and business models, and promoting a culture of innovation. Through ICT, creative people can connect time- and location independently, and virtual teams are becoming increasingly efficient in information sharing. Whereas practitioners welcome these advantages, many creatives still express the need for physical interaction and indicate they would opt for a hybrid solution. Extended screen time can impede creativity by inducing technostress and fatigue and negatively impacting mood. Moreover, on a team level, hybrid settings lack co-presence and hinder the development of psychological safety. As a result, team members appear to feel disconnected and hesitant to share ideas or provide constructive feedback, which is essential in creative group work.

The design requirements specify how to address technology and content preparation, meeting moderation, team building, and inclusion of virtual participants in hybrid meetings. In conclusion, hybrid work has the potential to become a powerful source of innovation if the interplay of human creativity and virtual collaboration is appropriately understood and applied. With a thoughtful design and application of design principles, hybrid work modes can improve efficiency, effectiveness, and sustainability while still fulfilling the needs and requirements for creativity, such as psychological safety, co-presence, and avoidance of technostress.

ACKNOWLEDGEMENT

This research was funded by the German Federal Ministry of Education and Research (BMBF) under the project Study Buddy (Grant # 21INVI06).

REFERENCES

Amabile, T.M., Conti, R., Coon, H., Lazenby, J., Herron, M. (1996). Assessing the Work Environment for Creativity. *The Academy of Management Journal,* 39, 1154–1184. https://doi.org/10.2307/256995

Aroles, J., Cecez-Kecmanovic, D., Dale, K., Kingma, S.F., Mitev, N. (2021). New ways of working (NWW): Workplace transformation in the digital age, *Information and Organization* 31, 100378. https://doi.org/10.1016/j.infoandorg.2021.100378

Baas, M., De Dreu, C. K. W., Nijstad, B. A. (2008). A Meta-Analysis of 25 Years of Mood-Creativity Research: Hedonic Tone, Activation, or Regulatory Focus? *Psychological Bulletin*, 134, 779–806. https://doi.org/10.1037/a0012815

Bailenson, J. N. (2021). Nonverbal Overload: A Theoretical Argument for the Causes of Zoom Fatigue. *Technology, Mind, and Behavior*, 2. https://doi.org/10.1037/tmb0000030

Brenner, W., Uebernickel, F., Abrell, T. (2016). Design Thinking as Mindset, Process, and Toolbox, in: Brenner, W., Uebernickel, F. (Eds.), *Design Thinking for Innovation: Research and Practice.* Springer International Publishing, Cham, pp. 3–21. https://doi.org/10.1007/978-3-319-26100-3_1

Brewer, M. B. (1999). The Psychology of Prejudice: Ingroup Love and Outgroup Hate? *Journal of Social Issues,* 55, 429–444. https://doi.org/10.1111/0022-4537.00126

Brod, C. (1984). Techno Stress: The Human Cost of the Computer Revolution. Longman Higher Education.

Brodbeck, F. C., Kerschreiter, R., Mojzisch, A., Schulz-Hardt, S. (2007). Group Decision Making Under Conditions of Distributed Knowledge: The Information Asymmetries Model. *AMR,* 32, 459–479. https://doi.org/10.5465/amr.2007.24351441

Bulu, S. T. (2012). Place presence, social presence, co-presence, and satisfaction in virtual worlds. *Computers & Education,* 58, 154–161. https://doi.org/10.1016/j.compedu.2011.08.024

Cropley, A. (2006). In Praise of Convergent Thinking. *Creativity Research Journal,* 18, 391–404. https://doi.org/10.1207/s15326934crj1803_13

Dennis, A. R., Valacich, J. S., Speier, C., Morris, M. G. (1998). Beyond Media Richness: An Empirical Test of Media Synchronicity Theory. *Proceedings of the Thirty-First Hawaii International Conference on System Sciences*, pp. 48–57. https://doi.org/10.1109/HICSS.1998.65308

Dul, J. (2019). The Physical Environment and Creativity: A Theoretical Framework, in: Kaufman, J.C., Sternberg, R.J. (Eds.), *Cambridge Handbooks in Psychology*. Cambridge University Press, Cambridge, pp. 481–510. https://doi.org/10.1017/9781316979839.025

Edmondson, A. C., Daley, G. (2020). How to Foster Psychological Safety in Virtual Meetings. *Harvard Business Review,* 25, 1–4.

Frich, J., Nouwens, M., Halskov, K., Dalsgaard, P. (2021). How Digital Tools Impact Convergent and Divergent Thinking in Design Ideation, in: *Proceedings of the Conference on Human Factors in Computing Systems.* Yokohama Japan, pp. 1–11. https://doi.org/10.1145/3411764.3445062

Furmanek, L., Daurer, S. (2019). Application of Media Synchronicity Theory to Creative Tasks in Virtual Teams Using the Example of Design Thinking, *Proceedings of the Wirtschaftsinformatik 2019.*

Gebbing, P., Lattemann, C., Siemon, D. (2022). Creativity Drivers: Design Principles for Virtual Creative Collaboration, in: PACIS 2022 Proceedings. Presented at the PACIS 2022. https://aisel.aisnet.org/pacis2022/165

Gebbing, P., Yang, X., Michalke, S., Lattemann, C. (2021). Kreativitätsförderung in der virtuellen Gruppenarbeit. *HMD Praxis der Wirtschaftsinformatik*, 58, 1364–1377.

Hardwig, T., Boos, M. (2023). Hybrid Work: Herausforderungen an das Change Management in Unternehmen. Gr Interakt Org. https://doi.org/10.1007/s11612-023-00686-5

Hite, D.M., Voelker, T., Robertson, A. (2014). Measuring Perceived Anonymity: The Development of a Context Independent Instrument. *Journal of Methods and Measurement in the Social Sciences*, 5, 22–39. https://doi.org/10.2458/v5i1.18305

Inie, N., Dalsgaard, P. (2020). How Interaction Designers Use Tools to Manage Ideas. *ACM Trans. Computer-Human Interaction 27*, 7:1-7:26. https://doi.org/10.1145/3365104

Lattemann, C., Siemon, D., Dorawa, D., Redlich, B. (2017). Digitization of the Design Thinking Process Solving Problems with Geographically Dispersed Teams, in: Marcus, A., Wang, W. (Eds.), Design, User Experience, and Usability: Theory, Methodology, and Management, *Lecture Notes in Computer Science*. Springer, Cham, pp. 71–88. https://doi.org/10.1007/978-3-319-58634-2_6

Maaravi, Y., Heller, B., Shoham, Y., Mohar, S., Deutsch, B. (2021). Ideation in the digital age: literature review and integrative model for electronic brainstorming. *Review Management Science*, 15, 1431–1464. https://doi.org/10.1007/s11846-020-00400-5

Meluso, J., Johnson, S., Bagrow, J. (2020). Making Virtual Teams Work: Redesigning Virtual Collaboration for the Future. *SocArXiv*. https://doi.org/10.31235/osf.io/wehsk

Möller, F., Guggenberger, T. M., Otto, B., (2020). Towards a Method for Design Principle Development in Information Systems, in: Hofmann, S., Müller, O., Rossi, M. (Eds.), Designing for Digital Transformation. Co-Creating Services with Citizens and Industry, *Lecture Notes in Computer Science*. Springer International Publishing, Cham, pp. 208–220. https://doi.org/10.1007/978-3-030-64823-7_20

Nemiro, J. E. (2007). The Building Blocks for Creativity in Virtual Teams, in: MacGregor, S.P., Torres-coronas, T. (Eds.), *Higher Creativity for Virtual Teams: Developing Platforms for Co-Creation*. IGI Global, pp. 98–121.

Neumayr, T., Saatci, B., Rintel, S., Klokmose, C. N., Augstein, M. (2021). What was Hybrid? A Systematic Review of Hybrid Collaboration and Meetings Research. *ACM Trans. Computer-Human Interact*.

Newman, A., Donohue, R., Eva, N. (2017). Psychological Safety: A Systematic Review of the Literature. *Human Resource Management Review* 27, 521–535. https://doi.org/10.1016/j.hrmr.2017.01.001

Nimrod, G. (2018). Technostress: Measuring a New Threat to Well-Being in Later Life. *Aging Mental Health,* 22, 1080–1087. https://doi.org/10.1080/13607863.2017.1334037

Pilcicki, R., Siemon, D., Lattemann, C. (2022). Constraints That Support Creativity – Design Principles for Next Generation Creativity Support Systems 18. *PACIS 2022 Proceedings*. 148.

Redlich, B., Siemon, D., Lattemann, C., Robra-Bissantz, S. (2017). Shared Mental Models in Creative Virtual Teamwork, *Proceedings of the 50th Hawaii International Conference on System Sciences*, Hawaii, pp. 464–473. https://doi.org/10.24251/HICSS.2017.057

Runco, M. A., Jaeger, G. J. (2012). The Standard Definition of Creativity. *Creativity Research Journal,* 24, 92–96. https://doi.org/10.1080/10400419.2012.650092

Sherman, L. E., Michikyan, M., Greenfield, P. M. (2013). The effects of text, audio, video, and in-person communication on bonding between friends. *Cyberpsychology: Journal of Psychosocial Research on Cyberspace,* 7. https://doi.org/10.5817/CP2013-2-3

Tarafdar, M., Cooper, C. L., Stich, J.-F. (2019). The technostress trifecta - techno eustress, techno distress and design: Theoretical directions and an agenda for research. *Information Systems Journal,* 29, 6–42. https://doi.org/10.1111/isj.12169

Tønnessen, Ø., Dhir, A., Flåten, B.-T. (2021). Digital knowledge sharing and creative performance: Work from home during the COVID-19 pandemic. *Technol. Forecast. Soc. Change* 170, 120866. https://doi.org/10.1016/j.techfore.2021.120866

Weritz, P., Matute, J., Braojos, J., Kane, J. (2022). How Much Digital is Too Much? A Study on Employees' Hybrid Workplace Preferences, *Proceedings of the ICIS 2022.* https://aisel.aisnet.org/icis2022/is_futureofwork/is_futureofwork/3

Yang, X., Gebbing, P., Lankut, E., Lattemann, C. (2023). Virtual Creativity – Bibliometric Literature Review on Measurements and Factors That Influence Creative Virtual Teamwork. *Creativity Research Journal*, 1–15. https://doi.org/10.1080/10400419.2023.2198300

WELL-BEING AND LIFE STAGES IN DIGITAL WORK ENVIRONMENTS

Maximilian Helms, Julia Bosbach, Pia Gebbing, Audris Umel and Christoph Lattemann
Constructor University Bremen
Campus Ring 1, 28759 Bremen, Deutschland

ABSTRACT

The drive for digital transformation (DT) reshaped various work aspects, leading to changed requirements not only for employees' skills and performance but also for their well-being. In return, employee well-being is crucial for the success of companies' DT. Drawing on the self-determination theory, this study investigates how DT affects employees' motivation considering their basic psychological needs and physical health across different life stages, which are the basis for well-being. Focus groups consisting of 20 experts from the consultancy industry were surveyed. Our findings illustrate both positive and negative impacts of DT on employees' well-being, depending on the life stage and work environment. In general, employees welcome the increased demand for more digital competencies. However, particularly for employees in their 30s, the new requirements are perceived to cause stress. The effects of DT on physical health are controversial; in the life stage 30-39, flexible working hours have a positive effect whereas parents in their 30s perceive a negative effect on physical health due to increased computer work. Flexibility emerges as a vital element for employee well-being across all age groups, yet remote work can adversely affect the relatedness to the employer. This research offers insights for further exploration of DT impacts and strategies for practical implementation.

KEYWORDS

Employee Well-Being, Digital Transformation, Remote Work, Basic Psychological Needs

1. INTRODUCTION

The COVID-19 pandemic accelerated digitalization and led to the widespread adoption of remote work in businesses wherever feasible. Remote work offers increased flexibility for employees, allowing them to organize their working hours and location autonomously (van Zoonen et al. 2023). The elimination of travel times to and from the office resulted in freed-up capacities. At the same time, new technologies make it possible to work from anywhere in the world. Digital transformation (DT) has therefore fundamentally changed the way we work (Burr et al. 2020). Given the shortage of skilled workers and high turnover rates, it seems counterproductive to demand a return to the office and thus take back the benefits of flexibility and freedom. In this changing working environment, well-being, and the associated motivation are of fundamental importance for long-term business success (Bonekamp and Sure 2015). Companies should therefore aim to ensure a high level of job satisfaction and promote employee well-being (Page and Vella-Brodrick 2009). Yet, researchers and practitioners could not provide a comprehensive answer to how well-being can be actively promoted in times of DT (Überbacher et al. 2020).

According to Deci and Ryan's (1985) well-established self-determination theory (SBT), well-being is significantly influenced by three basic psychological needs: autonomy, relatedness, and competence. An examination of these basic needs seems appropriate for systematically researching the extent to which DT influences well-being and allows further conclusions on how well-being can be promoted in the workplace.

In research on digital workplaces, Meske (2019) found that well-being is most positively influenced by the promotion of employee autonomy. Being able to choose your own workplace promotes autonomy, therefore it can be concluded that flexible working options promote well-being. On the other hand, remote work may create feelings of loneliness and isolation (Tapani et al. 2022) and presumably harm social ties with colleagues. A return to the office could thus be a step towards reinvigorating the need for connection. However, studies contradict this assumption (Brunelle and Fortin, 2021), revealing that connectedness does not diminish by remote work but is compensated for by social ties in the private sphere as the time freed up can be devoted to private activities. Therefore, an employee's entire environment is relevant for the well-being and not solely the social bond with colleagues in companies.

Finally, physical health, is considered separately in our analysis of well-being alongside psychological needs because it represents a distinct dimension—the body's physical state. Additionally, it plays a crucial role in long-term collaboration and is a significant contributor to employees' overall well-being (Joshanloo and Jovanović, 2018). Factors influencing these well-being dimensions may vary, and addressing them can lead to synergistic effects, where improvements in one aspect can positively impact the other. Still, negative effects could also arise from influences on either dimension. For instance, despite the enabling aspect of digital technology for remote work, which promotes autonomy, it also can increase screen time which has been shown to have adverse effects on physical health, thus affecting overall well-being. This separation between psychological needs and physical health enables a holistic understanding of well-being, facilitating interventions tailored to each dimension.

As the existing research in this area appears contradictory, we suggest that differentiation of individual life stages can bring a deeper understanding of the topic and more clarity to existing research. The overall research objective is to gain a deeper understanding of the influences of digital technologies on well-being across different life stages by answering the following research questions: First, what influence does DT have on employees' well-being in the consulting sector? Second, do the effects of DT differ in terms of basic psychological needs and physical health in consultants' different life stages? Third, does DT have a negative impact on attachment to the employer in times of remote work?

To answer these questions, qualitative data was collected from focus group interviews with 20 German experts from the consultancy industry and a preceding survey, conducted in July 2023. Following an introductory literature review on well-being in the digital work context, the research framework and the applied methodology are described. Based on a life-stage model and the SDT, a research framework was established to analyze the factors identified by the experts as influencing DT on basic psychological needs and physical health. The results of the analysis are presented and evaluated in a concluding discussion.

2. LITERATURE REVIEW: WELL-BEING IN TIMES OF REMOTE WORK

Diener (2006) describes well-being as the reflection of different values that people have concerning their lives, the events that happen to them, their bodies and minds, and the circumstances in which they live. Ryan and Deci (2022) see the satisfaction of basic psychological needs (autonomy, relatedness, and competence) as a prerequisite for well-being within the framework of SDT. Ryan and Deci (2020) describe the basic psychological needs as follows:

First, autonomy means acting independently and taking responsibility for one's own actions. Meske's (2019) research on digital work environments shows that autonomy is a key factor for well-being, which is promoted by flexible working options. Research by Brunelle and Fortin (2021) in a Canadian IT consulting firm confirms the positive effect of autonomy on well-being, although this seems to be far greater for employees working on-site compared to those working remotely.

Second, connectedness refers to the need for social bonding or integration. Johnson et al. (2009) examined the aspect of remote communication in their research. They found that positive aspects of communication with the team are significantly reduced when communication is almost exclusively remote. This seems to contradict the findings on connectedness by Brunelle and Fortin (2021), who found a significant positive effect for remote workers. When working from home, the private environment is an important aspect in this context. Social ties in the private sphere can compensate for a lack of personal interaction with colleagues.

Lastly, competence is the experience of mastering challenges and feeling competent in doing so. In times of DT, sufficient time should be available for the employee to master digital skills to increase well-being (Shultz et al. 2010). However, Brunelle and Fortin (2021) were only able to identify a significant positive effect of the need for competence on well-being among on-site workers. Nevertheless, in specific industries, i.e. the consulting industry, characterized by changing assignments, new customers, and cooperation across diverse sectors, Lechler and Huemann (2023), identified the need for competence as the most significant factor influencing motivation.

Well-being and job satisfaction are also directly related to physical health (Burr et al. 2020), as they influence performance and stress management. Research by Lange and Kayser (2022) shows that working from home is associated with increasing perceived work stress and can have a negative impact on health. Joshanloo and Jovanović (2018) also argue that factors influencing well-being should be considered in the context of physical health. Employers have an economic interest in promoting basic psychological needs to reduce costs associated with stress or dismissals and increase performance (Broeck et al. 2010). Yet, research findings appear to be partly contradictory in this area. Age and the respective stages of life further shape behavior and well-being (Hyde et al. 2013) and the consideration of the increasingly aging workforce is an important field for future research (Zacher and Froidevaux 2021). Current research has gathered both qualitative and quantitative data but the life stage-specific perspective is still novel in this research context. Consequently, additional foundational research on specific life stages is required to comprehend their significance.

In conclusion, the SDT suggests fostering independence, avoiding control that undermines autonomy, creating a positive working atmosphere, promoting team spirit and respectful interaction, and maintaining a continuous learning curve in the workplace. By considering the needs of SDT in their work design, leadership, and organizational culture, as well as providing security for physical health, organizations can create an environment for remote work that positively influences employee well-being and motivation (Gagné and Deci 2005). This in turn can lead to higher job satisfaction, better performance, and a positive organizational culture. Accordingly, the work environment is also of crucial importance in which the reference to SDT can be an approach to promote the satisfaction, well-being, and physical health of employees (Gomez-Baya and Lucia-Casademunt 2018).

3. RESEARCH FRAMEWORK AND METHODS

This study examines different life stages of employees to gain a more comprehensive understanding of the perceived impact of DT on well-being and the importance of life stages in work design (Skinner et al. 2014). The SDT and specific life stages form the research basis for investigating well-being under the influence of DT. More precisely, the influence of DT on autonomy, competence, connectedness, and physical health in different stages of life will be investigated (see Figure 1).

	< 20 Year		20-29 Year		.....		60+ Year	
	Child	w/o Child	Child	w/o Child	Child	w/o Child	Child	w/o Child
Autonomy								
Relatedness			←		Well-Being		→	
Competence								
physical Health								

Figure 1. Research Framework

The SDT is used as a framework for a multidimensional consideration of influences and effects, as its relevance has been proven and replicated over decades. This approach can be used to promote not only psychological but also physical well-being (Gagné et al. 2022). Since both psychological and physical aspects are changing within the life stages (Nilsson 2020, Wylleman and Lavallee 2021), it is to be expected that changes in the job across the life stages will influence the basic psychological needs of employees in very different ways. A life stage-specific view therefore provides a suitable framework for examining the effects of DT. Such a model aims to provide a structured understanding of the transitions individuals undergo from birth to old age, highlighting key milestones, changes, and responsibilities associated with each stage. Life stage models typically consider various aspects of human development, including factors like "age" and "parenthood", which have a significant impact on employees' flexibility and behaviors and often form the basis for the description of life stages in research (Roehling et al. 2001). Therefore, this paper utilizes a simplified model, focusing specifically on the factors of age and parenthood to identify fundamental differences between the phases. The selection of relevant phases was carried out in the focus group work.

As a methodological approach, the use of focus group interviews in combination with a preceding survey was chosen. According to Morgan (1996), this methodological approach offers the advantage of specifying the focus based on which the qualitative data and correlations are collected in the focus groups. As part of the survey, the relevant employee target groups and their life stages (including age, parenthood, and profession) were identified. Focus groups were assembled, comprising 20 selected experts, including German managers with 5 to 15 years of experience in management consulting.

An innovative research design was employed utilizing personas in focus group interviews (Schweibenz 2004) to investigate the impacts of DT on psychological and physical well-being at each life stage. The concept of personas offers the possibility of collecting user-centered needs, wishes, goals, fears, and resistances for archetypal users who are representative of real users. The benefits of personas in research have already been established in many studies, including in the field of health. The main advantage is that a variety of circumstances (e.g. working environment, tasks, skills) and their influences (including physical factors) on the well-being of fictitious individuals can be researched (Blomkvist 2002). With the help of the focus groups, the influence of DT on the goals, wishes, fears, and resistance of the personas was discussed and documented on whiteboards. In the next step, the impact of the collected results on the basic needs (autonomy, competence, and connectedness) and in relation to physical health was evaluated.

To gain a comprehensive understanding of well-being, it is necessary to consider the positive, negative, and neutral effects on work. Accordingly, the evaluation in this research work was carried out in three forms: positive, negative, and neutral. The evaluation was carried out by two research assistants (1st evaluation). Objectivity was ensured with the help of a peer review (2nd evaluation) by another independent research assistant. The reliability of the ratings was validated using Cohen's Kappa (Landis and Koch 1977).

4. ANALYSIS AND RESULTS

The data was collected in July 2023 in a workshop with N=20 German managers from the consultancy industry. With the help of a survey (via MS Forms) at the start of the workshop basic parameters for the creation of the persona were identified (see Figure 2). The survey asked the participants to determine the age group they would like to discuss in the persona creation (<20, 20-29, 30-39, 40-49, 50-59, and 60+ years), their parenthood (with child / without child) and their areas of activity.

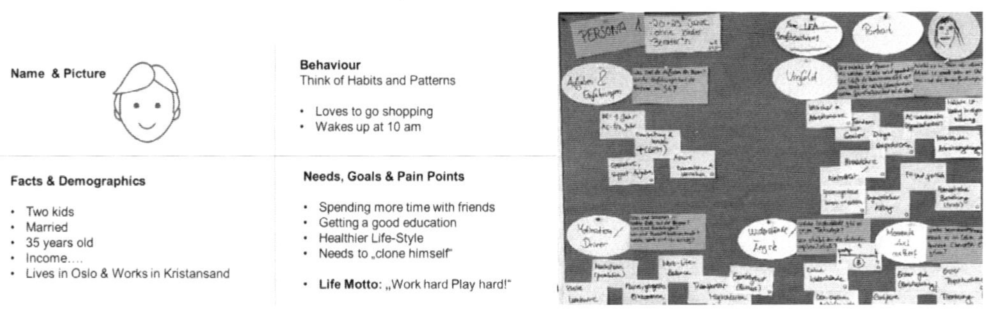

Figure 2. Examples of Personas; Figure 2a. (left): example template; Figure 2b. (right): result from a workshop

The age between 30 and 39 was most prevalent for the analysis with 11 participants in this life stage. The age ranges 20 to 29, and 40 to 49 were also selected for the next step of the analysis by the workshop participants, mentioned nine times, respectively two times. Other stages were not indicated. The other aspects of the respective stages of life were surveyed in the same way. Using the example of 30 to 39-year-olds, 54% of the responses for this age group opted to analyze personas without children. Using this basic data on the life stages, four personas were developed.

In the process, the experts collaboratively identified 19 influencing factors of DT and assessed their influence on the dimensions of autonomy, competence, connectedness, and physical health (e.g. positive effect of flexibility and negative effect of fear of AI on autonomy). This multidimensional evaluation (positive, negative, neutral) of the four dimensions resulted in a total of 34 ratings (see Figure 3). The robustness of the evaluation was confirmed using Cohen's Kappa (κ = 0.68) (Landis and Koch, 1977).

			20-29 Year				30-39 Year							40-49 Year			
		...	without Child			...	without Child			with Child			...	with Child			...
	Σ		positive	negative	neutral		positive	negative	neutral	positive	negative	neutral		positive	negative	neutral	
Autonomy	11		1		1		1	1	1	1				2	2	1	
Relatedness	8			2			1	1	1		1			1		1	
Competence	8		1				1	1	1		2			2			
physical Health	7		0				2				2			1	2		
Σ	34		2	2	1		5	3	3	1	5			6	4	2	

Figure 3. Evaluation

With regard to the four dimensions (autonomy, connectedness, competence, and physical health), 34 evaluations confirmed that DT influences well-being. Overall, the results (+14, -14) indicate a very balanced effect of DT on well-being. With 11 of the 34 ratings, the need for autonomy was most frequently mentioned as an influencing (positive and negative) factor on well-being (connectedness (8), competence (8), and physical health (7)). The overall influence of DT on well-being, positive and negative, increases with age. Thus, it can be concluded that the impairment of basic psychological needs by DT increases with age.

4.1 Analysis of Needs

Flexibility at the workplace and working hours have a perceived positive effect on the basic need for autonomy. Fears that artificial intelligence (AI) will take over interesting tasks and blur the boundaries between work and leisure are perceived negatively in terms of autonomy. Overall, the positive influences of flexibility on the need for autonomy predominate (+5, -3). The surveyed effects on connectedness illustrate a rather perceived negative effect on this basic need (+2, -4). In particular, the social bond with the employer is impaired by the opportunities to work remotely and at flexible times. The decline in personal contacts within the company therefore has a perceived negative impact on social ties with colleagues and the company. The basic need for competence (+4, -3) has a positive impact overall. Interesting and new project assignments and the opportunity to deal with new topics in the context of DT are perceived positively. Only in the life stage 30-39 did the new requirements cause stress for parents and were perceived negatively. The effects of DT on physical health (+3, -4) are slightly negative. At a young age (20-29), no effects are perceived; in the life stage 30-39 flexible working hours have a positive effect and parents perceive a negative effect on physical health due to expected more working hours at the computer.

4.2 Analysis of Life Stages

Overall, the influence of DT on the needs examined is balanced in the stage 20-29 (+2, -2). A more detailed analysis for this age stage shows a positive effect on autonomy due to greater perceived flexibility and a positive influence on competence due to the opportunities for condensed learning. However, greater flexibility through increased remote work is accompanied by a reduction in personal contact with colleagues and thus a weaker bond with the company, so that a negative effect on social connectedness is perceived. Effects on physical health caused by DT were not perceived in this life stage. With increasing age, the effects are more balanced, but the topic of health is relevant in this life stage, and a positive influence (+2.0) of DT is perceived in the 30-39 age group without children. Here, the possibilities of being able to plan more time for private activities through flexible working hours, remote work, and the reduction of tasks due to AI are seen.

On the other hand, the influence of AI (taking on interesting tasks) is perceived to have a negative impact on competence and autonomy due to the reduced choice of one's own activities. As DT leads to new types of projects, a positive effect is perceived on the bond through new exciting consulting assignments and the opportunity to build up new skills. In general, the negative effects for parents in this age group outweigh the positive effects in the comparison between without a child (+5.-3) and with a child (+1.-5). In contrast to the 30-39 age group without a child, only negative effects (+0.-2) are perceived in this age group in terms of physical health. The stress of having to stay up-to-date and not missing out on any trends influences physical health and also has a negative effect on competence. At this age, a negative effect on connectedness is also perceived in both life stages (with and without a child) due to a decrease in personal interaction with colleagues.

However, the increasing flexibility is perceived in a more differentiated way when comparing these two stages of life; a positive effect on autonomy is perceived (with & without child), although this has only a positive effect on physical health in the stage (30-39 without child). Free time is not directly perceived by parents as having a positive effect on physical health or associated with health-promoting activities. This is confirmed in the life stage 40-49 with a child, where free time is also perceived as having a positive effect on autonomy and no effect on physical health. At the same time, DT increasingly blurs the boundaries between work and leisure time, which in turn restricts autonomy. More time at the computer is also perceived as an increasing burden on physical health. Openness to new topics (including AI) and the desire to have answers from customers and colleagues to questions about DT have a positive effect on competence. In the years 40-49, the positive effects of DT therefore predominate (+6, -4).

The results of the analyses show that DT influences well-being, but that this is perceived very differently when comparing the needs and most frequently influences the need for autonomy. The detailed analysis of the life phases also made it clear that the perception of the effects on the dimensions examined differed greatly depending on age and parenthood.

5. DISCUSSION, CONCLUSION AND OUTLOOK

This study explores the impact of DT on well-being across diverse life stages, considering three basic psychological needs (autonomy, connectedness and competence) and physical health. In relation to the initial research questions, we will discuss how employees' well-being is affected by DT, particularly by remote work, with varying effects on basic psychological needs and physical health. The comparison across life stages adds value by revealing differentiated findings, emphasizing the importance of life stage-specific research. However, a limitation of this study is its incomplete coverage of life stages, highlighting the need for further research to achieve a comprehensive understanding.

Autonomy emerged as the basic psychological need most influenced by DT, thus confirming findings by Meske (2019). Our results show a positive effect across the life phases in terms of perceived autonomy. Targeted promotion of autonomy, for example through leadership (Sarmah et al. 2022), can be understood as one of the key factors for well-being. In times of remote work, increased connectivity can have a positive effect on autonomy, as it enables flexibility (van Zoonen et al. 2023). On the down side, the lines between work and leisure are increasingly blurred, which is perceived as detrimental. Yet, the positive effects of flexibility outweigh the challenges arising from the separation between work and private life. This means that the research results of Brunelle and Fortin (2021), which found the most positive effects of autonomy among employees working on-site, could not be confirmed.

Our findings also contribute to the ongoing debate about the impact of DT on autonomy. On the one hand tasks will increasingly be replaced by digital technologies (particularly AI) in the future (Bonekamp and Sure 2015). AI is expected to increase autonomy through automatization and reducing the workload. On the other hand, there are fears that digital technologies (particularly AI) will take on more interesting and responsible tasks and thus have a negative impact on the basic psychological need for autonomy.

Considering the basic psychological need for connectedness, a return to the office - based on the findings of this research - would only have a positive effect on the well-being of younger employees in the life stage 20-29 without children. In this life stage, a clear desire for direct social ties with colleagues was evident, indicating that remote work would have a negative impact on connectedness and well-being. For parents aged 30-39, however, a return to the office would not have a positive effect on connectedness and would simultaneously restrict autonomy and the opportunity to spend more time with the family and have a negative impact on well-being. In another life stage - especially if employees are parents - a lack of social ties at work can be compensated for by more time with the family. Our findings partly differ from the results of Brunelle and Fortin (2021), who recognized a significant positive effect for remote workers in terms of connectedness, providing a more detailed picture. Promoting proactive shutdowns through digital separation and more conscious use of smartphones can reduce the negative effects of remote work (Vanden Abeele and Nguyen 2022). We argue that creating an inclusive and collaborative corporate culture - for remote and on-site work - which also considers the respective family situation is an important factor for employee well-being (Lyngstadaas and Berg 2022), and thus, for sustainable corporate success.

Our findings show that competence is mainly enhanced by DT across life stages and can efficiently promote well-being and motivation. Lechler and Huemann (2023) found that competence has the strongest influence on employees' motivation. Only in the stage 30-39 years the new demands of DT cause stress for parents and were perceived as having a negative effect on competence.

Lastly, this research has also shown that especially parents' physical health is affected by DT. Remote working means that more time is spent in front of a computer. At the same time, the lack of separation between work and private life creates a higher level of stress, which can have a negative impact on physical health. We found that the detrimental effects described by Lange and Kayser (2022) could only be confirmed for the life stages where the employees have children.

The findings have broader relevance beyond just the consulting business since the everyday work life of a consultant shares similarities with employees in various industries, particularly those involving project-based work, client interaction, and problem-solving (e.g. IT and technology, management and strategy consulting, finance and accounting as well as marketing and communications). While this study provides valuable insights for the consulting business and industries with comparable working environments, it acknowledges limitations in its scope, addressing expert groups from a single company in a knowledge-intensive industry. Exploring the impacts of DT in different domains with distinct working conditions, for example industries marked by manual labor (e.g. craftsmanship) with less working flexibility, presents a promising avenue for future research. Furthermore, a more detailed life stage model with additional factors like (single, relationship, single parent or the effect of major events) offering potential for enriching our understanding of well-being in specific life stages through quantitative approaches.

In conclusion, this study offers a comprehensive exploration of the multifaceted impact of DT on well-being across different life stages. By considering three fundamental psychological needs (autonomy, connectedness, and competence) and physical health, the study provides a nuanced understanding of the complex interplay between DT and employee well-being. The research offers valuable insights into age-specific variations, highlighting the differential effects of DT on individuals in distinct life stages.

ACKNOWLEDGEMENT

This research was funded by the German Federal Ministry of Education and Research (BMBF) under the project HAMIZU (Grant#02K20D003)

REFERENCES

Blomkvist, S. (2002). Persona - The User as a personality. Using Personas as a tool for design. Position paper for the course workshop "Theoretical perspectives in Human-Computer Interaction" at IPLab, KTH, September 3, 2002.

Bonekamp, L., Sure, M. (2015). Consequences of Industry 4.0 on Human Labour and Work Organisation. Journal of Business and Media Psychology (JBMP) 1, 33-40.

Broeck, A., Vansteenkiste, M., Witte, H., Soenens, B., Lens, W. (2010). Capturing autonomy, competence, and relatedness at work: Construction and initial validation of the Work-related Basic Need Satisfaction scale. J. Occup. Organ. Psychol. 83, 981–1002.

Brunelle, E., Fortin, J.-A. (2021). Distance Makes the Heart Grow Fonder: An Examination of Teleworkers' and Office Workers' Job Satisfaction Through the Lens of Self-Determination Theory. SAGE Open 11, 215824402098551.

Burr, C., Taddeo, M., Floridi, L. (2020). The Ethics of Digital Well-Being: A Thematic Review. Sci. Eng. Ethics 26, 2313–2343.

Deci, E.L., Ryan, R.M. (1985). Intrinsic Motivation and Self-Determination in Human Behavior. Springer US, Boston, MA.

Diener, E. (2006). Guidelines for National Indicators of Subjective Well-Being and Ill-Being. J. Happiness Stud. 7, 397–404.

Gagné, M., Deci, E.L. (2005). Self-determination theory and work motivation: Self-Determination Theory and Work Motivation. J. Organ. Behav. 26, 331–362.

Gagné, M., Parker, S.K., Griffin, M.A., Dunlop, P.D., Knight, C., Klonek, F.E., Parent-Rocheleau, X. (2022). Understanding and shaping the future of work with self-determination theory. Nat. Rev. Psychol. 1, 378–392.

Gomez-Baya, D., Lucia-Casademunt, A.M. (2018). A self-determination theory approach to health and well-being in the workplace: Results from the sixth European working conditions survey in Spain. J. Appl. Soc. Psychol. 48, 269–283.

Hyde, A.L., Maher, J.P., Elavsky, S. (2013). Enhancing our understanding of physical activity and well-being with a lifespan perspective. Int. J. Wellbeing 3, 98–115.

Johnson, S., Bettenhausen, K., Gibbons, E. (2009). Realities of Working in Virtual Teams: Affective and Attitudinal Outcomes of Using Computer-Mediated Communication. Small Group Res. - SMALL GROUP RES 40.

Joshanloo, M., Jovanović, V. (2018). Subjective health in relation to hedonic and eudaimonic wellbeing: Evidence from the Gallup World Poll. J. Health Psychol. 135910531882010.

Landis, J.R., Koch, G.G. (1977). The Measurement of Observer Agreement for Categorical Data. Biometrics 33, 159.

Lange, M., Kayser, I. (2022). The Role of Self-Efficacy, Work-Related Autonomy and Work-Family Conflict on Employee's Stress Level during Home-Based Remote Work in Germany. Int. J. Environ. Res. Public. Health 19, 4955.

Lechler, R.C., Huemann, M. (2023). Motivation of Young Project Professionals: Their Needs for Autonomy, Competence, Relatedness, and Purpose. Proj. Manag. J. 87569728231195587.

Lyngstadaas, H., Berg, T. (2022). Harder, better, faster, stronger: digitalisation and employee well-being in the operations workforce. Prod. Plan. Control 1–18.

Meske, C. (2019). Digital Workplace Transformation - on the role of self-determination in the context of transforming work environments. Proc. 27th Eur. Conf. Inf. Syst. ECIS Stockh. Upps. Swed. June 8-14 2019 Res. Pap.

Morgan, D. (1996). Focus Groups. Annu. Rev. Sociol. 22, 129–152.

Nilsson, K. (2020). A sustainable working life for all ages – The swAge-model. Appl. Ergon. 86, 103082.

Page, K.M., Vella-Brodrick, D.A. (2009). The 'What', 'Why' and 'How' of Employee Well-Being: A New Model. Soc. Indic. Res. 90, 441–458.

Roehling, P.V., Roehling, M.V., Moen, P. (2001). The Relationship Between Work-Life Policies and Practices and Employee Loyalty: A Life Course Perspective. J. Fam. Econ. Issues. 22, 219-252

Ryan, R.M., Deci, E.L. (2020). Intrinsic and extrinsic motivation from a self-determination theory perspective: Definitions, theory, practices, and future directions. Contemp. Educ. Psychol. 61, 101860.

Ryan, R.M., Deci, E.L. (2022). Self-Determination Theory, in: Maggino, F. (Ed.), Encyclopaedia of Quality of Life and Well-Being Research. Springer International Publishing, Cham, pp. 1–7.

Sarmah, P., Van den Broeck, A., Schreurs, B., Proost, K., Germeys, F. (2022). Autonomy supportive and controlling leadership as antecedents of work design and employee well-being. BRQ Bus. Res. Q. 25, 44–61.

Schweibenz, W. (2004). Zielgruppenorientiertes Informationsdesign mit Personas. NFD Inf.-Wiss. Prax. 55, 151–156.

Shultz, K.S., Wang, M., Crimmins, E.M., Fisher, G.G. (2010). Age Differences in the Demand–Control Model of Work Stress. J. Appl. Gerontol. Off. J. South. Gerontol. Soc. 29, 21–47.

Skinner, N., Elton, J., Auer, J., Pocock, B. (2014). Understanding and managing work-life interaction across the life course: a qualitative study: Understanding and managing work-life interaction across the life course: a qualitative study. Asia Pac. J. Hum. Resour. 52, 93–109.

Tapani, A., Sinkkonen, M., Sjöblom, K., Vangrieken, K., Mäkikangas, A. (2022). Experiences of Relatedness during Enforced Remote Work among Employees in Higher Education. Challenges 13, 55.

Überbacher, R., Brozzi, R., Matt, D.T. (2020). Innovation in craftsmanship family SMEs in times of digitalization. Piccola Impresa Small Bus. 1, 67-85.

van Zoonen, W., Treem, J.W., Sivunen, A.E. (2023). Staying connected and feeling less exhausted: The autonomy benefits of after-hour connectivity. J. Occup. Organ. Psychol. 96, 242–263.

Vanden Abeele, M.M.P., Nguyen, M.H. (2022). Digital well-being in an age of mobile connectivity: An introduction to the Special Issue. Mob. Media Commun. 10, 174–189.

Wylleman, P., & Lavallee, D. (2004). A developmental perspective on transitions faced by athletes, in: Weiss M. R. (Ed.), Developmental sport and exercise psychology: a lifespan perspective. Fitness Information Technology, pp. 503-524

Zacher, H., Froidevaux, A. (2021). Life stage, lifespan, and life course perspectives on vocational behavior and development: A theoretical framework, review, and research agenda. J. Vocat. Behav. 126, 103476.

BEHAVIOURAL RESEARCH IN MANAGING INFORMATION TECHNOLOGY: A SYSTEMATIC LITERATURE REVIEW

Mark van der Pas, Jannika Leckebusch and Max Schrijen
European Center for Digital Transformation
Willem II singel 2, 6041HS, Roermond, The Netherlands

ABSTRACT

This paper seeks to deepen the understanding of IT management as well as of the rationality of decision-making, and the accuracy of information used in IT decision-making. More specifically, this study presents a systematic literature analysis of the research that has been published in the last five years. Comprehensive analysis will help identify the primary research gaps that still exist, while also offering a summary of the most recent advancements within the field. The findings of this paper are based on a systematic review of literature, conducted using electronic database searches, a manual search, as well as snowballing. After subjecting identified papers to a quality evaluation and study selection criteria, 49 relevant publications were identified for the analysis. The SLR identified research gaps in 'IT management,' including a lack of studies on the behaviour of organisational agents akin to the Theory of Planned Behaviour, an absence of research on decisions by gatekeeping boards and their accuracy, and a scarcity of studies on the realised quantitative benefits of IT investments.

KEYWORDS

IT Management, Systematic Literature Review, Human Behaviour, IT Decision-Making, IT Accuracy

1. INTRODUCTION

Since the start of the 21st century, businesses have witnessed a rapid surge in the development of new technologies, reshaping markets and transforming business operations (Demir et al. [2019]). These technologies, including Internet of Things (IoT), Big Data, Artificial Intelligence (AI), and Cloud Computing, not only enhance the efficiency of business processes but also introduce increased complexity and management challenges. This study is centred on Information Technology management, acknowledging its significant impact on technological advancements. There are multiple definitions of the concept of IT management. According to Hundal et al. [2022], IT management involves overseeing all Information Technology resources and infrastructure components to ensure efficient operations and minimise the risk of failure by understanding potential risks, capabilities, and constraints. Reichstein [2019] argues that focusing solely on IT issues is outdated, and IT competence has evolved from operational to strategic. This study adopts the Badawy [1998] definition, which states that IT management encompasses the exploration and understanding of (a) the management of IT itself, (b) the development of IT solutions, and (c) the usage of Information Technology, highlighting the challenge of formulating a definition that is both concise and broadly applicable due to diverse interpretations. This shows how broad and ambiguous the topic of IT management is, as nowadays, IT management is found in almost all organisational activities.

As per Ajzen [1991], behaviour refers to the actions exhibited by individuals, and in organisational contexts, it relates to the actions taken by organisational agents. While IT management decisions are often associated with senior executives like the CIO, they also involve non-IT managers such as the CFO, COO, and CMO (Kappelman et al. [2019]). However, decision-making isn't exclusive to senior executives, as research indicates individuals make thousands of decisions daily (Basu and Savani [2023]; Erwin [2023]). In IT management, decisions range from technical choices made by software developers to the actual usage of IT infrastructure. The impact of these decisions, spanning the development of IT solutions and their usage, can be profound, potentially leading to severe consequences like aeroplane crashes or bankruptcy.

Great decisions are timely and accurate and 'the only surefire way to evaluate the efficacy of a decision is to assess the outcomes' (Moore [2022]). Unfortunately, not all decisions are great, as a lot of 'inaccurate decisions' made in IT management today result in a waste of resources. Examples such as deciding on an inefficient architecture, selecting an inadequate IT supplier, underestimating the cost involved in an IT project or overestimating expected benefits (Flyvbjerg et al. [2022]) are not uncommon, which highlights the need to provide synthesis around the rationality of behaviour by organisational agents and the accuracy in Information Technology management.

Solberg et al. [2020] and literature reviews by Danesh et al. [2018] and Sharma and Sehrawat [2021] extensively explore technology acceptance and specific aspects of human behaviour. Despite the acknowledged contribution of IT management to the business revolution, systematic literature studies on human behaviour, especially decision-making in IT management, are limited. In contrast to existing studies, this work aims to synthesise existing research comprehensively, pinpointing current knowledge gaps and paving the way for future research. Therefore, a systematic literature review (SLR) approach was chosen to address the following research question: What are the main areas of focus in human behaviour in IT management, and how rational are decisions made in this field, taking into account the accuracy of the information used? Which issues have advanced, and which main research gaps within the field are relevant for future research? The SLR's approach and method are covered in section two, the findings of the SLR are presented in section three, and the last section provides an answer to the research question and draws conclusions from the SLR in light of the findings and identified research gaps.

2. METHODOLOGY

This SLR, conducted between July and October 2023, adheres to the guidance made by Booth et al. [2016] and Kitchenham and Charters [2007] and adopts their three-step approach: (1) identify search strategy and search scope; (2) locate, select and evaluate the quality of studies; (3) synthesise and analyse the results.

This study employs three methods to locate studies: electronic database searches, a manual search, and snowballing, ensuring both high recall and precision. To encompass diverse research communities, the electronic database Business Source Complete (via EBSCO HOST) was chosen for its scientific research relevance. The list of keywords was developed through a preliminary search, which gave an initial understanding and allowed the optimisation of both keywords and categories. The three categories include general human behaviour and technology acceptance, decision-making and governance, and instruments used in decision-making in IT management. Focused on IT management, this study primarily employs 'IT management' and 'Information Technology management' as the main key search terms. Nine distinct search strings were crafted, with the basic search string ('IT management' OR 'Information Technology Management') combined using the boolean AND operator with each of the nine groups (keywords with each group were also connected with 'OR'). This approach, examining keywords in Title, Abstract, and Keywords, ensures the inclusion of pertinent papers related to the research question while preventing oversight of relevant research.

The search outcome was refined in several ways. Firstly, the results were filtered to include only peer-reviewed papers, ensuring scientific rigour. Additionally, the publication date was restricted to research between 2018-2023 to focus on the most recent information in the dynamic IT management environment. Finally, the results were limited to topics relevant to this thesis. The database search (n=80), manual search (n=3), and snowballing (n=5) produced a sample of 88 papers. Removing duplicates led to 65 papers which were then screened for exclusion. To identify primary studies directly addressing the research question, seven exclusions were developed. The first four exclusions (Papers published before 2018 (EC1), without full text (EC2), not in English (EC3) and not peer-reviewed (EC4)) were applied during the title, keyword, and abstract screening. The second iteration involved a full-text screening, where the remaining three exclusions (Papers unrelated to IT management and human behaviour (EC5), not relevant to answer research question (EC6) and lacking sufficient quality (EC7)) were considered through an in-depth analysis of the paper's substance. The selection process resulted in the exclusion of an additional fifteen papers, which resulted in a total of 49 relevant publications. Following Booth et al. [2016] guidance, relevant data and metadata were extracted during the exclusion criteria and quality assessment process, and organised in a spreadsheet, aligning with the formulated research question. Descriptive (narrative) analysis and synthesis were chosen as the appropriate methods for handling the heterogeneity of the papers, rather than a statistical approach like meta-analysis.

3. RESULTS

The results of the SLR are presented in this section. The SLR findings about organisational agents' behaviour are discussed first. The results about the accuracy of IT management decision-making are then provided.

Within the identified studies, a large number focus on technology acceptance. Çelik and Uslu [2023] present in their literature review, 24 key acceptance components, such as gender (Johnson et al. [2020]) or experience (Haislip et al. [2020]; Kappelman et al. [2021]). Alongside these components, other predictors such as expectations (Khayer et al. [2020]) and social presence for technology acceptance were also studied. Mallmann and Maçada [2019] and Mallmann and Maçada [2021] highlighted a positive relationship between social presence and acceptance, making it a driver of shadow IT. If organisational agents do not accept the offered IT solution, workarounds are adopted, which mostly happens when ERP systems are implemented (Pinto et al. [2018]). Another driver of technology acceptance found is the organisational culture (Wiesböck and Hess [2020]). Besides technology acceptance, organisational agents exhibit individual behaviour, a topic explored in the following paragraph.

Hanus et al. [2022] explored organisational agents' behaviour in a phishing experiment, categorising them as 'vulnerable' or 'immune' based on predictors the most significant being age, compensation, and job characteristics. A security-related study by Elifoglu et al. [2018] addressed insider threats, emphasising the human aspect, proposing subjects such as alcohol, legal restraining orders, and disregard for authority as indicators of insider threat. Solberg et al. [2020] investigated the 'digital mindset,' finding that beliefs about personal and situational resources influence agents' engagement in digital transformation. Organisational agents use various tactics such as exchange, rational persuasion, personal appeal, and coalition, to influence peers and superiors, as explored by Pang and Lee [2022].

Some organisational changes indirectly relate to individual agent behaviour, as seen in studies associating concrete language usage in IS project business cases with bigger budgets and schedule overruns than in IS projects with more abstract language (Benschop et al. [2020]). Pang and Lee [2022] find that the overrun of IT projects in federal US organisations is negatively correlated to the number of managerial IT officers. Complex studies, such as Hartzel and Spangler [2021], focus on 'management principles and behaviour' for IT risk management in high-reliability organisations, proposing guidelines like 'build, execute, and continuously monitor the entire risk management process' and 'establish a culture of shared ownership.' These guidelines differ from individual behavioural indicators but are influenced by organisational agents' decisions or contributions to them. Culture poses challenges in implementing agile IT management in public organisations, emphasising stability (Ylinen [2021]). Even culture is identified as a driver for digital innovations (Wiesböck and Hess [2020]), and a digital mindset drives digital strategy, it is a challenge to implement agile IT management in public organisations, as they value stability (Ylinen [2021]).

Research on the characteristics and behaviour of managers in IT management is extensive. The identified papers frequently emphasise the impact of CEOs' IT competence on technology adoption, highlighting a lack of IT expertise at the top level as detrimental to organisational performance (Haislip et al. [2020]). Higher IT experience, awareness, and knowledge among board members positively influence firm performance (Reichstein [2019]; Zhang et al. [2018]). Roy et al. [2018] explore the cascading effect of management actions on new product development, showing a positive correlation between top management support and IT management. CEOs with IT expertise report Form 8-K more promptly than those without, and managerial IT capability significantly impacts cloud computing success (Haislip et al. [2020]; Khayer et al. [2020]). Roy et al. [2018] underscore the importance of upper management conduct in new product creation and financial prosperity. Technical aspects and organisational culture are identified as critical success factors influencing competitive success in business-managed IT (Klotz et al. [2022]).

The identified studies in the SLR often also center on CIOs, and they show that a company's attitude towards artificial intelligence is positively correlated with having a CIO position (Li et al. [2021]). According to Johnson et al. [2020], who studied the gender of IT managers, the proportion of women in IT leadership roles is growing, with female CIOs in 'predominantly female industries' and in companies with larger IT budgets/revenues. Kappelman et al. [2019] present the top ten most difficult-to-find soft skills for IT managers a.o. these are communication, collaboration, decision-making, and change management. Effective assimilation of emerging technology into existing infrastructure requires IT managers' coordination of intricate tasks (Khayer et al. [2020]).

This SLR not only unveiled extensive research on the behaviour of organisational agents and management but also emphasised collaboration within and across departments. European CIOs spend a considerable amount of time coordinating with their IT unit (26,4%) and C-level colleagues (19,1%) (Kappelman et al. [2019]). Collaboration extends beyond senior managers, involving IT specialists and senior management to align technology architecture with business goals (Patterson [2020]). IT management, often distributed among various agents (Juiz and Gomez [2021]; Klotz et al. [2022]), involves cross-functional teams and diverse roles such as deciders, gatekeepers, users, and buyers, in processes like enterprise software selection (Turel et al. [2019]; Raghavan et al. [2020]). Successful IT outsourcing requires managing collaboration between customers and providers (Juiz and Gomez [2021]). New cooperation methods, such as co-design and co-creation, are recommended for cross-functional teams (Wiesböck and Hess [2020]).

Research not only acknowledges cross-organisational cooperation but emphasises its importance. Business IT alignment enhances IT performance, innovation, and firms' profitability (Raymond et al. [2019]). Additionally, effective IT utilisation relies on cooperation among organisational agents (Haislip et al. [2020]). The value of business intelligence and analytics depends on the complementarity of IT and organisational resources (Moreno et al. [2019]). Siloed IT structures hinder collaboration, impacting the sharing of the agile mindset (Ylinen [2021]). Miscommunication between senior management and IT specialists is a significant contributor to projects failing to deliver the desired values (Patterson [2020]).

In the following, the SLR findings on decision-making in IT management are presented. The initial part provides insights into decisions, decision-makers, and decision-making tools, with a focus on the accuracy of information. The subsequent segment covers the latest discoveries related to risk management in IT management. The findings of the SLR covered various issues, including high-impact decisions on architecture, infrastructure, and strategy (Kappelman et al. [2019]), prioritising IT investments (Lima et al. [2018]) and terminating projects (Thornley and Crowley [2018]). Pang and Lee [2022] categorise IT management decisions into control and management rights, addressing performance monitoring, project setup approval, resource utilisation, and ratified decision execution. Specific IT management decisions pertain to technologies like artificial intelligence (Li et al. [2021]), business intelligence (Moreno et al. [2019]), and cloud computing (Coppolino et al. [2021]; Khayer et al. [2020]; Mallmann and Maçada [2018]), human resource information systems (Barisic et al. [2018]), robotic process automation (Hofmann et al. [2020]), shadow IT (Mallmann and Maçada [2019]) and Software as a Service (Raghavan et al. [2020]). The following paragraph addresses the decision-makers or authorities in IT management.

CIOs play a crucial role in selecting enterprise software to align with organisational demands (Raghavan et al. [2020]). However, decision-making in IT management is evolving, with SaaS causing a shift from the IT department to business units (Raghavan et al. [2020]). Pang and Lee [2022] show that time overruns and the degree of decision-making authority held by an IT unit are inversely associated and according to Reichstein [2019] businesses with influential IT departments do better both financially and non-financially. Decision power often rests with committees, such as IT management committees or IT steering committees, emphasising a collective approach to decision-making (Juiz and Gomez [2021]; Lima et al. [2018]). These committees, termed 'gatekeeping boards' in this study, are normally cross-functional groups deciding on and prioritising IT projects (Carlsson-Wall et al. [2021]; Juiz and Gomez [2021]). Decentralised decision-making gains prominence, with employee empowerment seen as vital for implementing agile practices and addressing challenges autonomously (Ylinen [2021]). The responsibility for IT management is progressively shifting from senior management to IT staff (Mallmann and Maçada [2019]; Pinto et al. [2018]).

IT decision-making is integral to IT governance, defined by the IT Governance Institute as the leadership, structures, and processes ensuring IT aligns with organisational strategies (ITGI [2003]). IT governance is not a new topic; an overview of standards and related research can be found in Yokkhun and Papasratorn [2018]. Academics and practitioners agree that there are three crucial mechanisms for successful IT governance: communication, decision-making, and alignment processes (Juiz and Gomez [2021]). Financial aspects of IT governance, focusing on the value derived from IT investments supporting the business, gain importance, as businesses fail to derive a competitive advantage from their large-scale investments (Zong and Wang [2022]). Challenges in IT governance include practitioners lacking a holistic understanding of ongoing IT projects, leading to low decision-making, and the potential negative impact on decision-making authority when taking on too many IT projects at once (Ylinen [2021]; Pang and Lee [2022]).

IT project termination becomes essential to avoid project overload, with challenges encompassing governance, cultural issues, and the need for cooperation across multiple departments (Thornley and Crowley [2018]). Whereas studies predominantly assume behaviour based on efficient choices, Akhlaghpour and

Lapointe [2018] suggest that decision-making incorporates economically rational efficient choice, forced selection (e.g. on regulatory obligations), fashion (mass media), and fad-based perspectives (following 'neighbouring' organisations) (Akhlaghpour and Lapointe [2018]). A literature review by Mallmann and Maçada [2018] identifies variables affecting decision-making, including cost, availability, flexibility, security, risk, regulations, and contract concerns. Kuhlen and Speck [2023] use software production process simulation to explore inputs influencing managers' decisions on costs, skills, quality, and reusability. Their study, notable for incorporating agents' behaviour into simulations, provides valuable insights into decision-making processes in IT management.

Risk management is another key subject for IT management in general and decision-making in particular (Yokkhun and Papasratorn [2018]). The first risk addressed is the inaccuracy of cost and benefit estimations. Decision-making in IT management heavily relies on monetised metrics and business cases (Lima et al. [2018]; Juiz and Gomez [2021]). According to Flyvbjerg et al. [2022], the evaluation of IT project performance encompasses both objective and subjective measurements.

On average, IT projects experience an 80% overrun, with much higher overruns in the public sector (110%) compared to the private sector (40%) and supply chain projects having the highest average overruns at 120% (Flyvbjerg et al. [2022]). Increasing the accuracy of cost estimates is necessary, as studies like Benschop et al. [2020], Flyvbjerg et al. [2022], and demonstrate. Efforts to enhance cost estimation accuracy are ongoing, with studies like Relich and Pawlewski [2018] employing neural network models for more precise predictions. Risk can also be assessed qualitatively (e.g. on an ordinal scale) (Danesh et al. [2018]), including elements like unavailability, information security, data privacy, and financial components. Flyvbjerg et al. [2022] underscore the riskiness of large IT projects based on quantitative financial analysis. Beyond financial considerations, researchers explore various components influencing IT decision-making, such as sustainability within a green IT framework (Patón-Romero et al. [2019]). Techniques like multicriteria decision-making are proposed by Coppolino et al. [2021] and Danesh et al. [2018] to refine assessment and selection processes for IT projects, introducing a weighted scale for criteria.

Besides evaluating risk for individual projects, assessing project portfolio outcomes is vital, with Pang and Lee [2022] revealing, at the portfolio level, an increase of one percentage point in the ranks of IT managers corresponds to a reduction of 13,8 days in the average overrun of project activities. Portfolio performance becomes crucial, as the success of one IT project can impact others, emphasising the relative nature of prioritisation (Carlsson-Wall et al. [2021]).

Risk management is integral to IT governance, with a focus on minimising security risks (Mallmann and Maçada [2019]). Strategies like Lean Six Sigma are proposed to reduce risks (Hundal et al. [2022]), emphasising the alignment of policies, strategies, and operational activities with risk evaluation (Juiz and Gomez [2021]). However, many decision-making models overlook risk considerations, leading to potential suboptimal decisions, like taking on extremely risky IT projects (Flyvbjerg et al. [2022]). The subjective component of decision-making underscores the significance of human behaviour (Danesh et al. [2018]). Wiesböck and Hess [2020] state that cultural attitudes towards risk impact an organisation's approach to digital technologies. For high-risk, high-complexity IT projects to be successful, Hartzel and Spangler [2021] suggest continuous risk monitoring as a guideline for success. This summarises the SLR findings on human behaviour in managing Information Technology, providing valuable insights into the current state of research in this domain.

4. DISCUSSION AND CONCLUSIONS

A variety of research methodologies ranging from experiments, interviews, surveys and archival research are used in IT management research. As far as theories are concerned, the typical behaviour-based theories are used, but most papers are exploratory in nature. The field lacks a strong theoretical basis for organisational agents' behaviour beyond the acceptance of technology.

In the study by Çelik and Uslu [2023], twenty-four key components of TAM were identified, with some components studied in this SLR. Additional components like culture, social presence, digital mindset, consultation, and overcoming anomalies were found (Akhlaghpour and Lapointe [2018]; Elifoglu et al. [2018]; Hanus et al. [2022]; Mallmann and Maçada [2018]; Pang and Lee [2022]; Pinto et al. [2018]; Raghavan et al. [2020]; Solberg et al. [2020]; Ylinen [2021]; Wiesböck and Hess [2020]). The financial impact on human behaviour in managing IT was explored by Benschop et al. [2020], Flyvbjerg et al. [2022], and Zong and Wang [2022].

Numerous studies have been conducted on IT governance, and one aspect of IT governance that is frequently addressed is human behaviour (Juiz and Gomez [2021]; Turel et al. [2019]; Wiesböck and Hess [2020]; Yokkhun and Papasratorn [2018]). In the SLR, studies explore how organisations decide on IT projects, addressing issues like a lack of holistic views (Ylinen [2021]), managing simultaneous projects (Danesh et al. [2018]; Pang and Lee [2022]), and project termination (Thornley and Crowley [2018]). Other studies focus on decision-making processes, information system adoption (Barisic et al. [2018]; Coppolino et al. [2021]; Hofmann et al. [2020]; Moreno et al. [2019]; Raghavan et al. [2020]), and gatekeeping boards (Carlsson-Wall et al. [2021]; Danesh et al. [2018]; Haislip et al. [2020]; Juiz and Gomez [2021]; Kappelman et al. [2019]; Lima et al. [2018]; Raghavan et al. [2020]; Turel et al. [2019]). Financial information supporting IT decision-making is explored by Flyvbjerg et al. [2022], Juiz and Gomez [2021], Lima et al. [2018], and Zong and Wang [2022]. Additionally, studies by Danesh et al. [2018] and Patón-Romero et al. [2019] focus on managing non-financial inputs in IT management decision-making. IT leaders are currently finding that security, business alignment, and continuity are the most challenging issues to address (Kappelman et al. [2021]). Flyvbjerg et al. [2022], Juiz and Gomez [2021], Mallmann and Maçada [2018], Mallmann and Maçada [2019], and Yokkhun and Papasratorn [2018] address these issues.

After a comprehensive analysis of the existing literature on human behaviour in IT management, several unaddressed gaps have surfaced. Firstly, research on organisational agents' adoption of technology is widely studied, however, less is known about the motivations behind and methods by which they actively and voluntarily participate in IT management (Solberg et al. [2020]). Moreover, no current studies on the factors influencing organisational agents' behaviour in managing Information Technology, as described by Ajzen [1991], were identified. Therefore, a research gap is identified, specifically the application of the Theory of Planned Behaviour to modern Information Technology management. This could be relevant as, for example, understanding the personal traits of CIOs and business users, as suggested by Raghavan et al. [2020], can contribute to a more comprehensive comprehension of Software as a Service adoption.

Secondly, exploring gatekeeping boards' performance in managing Information Technology reveals a substantial gap in empirical information on their decisions. No statistics on the number of decisions, approval rates, or their role in preventing failed initiatives were found. This gap extends to risk management, with a lack of studies applying machine learning to quantify and mitigate risks. Since risk management is typically dependent on subjective decisions, there is a substantial research gap caused by the lack of machine learning models supporting project cancellation probability for gatekeeping boards as well as the absence of studies on their prediction accuracy (Danesh et al. [2018]). As gatekeeping boards often make critical decisions swiftly with incomplete information, supporting them automatically becomes crucial.

Lastly, in the realm of decision-making in managing Information Technology, literature predominantly evaluates success based on process and product performance. While Flyvbjerg et al. [2022] delve into the power law distribution of cost overruns, a research gap exists, as much of the review is dated. A significant gap emerges regarding quantitative financial performance, especially in assessing the benefit component of IT investments. The literature lacks objective characterisation of the disparity between expected and actual financial returns on IT investments. This research gap is relevant for addressing challenges in portfolio management, such as having incorrect information (Danesh et al. [2018]) and inaccurate business cases Thornley and Crowley [2018]. Additionally, the failure to assess the accuracy of business cases restricts continual learning and successful project completion (Benschop et al. [2020]).

The identified gaps align with Thornley and Crowley [2018], who suggested that future research should prioritise enhancing the business case, alongside areas such as change and people management, governance, stakeholder management, and staged delivery. Despite efforts to avoid biases, this study has limitations, aiming to provide a comprehensive overview of recent advancements in IT Management. The authors acknowledge limitations in scope and time frame, ensuring relevance but potentially excluding relevant work. Future research could explore multiple databases or broaden the scope to include other technologies like production technology and logistics technology for additional insights into managing IT. The relevance of IT management for the functioning of modern society, for those employed in the field, and for financial investments in IT management was highlighted throughout this SLR.

REFERENCES

Ajzen, I. (1991). The theory of planned behaviour. *Organizational Behavior and Human Decision Processes*, 50(2): 179-211.

Akhlaghpour, S. and Lapointe, L. (2018). From placebo to panacea: Studying the diffusion of IT management techniques with ambiguous efficiencies: The case of capability maturity model. *Journal of the Association for Information Systems*, 19:441–502.

Badawy, M. K. (1998). Technology management education: Alternative models. *California Management Review*, 40(4): 94–116.

Barisic, A. et al. (2018). Human resources information systems and its impact on organizational performance. *Conference Proceedings: International Conference of the Faculty of Economics Sarajevo (ICES)*, pages 81–96.

Basu, S. and Savani, K. (2023). To make better choices, look at all your options together. *Harvard Business Review*, Fall: 70–72.

Benschop, N. et al. (2020). Detection of early warning signals for overruns in is projects: linguistic analysis of business case language. *European Journal of Information Systems*, 29(2): 190–202.

Booth, A. et al. (2016). *Systematic Approaches to a Successful Literature Review*. SAGE Publications.

Carlsson-Wall, M. et al. (2021) Exploring the role of management control anchor practices in new product development. *European Accounting Review*, 30(2):251–276.

Çelik, Z. and Uslu, A. (2023). A bibliometric analysis of the literature on the origins of the technology acceptance model (tam) and a marketing-sided approach to tam. *Öneri Dergisi*, 18(59):1–14.

Coppolino, L. et al. (2021). Fuzzy set theory-based comparative evaluation of cloud service offerings: an agro-food supply chain case study. *Technology Analysis Strategic Management*, 33(8): 900–913.

Danesh, D. et al. (2018). Multi-criteria decision-making methods for project portfolio management: a literature review. *International Journal of Management and Decision Making*, 17(1):75–94, 2018.

Demir, K. et al., (2019). Industry 5.0 and human-robot co-working. *Procedia computer science*, 158 (13):688–695.

Elifoglu, I. et al. (2018). Minimizing insider threat risk with behavioral monitoring. Review of Business, 38(2):61–73.

Erwin, M. (2023). Six reasons we make bad decisions, and what to do about them. *Harvard Business Review*, Fall:64–65.

Flyvbjerg, B. et al. (2022). The empirical reality of IT project cost overruns: Discovering a power-law distribution. *Journal of Management Information Systems*, 39(3):607–639, 2022.

Haislip, J. et al. (2020). The influences of ceo IT expertise and board-level technology committees on form 8-k disclosure timeliness. *Journal of Information Systems*, 34(2):167–185.

Hanus, B. et al. (2022). Phish me, phish me not. *Journal of Computer Information Systems*, 62(3): 516–526, 2022.

Hartzel, K. and Spangler, E. (2021). A high-reliability approach to risk management in an IT project. *Journal of Computer Information Systems*, 61(2):130–140.

Hofmann, P. et al. (2020). Robotic process automation. *Electronic Markets*, 30(1):99–106.

Hundal, G. et al. (2022). The impact of lean six sigma practices on supply chain resilience during covid 19 disruption: a conceptual framework. *Total Quality Management Business Excellence*, 33(15/16):1913–1931.

Johnson, V. et al. (2020). Women in IT management: Significant gains and continuing challenges. *Journal of Computer Information Systems*, 60(3):244–255, 2020.

Juiz, C. and Gomez, B. (2021). Delving into the IT governance- management communication interface: A scoping review. *International Journal of Digital Strategy, Governance, Business Transformation (IJDSGBT)*, 11(1):1–37.

Kappelman, L. et al. (2019). A study of information systems issues, practices, and leadership in europe. *European Journal of Information Systems*, 28(1):26–42.

Kappelman, L. et al. (2021). The 2020 sim IT issues and trends study. *MIS Quarterly Executive*, 20(1):69–107.

Khayer, A. et al. (2020). Understanding cloud computing success and its impact on firm performance: an integrated approach. *Industrial Management Data Systems*, 120(5):963–985.

Kitchenham, B. and Charters, S. (2007). *Guidelines for performing systematic literature reviews in software engineering*.

Klotz, S. et al. (2022). Critical success factors of business-managed it: It takes two to tango. *Information Systems Management*, 39(3):220–240.

Kuhlen, D. and Speck, A. (2023). Extension of a simulation software to incorporate quality-related factors in investigations on software engineering economics. *International Journal of Software Engineering Knowledge Engineering*, 33 (1): 1–21.

Li, J. et al. (2021). Strategic directions for ai: The role of cios and boards of directors. *MIS Quarterly*, 45(3):1603–1643.

Lima, A. et al. (2018). A consensus-based multicriteria group decision model for information technology management committees. 65:1–17, 2018.

Mallmann, G. and Maçada, A. (2018). Adoption of cloud computing: A study with public and private hospitals in a developing country. *International Journal of Innovation and Technology Management*, 15(5).

Mallmann, G. and Maçada, A. (2019). Shadow IT and computer-mediated collaboration: Developing a framework based on social presence theory. Brazilian Journal of Management / Revista de Administração da UFSM, 12 (4):821–839.

Mallmann, G. and Maçada, A. (2021). The mediating role of social presence in the relationship between shadow IT usage & individual performance: a social presence theory perspective. *Behaviour Information Technology*, 40(4):427–441.

Moore, G. (2022). How to make great decisions, quickly (online accessed on 2023.08.09*). Harvard Business Review*, 2022. URL https://hbr.org/2022/03/how-to-make-great-decisions-quickly.

Moreno, V. et al. (2019). Complementarity as a driver of value in business intelligence and analytics adoption processes. *Revista Ibero-Americana de Estratégia (RIAE)*, 18(1):57–70.

Pang, M. and Lee, G. (2022). The impact of IT decision-making authority on IT project performance in the u.s. federal government. *MIS Quarterly*, 46(3):1759–1776.

Patón-Romero, J. et al. (2019). Maturity model based on cmmi for governance and management of green it. *IET Software* (Wiley-Blackwell), 13(6):555–563, 2019.

Patterson, M. (2020). A structured approach to strategic alignment between business and information technology objectives. *South African Journal of Business Management*, 51(1):1–12.

Pinto, A. et al. (2018). Workaround behaviour in information systems research. *Journal of Manufacturing Technology Management*, 25(4):430–446.

Raghavan, S. et al. (2020). Impact of software as a service (saas) on software acquisition process. *Journal of Business Industrial Marketing*, 35(4):757–770.

Raymond, L. et al., (2019). Determinants and outcomes of IT governance in manufacturing smes: A strategic IT management perspective. *International Journal of Accounting Information Systems*, 35:100422.

Reichstein, C. (2019). Strategic IT management: how companies can benefit from an increasing IT influence. *Journal of Enterprise Information Management*, 32(2):251–273.

Relich, M. and Pawlewski, P. (2018). A case-based reasoning approach to cost estimation of new product development. *Neurocomputing*, 272(C):40–45.

Roy, S. et al. (2018). Cascading effects of management actions on npd in the manufacturing sector. *Journal of Manufacturing Technology Management*, 29(7):1115–1137.

Sharma, M. and Sehrawat, R. (2021). Decision-making in management of technology: a literature review. *International Journal of Technology Intelligence and Planning,* 13(1):38–62.

Solberg, E. et al. (2020). Digital mindsets: Recognizing and leveraging individual beliefs for digital transformation. *California Management Review,* 62(4):105–124, 2020.

Thornley, C. and Crowley, C., (2018). Developing the capability to terminate IT projects when they can no longer deliver business value. *International Journal of Managing Projects in Business*, 11(2):406–431.

Turel, O. et al. (2019). Is board IT governance a silver bullet? a capability complementarity and shaping view. *International Journal of Accounting Information Systems*, 33(2):32–46.

Wiesböck, F. and Hess, T. (2020). Digital innovations: Embedding in organizations. *Electronic Markets*, 30(1):75–86.

Ylinen, M. (2021). Incorporating agile practices in public sector IT management: A nudge toward adaptive governance. Information Polity: *The International Journal of Government Democracy in the Information Age*, 26(3):251–271.

Yokkhun, A. and Papasratorn, B. (2018). An IT governance framework for virtual enterprise in tourism industry: Evidence from small tourism enterprises in thailand. *International Journal of Innovation Technology Management,* 15 (3).

Zhang, P. et al. (2018). How IT awareness impacts IT control weaknesses and firm performance. *Journal of International Technology Information Management*, 27(2):99–120.

Zong, K. and Wang, Z. (2022). An empirical study on impact of management capabilities for the multinational company's sustainable competitive advantage. *Journal of Organizational End User Computing*, 34(8):1–23.

ON THE APPLICATION OF STATIC CODE ANALYSIS TOOLS IN THE SERBIAN IT INDUSTRY: AN EMPIRICAL STUDY

Aleksa Komosar, Sara Kijanovic, Vladimir Mandic, Danilo Nikolic and Teodora Vuckovic
Faculty of Technical Sciences, University of Novi Sad, Trg Dositeja Obradovica 6, Novi Sad, Serbia

ABSTRACT

The rapid development of information technologies and the increase in client demands in the sphere of software product production create motivation for the development and improvement of static code analysis tools. The aim of this paper is to investigate the impact of seniority on the opinion of tools for static code analysis, as well as the impact of tools on the deployment pipeline. This paper presents an empirical study based on the survey, where the questions are separated into three sections that refer to demographic data, static code analysis tools, and tool evaluation. The target group is technical persons in the IT industry in Novi Sad and Belgrade. Data processing was performed using the JASP tool and Pearson's tests were performed to obtain the results. It was observed that a higher level of seniority determines a lower evaluation of the tool. In addition, all the participants for whom static code analysis is a mandatory part of pipeline deployment will use the tool more often. Therefore, static code analysis tools are a powerful tool that facilitates work in the IT industry, but there are many parts that are suitable for improvement. The full survey is available on request.

KEYWORDS

Static Code Analysis, IT Industry, Software Development, Empirical Study, Survey

1. INTRODUCTION

Static code analysis, as a way of identifying problems of different levels within the code of a project, is widely used today (Gomes et al.). Using static code analysis tools can increase the effectiveness and efficiency of development teams working on projects. The rapid development of information technologies requires fast, efficient, and effective code delivery. In order for the code to be highly performant, it is necessary not only to optimize the compiler time but also to detect bugs and vulnerabilities in parts of the code, which is the basic role of static code analysis (Stefanović et al. 2021). In 2009, Matti Mantere et al. (Mantere et al. 2009) compared SCA, Frama-C, and Splint code analysis tools. Today, the number of tools for static analysis of code has increased significantly, where their importance for further development and application in the IT industry can be seen. In their research conducted on a large sample, Herbert Prähofer et al. (Prahofer et al. 2017) observed the importance of developing tools for static code analysis and contributed to the development of this field.

Successful static code analysis is influenced by numerous factors, among which the experience of the developer within the development team can be highlighted (Baca et al. 2009). In addition to the developer's experience, the approach to software development, as well as the methodology, can also be highlighted. Static code analysis brings a large number of benefits that today, employees in IT companies understand (Aurum et al. 2002). There are defined different ways of evaluating the code, where the development team on the project plays a big role (Aurum et al. 2002). Today, with the existence of a large number of tools for statistical code analysis, a completely new approach can develop better understanding of the problems and how to resolve them (Nikolic et al. 2021; Stefanović et al. 2021).

Tools for static code analysis are increasingly used in the IT industry, which encourages the use of tools for static code analysis even at entry-level levels when it comes to the seniority of employees in IT companies (Katin et al. 2022; Nikolic et al. 2021). By improving aspects of the static code analysis tool, the overall quality of the static code analysis tool itself is improved. Different seniorities have different experiences in using different tools. As required code revisions affect the frequency of tool usage, there is a dependency that can be used to determine their relationship. More than 40.000 people in Serbia work in the IT industry and generate 10 percent of its GDP (*Serbia - Information and Communications Technology Market* 2022). Accordingly, two major cities – Novi Sad and Beograd are used as a relevant cities to explore usage of static code analysis.

As the importance of tools for static code analysis has been observed, this paper will present the state of the art in the field of empirical and related research on the use of tools for static code analysis, as well as modern code analysis. The section after that refers to the methodology and research questions, where at the end of the paper the results will be presented, as well as the conclusion. The research was conducted on the territory of the Republic of Serbia in the largest cities - Novi Sad and Belgrade, as mentioned previously. The survey participants work for various IT companies and possess expertise in utilizing tools for static code analysis.

2. STATE OF THE ART

Static code analysis, as well as its tools, are often a sphere of interest for conducting empirical research with the aim of acquiring new knowledge and improving this field. Over the last few years, many authors have been conducting empirical research in the field of both modern and static code analysis. In order to pay attention to current trends in the field of statistic code analysis, Scopus and Web of Science databases were searched. All papers in the past five years related to empirical research in the field of static code analysis and this specific problem given in this paper were taken into account.

Caitlin Sadowski et al. (Sadowski et al. 2018) conducted research in the field of modern code analysis at Google. They posed three research questions, relating to the motivation for code analysis, the practice used at Google, and how developers perceive code analysis. They collected a total of 44 responses from developers. The research results indicate that developers at Google expect static code analysis to provide education, prevention, and easier maintenance of software products. In addition, developers believe that code analysis is still vulnerable and not sufficiently good, and that there is motivation for further development.

The prediction of high-impact design changes in modern code analysis was conducted by Anderson Uchoa et al. (Uchoa et al. 2021), finding that Random Forest and Gradient Boosting are best for predicting changes that significantly affect the design. Previously, Anderson Uchoa and colleagues (Uchoa et al. 2020) analyzed code from seven projects, concluding that code analysis does not degrade the design of software products.

On the other hand, Andrej Katin et al. (Katin et al. 2022) conducted an empirical study examining the SonarQube tool and its application among junior developers, involving a total of 133 students from Serbia and Finland. It was observed that juniors estimate the time needed to resolve technical debt as less than what the tool suggests, and their perceptions differ based on the level of criticality of code issues and vulnerabilities.

Besides the study concluding that junior developers and static code analysis tools perceive the levels of criticality of code vulnerabilities differently (Katin et al. 2022), Sebastiano et al. (Panichella & Zaugg 2020) review necessary changes for improving static code analysis. Their empirical study involves 52 developers and identifies the use of cloud computing technologies for static code analysis as suitable for developing this field.

Carmine Vassallo et al. (Vassallo et al. 2018) include 42 developers in their empirical study, with 69% working in IT companies and the rest on open-source projects. FindBugs, Checkstyle, and SonarQube are mentioned as tools used by the participants, primarily for local environments, code analysis, and continuous integration. All developers configure static code analysis tools at least once during a project, and approaches to prioritizing and solving problems vary depending on project complexity, organization, and goals.

Conversely, Vladimir Mandić et al. (Mandić et al. 2020) investigated the prevalence of the technical debt concept in Serbia, noting the use of static code analysis tools as a means to reduce technical debt. The study considered company size and other factors significant at the national level, confirming a positive response regarding familiarity with the concept of technical debt and its resolution using static code analysis tools.

3. METHODOLOGY

In this chapter, the methodology for collecting and creating the questionnaire will be presented. In addition, the research questions of this study, as well as the process of data processing and obtaining results, are also introduced.

3.1 Research Questions

With the aim of better understanding the use of static code analysis tools, two research questions have been posed:

RQ1: How does seniority affect the respondents' experience in terms of using static code analysis tools?

RQ2: To what extent does the requirement for code analysis during the deployment pipeline influence the frequency of the tools in use?

3.2 Data Collection

All the data within this empirical study were collected using a Google Forms survey. The survey was divided into three sections, respectively the demographic section, tool usage, and tool ratings. Before releasing the survey to the public, it was filled out by test subjects, and based on their feedback, the questions were clarified for better understanding. All respondents answer anonymously, which gives them the freedom to give honest answers, based on the context of the survey. Authors approached to different IT company that are using software for static code analysis.

40 respondents answered a total of 35 questions, with 15 questions being single-choice (SC), 14 rated on a linear scale (LS) from 1 to 5, three questions were multiple-choice (MC), and 3 questions were open-ended and optional for respondents, where they could leave their comments and suggestions for improvements.

3.3 Data Analysis

Based on the set research questions, both qualitative and quantitative methods were further used to draw conclusions. In the following chapter, graphical representations of the obtained results are presented, as well as the results of Pearson's $\chi 2$ test, to determine whether there is a correlation between the defined variables and to characterize whether the dependent variable influences the independent one.

For data analysis, the open-source statistical program JASP (*JASP - A Fresh Way to Do Statistics*) was used. The limitation of the JASP statistical program relates to the types of data that can be processed.

Considering the nature of Pearson's test, it was necessary to transform the answers into an appropriate format. Question Q3, relating to the level of seniority, was transformed into numerical values. All responses with junior values were replaced with 1, medior with 2, and senior with 3. Accordingly, the same procedure was applied to the other questions.

4. ANALYSIS OF RESEARCH RESULTS

According to the different sections of the survey, the first two sections will be briefly analyzed in a descriptive way. The first section of the survey was based on demographic data. The demographic data based on the survey, provide insight into the size of the company and the project team in which the respondents work, position, level of seniority, and years of work experience in the industry. The majority of respondents (47.5%) are employed in companies sized between 101-500 employees. All types of seniority are evenly distributed, while regarding years of work in the industry, it is observed that half of the respondents have been working in the industry for up to 3 years, with 10% of respondents working less than one year, and 40% between 1 and 3 years. 57.5% of respondents are employed as software developer/engineer, then 15% as Technical Team Lead, while other technical positions are less represented. Respondents answered questions in the context of the project or projects on which they used static code analysis tools. Regarding the approach to software development on projects where tools were used, 77.5% of respondents use an agile approach, with SCRUM being the chosen methodology in the majority of cases, i.e., 81.3%. One question that relates to the size of the team using static code analysis tools, evidently indicates the choice of approach and methodology in project realization, as 47.5% of respondents work in teams of 5 to 10 people, and 30% in teams of 3 to 5 people.

The second section of the survey provides questions related to the use of static code analysis tools. Questions are based on the principle of a single answer or the selection of multiple different answers. The majority of respondents stated that they use static code analysis tools on outsourcing projects (57.5%), while 25% of respondents use tools in combination, both on outsourcing projects and on projects that represent the company's own product.

Additionally, second section provides data about frequency of tool usage in the context of real projects, and it can be concluded that this depends on whether code analysis is mandatory as part of the deployment pipeline. 60% of respondents indicated that it is not possible to execute deployment without code analysis, and 25% perform code analysis upon request. Within the responses related to mandatory code analysis, data is provided that gives insight into the frequency of tool usage in this case.

Table 1. Mean values per question

Evaluation variable	**Average grade**
Q16. Satisfaction with the tool's performance	3.77
Q17. Intuitveness of tool usage	3,8
Q18. Simplicity of the tool's control panel	3.77
Q19. Clarity and accuracy of information	3.82
Q20. The platform's capability for quality code writing	3.87
Q21. The platform's contribution to efficiently executing tasks	3,6
Q22. Satisfaction with problem classification	3,8
Q23. Satisfaction with the platform's assistance in resolving code issues	3,9
Q25. Experience in using the tool	3.82
Q26. Display of an overview of flaws in the source code	3,7
Q27. Frequency of recognizing false positive issues	3,25
Q28. Frequency of recognizing false negative issues	2.92
Q29. Suggestion of good solutions	3.37
Q30. Prediction of the time needed for correcting flaws	3.02

Table 1 presents the mean values, namely the average ratings of linear scales marked by the respondents within the posed questions. None of the average ratings exceed the range of 4 to 5, which provides further reason for considering the efficiency of all static code analysis tools that are frequently in use. It is primarily important to consider the reasons why the questions (Q17, Q18, Q19) have an average rating of 3.8. Tools that are insufficiently intuitive and not easy to use for professionals and information that is not at a satisfactory level of clarity and precision, undoubtedly affect all other metrics that are further derived.

Clarity and accuracy of information has a higher average grade than frequency of recognizing false negative issues. Based on the achieved results, an assumption can be made for removing generalization view of point and looking from multiple seniority perspectives. In addition, there may be an expansion of investigations related to these two questions.

The lowest rating relates to the frequency of recognizing false negative issues, where the average score is 2.92. Additionally, the majority of respondents listed the excessive detection of false negative issues as a characteristic of the tool they are dissatisfied with.

The respondents indicated that they are generally satisfied with the tool or tools for static code analysis, in the context of resolving issues in the code. The average satisfaction rating of the respondents is 3.9.

The conducted Pearson test answers the first research question (RQ1.), indicating that the test showed that the variables relating to seniority (Q3.) and the rating of the tool in terms of code writing quality (Q20.) are related. The test shows that the higher the seniority, the lower the rating of the static code analysis tool in terms of quality.

Table 2 presents the mean values of the observed variables in relation to seniority. Q3. the question refers to the current seniority of the respondents, where there is an even distribution by seniority, respectively 35% juniors and 32.5% middle and seniors. Consequently, in the context of the influence of seniority on the observation of the average score of the variables, it is valid to observe the scores of the respondents in relation to an even distribution. It is evident that according to the higher rank of seniority, there are more rigorous grades for almost all observed parameters, but not in a significant range. In most cases, seniors are focused mostly on the more prioritized issues and problems that the tool displays after the code analysis has been performed. In this context issues, such as blocker and critical and identification of security risks are observed. Juniors often pay more attention to other types of issues and problems detected by the tool (minor, major, info).

Consequently, seniors will spend much less time working on debugging than juniors, due to their focus on the most important aspects in terms of code quality. It is important to point out that it is of additional importance to observe issues and problems at all levels, so that the code that needs to be released into production is of high quality. Better grades for most parameters among respondents in junior positions is expected, due to the fact that through the various functionalities of the tool, they have the opportunity to spot different types of issues and thus improve their knowledge and skills in the context of quality implemented code. Also, respondents in senior positions can more easily notice the worse performance of tools for static code analysis, according to the experience of working on projects.

Table 2. Mean of variables by seniority

Evaluation variable	*Average grade by juniors*	*Average grade by mediors*	**Average grade by seniors**
Q16.	4.07	3.61	3.61
Q17.	3.93	3.77	3.69
Q18.	4.14	3.61	3.54
Q19.	3.86	3.08	3.54
Q20.	4.14	3.85	3.62
Q21.	3.57	3.85	3.35
Q22.	4	3.85	3.53
Q23.	4.07	3.85	3.77
Q25.	4.07	3.7	3.69
Q26.	3.71	3.7	3.69
Q27.	3.21	3.23	3.3
Q28.	3	2.69	3.07
Q29.	3.64	3.23	3.23
Q30.	3.21	3.07	2.77

It is also important to point out that there is an evident similarity in the average grades for junior and senior positions, for almost all aspects, that is, the observed variables. Q25. in table 2 represents the average score with which the respondents evaluated the experience in using the tool. Analogously, and taking into account all the previously mentioned reasons, the best average grade was given by the group of respondents in junior positions, while the difference between the average and senior answers is 0.01.

In addition to descriptive statistics, statistical tests were also used for research purposes, in order to see the correlation between variables. Pearson's $\chi2$ test was used. The following questions were asked for variables: Q3, Q16, Q17, Q18, Q19, Q20, Q21, Q22, Q23, Q25, Q26, Q27, Q28, Q29 and Q30. Question Q3 refers to the seniority of the respondents. Taking into account the seniority that corresponds to the respondents can be 1 - junior, 2 - mediocre and 3 - senior, based on the Pirosno test, it is concluded that it does not affect other variables to a large extent.

In addition, it is observed that seniority has a negative correlation with the question Q20. Question Q20. refers to the evaluation of static code analysis tools in the context of code quality. By increasing seniority, the grade on question Q20. is decreasing. On the other hand, based on the results, it can be seen that questions Q20. and Q25. have a statistically significant influence on most other variables, that is, questions. Question Q20 has a statistically significant positive correlation with questions Q16, Q17, Q18, Q19, Q21, Q22, Q23, Q25, Q26 and Q29. As the questions refer to the performance of the tools themselves in terms of their technical features, possibilities and intuitive use, it is seen that a positive correlation between the mentioned variables leads to a higher evaluation of the quality of code writing with the help of static code analysis tools.

Question Q25. which refers to the evaluation of previous experience with the tool achieves a statistically significant positive correlation with questions: Q16, Q17, Q18, Q19, Q20, Q21, Q22, Q23, Q26, Q29. It is observed that all aspects have a positive effect on increasing the evaluation of the respondents' past experience. By improving certain aspects of the tool for static code analysis, it greatly affects the generally formed attitude and opinion of users.

Based on the presented heat map, it can be seen that seniority has a negative correlation with the rating of the static code analysis tool as a tool for quality code writing. The previously described demographic characteristics of the respondents can also be taken into account, where all seniors have an average of over 7 years of experience, which implies an increase in demands on their part.

Furhetmore, results shows that 58% of the respondents use static code analysis tools daily, 25% once a week, while several times a week are used by the respondents in the mentioned case.

The frequency of use of tools for static code analysis is interesting to observe in relation to whether code analysis is an integral part of the deployment pipeline. In order to determine the correlation between these two variables, namely question Q12. and Q15, Pearson's $\chi2$ test was performed. The answers are presented as follows: for Q12. question 1 - once a week, 2 - several times a week, 3 - daily, while for question Q15 the marks are 1 - it is not possible to perform deployment without prior code analysis, 2 - code analysis is done on request, if necessary, 3 - code analysis is not part of the pipeline.

Table 3. Pearson's correlation test for Q15. and Q12

Pearson's Correlations			
Variable		**Q15.**	**Q12.**
1. Q15.	Pearson's r	—	
	p-value	—	
2. Q12.	Pearson's r	-0.450**	—
	p-value	0.004	—
*** p < .05, ** p < .01, *** p < .001**			

Table 3 presents the test results where the correlation between the two observed variables can be clearly seen. From this it can be concluded that if the static analysis of the code is required within the deployment pipeline, the frequency of use is higher. Pearson's r coefficient is negative due to the fact that the scales of the variables themselves are set as previously indicated. Consequently, the answer to the second research question (RQ2.) is that if code analysis is required within the deployment, it is inevitable that it will be used more often. That is, the higher the conditionality score on the scale, the less often the use of static code analysis tools.

When asked whether the tool used is paid for, 47.5% of respondents stated that the tool is paid for, 30% did not say, and 22.5% of respondents use free versions. Static code analysis tools used on commercial projects are expected to be paid for, and according to the answers to the question about the most used tools, the answers partially match. The SonarQube Community (*Open Source Edition*) tool is free, while all other versions are paid. SonarCloud is available as a free version exclusively for open-source projects (*Plans & Pricing*).

Results for the purpose of using the static code analysis tool shows that 92.5% of respondents indicated that they use tools for the purpose of identifying code smells, 57.5% of respondents use tools to identify security risks, and 52.5% of respondents use them for test coverage statistics. 18 (45%) and 15 (37.5%)

respectively use it for the purpose of stylistic problems in writing code and assessing technical grief. It is important to point out that respondents use static code analysis tools on average for the three mentioned categories, and for the purpose of better-quality code writing within projects.

5. THREATS TO VALIDITY

In order to validate the achieved results, but also to set limitations, the following part will describe how the research was carried out.

Construct validity: In this domain, the answers to the questions could have been a threat to the successful research. All responses were related to the context of one project and included only respondents in technical positions who used the static code analysis tool. All those who do not meet these criteria are not taken into account.

Validity of inference: In this domain some of the answers had to be encoded into numerical values for further static analysis.

Internal validity: The data have been subjected to tests to infer correlation, so they are not subject to internal threats to validity.

External validity: The diversity of the different positions held by the respondents is represented. In addition, the survey was conducted in the area of two large cities in Serbia. However, any validity outside the context of Serbia may be the subject of future investigations.

6. CONCLUSION

This paper presents the results of research conducted in Novi Sad and Belgrade, regarding the use of static code analysis tools in the IT industry. A total of 40 responses were analyzed. It is important to point out that there is a growing need to use tools for static code analysis in the industry and on specific projects, according to the fact that 58% of the respondents answered that they have a mandatory code analysis as part of code deployment on the project.

It is necessary to see how to improve the user experience, so that the tools in future research have higher ratings in terms of basic parameters such as ease, intuitiveness, simplicity and clear and precise information. Respondents point out that the documentation for certain tools is poor, and the largest number of respondents state that setting up the tool and uploading projects to it is difficult.

The level of seniority affects the evaluation of static code analysis tools as a means of writing quality code. In addition, the frequency of using static code analysis tools depends on the deployment pipeline of a given project. Future work on this topic is reflected in the research of the use of tools in different aspects, with the aim of understanding in which segments tools for static code analysis best contribute to the development and implementation of projects in the domestic IT industry.

For further steps, this type of research can be continued for companies working on different projects. In addition, seniority levels can be separated as potential dependent variables that influence other aspects of using static code analysis tools. The survey taken for this research is available on request.

REFERENCES

Aurum A, Petersson H, Wohlin C. (2002). State-of-the-art: software inspections after 25 years. *Softw. Test. Verif. Reliab.* 12(3):133–54.

Baca D, Petersen K, Carlsson B, Lundberg L. (2009). Static Code Analysis to Detect Software Security Vulnerabilities - Does Experience Matter? *2009 International Conference on Availability, Reliability and Security*, pp. 804–10. Fukuoka, Japan: IEEE.

Gomes I, Morgado P, Gomes T, Moreira R. An overview on the Static Code Analysis approach in Software Development

JASP - A Fresh Way to Do Statistics. JASP - Free and User-Friendly Statistical Software. https://jasp-stats.org

Katin A, Lenarduzzi V, Taibi D, Mandić V. (2022). On the Technical Debt Prioritization and Cost Estimation with SonarQube Tool. In *Proceedings on 18th International Conference on Industrial Systems – IS'20*, eds. B Lalic, D Gracanin, N Tasic, N Simeunović, pp. 302–9. Cham: Springer International Publishing.

Mandić V, Taušan N, Ramač R. (2020). The prevalence of the technical debt concept in serbian IT industry: results of a national-wide survey. *Proceedings of the 3rd International Conference on Technical Debt*, pp. 77–86. Seoul Republic of Korea: ACM.

Mantere M, Uusitalo I, Roning J. (2009). Comparison of Static Code Analysis Tools. *2009 Third International Conference on Emerging Security Information, Systems and Technologies*, pp. 15–22. Athens/Glyfada, Greece: IEEE.

Nikolic D, Stefanovic D, Dakic D, Sladojevic S, Ristic S. (2021). Analysis of the Tools for Static Code Analysis. *2021 20th International Symposium INFOTEH-JAHORINA (INFOTEH)*, pp. 1–6. East Sarajevo, Bosnia and Herzegovina: IEEE.

Open Source Edition. www.sonarsource.com

Panichella S, Zaugg N. (2020). An Empirical Investigation of Relevant Changes and Automation Needs in Modern Code Review. *Empir Software Eng*. 25(6):4833–72.

Plans & Pricing. www.sonarsource.com

Prahofer H, Angerer F, Ramler R, Grillenberger F. (2017). Static Code Analysis of IEC 61131-3 Programs: Comprehensive Tool Support and Experiences from Large-Scale Industrial Application. *IEEE Trans. Ind. Inf.* 13(1):37–47.

Sadowski C, Söderberg E, Church L, Sipko M, Bacchelli A. (2018). Modern code review: a case study at google. *Proceedings of the 40th International Conference on Software Engineering: Software Engineering in Practice*, pp. 181–90. Gothenburg Sweden: ACM.

Serbia - Information and Communications Technology Market. (2022). www.trade.gov

Stefanović D, Nikolić D, Havzi S, Lolić T, Dakić D. (2021). Identification of strategies over tools for static code analysis. *IOP Conf. Ser.: Mater. Sci. Eng.* 1163(1):012012.

Uchoa A, Barbosa C, Coutinho D, Oizumi W, Assuncao WKG, et al. (2021). Predicting Design Impactful Changes in Modern Code Review: A Large-Scale Empirical Study. *2021 IEEE/ACM 18th International Conference on Mining Software Repositories (MSR)*, pp. 471–82. Madrid, Spain: IEEE.

Uchoa A, Barbosa C, Oizumi W, Blenilio P, Lima R, et al. (2020). How Does Modern Code Review Impact Software Design Degradation? An In-depth Empirical Study. *2020 IEEE International Conference on Software Maintenance and Evolution (ICSME)*, pp. 511–22. Adelaide, Australia: IEEE.

Vassallo C, Panichella S, Palomba F, Proksch S, Zaidman A, Gall HC. (2018). Context is king: The developer perspective on the usage of static analysis tools. *2018 IEEE 25th International Conference on Software Analysis, Evolution and Reengineering (SANER)*, pp. 38–49. Campobasso: IEEE.

A GREY WOLF ALGORITHM FOR INDEX OPTIMIZATION IN RELATIONAL DATABASES

Fernando Verástegui, Rony Cueva and Manuel Tupia
Pontificia Universidad Católica del Perú, Department of Engineering
Universitaria Avenue 1801, San Miguel, Lima, Peru

ABSTRACT

Optimizing indexes in relational databases is crucial for enhancing information system performance, productivity, and decision-making. Indexes are structures that expedite data retrieval, offering swift access to records. Optimization yields faster data access, reducing query delays and enhancing application responsiveness, crucial in competitive enterprise settings. It also eases server load and resource use, resulting in long-term cost savings. Proper index management preserves database integrity, ensuring accurate, consistent data retrieval. Poor design can lead to locking and performance issues, affecting system reliability. The Grey Wolf Optimization (GWO) algorithm, introduced by Seyedali Mirjalili in 2014, is a metaheuristic inspired by grey wolf social behavior. It aids in solving optimization problems, including data management. This algorithm models the social hierarchy and hunting dynamics of grey wolf packs, including four wolf types: alpha, beta, delta, and omega, representing the pack's dominant individuals. This paper presents a GWO algorithm to solve the optimization problem in the indexing of large relational databases.

KEYWORDS

Grey-Wolf Algorithm, Bio-Inspired Algorithm, Database, Optimization, Indexation

1. INTRODUCTION

Optimizing indexes in relational databases is essential to boost the performance of information systems and has a significant impact on productivity and business decision making. Indexes are data structures that speed up the search and retrieval of information in a database, acting as a quick access mechanism to records. Index optimization results in faster access to data, which reduces query latency and improves application responsiveness. This is critical in an enterprise environment where data processing speed is essential to remain competitive. In addition, index optimization can reduce the load on servers and minimize resource consumption, resulting in significant cost savings in the long run. In addition, proper index management is essential for maintaining database integrity and ensuring that data is retrieved accurately and consistently. Poor index design can lead to locking problems and inefficient performance, affecting system reliability and availability. To this end, this paper shows the proposed Grey Wolf Optimization (GWO) algorithm is a metaheuristic optimization algorithm inspired by the social behavior of grey wolves. It was proposed by Seyedali Mirjalili in 2014 and is used to solve optimization problems in various areas, such as data management. The Grey Wolf algorithm is based on the social hierarchy and hunting behavior of a pack of grey wolves. In its operation, four types of wolves are considered: alpha, beta, delta and omega, which represent the most dominant individuals in the pack hierarchy. Each wolf moves in search of prey (optimal solution) following certain rules and mathematical equations that simulate the social and hunting dynamics of wolves.

This paper is divided into the following sections: section 2 shows the problems addressed in relational databases; section 3 presents key concepts for understanding the proposal; section 4 shows the proposed GWO algorithm; section 5 shows the numerical experimentation that confronts the GWO algorithm with a genetic algorithm in order to measure the quality of the responses of the former; and finally, section 6 shows the conclusions of the present work.

2. PROBLEMATIC

In today's business world, data is of crucial importance for the development of a company, whether it is for analysis, commercial monitoring, business strategies, among others. Therefore, its storage and extraction are an important part of its use. Databases are used to store this information, so that it can later be consulted. These can be both relational and non-relational, the former being where the data that is stored is related to each other. The information is organized in tables, which include columns and rows, and this data can be accessed in different ways (AWS, n.d.).

For database administrators (DBAs) and researchers, improving database performance has been a persistent challenge over the years. This challenge is strongly related to the way records are logically organized and, especially, how quickly they are accessed and processed. In that sense, indexes act as a faster way of accessing information. As an example, when data is requested, the database management system first verifies whether an index exists and its structure, which is ordered and contains the physical address of the data, thus allowing the information to be retrieved directly from the database hard drive, simplifying the search work (Pedrozo & Vaz, 2014).

While indexes serve to speed up data retrieval, a poorly designed index degrades the overall performance. This is due to the different aspects that influence its creation, such as: the type of data, the structure of the table, the number of times a specific field was searched, the frequency of certain queries, the frequency of different values in a column, the workload, the number of reading and writing operations, among others (Naik, 2018).

Finding an optimal index setting in order to obtain the minimum implementation cost, balancing both search and maintenance queries on the application workload data, is formally known as the index selection problem (Kovačević & Filipič, 2006).

Among the main problems of index selection, most approaches do not use the same variables, while some focus on input variables (Neuhaus et al., 2019) (Boronski & Bocewicz, 2014) (Kołaczkowski & Rybiński, 2011b) (Kołaczkowski & Rybiński, 2009) (Kovačević & Filipič, 2006) (Korytkowski et al., 2004) (Chaudhuri et al., 2004); others focus on the algorithm's own variables (Kołaczkowski & Rybiński, 2011a) (Calle et al., 2011) (Kratica et al., 2003).

Another very important problem is found in the research, because almost all of it is based on genetic algorithms, which have been used on the market for more than 20 years (Katoch et al., 2021), and others are based on proprietary tools of each database engine (Naik, 2018), so they cannot be applied to any engine.

Finally, these alternative solutions have not given satisfactory results and comparisons need to be done, since, even though each one presents interesting attempts to solve the problem and has many benefits, they are not enough to be implemented in practice for any engine (Boronski & Bocewicz, 2014).

As it has been shown in various investigations, even though each one proposes a new solution, they have not been able to comply with the needs of the user. Therefore, the objective of this project is to optimize the resource consumption (response time and disk space) of the queries through the use of indexes, providing the best option for creating these, on the tables within a relational database management system.

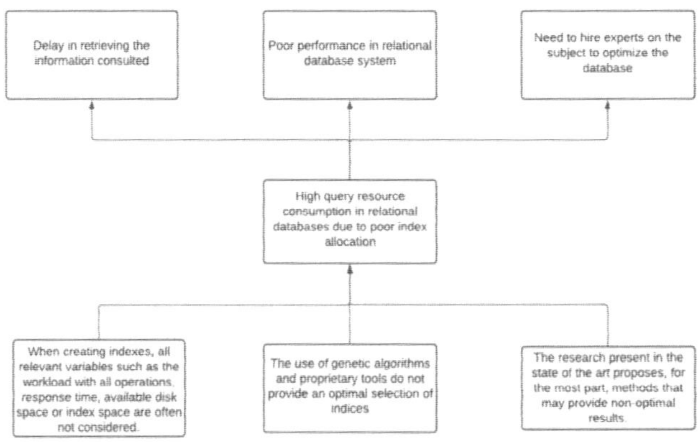

Figure 1. Problem tree. Central zone: Main problem. Lower zone: Problems causes. Upper area: Effects problems

3. KEY CONCEPTS

3.1 Relational Database

First, a database is a type of information storage so that information can be retrieved from it (A Relational Database Overview, n.d.). In that sense, a relational database is a based on the relational data model proposed by Edgar Frank Codd (F., 1970). Frank's system can be defined by two terms. The first, an instance, a table with rows and columns; the second, a scheme, in which the structure, the name of the relationship, name and type of column are specified (Berg et al., 2013).

In this model, each row in a table is a record with a unique identifier called a key. The columns of the table contain attributes of the data and, generally, each record has a value for each attribute, which makes it easy to establish relationships between the data (What Is a Relational Database | Oracle, n.d.).

3.2 Database Optimization

Analyzing and improving the performance of the database management system is called database optimization (Almeida et al., 2019). Performance modification requires the database administrator to possess vast knowledge about the internal aspects of the database (Kołaczkowski & Rybiński, 2011a). In order to make the system faster, this process commonly involves modifying data structures, system parameters, operating system settings, or hardware (Almeida et al., 2019). Additionally, the number of all possible settings grows exponentially with the size of the database scheme (Kołaczkowski & Rybiński, 2011a).

3.3 Index Selection Problem

According to Calle et al. (2011), "The index selection problem can be defined as the search for a particular combination of indexes so that the cost of a given database workload is minimized" (p. 485).

This task is challenging for several reasons. The first, since database schemes of real applications can be large, in terms of tables and columns, and indefinite indexes can be created for a sequence of one or more columns, the space it occupies for the workload can be very big. Second, current query optimizers are able to exploit available indexes using sophisticated techniques. Therefore, it is important to take into consideration the interactions between indexes. Third, the choice of indexes is under certain restrictions, such as limiting the amount of storage space allocated to the indexes. In summary, index selection is stated as an optimization problem where the objective is to find the most productive subset of indexes relevant to the workload under the given constraints (Chaudhuri et al., 2004).

3.4 Grey Wolf Algorithm

The Grey Wolf Algorithm is a metaheuristic algorithm that imitates the leadership hierarchy and hunting mechanism of grey wolves. From this inspiration in nature, four types of grey wolves are used: Alpha, Beta, Delta and Omega, to simulate the leadership hierarchy. Furthermore, three main hunting steps or methods are implemented to perform optimization (GWO, n.d.): Prey Search, Prey Fencing, and Prey Attack. This metaheuristic algorithm has been selected since it has shown to have good results in assignment problems of similar complexity (Mirjalili et al., 2014).

4. PROPOSED ALGORITHM

Our goal is to find subsets of columns that make up the index among all possible subsets of combinations. Therefore, different data structures have been defined for the subsequent adaptation of the Grey Wolf Algorithm for the index selection problem.

4.1 Data Structures

I define three data structures to help implement the Grey Wolf Algorithm: the "Table" structure, that stores table's names, its corrective number, and the number of rows; the "Column" structure, that stores the name, data type and the correlative of the column; the "Wolf" structure, used to represent a population agent. This structure stores the query, the execution time in seconds, the space in GB, the frequency, total penalty of the columns to be indexed, an array of the candidates' columns to be indexed and the fitness.

4.2 Grey Wolf Implementation

The algorithm is divided into three phases: initialization, iteration and update. During the initialization phase, wolves are created and initial values, such as the query, the inputs related to create data structures and algorithm's constants, are assigned to their positions and speeds. During the iteration phase, each wolf is evaluated for fitness and its positions and speeds are updated. The update phase is used to update the parameter values of the algorithm. The algorithm uses several functions, including the fitness function, which evaluates the quality of a solution, and the selection function, which selects the best solutions for the next iteration.

```
Function greyWolfAlgorithm (querys, tables, columns, populationSize, alpha, beta, dSpace)
  population <- generateInitialPopulation (querys, tables, columns, populationSize, alpha, beta, dSpace)
  getThreeBestSolutions (population, tables, alpha, beta, dSpace, alphaWolf, betaWolf, gammaWolf)
  t <- 1
  WHILE t <= maxIter
    a <- 2 * (1 - t/maxIter)
    FOR EACH agent in population
      agent <- updatePopulation (agent, a, alpha, betaWolf, gammaWolf, alpha, beta, dSpace, tables, population)
    END FOR
    getThreeBestSolutions (population, tables, alpha, beta, dSpace, alphaWolf, betaWolf, gammaWolf)
    t <- t + 1
  END WHILE

End Function
```

Figure 2. Grey Wolf Algorithm adapted pseudocode

4.2.1 Initial Population Generation

This method generates the initial population. First, it obtains the columns of the query. Then, it enters a loop until the necessary amount is reached. In each iteration, a new agent is created randomly and it is added to the population if it satisfies all the restrictions in the method "as valid".

```
Function population <- generateInitialPopulation(querys, tables, columns, populationSize, alpha, beta, dSpace)
    columns <- getColumns(querys, tables, columns)
    cont <- 1
    population <- []
    WHILE cont <= populationSize
        agent <- generateAgent(columns, querys)
        IF isValid(agent, population, alpha, beta, dSpace, tables) THEN
            add(agent, population)
            cont <- cont + 1
        END IF
    END WHILE
End Function
```

Figure 3. Initial population generation pseudocode

4.2.2 Aberration Control

This method implements the restrictions for the algorithm. The first one is about the number of indexes per table, which must be a maximum of 4. The second one is about the number of columns that make up the proposed index, which should not exceed 3. The third one is the new possible combination should not already exist in the population. The fourth, space of the new index is not greater than the available disk space. The last, the proposed index is not the primary key of the table.

```
Function flagError <- isValid ( agent, population, alpha, beta, dSpace, tables )
    flagError <- 0

    indexTable <- [ ]
    getIndexQuantityByTable( agent, indexTable )
    FOR EACH tableAmount IN indexTable
        IF tableAmount > 5 THEN
            flagError <- 1
            RETURN flagError
        END IF
    END FOR

    indexColumn <- [ ]
    getColumnQuantityByIndex( agent, indexColumn )
    FOR EACH columnAmount IN indexColumn
        IF columnAmount > 4 THEN
            flagError <- 1
            RETURN flagError
        END IF
    END FOR

    calculateFitness( agent, tables, alpha, beta, dSpace )

    agentColumns <- selectColumns( agent )
    FOR EACH agentP IN population
        agentColumnsP <- selectColumns( agentP )
        IF checkSame( agentColumns, agentColumnsP ) THEN
            flagError <- 1
            RETURN flagError
        END IF
    END FOR

    IF getSpace( agent ) > dSpace THEN
        flagError <- 1
        RETURN flagError
    END IF

    indexColumnPK <- [ ]
    getColumnsPkQuantityByIndex( agent, indexColumnPK )
    i<-1
    WHILE i <= longitud( indexColumnPK )
        IF indexColumnPK[ i ] == indexColumn[ i ] Y indexColumn[ i ] <> 0 THEN
            flagError <- 1
            RETURN flagError
        END IF
        i<-i+1
    End WHILE

End Function
```

Figure 4. Aberration control pseudocode

4.2.3 Fitness Function Calculation

This method calculates the fitness based on the proposed objective function. First, it calculates the frequency, the total space and the execution time of the new index. After calculating all previous values, the objective function is composed by the execution time, multiplied by one plus the inverse of the frequency times the constant Alpha, multiplied by one plus the index space divided by the available space times the constant Beta.

```
Function calculateFitness ( agent, tables, alpha, beta, dSpace )
    agentColumns <- selectColumns( agent )

    setFrequency( agent, agentColumns )
    setSpace( agent, agentColumns, tables )
    setTime( agent, agentColumns, tables )

    agent <- getTime( agent ) * ( 1 + alpha * 1 / getFrequency(agent) ) * ( 1 + beta * getTime(agent) / dSpace )
End Function
```

Figure 5. Fitness calculation pseudocode

After the implementation of the metaheuristic algorithm, the data structures designed allow the various data to be organized in order to facilitate their future use.

Additionally, thanks to the design proposed for the solution, in its adapted pseudocode and its most relevant subfunctions, it helped to understand the characteristics of each method in a simple way, in addition to reducing possible errors during implementation.

On the other hand, based on the review of the state of the art carried out, no research was found that has implemented the Grey Wolf Algorithm for the problem of index selection in relational databases, being almost entirely algorithms genetics, it is expected that this adaptation will mean a contribution to the state of the art of index selection.

5. NUMERICAL EXPERIMENTATION

In order to validate the results obtained from the Grey Wolf Algorithm, the performance of the proposed algorithm will be compared with the most relevant solution found in the state of the art for the index selection problem, being a genetic algorithm.

5.1 Data Collection

For data collection, the *"northwindextended"* database was used (Google Code Archive - Long-Term Storage for Google Code Project Hosting., n.d.) and the same input data is shared for both algorithms.

5.2 Statistical Testing

First, the results were subjected to the Shapiro-Wilk and Bartlett test to evaluate normality for each algorithm and homogeneity respectively. It was found that the results of the measurements have a normal distribution and homogeneous variation.

After guaranteeing normality and homogeneous variations between the results, the Z Test is performed. Given the resulting P-value, there is sufficient evidence to reject the null hypothesis. Therefore, it is concluded that the mean of the Grey Wolf Algorithm is different from that of the genetic algorithm.

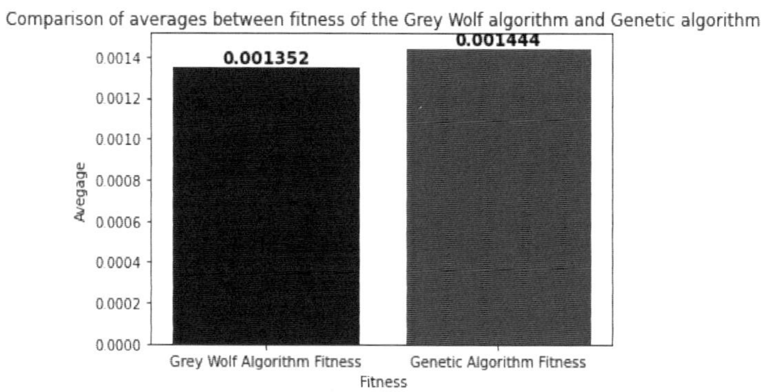

Figure 6. Comparison of averages

Finally, as detailed in the results, the average of the Grey Wolf Algorithm is lower than that of the genetic algorithm, so it can be stated that the former provides better quality solutions.

6. CONCLUSION

First, the proposed objective function was easily coupled to the development of the algorithms because the solutions provided by the latter contain all the necessary elements for its evaluation.

Second, both algorithms could be correctly adapted to the index selection problem. Both the genetic algorithm and the Grey Wolf Algorithm provided the expected solutions.

Third, thanks to the results of numerical experimentation, it can be seen that the Grey Wolf Algorithm provides better results than the genetic algorithm. This is result of the working mode of the Grey Wolf Algorithm, that emphasizes continuing the search for the global optimum, avoiding relapse into local optima. On the other hand, the genetic algorithm is only based on inheriting the best solutions and trying to improve iteration after iteration, which can end up in a local optimum. Despite this, as it can be seen in the fitness obtained for numerical experimentation, the results of the Grey Wolf Algorithm are not different from those of the genetic algorithm to a large extent.

REFERENCES

A Relational Database Overview. (n.d.). Retrieved September 26, 2021, from https://docs.oracle.com/javase/tutorial/jdbc/overview/database.html

Abdel-Basset, M., Abdel-Fatah, L., & Sangaiah, A. K. (2018). Metaheuristic Algorithms: A Comprehensive Review. Computational Intelligence for Multimedia Big Data on the Cloud with Engineering Applications, 185–231. https://doi.org/10.1016/B978-0-12-813314-9.00010-4

Ae, L. B., Dorigo, M., Luca, A. E., Ae, M. G., & Gutjahr, W. J. (2008). A survey on metaheuristics for stochastic combinatorial optimization. https://doi.org/10.1007/s11047-008-9098-4

Almeida, F., Silva, P., & Araújo, F. (2019). Performance analysis and optimization techniques for Oracle Relational Databases. Cybernetics and Information Technologies, 19(2), 117–132. https://doi.org/10.2478/CAIT-2019-0019

AWS. (n.d.). What is a Relational Database?. Retrieved August 19, 2021, from https://aws.amazon.com/relational-database/?nc1=h_ls

Berg, K. L., Seymour, T., & Goel, R. (2013). History Of Databases. International Journal of Management & Information Systems (IJMIS), 17(1), 29–36. https://doi.org/10.19030/IJMIS.V17I1.7587

Boronski, R., & Bocewicz, G. (2014). Relational Database Index Selection Algorithm. In Communications in Computer and Information Science (Vol. 431). https://doi.org/10.1007/978-3-319-07941-7_34

Calle, J., Sáez, Y., & Cuadra, D. (2011). An evolutionary approach to the index selection problem. Proceedings of the 2011 3rd World Congress on Nature and Biologically Inspired Computing, NaBIC 2011, 485–490. https://doi.org/10.1109/NABIC.2011.6089637

Castellano Lendínez, L. (2019). Kanban. Metodología para aumentar la eficiencia de los procesos. 3C Tecnología. Glosas de innovación aplicadas a la pyme. 8(1), 30–41. https://doi.org/10.17993/3ctecno/2019

Chaudhuri, S., Datar, M., & Narasayya, V. (2004). Index selection for databases: A hardness study and a principled heuristic solution. IEEE Transactions on Knowledge and Data Engineering, 16(11), 1313–1323. https://doi.org/10.1109/TKDE.2004.75

F., CoddE. (1970). A relational model of data for large shared data banks. Communications of the ACM, 13(6), 377–387. https://doi.org/10.1145/362384.362685

Git. (n.d.). Retrieved October 25, 2021, from https://git-scm.com/

Gómez, M. G.-, Danglot-Banck, C., & Vega-Franco, L. (2003). Sinopsis de pruebas estadísticas no paramétricas. Cuándo usarlas. Revista Mexicana de Pediatría, 70(2), 91–99.

Google Code Archive - Long-term storage for Google Code Project Hosting. (n.d.). Retrieved April 4, 2022, from https://code.google.com/archive/p/northwindextended/

¿Qué es Java y para qué es necesario? (n.d.). Retrieved October 24, 2021, from https://www.java.com/es/download/help/whatis_java.html

Gupta, M., & Badal, D. (2012). COMPARATIVE STUDY OF INDEXING TECHNIQUES IN DBMS.

GWO. (n.d.). Retrieved May 17, 2022, from https://seyedalimirjalili.com/gwo

How to conduct a systematic review from beginning to end - Covidence. (n.d.). Retrieved August 23, 2021, from https://www.covidence.org/blog/how-to-conduct-a-systematic-review-from-beginning-to-end/?campaignid=13271466385&adgroupid=123024099579&adid=524233276792

IntelliJ IDEA overview | IntelliJ IDEA. (n.d.). Retrieved October 24, 2021, from https://www.jetbrains.com/help/idea/discover-intellij-idea.html#IntelliJ-IDEA-supported-languages

Katoch, S., Sumit, &, Chauhan, S., & Kumar, V. (2021). A review on genetic algorithm: past, present, and future. Multimedia Tools and Applications, 80, 8091–8126. https://doi.org/10.1007/s11042-020-10139-6

Kołaczkowski, P., & Rybiński, H. (2009). Automatic index selection in RDBMS by exploring query execution plan space. In Studies in Computational Intelligence (Vol. 223). https://doi.org/10.1007/978-3-642-02190-9_1

Kołaczkowski, P., & Rybiński, H. (2011a). An interactive tool for automatic index selection in relational database management systems. In Studies in Computational Intelligence (Vol. 369). https://doi.org/10.1007/978-3-642-22732-5_6

Kołaczkowski, P., & Rybiński, H. (2011b). Online index selection in RDBMS by evolutionary approach. In Lecture Notes in Computer Science (including subseries Lecture Notes in Artificial Intelligence and Lecture Notes in Bioinformatics): Vol. 6861 LNCS (Issue PART 2). https://doi.org/10.1007/978-3-642-23091-2_41

Korytkowski, M., Gabryel, M., Nowicki, R., & Scherer, R. (2004). Genetic algorithm for database indexing. Lecture Notes in Artificial Intelligence (Subseries of Lecture Notes in Computer Science), 3070, 1142–1147. https://doi.org/10.1007/978-3-540-24844-6_179

Kovačević, V., & Filipič, B. (2006). A genetic algorithm with an adaptation mechanism for database index optimization. Bioinspired Optimization Methods and Their Applications - Proceedings of the 2nd International Conference on Bioinspired Optimization Methods and Their Applications, BIOMA 2006, 111–120.

Kratica, J., Ljubić, I., & Tošić, D. (2003). A Genetic Algorithm for the Index Selection Problem. Lecture Notes in Computer Science (Including Subseries Lecture Notes in Artificial Intelligence and Lecture Notes in Bioinformatics), 2611, 280–290. https://doi.org/10.1007/3-540-36605-9_26

lerocha/chinook-database: Sample database for SQL Server, Oracle, MySQL, PostgreSQL, SQLite, DB2. (n.d.). Retrieved April 16, 2022, https://github.com/lerocha/chinook-database

Lieponienė, J. (2020). Recent Trends in Database Technology. Baltic J. Modern Computing, 8(4), 551–559. https://doi.org/10.22364/bjmc.2020.8.4.06

Mirjalili, S., Mirjalili, S. M., & Lewis, A. (2014). Grey Wolf Optimizer. Advances in Engineering Software, 69, 46–61. https://doi.org/10.1016/J.ADVENGSOFT.2013.12.007

MySQL : Employees Sample Database. (n.d.). Retrieved April 16, 2022, from https://dev.mysql.com/doc/employee/en/

MySQL : MySQL 8.0 Reference Manual :: 8.9.4 Index Hints. (n.d.). Retrieved April 17, 2022, from https://dev.mysql.com/doc/refman/8.0/en/index-hints.html

Naik, S. (2018). TIER: Table index evaluator and recommender - A proposed model to improve transaction performance in distributed heterogeneous database. 2017 International Conference on Soft Computing and Its Engineering Applications: Harnessing Soft Computing Techniques for Smart and Better World, IcSoftComp 2017, 2018-January, 1–8. https://doi.org/10.1109/ICSOFTCOMP.2017.8280085

Neuhaus, P., Couto, J., Wehrmann, J., Ruiz, D. D., & Meneguzzi, F. (2019). GADIS: A genetic algorithm for database index selection. Proceedings of the International Conference on Software Engineering and Knowledge Engineering, SEKE, 2019-July, 39–42. https://doi.org/10.18293/SEKE2019-135

Nita, S., & Kartikawati, S. (2020). Analysis Of The Impact Narrative Algorithm Method, Pseudocode And Flowtable Towards Students Understanding Of The Programming Algorithm Courses. IOP Conference Series: Materials Science and Engineering, 835(1), 012044. https://doi.org/10.1088/1757-899X/835/1/012044

Pedrozo, W. G., & Vaz, M. S. M. G. (2014). A Tool for Automatic Index Selection in Database Management Systems. 2014 International Symposium on Computer, Consumer and Control, 1061–1064. https://doi.org/10.1109/IS3C.2014.277

RDBMS Definition. (n.d.). Retrieved September 25, 2021, from https://techterms.com/definition/rdbms

Response time - IBM Documentation. (n.d.). Retrieved September 29, 2021, from https://www.ibm.com/docs/en/informix-servers/12.10?topic=performance-response-time

RStudio - RStudio. (n.d.). Retrieved October 26, 2021, from https://www.rstudio.com/products/rstudio/

Sánchez, M., Bahamondez, E. V., & de Clunie, G. T. (2020). Use of PSeInt in teaching programming: A case study. ACM International Conference Proceeding Series, Part F166737. https://doi.org/10.1145/3401895.3402083

Silberschatz, A., Korth, H. F., & Sudarshan, S. (2019). DatabaseSystem Concepts.

Space requirements for indexes - IBM Documentation. (n.d.). Retrieved April 17, 2022, from https://www.ibm.com/docs/en/db2/11.5?topic=indexes-space-requirements

What Is a Relational Database | Oracle. (n.d.). Retrieved September 25, 2021, from https://www.oracle.com/database/what-is-a-relational-database/

Wijesiriwardana, C., & Firdhous, M. F. M. (2019). An Innovative Query Tuning Scheme for Large Databases. 2019 International Conference on Data Science and Engineering, ICDSE 2019, 154–159. https://doi.org/10.1109/ICDSE47409.2019.8971483

A CAPABILITY SYSTEM PERSPECTIVE TO CONCEPTUALIZE A BUSINESS MODEL

Mikko H. Hirvonen
Lappeenranta University of Technology, School of Business and Management, Finland
P.O. Box 20, FIN-53851 Lappeenranta, Finland

ABSTRACT

In this conceptual article, a 'capability system perspective' to conceptualize a business model (BM) is suggested. First, a theoretical framework is constructed by giving a brief overview of the business model (BM) research and of the Pyramid model (Hirvonen 2022b) - a generic socio-technical framework to conceptualize an organizational capability. The BM is defined to consist of three interdependent elements: Customer Value Proposition (CVP), Capability System (CS), and 'Financial system & Risk exposure'. The 'CS' is conceptualized with the Pyramid model complemented with financial and risk dimensions. Suggested conceptualization is a novel framework for Business Model Innovation (BMI) and IT investment design. The 'capability system perspective' concretizes the role of BM between business strategy and processes and it is expected to be highly valuable in practice.

KEYWORDS

Capability System Perspective, Business Model Research, IT Investments, Organizational Capabilities, Conceptual, Pyramid Model, Framework

1. INTRODUCTION

Innovations in information technology (IT) enable product, process, organization, and even *business model* innovations. In these more extensive *technological innovations*, one or multiple IT innovation(s) are embedded to the wider system. The *business model* is defined as a system consisting of interdependent and interacting elements to execute the business strategy according to defined logic to do business. It is defined to consist of three elements: Customer Value Proposition (CVP), Capability System (CS), and 'Financial system & Risk exposure'. In this article, the focus is on *business model innovation* and particularly on the CS. The *CS* is defined as a *business strategy specific systemic set of required organizational capabilities to create, deliver, and capture value, and to adjust the BM to maintain its internal and external equilibrium*. It is conceptualized here with the socio-technical Pyramid model (Hirvonen 2022b). *Business model innovation* (BMI) is defined as development of a new BM, or adjustment of an existing one.

BM and BMI have gained lots of attention during the last 25 years both in research and practice (Burkhart et al. 2011; Massa et al. 2017). This disputed construct (Prescott and Filatotchev 2021), is seen as a reflection of the firm's realized strategy (Casadesus-Masanell and Ricart 2010; Osterwalder 2004; Shafer et al. 2005), bridging strategy formulation and execution (Richardson 2008; Zott et al. 2011). As an evolving construct (Chesbrough and Rosenbloom 2002; Demil and Lecocq 2010) and as an own domain of innovation (Casadesus-Masanell and Zhu 2013; Doganova and Eyquem-Renault 2009; Gassmann et al. 2013; Massa and Tucci 2013b; Massa et al. 2017; Teece 2010; Zott et al. 2011), the BM is a potential source of competitive advantage in itself (Christensen 2001; Massa et al. 2017; Zott and Amit 2008).

Designing the BM and BMI is complex. It has been approached from multiple *perspectives* (Ritter and Lettl 2017) and with different background theories (see e.g., Amit and Zott 2001). *Tools* to conceptualize a BM (see review e.g., by Zott, Amit, & Massa, 2011) with varying levels of abstraction (Massa and Tucci 2013a) and *design principles* (Snihur et al. 2021) have been suggested. Regardless of the gained consensus, the field is diverse (Massa et al. 2017), siloed (Zott et al. 2011), with limited attention to the *context* (dos Santos et al. 2015; Zott and Amit 2013). This has plagued theory development making utilization of the research findings difficult (Fjeldstad and Snow 2018) and thus necessitating conceptual consolidation (Zott et al. 2011).

IT as an enabler of digital transformation, does not generate transformation with business value by itself, but necessitating complementary investments (Hirvonen 2022a; Kohli and Grover 2008). *Large-scale digital transformation*, defined here as an extensive and fundamental adjustments of an organization's operating models enabled by IT, typically necessitates adjustments to the existing BM(s), or enables completely new ones.

The *purpose* of this article is to suggest a novel and unifying *capability system perspective* to conceptualize a BM which helps to design large-scale digital transformations. The research question of this article is: *How to conceptualize a BM to design BMIs?*

The *motivation* is to develop a unifying approach to the BM conceptualization in its context in the scattered field of BM research, where the research findings have been difficult to utilize in practice. In suggested conceptualization the BM seamlessly mediates business strategy and business processes and enables development of BMI investments to achieve required set of organizational capabilities (the CS). The Pyramid model (Hirvonen 2022b) is based on RBV and DCF from strategic management research to conceptualize an organizational capability - the basic building block of competitive advantage - provides a basis for the conceptualization of the CS of the BM.

In Chapter 2, a brief background to the BM concept with previous research and to the applied '*Pyramid model*' is provided. In Chapter 3, the conceptualization of the *CS* with the Pyramid model is developed. Finally, in Chapter 4, the discussion and conclusions are presented.

2. BACKGROUND

2.1 Business Model (BM) Concept

The BM concept has significantly gained attention during the last three decades (Massa et al. 2017; Maucuer and Renaud 2019). There is plethora of views of the concept itself, its relevance (see e.g., Porter 2001), and relationship to other concepts like *strategy* (Massa et al. 2017; Seddon et al. 2004). Commonly accepted main tasks of a BM are *value creation*, value *delivery*, and *value capture* (Dubosson-Torbay et al. 2002; Ritter 2014; Teece 2010; Teece 2018; Zott et al. 2011). The BM is a *contextual*, *situational*, and *evolutionary* construct (Casadesus-Masanell and Ricart 2010; Chesbrough and Rosenbloom 2002; Demil and Lecocq 2010; dos Santos et al. 2015; Osterwalder 2004; Shafer et al. 2005; Teece 2010; Winter and Szulanski 2001) which outlines the *business logic* (Slywotzky 1995; Teece 2010).

Typically, the BM choices are based on customer and CVP (Chesbrough and Rosenbloom 2002; Johnson 2018; Johnson et al. 2008; Teece 2010). As a networked (Hamel 2000; Zott et al. 2011) and boundary-spanning concept (Shafer et al. 2005; Zott and Amit 2008) the *locus of value creation* is not limited to a focal firm, but also covers all stakeholders of the value constellation.

The BM is a potential source of *competitive advantage* itself (Christensen 2001; Massa et al. 2017; Zott and Amit 2008) and an own domain of innovation (Doganova and Eyquem-Renault 2009; Teece 2010; Zott et al. 2011) - often complementary to product, process, and organization domains (Casadesus-Masanell and Zhu 2013; Gassmann et al. 2013; Massa and Tucci 2013b; Massa et al. 2017). The BM mediates strategic planning and execution (Richardson 2008; Zott et al. 2011), and on the other hand strategy and *business processes* (Osterwalder and Pigneur 2002b).

The BM concept and research has also been criticized (see e.g., Massa et al. 2017). The lack of theoretical consensus and clarity about the concept (Zott et al. 2011), relationship with business strategy (Burkhart et al. 2011; Porter 2001; Seddon et al. 2004), and multiple *perspectives* (Ritter and Lettl 2017), *interpretations* (Massa et al. 2017) with different definition focus (Andreini and Bettinelli 2017; Burkhart et al. 2011; Fielt 2013; Maucuer and Renaud 2019; Osterwalder et al. 2005; Timmers 1998; Weill et al. 2011), and differences in opinions inside these perspectives have made the research field scattered and siloed (George and Bock, 2011; Massa et al., 2017; Zott et al., 2011; Wirtz et al., 2016). High focus on development of the concept itself has left the support of BM research to practice relatively limited (Mangematin et al. 2017). *Capability system perspective* is integrative, and it is expected to support practice.

For example, in *configurational approach* (Boulding 1956; Meyer et al. 1993; Miller 1987; Miller 1996; von Bertalanffy 1968) the BM is depicted as a system consisting of complementing and aligned design elements, interdependencies and dynamics between them, and their evolution (Afuah and Tucci 2001;

Baden-Fuller and Haefliger 2013; Demil and Lecocq 2010; Fjeldstad and Snow 2018; Gassmann et al. 2013; Osterwalder and Pigneur 2002a; Osterwalder and Pigneur 2010). *Performance* is the function of '(strategic) fit' of interacting elements (Demil et al. 2018; Porter 1996; Zajac et al. 2000; Zott et al. 2011) and their relationships and dynamics (Afuah and Tucci 2001). However, there is no common view which are the BM elements (Andreini and Bettinelli 2017; Gassmann et al. 2013; Wirtz et al. 2016), their interdependencies, dynamics (Burkhart et al. 2011), nor evolution (Demil and Lecocq 2010). Suggested *capability system perspective* can be characterized as configurational, logical, and systemic where the BM is defined to consist of three interdependent elements: *CVP*, *CS*, and '*Profit system & Risk exposure'*.

Activity system perspectives conceptualizes a BM as a *system* of interdependent activities (Zott and Amit 2010) orchestrated as a holistic system (Massa and Tucci 2013b; Zott et al. 2011) with different types of *fit* (Porter 1996). In this research, *organizational capabilities,* welling from the Resource-Based View (RBV) of the firm and Dynamic Capabilities Framework (DCF), are the basic building blocks of the '*CS'* and *sustained competitive advantage*. In the applied Pyramid model (Hirvonen 2022b), the potential capability (what could be done) and realized capability (what is done i.e., activity) is separated. Accordingly, activities utilize organizational capabilities.

2.2 The 'Pyramid Model'

In the '*Pyramid model'* (Hirvonen 2022b) an organizational capability is defined to consists of three interdependent and partially overlapping levels *i.e., types of capabilities* (operational, dynamic, and managerial). Each type of capability (level of an organizational capability) is defined to consists of four interdependent *capability variables* ('*Tasks, Abilities & Qualities'*, '*Technologies*', '*Resources & Capabilities*', and '*Structure & Culture'*) interacting with their *operating environment and* striving towards equilibrium. Generic main 'responsibilities' are identified on each level. In this research, the *'Pyramid model'* is applied on BM level which is also the unit of analysis.

3. CONCEPTUALIZING A CAPABILITY SYSTEM (CS)

3.1 Business Strategy Provides the Context for Conceptualization

Business strategy is defined as a plan to *move into a targeted unique and valuable position by designing, building, and utilizing an available set of capabilities.* The BM is defined here as a part of the *business strategy* (cf. Burkhart et al. 2011; Seddon et al. 2004).

Sustained competitive advantage & value appropriation is formed inside the BM in relation to its operating environment. A *sustained competitive advantage* is defined as an ability to fulfill the addressed customer need, or a combination of needs, in a more valuable way than competitors, perceived by the customer, over time in changing operating environment. It is based on a unique and appropriate '*CS'*, and its utilization. Competitive advantage materializes as an overwhelming CVP. *Value appropriation* is the ability of a focal company to capture the share of generated value to make (or not) targeted profit while the rest of the BM partners capture sufficient share of revenue.

Success in achieving competitive advantage and value appropriation is the outcome of the BM consisting of the three interacting BM elements. *CVP* is the value of an offered solution to the targeted customer need with its delivery model. The background assumption is that the customer selects the solution with highest value, and that it is able and willing to pay the requested price. *CS* is an aligned set of systemic organizational capabilities enabling value creation, delivery, and capture over time in a changing operating environment. *Financial system & Risk exposure* is a projection of the business from a financial and risk point of view monitoring adequacy of capital in every moment for different purposes, and isolated and systemic risks.

BM choices are decisions regarding the BM, its elements, and their configuration to achieve or strengthen competitive advantage, and to prepare for discontinuities in prevalent contingencies or sequential strategic moves. *Configurational choices* are decisions how the BM elements are configured – e.g., solution elements creating CVP or *governance choices* (make-buy-ally) as part of the *capability configurations*. To design the required '*CS'*, an appropriate conceptualization is needed. This is done next with the *Pyramid model* (Hirvonen 2022b).

3.2 Capability System (CS)

A *competitive advantage* can only be gained if there is the right set of *ordinary capabilities* to create, commercialize, and deliver a solution with the best CVP. Ordinary capabilities (Winter 2003) are defined as organizational capabilities to conduct 'operational tasks' and 'operational managerial tasks'. Because the operating environment is under constant change, the '*CS*' needs to be adjusted and rebuilt from time to time. For this purpose, an aligned set of *dynamic capabilities* is needed.

To capture this complexity, the Pyramid model (Hirvonen 2022b) is applied to conceptualize the '*CS*'. Each level consists of four interdependent *capability variables*. Value capture necessitates financial viability with risk exposure, the Pyramid model is complemented with these dimensions.

3.2.1 Operational Level – The Operational System

Tasks, Abilities & Qualities. The operational level is the *raison d'être* of the BM. The *task* is to create, commercialize, and deliver the planned solution to the targeted customer need with an overwhelming CVP. *Abilities* are potential *evolution paths* consisting of untapped potential of operational *capability*, and *readiness* for future development. *Qualities* define the non-functional criteria (e.g., profitability and sustainability).

Technologies. Technologies variable consists of three types of technologies. *Product technology* defines the solution details. *Value configuration technology (VCT) with frequency* defines *what* needs to be done to generate targeted outcomes by utilizing resources and combining inputs, and what is the frequency to produce those. VCT is the link to a more detailed description of *how* value is created (e.g., business processes). *Information systems (IS) technology* defines how the data/information is managed and utilized on an operational level.

Resources & Sub-capabilities. Resources & Sub-capabilities consists of a set of available resources and operational capabilities to conduct operational task(s). On the BM level, this is about doing business according to defined business strategy and designed BM. It is the feasibility and uniqueness of this CS, interaction of the capabilities, and its effective utilization to provide the targeted solution with the best CVP, which defines if *competitive advantage* is achieved.

Structure & Culture. Structure & Culture are aligned with *strategic choices.* They are created by the management to support *BM execution,* but on the other hand needs to be taken into account when doing strategic choices (cf. Birkinshaw and Ansari 2015; Chandler 1962). *Governance structure* consists of formal ways to organize, coordinate, and control the BM. Organizational *culture*, with possible micro cultures, define common beliefs and values steering and governing the behavior of individuals.

3.2.2 Dynamic Level – The System of Change

Tasks, Abilities & Qualities. The *dynamic level* is responsible of striving the BM towards internal and external equilibrium (see also Ch 3.4)., or sometimes to change the *equilibrium state* purposefully. Based on the generic main tasks of the dynamic level defined in the Pyramid model, *dynamic operative task* is to adjust and develop existing BM without changing the BM itself. *Dynamic managerial task* is to innovate by reconfiguring the BM to react to the changes in operating environment (as a context dependent complex adaptive system) and to improve its *evolutionary fitness* (Helfat et al. 2007) to prepare for future changes (*internal domain)*, or to create favorable conditions by *shaping the operating environment* (*external domain)* e.g., by changing the *equilibrium state* purposefully to a more favorable (e.g., by impacting on customer needs or behavior). *'Abilities'* are untapped part of the *dynamic capabilities* (potential) what could be utilized immediately or *readiness* to develop those in a certain way. *'Qualities'* define the non-functional criteria for a dynamic level.

Technologies. *Product technology* defines technical details of the outcomes of dynamic level (e.g., scenarios, analysis, proposals, etc.). *VCT* with *frequency* defines what needs to be done to generate the expected outcomes on dynamic level and on what frequency. *IS technology* defines how relevant data/information is managed and utilized on dynamic level.

Resources & Sub-capabilities. Resources & Sub-capabilities of the dynamic level consist of resources and a set of dynamic capabilities including *abilities* of existing capabilities to change. This 'system of change' consists of coherent and strategy-specific, mutually aligned, reinforcing, and optimized dynamic capabilities. Additionally, it is aligned with operational and managerial levels, and operating environment. Three main types of dynamic capabilities follow the categorization of the main tasks of dynamic level: *dynamic operational* *capabilities* are utilized to develop the existing *BM*, dynamic managerial capabilities are utilized to *reconfigure* it, or to *shape the operating environment*.

Structure & Culture. The *structure* of the dynamic level defines the formal allocation of resources and governance mechanisms to organize, coordinate, and control the 'system of change'. Organizational *culture*, and possible micro cultures, of dynamic level define the values and beliefs governing the behavior of individuals. The management strives to shape the culture to support and enable execution of dynamic level tasks.

3.2.3 Managerial Level – The Management System

Tasks, Abilities & Qualities. The managerial level of the BM is responsible for leading and managing the business to achieve the targets in its operating environment. The task is divided into operative and dynamic managerial tasks. The operative managerial task consists of *BM execution* and *maintenance of external relations*. The *BM execution* is about serving, enabling, and managing day-to-day activities. It is resource allocation, coordination and controlling, but also leading and motivating actors in all levels of the BM. *Maintaining external relations* is an ongoing mediation of the business with stakeholders within its internal and external operating environment. The *dynamic managerial task* to *reconfigure the BM* and *shape the operating environment* was covered above as an overlapping part of the dynamic level. *Abilities* are potential evolution paths of managerial capabilities consisting of untapped *potential* in management system, or *readiness* for its future development. *Qualities* are non-functional criteria, or requirements, for how business needs to be managed.

Technologies. Technologies define how management tasks are conducted. *Product technology* defines the details of expected outcomes of management activities. Effective BM execution necessitates coherent and aligned *management model* and methods (*VCT*), and the required frequency, to achieve targeted outcomes on operational and dynamic levels. *IS technology* defines how data and information is treated to generate insight needed for decision making, and shared to communicate decisions.

Resources & Sub-capabilities. Resources & Sub-capabilities on the management level consist of available resources and a system of managerial sub-capabilities. Strategic choices, *data/information* of the organization, governance mechanisms, and organizational *culture* are resources for management when conducting managerial tasks. In other words, *governance mechanisms* and *culture* give structure to the BM, but at the same time serve as communication and coordination devices i.e., as resources for management.

Structure & Culture. The governance mechanism for management is set by higher level management and social systems. It contains e.g., responsibilities and objectives, reporting structures, incentives, legal norms, etc. Like in any other level, the behavior of actors i.e., managers, is influenced by the *culture*.

3.3 Financial Viability

To be economically feasible, the BM needs to ensure sufficient *value capture* and appropriate retainment of the surplus for the focal company. The BM needs to meet profitability expectations and operate under potential capital limitations (e.g., investment budget). The *BM choices* have implications for the financial viability of the BM, which is projected with two mutually dependent sub-systems: *Profit system* and *Capital system*.

Profit system. The profit system projects the profitability of the BM with different volumes. A profit system consists of four elements (see also Johnson et al. 2008). *Revenue model* depends on the revenue potential of an addressable market, revenue streams, and pricing mechanisms. *Cost structure* indicates the share of fixed and variable costs with different volumes defining the cost behavior (e.g., *scale economies*). *The margin model* gives the gross and net margins. When targeted volume and/or profits, and available resources are known, *resource velocity* defines how efficiently resources need to be turned over (e.g., inventory) or an activity repeated (frequency) in certain time frame.

Capital system. Capital system is a projection of capital requirements of the BM at different times and with different volumes. Strategic choices, volume, and resource velocity impact on required capital (*investments* and *working capital). Cash flow* gives a temporal view to the in- and outflows of money helping to manage liquidity.

3.4 Risk Exposure Explained with Degree of Equilibrium

Alignment and *fit,* inside and between BM elements, and with operating environment, define *effectiveness* and *efficiency* of the BM. *Dynamic level* strives to move the BM towards internal and external equilibrium.

External equilibrium. An *external equilibrium* is defined as BM's compatibility and interaction with its operating environment. The relationship is bidirectional. While the operating environment has expectations towards BM, the BM has also expectations towards operating environment. The degree of external equilibrium defines *effectiveness* of the BM (does it deliver what is expected) and how well the operating environment supports it (does it receive what is expected like public infrastructure, skilled workforce, etc.?). Although the external equilibrium is an absolute measure, it's the *relative external equilibrium* compared to competitors what matters from a competitive advantage point of view. Therefore, disrupting the operating environment purposefully might be beneficial, if the focal company is able to gain relatively better position than competitors.

Internal equilibrium. An *internal equilibrium* is the compatibility and interaction of *BM components* (CVP, *CS*, and '*Financial system & Risk exposure*') and their constituting *elements*. The CS needs to be aligned and optimized to create, commercialize, and deliver solutions with planned CVP i.e., organizational capabilities, and capability levels and capability variables as their constituting elements need to be aligned. The degree of internal equilibrium defines *efficiency*.

Risk exposure. *The risk exposure* of the BM is defined as a projection of individual, potentially interconnected, and systemic risks and uncertainties springing from the *internal* or *external disequilibrium*. *Risk* is defined as a possible future development with a certain probability of a known outcome whereas *uncertainty* is an unknown future development with unknown outcome. *Systemic* refers to the risks and uncertainties of an entire system rather than its individual parts. BM choices and changes in operating environment impact on risk exposure reflecting the viability of the BM.

4. DISCUSSION AND CONCLUSIONS

In this article, a novel theory-anchored *capability system perspective* to the BM research has been suggested.

4.1 Theoretical Contribution

Conceptualization of the business model. The BM was defined to consist of three elements: CVP, *CS*, and '*Financial viability & risk exposure*'. Addressed customer need(s) is the basis for BM design. Targeted solution with overwhelming CVP, planned actions, and operating environment were considered as starting points for *CS* design. BM choices, including configurational choices, are seen to have financial and risk implications.

The *CS* was conceptualized in a novel way with the Pyramid model (Hirvonen 2022b) - an advanced and generic framework to design organizational capabilities. This *capability system perspective* provides a new perspective to BM research increasing clarity to the BM concept (see e.g., Prescott and Filatotchev 2021) and contributing to the siloed and insufficient theoretical foundation of the BM research (Fjeldstad and Snow 2018; Massa et al. 2017).

Suggested approach provides both a *static* view to design competitive advantage, and a *transformational/dynamic* view to make it sustainable (Demil and Lecocq 2010; Teece 2018). Required *ordinary capabilities* are the building blocks of temporary *competitive advantage* which can only be realized on a system level. *Sustained competitive advantage* is achieved by designing required *evolutionary fitness* i.e., incorporating dynamic capabilities as an integral part into the *CS* design.

BM as a mediator. Suggested *capability system perspective* makes the role of BM as a mediator between strategy and business processes concrete (cf. Osterwalder and Pigneur 2002b). The *value configuration technology* (VCT) -element in 'Technology' -variable describing 'what' needs to be done to achieve targeted outcomes, is the linkage from capabilities to a more detailed process level describing 'how' something is done.

Financial and Risk views. To conceptualize a BM, the Pyramid model was complemented with *financial and risk views*. Both views have been recognized in BM research, but especially *capital requirements and limitations* and *risk exposure* have gained relatively little attention. In suggested conceptualization, financial and risk view are an integral part when designing the *CS*. In the Pyramid model (Hirvonen 2022b), internal and external equilibrium were already recognized, but here the bidirectionality of *external equilibrium* was suggested, which is new according to the author's knowledge. This conceptualization is seen novel in BM research providing a structure to identify *risks* and inefficiencies.

4.2 Contribution to Practice

The purpose of this research was also to contribute to the calls to support practice (Maucuer and Renaud 2019). Suggested conceptualization is a tool to design BMs.

BMI investments. Organizations have often been claimed to lack *capabilities* to innovate BMs. This means either development of better BMs enabled e.g., by IT innovations; or to enable scaling and value realization from product and process innovations (Collins et al. 2020; Hart and Dowell 2011; Kanioura and Lucini 2020; Lancry et al. 2019; Mangematin et al. 2017; McKinsey 2019; WEF 2018). The suggested *capability system perspective* is expected to support *investment design* by helping to identify required capabilities and capability variables to be adjusted.

Agility and resilience. Suggested conceptualization integrates organization's '*system of change'* into operating environment helping to prepare for discontinuities. A practical application could be scenario planning, where the suggested *capability system perspective* helps to understand and prepare for CS requirement in different scenarios. In a same way, it also helps to prepare for self-initiated changes in strategy increasing agility and resilience.

4.3 Drawbacks and Limitations

Parallel BMs with potential *incidental/external effects* were not considered.

4.4 Future Research

This article is conceptual. To further advance the suggested *capability system perspective*, at least two streams of future research can be identified:

Theoretical and empirical testing. Although the Resource-Based View (RBV) and the Dynamic Capabilities Framework (DCF) have been extensively applied in BM research, the suggested *capability system perspective* is unique in BM research. Applied *Pyramid model* (Hirvonen 2022b) with complementing financial and risk dimensions is new necessitating both theoretical and empirical testing, and potentially iterations.

Extending the context. In this article, the unit of analysis is an individual BM. Extending conceptualization to multi-business and multi-BM environments and to ecosystems could be a next step to advance conceptually the suggested perspective.

REFERENCES

Afuah, A., and Tucci, C. L. (2001). Internet Business Model and Strategies: Text and Cases. New York City, USA: McGraw-Hill/Irwin.

Amit, R., and Zott, C. (2001). "Value Creation in E-Business," Strategic Management Journal (22:6-7), pp. 493-520.

Andreini, D., and Bettinelli, C. (2017). Business Model Innovation: From Systematic Literature Review to Future Research Directions. Springer.

Baden-Fuller, C., and Haefliger, S. (2013). "Business Models and Technological Innovation," Long Range Planning (46:6), pp. 419-426.

Birkinshaw, J., and Ansari, S. (2015). "Understanding Management Models: Going Beyond "What" and "Why" to "How" Work Gets Done in Organizations," in Business Model Innovation: The Organizational Dimension, N.J. Foss and T.E. Saebi (eds.). Oxford: Oxford University Press.

Boulding, K. E. (1956). "General Systems Theory: The Skeleton of Science," Management Science (2), pp. 197-208.

Burkhart, T., Krumeich, J., Werth, D., and Loos, P. (2011). "Analyzig the Business Model Concept: A Comprehensive Classification of Literature," in: Thirty Second International Conference on Information Systems. Shanghai 2011.

Casadesus-Masanell, R., and Ricart, J. E. (2010). "From Strategy to Business Models and onto Tactics," Long Range Planning (43:2-3), pp. 195-215.

Casadesus-Masanell, R., and Zhu, F. (2013). "Business Model Innovation and Competitive Imitation: The Case of Sponsor-Based Business Models," Strategic Management Journal (34:4), pp. 464-482.

Chandler, A. D. j. (1962). Strategy and Structure: History of the Industrial Enterprise. Cambridge: MIT Press.

Chesbrough, H., and Rosenbloom, R. S. (2002). "The Role of the Business Model in Capturing Value from Innovation: Evidence from Xerox Corporation´S Technology Spin-Off Companies," Industrial & Corporate Change (11:3), pp. 529-555.

Christensen, C. M. (2001). "The Past and Future of Competitive Advantage," MIT Sloan Management Review (42:2), pp. 105-109.

Collins, S., Dreischmeier, R., Ligarikian, A., and Unni, U. (2020). "Why Business Building Is the New Priority for Growth," McKinsey Digital:December).

Demil, B., and Lecocq, X. (2010). "Business Model Evolution: In Search of Dynamic Consistency," Long Range Planning (43:2-3), pp. 227-246.

Demil, B., Lecocq, X., and Warnier, V. (2018). ""Business Model Thinking", Business Ecosystems and Platforms: The New Perspectives on the Environment of the Organization," M@n@gement (21:4), pp. 1213-1228.

Doganova, L., and Eyquem-Renault, M. (2009). "What Do Business Models Do? Innovation Devices in Technology Entrepreneurship," Research Policy (38:10), pp. 1559-1570.

dos Santos, J. F. P., Spector, B., and Van der Heyden, L. (2015). "Towards a Theory of Business Model Innovation within Incumbent Firms," in Business Model Innovation: The Organizational Dimension, N.J. Foss and T.E. Saebi (eds.). Oxford University Press, pp. 43-63.

Dubosson-Torbay, M., Osterwalder, A., and Pigneur, Y. (2002). "E-Business Model Design, Classification, and Measurements," Thunderbird International Business Review (44:1), pp. 5-23.

Fielt, E. (2013). "Conceptualizing Business Models," Journal of Business Models (1:1), pp. 85-105.

Fjeldstad, O. D., and Snow, C. C. (2018). "Business Models and Organizational Design," Long Range Planning (51:1), pp. 32-39.

Gassmann, O., Frankenberger, K., and Csik, M. (2013). "The St. Gallen Business Model Navigator," University of St. Gallen.

Hamel, G. (2000). Leading the Revolution: How to Thrive in Turbulent Times by Making Innovation a Way of Life.

Hart, S. L., and Dowell, G. (2011). "A Natural-Resource-Based View of the Firm: Fifteen Years After," Journal of Management (37:5), pp. 1464-1479.

Helfat, C. E., Finkelstein, S., Mitchell, W., Peteraf, M., Singh, H., Teece, D. J., and Winter, S. G. (2007). Dynamic Capabilities: Understanding Strategic Change in Organizations. Blackwell, Place, Oxford.

Hirvonen, M. (2022a). "Capability Diamond - Designing It Investments to Develop Operational Capabilities," International Journal of Business Information Systems (In Press).

Hirvonen, M. H. (2022b). "The Pyramid Model: Conceptualizing an Organizational Capability to Design It Investments," Journal of Electronic Commerce in Organizations (20:1).

Johnson, M. W. (2018). Reinvent Your Business Model: How to Seize the White Space for Transformative Growth. Harvard Business School Press.

Johnson, M. W., Christensen, C. M., and Kagermann, H. (2008). "Reinventing Your Business Model," Harvard Business Review (86:12), pp. 50-59.

Kanioura, A., and Lucini, F. (2020). "A Radical Solution to Scale Ai Technology," Harvard Business Review:April).

Kohli, R., and Grover, V. (2008). "Business Value of It: An Essay on Expanding Research Directions to Keep up with the Times," Journal of the Association for Information Systems (9:1), pp. 23-39.

Lancry, O., Anderson, N., Caimi, G., Colombani, L., Cummings, L., and Morrissey, R. (2019). "Scaling Your Digital Transformation: How You Can Succeed Where Other Fail." Bain & Company, Inc.

Mangematin, V., Ravarini, A. M., and Sharkey Scott, P. (2017). "Practitioner Insights on Business Models and Future Directions," Journal of Business Strategy (38:2), pp. 3-5.

Massa, L., and Tucci, C. L. (2013a). "Business Model Innovation," in The Oxford Handbook of Innovation Management, D.M. Dodgson, D.M. Gann and N.E. Phillips (eds.).

Massa, L., and Tucci, C. L. (2013b). "Business Model Innovation," in The Oxford Handbook of Innovation.

Massa, L., Tucci, C. L., and Afuah, A. (2017). "A Critical Assessment of Business Model Research," Academy of Management Annals (11:1), pp. 73-104.

Maucuer, R., and Renaud, A. (2019). "Business Model Research: A Bibliometric Analysis of Origins and Trends," M@n@gement (22:2), pp. 176-215.

McKinsey. (2019). "Industry 4.0: Capturing Value at Scale in Discrete Manufacturing," McKinsey article:September).

Meyer, A. D., Tsui, A. S., and Hinings, C. R. (1993). "Configurational Approaches to Organizational Analysis," Academy of Management Journal (36:6), pp. 1175-1195.

Miller, D. (1987). "The Genesis of Configuration," Academy of Management Review (12:4), pp. 686-701.

Miller, D. (1996). "Configurations Revisited," Strategic Management Journal (17:7), pp. 505-512.

Osterwalder, A. (2004). "The Business Model Ontology: A Proposition in a Design Science Approach." Lausanne: University of Lausanne.

Osterwalder, A., and Pigneur, Y. (2002a). "Business Models and Their Elements," in: International Workshop on Business Models, Lausanne, Switzerland, 4-5 October 2002.

Osterwalder, A., and Pigneur, Y. (2002b). "An Ebusiness Model Ontology for Modeling Ebusiness, Proceedings of the Bled Electronic Commerce Conference - Ereality: Constructing the Eeconomy, Bled, Slovenia, June 17-19."

Osterwalder, A., and Pigneur, Y. (2010). "Aligning Profit and Purpose through Business Model Innovation," in Responsible Management Practices for the 21st Century, G. Palazzo and M.E. Wentland (eds.). Pearson International, pp. 61-76.

Osterwalder, A., Pigneur, Y., and Tucci, C. L. (2005). "Clarifying Business Models: Origins, Present, and Future of the Concept," Communications of the Association for Information Systems (15:May).

Porter, M. E. (1996). "What Is Strategy?," Harvard Business Review (74:6), pp. 61-78.

Porter, M. E. (2001). "Strategy and the Internet," Harvard Business Review (79:3), pp. 62-78.

Prescott, J. E., and Filatotchev, I. (2021). "The Business Model Phenomenon: Towards Theoretical Relevance," Journal of Management Studies (58:2), pp. 517-527.

Richardson, J. (2008). "The Business Model: An Integrative Framework for Strategy Execution," Strategic Change (17:5/6), pp. 133-144.

Ritter, T. (2014). Alignment2: Driving Competitiveness and Growth through Business Model Excellence. Cbs Competitiveness Platform. Frederiksberg, Denmark:

Ritter, T., and Lettl, C. (2017). "The Wider Implications of Business-Model Research," Long Range Planning (51:1), pp. 1-8.

Seddon, P. B., Lewis, G. P., Freeman, P., and Shanks, G. (2004). "The Case for Viewing Business Models as Abstractions of Strategy," Communications of the Association for Information Systems (13:Article 25), pp. 427-442.

Shafer, S. M., Smith, H. J., and Linder, J. C. (2005). "The Power of Business Models," Business Horizons (48:3), pp. 199-207.

Slywotzky, A. J. (1995). Value Migration: How to Think Several Moves Ahead of the Competition. Boston: Harvard Business School Press.

Snihur, Y., Zott, C., and Amit, R. (2021). "Managing the Value Appropriation Dilemma in Business Model Innovation," Strategy Science (6:1).

Teece, D. J. (2010). "Business Models, Business Strategy and Innovation," Long Range Planning (43:2-3), pp. 172-194.

Teece, D. J. (2018). "Business Models and Dynamic Capabilities," Long Range Planning (51:1), pp. 40-49.

Timmers, P. (1998). "Business Models for Electronic Markets," Electronic Markets (8:2), pp. 3-8.

von Bertalanffy, L. (1968). General System Theory: Foundations, Development, Applications. New York: Braziller.

WEF. (2018). "The Digital Enterprise: Moving from Experimentation to Transformation," Worl Economic Forum, Cologny/Geneva, Switzerland.

Weill, P., Malone, T. W., and Apel, T. G. (2011). "The Business Models Investors Prefer," MIT Sloan Management Review (52:4), pp. 17-19.

Winter, S. G. (2003). "Understanding Dynamic Capabilities," Strategic Management Journal (24:10), pp. 991-995.

Winter, S. G., and Szulanski, G. (2001). "Replication as Strategy," Organization Science (12:6), pp. 730-743.

Wirtz, B. W., Pistoia, A., Ullrih, S., and Göttel, V. (2016). "Business Models: Origin, Development and Future Research Perspectives," Long Range Planning (49:1), pp. 36-54.

Zajac, E. J., Kraatz, M. S., and Bresser, R. K. F. (2000). "Modeling the Dynamics of Strategic Fit: A Normative Approach to Strategic Change," Strategic Management Journal (21:4), pp. 429-453.

Zott, C., Amit, R., and Massa, L. (2011). "The Business Model: Recent Developments and Future Research," Journal of Management (37:4), pp. 1019-1042.

Zott, C., and Amit, R. (2008). "The Fit between Product Market Strategy and Business Model: Implications for Firm Performance," Strategic Management Journal (29:1), pp. 1-26.

Zott, C., and Amit, R. (2010). "Business Model Design: An Activity System Perspective," Long Range Planning (43:2-3), pp. 216-226.

Zott, C., and Amit, R. H. (2013). "The Business Model: A Theoretically Anchored Robust Construct for Strategic Analysis," Strategic Organization (11), pp. 403-411.

INSTANTIATION OF ONTOUML MODELS IN MULTI-LABELED GRAPH DATABASES

Jaroslav Pokorný[1,3], Zdeněk Rybola[2], Michal Valenta[2], Jiří Zikán[2] and Robert Pergl[2]
[1]*Faculty of Mathematics and Physics, Charles University, Prague, Czech Republic*
[2]*Faculty of Information Technology, Czech Technical University, Prague, Czech Republic*
[3]*Škoda Auto University, Mladá Boleslav, Czech Republic*

ABSTRACT

The importance of conceptual modeling in software engineering is constantly growing along with the complexity of business domains. In order to handle this increasing complexity, it is essential to use modeling notations that provide a high level of abstraction and expressiveness. For this reason, we specifically focus on ontology-driven conceptual modeling and OntoUML notation in our research. In this paper, we present the main ideas behind our novel approach to OntoUML model instantiation using multi-labeled property graph databases, such as Neo4j. Our approach should not only serve to ensure data integrity in graph databases but also provide domain experts with a convenient way to verify the correctness and completeness of their conceptual models. Although there already exist approaches to instantiate OntoUML models using relational databases, our research shows that multi-labeled property graph databases are better suited for this purpose as their versatile data model better correlates to the essential principles of OntoUML.

KEYWORDS

Conceptual Modelling, OntoUML, Neo4j, Multi-Labeled Graph Database, Model Instantiation, Model Transformation

1. INTRODUCTION

Nowadays, business tends to get very complicated. Business processes are usually very complex, and data processed in the processes are regulated by lots of complex rules (Schäfermeyer 2012; van Grondelle 2012). In order to support further improvements of the processes and advances in the business, creating models is a necessity (Guizzardi, Proper 2021). To model the processes, various notations are used including BPMN (Kocbek et al 2015), DEMO (Mulder 2019), and others. To model the information and data used in the processes, conceptual models are usually created using UML class diagram notation (Bavota et al 2011). In our research, we focus only on the data modeling aspect.

The conceptual models of complex business domains tend to contain up to hundreds of types with even more attributes and relations. However, many of the important constraints and rules of the domain cannot be simply modeled using the UML class diagram notation and must be captured in the form of complex textual descriptions. Unfortunately, in this form, it is difficult to notice them and keep them in mind when working with the model. Luckily, there is a better notation for conceptual modeling offering a much more precise distinction of different kinds of types with different intrinsic constraints and properties – OntoUML.

OntoUML is a modeling language defined as an extension for the UML class diagram notation based on Unified Foundational Ontology (UFO). It was introduced by (Guizzardi 2004) and improved ever since (Fonseca et al 2019; Guizzardi et al 2021, 2022). UFO is based on cognitive science and modal logic and related mathematical foundations such as sets and relations. Thanks to this fact, it provides expressive and precise constructs for modelers to capture the domain of interest. Unlike other extensions of UML, OntoUML does not build on the UML's ontologically vague class notion but builds on the notion of *universals* and *individuals*. Universals are general classifiers of objects with certain properties. Individuals, on the other hand, are the objects in the reality having their own identity and carrying properties defined by the universals they instantiate. However, unlike UML where an object is always an instance of a single type, carrying the properties of the type and its eventual ancestors (via generalization), individuals can instantiate many different universals, combining their properties. Moreover, an individual can change their instantiation relation to the universals during their life – becoming an instance of universal means getting its properties, while ceasing to be an instance of a universal means losing its properties. The only limitation is the *identity principle* of the universals – all instantiated *sortal universals* (i.e., universals having identity) must be based on the same identity principle provided by an *ultimate sortal universal* (i.e., universal providing identity).

UFO distinguishes different types of universals, each with its own implicit constraints and limitations. *Kinds* represent ultimate sortal universals defining the identity principle and properties for their instances. *Subkinds* represent specializations of a Kind or another Subkind, extending the identity principle and adding properties to their instances. Both Kinds and Subkinds are *rigid universals* – their instances must always be their instances (in the modal sense). On the other hand, *Roles* and *Phases* are *anti-rigid universals* – individuals can be instances of these universals only in some situations. Roles define properties of individuals with certain identity principle (defined by the generalization relation between the Role and some other sortal universal) when related to instances of some other universal. Phases define properties of individuals with certain identity principle (defined by the generalization relation between the Phase and some other sortal universal) in certain phase of the existence of the individual.

OntoUML uses the original notation of a class from the UML to model the universals identified in the domain of interest. To distinguish the different kinds of universals, OntoUML uses stereotypes such as *«Kind»* or *«Role»*. Thanks to that, it is easier to notice the constraints and understand them when browsing the conceptual model in contrast to reading documentation attached to standard UML Class diagrams. OntoUML has been successfully used for creating conceptual models in many domains, such as medicine (Gonçalves et al 2011), biology (Martínez Ferrandis et al 2013), telecommunications (Barcelos et al 2011), virtual network function marketplaces (Guizzardi et al 2019), or payments and obligation settlements (Amaral et al 2022). Also, the understanding of UFO concepts leads to a higher quality of models in general as many constraints are not missed or are identified sooner in the modeling process (Verdonck et al 2018).

Even with OntoUML, the conceptual model's complexity can be very high, containing tens or hundreds of universals. To verify a conceptual model's correctness and completeness, the best practice is to instantiate the model by creating various instances of the identified types, simulating the reality of the domain (Burgueño et al 2019). Then, it is possible to inspect the instances and verify their properties and relations. A usual approach is creating a relational database where each type is represented by a table and the instances of the type are stored as rows in that table. SQL can then be used to query the data with specific properties and relations. Also, objects not conforming to the defined structures point out missing concepts in the model.

The problem with instantiation in a relational database is that each table has a strictly defined set of columns for a strictly defined set of object properties. For properties relevant only to specific situations, such as the properties of Role universals, an additional table must be defined. Objects are then partitioned over multiple tables, complicating the inspection. However, in such situations, our novel approach based on graph databases can be used. In graph databases, objects are stored as nodes with relationships to other nodes representing related objects (Pokorný 2015). Unlike tables in a relational database, in graph databases there do not have to be any specific restrictions regarding a node's properties. Any node can carry any set of properties. This approach aligns closely to the OntoUML approach to conceptual modeling, as it enables the storage of a single individual in a single node, carrying all properties defined by all universals it instantiates.

Although there is no strictly defined schema in graph databases, data consistency should be preserved here as well. To keep the data consistent, any database should only allow storing data that conforms to the original model. Therefore, it is necessary to check that all nodes carry only valid combinations of properties. To achieve that, it is necessary to identify which types the object stored in the node instantiates. In *typed-property graph databases*, a *type* is assigned to each node. However, only a single type can usually be assigned, preventing a node from effectively combining multiple types dynamically. This results in a situation similar to that of relational databases, where a single real-world object is decomposed into different nodes. However, in *labeled-property graph databases* like the Neo4j, the situation is much more convenient. They usually allow assigning multiple *labels* to a single node. Therefore, a node can be labeled with labels representing all universals an individual is an instance of. Even more, it is possible to attach or remove a label dynamically, conforming to the notion of anti-rigid universals such as Roles or Phases. Finally, with such labels, it is possible to define database triggers to check the valid combination of labels as well as the existence of specific properties of a node with those labels assigned (Pokorný et al 2017).

Our approach can be used not only to inspect and verify the conceptual model, but also to create an actual database for storing the data corresponding to this model. The OntoUML model can be instantiated as a graph database accompanied by triggers ensuring its data consistency.

The rest of the paper is structured as follows: in Section 2, related work is discussed; in Section 3, an example of our approach is provided with further discussion; in Section 4, our future plans are outlined; and in Section 5, the conclusions of the paper are given.

2. RELATED WORKS

In (Rybola 2017; Rybola, Valenta 2018) the authors discussed the transformation of OntoUML models into relational database schemas. In this relational approach, they applied the model-driven development (MDD) by consecutively transforming the original domain model in OntoUML into a UML domain model, into a relational database schema, and finally into the SQL code of the relational database. All along, the original implicit constraints defined by the original OntoUML model were transformed into Object Constraint Language (OCL) constraints accompanying the UML and relational database schemas and their realization in the relational database in the form of triggers and other SQL constructs. The resulting schema can be used for the original model verification by its instantiation in the database, however as pointed out in the introduction, storing the properties of the objects defined by anti-rigid universals they instantiate, such as Roles and Phases, forces the objects to be decomposed into multiple tables.

In this paper, we discuss the instantiation in graph databases. As graph databases do not define any strict schema and different nodes can combine various properties, it is not possible to apply the MDD approach by consecutively transforming the OntoUML model into a graph database schema and then its realization. Therefore, in this paper, we discuss the direct transformation of the OntoUML model into its realization in the form of *integrity constraints* (ICs) for the Neo4j graph database to verify the data stored in the individual nodes conform to the original model.

As for IC implementation in graph databases, in (Pokorný et al 2017) the authors suggested an extension of Cypher language in order to implement complex ICs in Neo4j. The paper was inspired by IC implementation in relational databases, especially SQL DDL. The development team of Neo4j actually introduced an extension of Cypher language which implements ICs in a similar way a few years later. Unfortunately, there is still a long way to a unified, community accepted, and complex enough approach to IC implementation in graph databases. The main reason for this situation is that implementations of individual graph databases use significantly different data models. Therefore, the research in the IC implementation in graph databases continues.

In (Masson et al 2020), the authors provided a systematic discussion of the concept of referential ICs in graph databases and an extension in the Neo4j that allows the specification of these ICs in a *domain-specific language* (DSL). Then they ran generated Cypher queries which checked ICs over an existing database.

In (Reina et al 2020), the authors introduced six types of complex ICs, implemented them in OrientDB, and provided a demo application with a small comparison of the effectivity of IC checking. This work also provided an overview of several different IC implementations in OrientDB, Neo4j, and extensions presented in (Pokorný et al 2017) and (Masson et al 2020). The approach presented in (Reina et al 2020) used a formal definition of the graph database data model. ICs were then defined based on this data model. Unlike our approach, the authors explicitly excluded a multi-label feature from their data model.

As mentioned in the introduction, the multi-label feature of a graph database data model is crucial for our approach due to the convenient instantiation of multiple inheritance. In this paper, we decided to use a different strategy. Instead of defining various ICs on the level of a graph database, we suppose that ICs have already been specified on a conceptual level (in the OntoUML), and we try to implement them directly in the Neo4j using database triggers. Of course, we are also using our own DSL represented as trigger names in order to instantiate the OntoUML model accurately, but this DSL can be hidden from the end users.

3. PRACTICAL EXAMPLE

To illustrate our approach, we use a limited example of an OntoUML conceptual model containing only Kind and Subkind types. On the other hand, we discuss all possible variants of their generalization set regarding the completeness and disjointness of the relation. A larger example is mentioned in Section 4.

The example shown in Figure 1 describes the type Animal, classified as a Kind, with two special subtypes Lion and Tiger, classified as Subkinds. Regarding the generalization set of Lion and Tiger towards Animal, we discuss three possible combinations of the completeness and disjointness properties.

Variant 1: No restrictions are applied; the generalization set is incomplete and overlapping by default. There can be individuals of any combination of the types, including a generic Animal.

Variant 2: The generalization set is complete and disjoint. Each individual of the Animal Kind must be either an instance of the Lion or Tiger type at the same time.

Variant 3: The generalization set is complete but overlapping. Similar to the previous case, but the individual can instantiate both the Lion and Tiger types simultaneously.

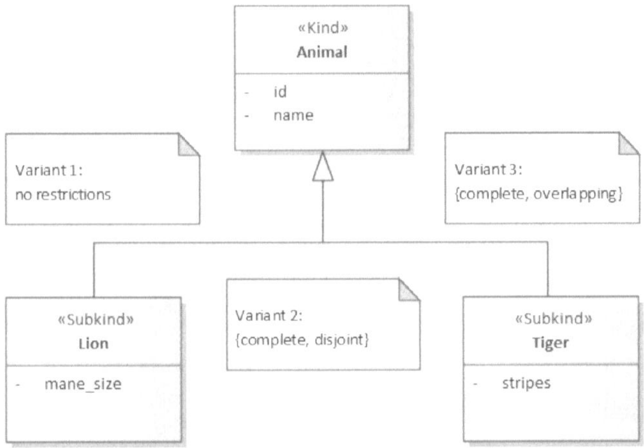

Figure 1. Example OntoUML domain model

In the following subsections, we show how the ICs resulting from the OntoUML model are implemented in Neo4j graph database. Also, we demonstrate how the Neo4j console can be utilized to validate original model by testing the creation of both valid and invalid objects.

3.1 Constraints Implementation in Neo4j

The reasons we chose Neo4j as the target database engine for the instantiation of the OntoUML model are the following:

- a multi-label property graph data model is well suitable for implementation of OntoUML constructs,
- declarative constraints which can be directly used to implement some of the OntoUML constructs (only a UNIQUE constraint was used because other constraint types are not provided in the Neo4j community edition),
- database triggers mechanism which can be used to implement all constraints resulting from OntoUML constructs,
- Cypher language – a high-level language that is intuitively understandable and can be directly used to create objects (instances) in the Neo4j database,
- Neo4j console which runs in a web browser and is a suitable tool for model validation by object instantiation.

Let us now discuss how ICs resulting from individual OntoUML constructs of our simple example are implemented in the Neo4j graph database.

3.1.1 Mandatory and UNIQUE Attributes

Cypher language provides constraints for both constructs, but mandatory attributes are supported only in the Neo4j enterprise editions. Therefore, we used only UNIQUE constraint. There is only one identifier in our example – the id attribute in the type Animal. In Cypher, it is specified in the following form:

```
//PROPERTY_MUST_BE_UNIQUE (Animal, id)
CREATE CONSTRAINT animal_id_must_be_unique ON (z:Animal)
ASSERT z.id IS UNIQUE;
```

To implement the check for a mandatory property, we must use a trigger. For example, the property name of the Animal type is mandatory, i.e., each node with the label Animal) must have this property. The trigger implementing this feature using Neo4j APOC extension can be defined as follows:

```
//PROPERTY_MUST_BE_PRESENT(Animal, name)
CALL apoc.trigger.add('animal_name_must_be_present',
'UNWIND(
    $createdNodes +
    apoc.trigger.nodesByLabel($assignedLabels, "Animal") +
    apoc.trigger.nodesByLabel($removedNodeProperties, "Animal")
) AS node
CALL apoc.util.validate(
    apoc.label.exists(node, "Animal") and not exists(node.name),
    "name property of Animal must be present", null
) RETURN null', {phase:'before'});
```

Notice that the trigger has the name `animal_name_must_be_present` (names of triggers are important in our example). In the body, all nodes with the label Animal are looked up and validated to have the name property. If the validation succeeds, the object is updated correctly. If not, an error message is returned: "name property of Animal must be present".

3.1.2 Generalization and Generalization Sets

The generalization relationship and completeness and disjointness of generalization set can be checked using a combination of the following three types of triggers:

```
//LABEL_MUST_BE_IN_COMBINATION(Lion, {Animal})
CALL apoc.trigger.add('lion_must_be_with_animal',
'UNWIND(
    apoc.trigger.nodesByLabel($assignedLabels, "Lion") +
    apoc.trigger.nodesByLabel($removedLabels, "Animal")
) AS node
CALL apoc.util.validate(
    apoc.label.exists(node, "Lion") and not
    (apoc.label.exists(node, "Animal")),
    "Lion label must be in a combination with Animal", null
) RETURN null', { phase:'before' });
//LABEL_MUST_BE_IN_COMBINATION(Animal, {Lion, Tiger})
CALL apoc.trigger.add('animal_must_be_with_lion_or_tiger',
'UNWIND(
    apoc.trigger.nodesByLabel($assignedLabels, "Animal") +
    apoc.trigger.nodesByLabel($removedLabels, "Lion") +
    apoc.trigger.nodesByLabel($removedLabels, "Tiger")
) AS node
CALL apoc.util.validate(
    apoc.label.exists(node, "Animal") and not (
    apoc.label.exists(node, "Lion") or apoc.label.exists(node, "Tiger")
    ), "Animal label must be in combination with Lion or Tiger", null
) RETURN null', { phase:'before' });
//LABEL_CANNOT_BE_IN_COMBINATION(Lion, {Tiger})
CALL apoc.trigger.add('lion_cannot_be_with_tiger',
'UNWIND(
    apoc.trigger.nodesByLabel($assignedLabels, "Lion")
) AS node
```

```
CALL apoc.util.validate(
    apoc.label.exists(node, "Tiger"),
    "Lion label cannot be in a combination with Tiger", null
) RETURN null', { phase:'before' });
```

According to our example, all three variants of the model can be implemented by the combination of UNIQUE constraints and the triggers described above. Here are individual variants of the model and generated implementations in Neo4j.

Variant 1 {no restrictions}:

```
// ----- CONSTRAINTS
    PROPERTY_MUST_BE_UNIQUE(Animal, id)
// ----- ATTRIBUTES
    PROPERTY_MUST_BE_PRESENT(Animal, id)
    PROPERTY_MUST_BE_PRESENT(Animal, name)
    PROPERTY_MUST_BE_PRESENT(Lion, mane_size)
    PROPERTY_MUST_BE_PRESENT(Tiger, lanes_amount)
// ----- GENERALIZATIONS
    LABEL_MUST_BE_IN_COMBINATION(Lion, {Animal})
    LABEL_MUST_BE_IN_COMBINATION(Tiger, {Animal})
```

Variant 2 {complete, disjoint}:

```
    ... initial lines are same as Variant 1 ...
// ----- GENERALIZATION SETS
    LABEL_MUST_BE_IN_COMBINATION(Animal, {Lion, Tiger})
    LABEL_CANNOT_BE_IN_COMBINATION(Lion, {Tiger})
    LABEL_CANNOT_BE_IN_COMBINATION(Tiger, {Lion})
```

Variant 3 {complete, overlapping}:

```
    ... initial lines are same as Variant 1 ...
// ----- GENERALIZATION SETS
    LABEL_MUST_BE_IN_COMBINATION(Animal, {Lion, Tiger})
```

It is important to note that all these constraints and triggers have been generated automatically, as described in the Section 4 of this paper.

3.2 Usage – Instantiation during Model Validation Phase

Suppose we have three sets of Cypher statements (scripts) consisting of triggers and constraints. Each script implements one variant of the model discussed above. Instantiation is then straightforward; it consists of the following two steps:

1. Load the model implementation into Neo4j database (i.e., run the script).
2. Try to create objects (instances) and check which are allowed, and which are not.

To validate the model, we use five distinct instances of the Animal type. Cypher language syntax is used because it is intuitively understandable – labels use the first letter in capital, individual properties and their values are enclosed in brackets, nodes (objects) in our example are assigned to variables a1-a5.

```
CREATE (a1:Animal {id:1, name:"celestyn"});
CREATE (a2:Animal :Tiger {id:2, name:"serchan", lanes_amount:20});
CREATE (a3:Animal :Lion {id:3, name:"maruska", mane_size:5.0});
CREATE (a4:Animal :Lion :Tiger {id:4, name:"alex", mane_size:4.0,
    lanes_amount:15});
CREATE (a5:Animal :Tiger :Lion {id:5, name:"mirek", mane_size:8.0,
    lanes_amount:42});
```

Let us now discuss all three model variants in terms of allowing or disallowing the insertion of the objects listed above.

Variant 1: no restrictions. All individuals listed above are allowed here, even a1 which is not Tiger nor Lion, even a4 and a5 which are both Lion and Tiger. But still, there are restrictions that are expressed in the model and are implemented in the script as well:

- property `name` for Animal Kind is mandatory, the same holds for attribute `mane_size` of a Lion Subkind and for attribute `lanes_amount` of Tiger Subkind,
- each Tiger or Lion instance must also be Animal instance,
- attribute `id` is mandatory and unique for each Animal Kind (it is an identifier).

For example, object construction `CREATE (a6:Animal {id:6});` fails. The important part of the error message says: "Error executing triggers {animal_name_must_be_present=failed...", where the name of the trigger is generated by our constraint generator, and it is self-explaining. Similarly, object construction `CREATE (a7:Tiger {lanes_amount:8});` causes the error `tiger_must_be_with_animal`, and object construction `CREATE (a8:Animal {id:1, name:"Boris"});` fails with error message "Node(0) already exists with label 'Animal' and property 'id' = 1". Let us note that this last validation had been done not by the trigger but using a Cypher UNIQUE constraint declaration. Of course, it can be checked by trigger as well, but we decided to use standard constraints when they are applicable.

Variant 2: {complete, disjoint}. Animal a1 is not allowed to create due to trigger (and corresponding error) `animal_must_be_with_lion_or_tiger`. In the model, it is expressed by complete restriction.

Also, Animal a4 and Animal a5 are not allowed in this variant, because they are labelled by both Subkinds which is not possible due to the disjoint restriction.

Variant 3: complete, overlapping. Animal a1 is not allowed (due to the complete restriction in the model), but due to the overlapping restrictions, the individuals a4 and a5 are allowed.

4. FUTURE AND ONGING WORK

The point of the simple example presented above is only to demonstrate the essential idea behind our approach. We are working intensively to make our methods directly applicable in production and we have already taken several significant steps towards this goal.

4.1 Other OntoUML Constructs and Neo4j Constraints Generator

Implementation of many other OntoUML constructs in the Neo4j has already been described in the master's thesis of one of the co-authors of this paper (Zikán 2023). At this moment, the following constructs have already been analyzed, and their implementation using Neo4j has been designed: Kind, Subkind, Category, Phase, Role, RoleMixin, Relator, and their mutual relationships with potential relationship restrictions (disjoint, complete, overlapping). It seems it will be possible to cover all OntoUML constructs.

The thesis also includes a prototype of a fully automated constraint generator that we have also used to generate scripts with constraints and triggers discussed in the example in the Section 3 of this paper.

4.2 Practical Infrastructure for Domain Experts

The next step to make the suggested methods directly applicable in production is to include the Neo4j constraints generator into a suitable CASE tool that supports OntoUML modeling. We are going to use the OpenPonk modeling platform (Uhnák, Pergl 2016) which has been created in the Centre for Conceptual Modelling and Implementation at Faculty of Informaton Technology, Czech Technical University in Prague. This tool is currently used in several projects where large OntoUML models have emerged. Therefore, there are enough real models and domain experts for further testing.

The usage of the model validation infrastructure for domain experts consists of the following steps:

1. Domain expert creates an OntoUML model in the OpenPonk tool.
2. Domain expert "clicks" on a button that creates the corresponding script with Neo4j ICs and uploads it directly to the selected Neo4j database.
3. Domain expert uses a tool like Neo4j console to validate the model by instantiation. If there are some unallowed cases, the domain expert changes the model.

5. CONCLUSION

The idea of automatic or semi-automatic generation of database schema from a conceptual model is the subject of many papers, and it is implemented in many tools. Our contribution to this topic can be summarized as follows:

1. We have described the idea of using a graph database with a multi-labeled property graph data model together with the concept of database triggers to instantiate OntoUML models. As is justified in this paper, this approach is better suited for the straightforward implementation of OntoUML constructs than standard approaches based on the transformation of models into relational database schemas.
2. We have also demonstrated our new approach with a simple example. This example should serve as a proof of concept that full-fledged instantiation of OntoUML models in graph databases is possible.
3. Finally, we have discussed where the research should go further. Together with our automated constraint generator and the OpenPonk platform, our approach is promising to be used as an infrastructure supporting domain experts in conceptual modeling.

Although it is still research in progress, the potential benefits are already apparent. Thanks to our approach, OntoUML models can become the high-level schemas for otherwise schema-free graph databases.

REFERENCES

Amaral G. et al, (2022). Modeling Payments and Linked Obligation Settlements. *Advances in Enterprise Engineering XV, Lecture Notes in Business Information Processing*. Cham, Germany. pp. 21-41.

Barcelos P. P. F. et al, (2011). Ontological evaluation of the itut recommendation g. 805. *18th International Conference on Telecommunications*. Ayia Napa, Cyprus. pp. 232-237.

Bavota G. et al, (2011). Identifying the Weaknesses of UML Class Diagrams during Data Model Comprehension. *14th International Conference, MODELS 2011*. Wellington, New Zealand. pp. 168-182.

Burgueño L. et al, (2019). A Systematic Approach to Generate Diverse Instantiations for Conceptual Schemas. *Conceptual Modeling, Lecture Notes in Computer Science*. Cham, Germany. pp. 513-521.

Fonseca C. et al, (2019). Relations in Ontology-Driven Conceptual Modeling. *Conceptual Modeling, Lecture Notes in Computer Science*. Cham, Germany. pp. 28-42.

Gonçalves B. et al, (2011). Using an ecg reference ontology for semantic interoperability of ecg data. *Journal of biomedical informatics*, vol. 44, pp. 126-136.

Guizzardi G., (2005). *Ontological foundations for structural conceptual models*. University of Twente, Enschede.

Guizzardi G. and Proper H., (2021). On Understanding the Value of Domain Modeling. *15th International Workshop on Value Modelling and Business Ontologies*. Bolzano, Italy.

Guizzardi G. et al, (2021). Types and taxonomic structures in conceptual modeling: A novel ontological theory and engineering support. *Data & Knowledge Engineering*, vol. 134, pp. 101891.

Guizzardi G. et al, (2022). UFO: Unified Foundational Ontology. *Applied Ontology*, vol. 17, no. 1, pp. 167-210.

Guizzardi R. et al, (2019). A Reference Conceptual Model for Virtual Network Function Online Marketplaces. *Conceptual Modeling, Lecture Notes in Computer Science*. Cham, Germany. pp. 302-310.

Kocbek M. et al, (2015). Business process model and notation: The current state of affairs. *Computer Science and Information Systems 2015*, vol. 12, iss. 2, pp. 509-539.

Martínez Ferrandis A. M. et al, (2013). Applying the principles of an ontology-based approach to a conceptual schema of human genome. *32nd International Conference on Conceptual Modeling, ER 2013*. Hong-Kong, China. pp. 471-478.

Masson T. et al, (2020). Defining referential integrity constraints in graph-oriented datastores. *Proceedings of the 8th International Conference on Model-Driven Engineering and Software Developmen*. Valletta, Malta. pp. 409-416.

Mulder M., (2019). A Design Evaluation of an Extension to the DEMO Methodology. *9th Enterprise Engineering Working Conference, EEWC 2019*. Lisbon, Portugal. pp. 55-65.

Pokorný J., (2015). Graph databases: their power and limitations. *Computer Information Systems and Industrial Management: 14th IFIP TC 8 International Conference*. Warsaw, Poland. pp. 58-69.

Pokorný J. et al, (2017). Integrity constraints in graph databases. *Procedia Computer Science*, vol. 109, pp. 975-981.

Reina F. et al, (2020). Modeling and enforcing integrity constraints on graph databases. *Database and Expert Systems Applications*. Cham, Germany. pp. 269-284.

Rybola Z., (2017). *Towards OntoUML for Software Engineering: Transformation of OntoUML into Relational Databases*. Faculty of Informaton Technology, Czech Technical University in Prague, Prague.

Rybola Z. and Valenta M., (2018). Towards OntoUML for software engineering: Experimental evaluation of exclusivity constraints in relational databases. *Model and Data Engineering, MEDI 2018*. Marrakesh, Morocco. pp. 58-73.

Schäfermeyer M. et al, (2012). The Impact of Business Process Complexity on Business Process Standardization. *Business & Information Systems Engineering*, vol. 4, pp. 261-270.

Uhnák P. and Pergl R., (2016). The OpenPonk modeling platform. *11th International Workshop on Smalltalk Technologies*. Prague, Czech Republic. pp. 1-11.

van Grondelle J., (2012). New Audiences for Ontologies: Dealing with Complexity in Business Processes. *The Semantic Web: Research and Applications, Lecture Notes in Computer Science*. Berlin, Germany, pp. 2-2.

Verdonck M. et al, (2018). Comparing traditional conceptual modeling with ontology-driven conceptual modeling: An empirical study. *Information Systems*, vol. 81, pp. 92-103.

Zikán J., (2023). *Implementation of OntoUML schemas in graph databases - case study*. Faculty of Informaton Technology, Czech Technical University in Prague, Prague.

TOWARDS AN ARTIFICIAL INTELLIGENCE PROJECT METHODOLOGY WITH AN INTEGRATIVE APPROACH TO DELIVER INNOVATIVE SOLUTIONS

Nilo Sergio Maziero Petrin, Henrique Cordeiro Mariano and João Carlos Néto
SENAC University Center, Brazil

ABSTRACT

Artificial Intelligence (AI) has transformed countless sectors, bringing innovative solutions to complex challenges. However, effective implementation of AI projects requires a systematic and integrative approach that can keep up with recent advances in the field. This study presents an innovative methodology for AI projects, aiming to overcome emerging challenges and deliver efficient solutions. The proposed methodology offers a comprehensive framework that guides teams through all project phases, from understanding business needs to operationalizing the AI system. It has proven effective in managing today's AI challenges, including adequately addressing the needs of the business, data, methods, and teams involved. Furthermore, the proposed methodology stands out for its flexibility and adaptability to rapid changes in the field of AI. This study contributes significantly to the existing literature by presenting a new methodology for AI projects capable of facing the challenges posed by recent advances in the field.

KEYWORDS

Artificial Intelligence, AI Project Methodology, AI Integrative Approach, AI Solution Development

1. INTRODUCTION

Artificial Intelligence (AI) has revolutionized several sectors, offering innovative solutions to complex problems. However, successful implementation of AI projects requires a systematic and integrative approach. The design, management, and development of AI systems present unique challenges. Designers often need help to create systems that solve complex problems and do so ethically and impartially. It is imperative to ensure that the AI system is transparent and understandable, which is a significant challenge given the black-box nature of many AI algorithms. As Timnit Gebru, a leading researcher in the field of ethics and AI, stated: “Transparency in AI systems is critical to building trust and accountability.” (Gebru, 2022).

AI project managers are tasked with assembling diverse teams with skills in data science, machine learning, software engineering, and business domain experience. They must also navigate the complexities of integrating AI systems into existing workflows and processes. As a renowned AI expert, Andrew Ng, once said, "Much of our work in AI is about closing the gap between what AI can do and what users need" (Ng, 2017). This point highlights the importance of managing stakeholder expectations and integrating AI systems with the existing ecosystem. Furthermore, it is necessary to manage stakeholder expectations, as there often needs to be more clarity between what AI can realistically achieve and what is expected.

Developers must deal with issues such as data quality and availability, model selection and tuning, system scalability, deployment, and operationalization. They also need to keep up with the rapidly evolving field of AI and continually update their skills. Furthermore, as Jeff Dean of Google Brain once said, "In machine learning, you are only as good as your data" (Dean, 2021). This point emphasizes the importance of data quality and availability in developing AI systems. These quotes highlight the complexities of designing, managing, and developing AI systems.

AI is a multidisciplinary field that involves concepts from computer science, statistics, mathematics, and domain-specific knowledge. Some key concepts include machine learning, deep learning, natural language processing, and computer vision. As Yann LeCun stated: “Deep Learning allows computational models composed of multiple layers to process data with multiple levels of abstraction.” (LeCun, 2015). To address these challenges, this article proposes a comprehensive methodology for AI projects that ensures effective solution delivery by providing a structured approach to implementation. This methodology guides the team through each project phase, from understanding business needs to operationalizing the AI system. Furthermore, it emphasizes the importance of continuous learning and iteration, as AI systems need to evolve with changing business needs and technological advances.

Considering the evolution of the use of AI by organizations and the development of different approaches with this technology, a large flow of investment was generated for this type of application. It significantly increased the number of solutions available, promoting a considerable impact on the market. Therefore, this article aims to align with the trends and demands generated by this evolution and consider the acceleration with which organizations are working to quickly increase the number of related projects and the expected quality level. Due to this situation, it is essential to describe an Artificial Intelligence Methodology that combines this technology with other associated disciplines, such as Data Management, Software Development, and Project Management, to organize and improve the success rate of these projects.

This article is organized as follows: Initially, in the Introduction, we describe a contextualization of the problem and the importance of the need to seek a methodological solution, the objective of this work. Next, we present the Proposed Methodology and detail each stage of the life cycle for AI projects. In the section Use and Practical Cases, we show some trends and case studies with their results. Next, we discuss the current AI Design Methodologies and contrast them with the modern needs. Finally, we make Final Considerations and point future work out.

2. PROPOSED METHODOLOGY OF AI PROJECT DEVELOPMENT

This section presents the proposed methodology for developing AI projects. The methodology is designed to provide a comprehensive and systematic framework that guides project teams through all phases of the AI project lifecycle, from understanding business needs to operationalizing the AI system.

The macro framework of the proposed methodology is presented in Figure 1. This framework provides an overview of the main phases of the AI project life cycle. Each phase is designed to address specific aspects of the project, ensuring that all important aspects are considered.

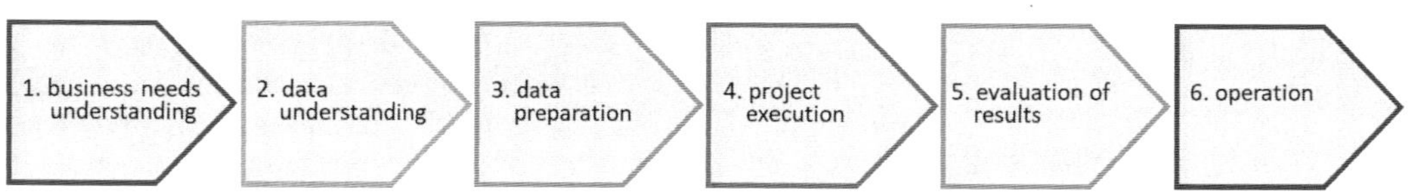

Figure 1. Macro framework from the proposed methodology. Source: prepared by the authors

Therefore, Figure 2 presents details of the proposed methodology. This framework expands on the previous by providing specific activities in each project life cycle phase.

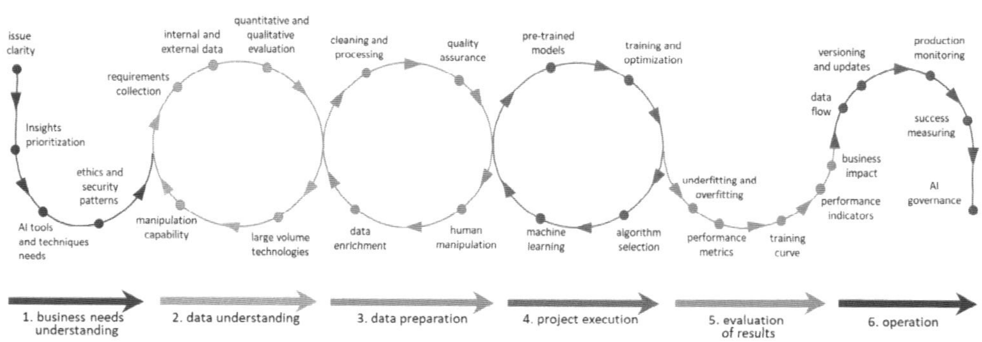

Figure 2. Detailed framework of the proposed methodology. Source: prepared by the authors

Figure 3. Business Needs Understanding

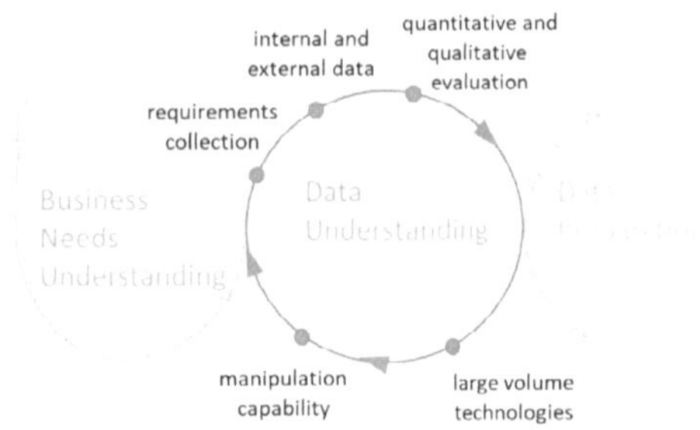

Figure 4. Data Understanding

Figure 5. Data Preparation

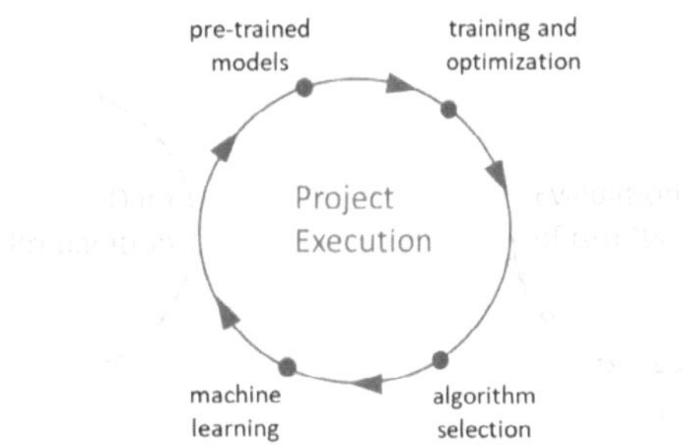

Figure 6. Project Execution

Figure 7. Evaluation of results

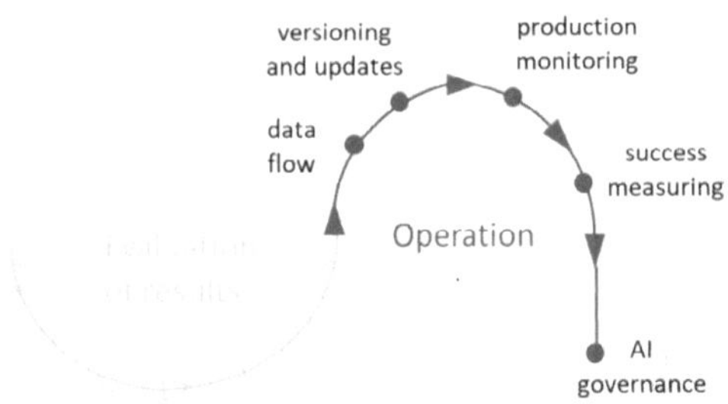

Figure 8. Operation

2.1 Phase I: Business Needs Understanding

The first phase in any AI project is understanding the business or organizational requirements. To achieve this, one must focus on clearly analyzing the problem the AI system intends to solve, evaluate the suitability of AI to address that problem, identify the parts of the project that will benefit from AI, select appropriate AI standards, establish criteria success, specify essential requirements for the successful completion of the project, define ethical, safety and limitations guidelines, and identify the skills needed for the team.

This phase is organized into stages, as shown in Figure 3, including Identification of the problem to be solved and confirmation of the need for an AI system. Furthermore, it is vital to prioritize the insights generated based on analyzing the parts of the project that require AI. Choosing the AI standards to be implemented and their tools and techniques is also essential. Finally, standards and ethical considerations, security, and limits are analyzed to structure business needs.

2.2 Phase II: Data Understanding

After understanding the business requirements, the next step involves understanding the data involved in the AI project. This step requires identifying essential data, assessing its quantity and quality, determining necessary internal and external data, establishing requirements to enhance existing data, defining processes for ongoing data collection, and identifying the technologies necessary for effective data manipulation.

This phase is structured into five steps, as shown in Figure 4, considering the Identification of the data necessary to achieve the objectives through the collection of requirements. The necessary internal and external data is then defined, followed by an assessment of the quantity and quality of data, the statistical processing of the data and as well validation, an analysis of technologies for processing large volumes, and a consequent review of the capabilities for handling, storing, and processing data effectively, including technological requirements for data processing.

2.3 Phase III: Data Preparation

With business and data requirements established, data preparation becomes crucial. This step involves transforming data to meet specific project requirements, performing data cleansing, aggregation, augmentation, labeling, normalization, transformation, and implementing continuous data quality monitoring and ethical integration of third-party data when necessary.

Initially, data transformation is conducted, as shown in Figure 5, to meet the project requirements, including data cleaning, transformation, and manipulation. Next, continuous data quality monitoring is conducted, considering that the data may not be static and will continue to be updated, thus requiring constant verification. Next, data is annotated and manipulated with human involvement. Finally, additional data augmentation steps are taken to improve the quantity and quality of data when necessary.

2.4 Phase IV: Project Execution

At this stage, the focus is on developing the AI system. These steps include transforming data into a machine learning model, selecting suitable tools, frameworks, programming development languages, as well as hardware infrastructure, such as servers (including servers, GPUs - Graphics Processing Units), establishment of a private and/or cloud computing environment, meticulous training and optimizing model hyperparameters, choosing appropriate algorithms and configurations, and incorporating pre-trained models if necessary.

This phase is structured in four stages, as shown in Figure 6. The first step involves transforming the data into a pre-trained machine-learning model. The second step involves selecting AI tools and frameworks that integrate well with the existing ecosystem and preferably use open-source solutions. The third step involves training the model and optimizing the hyperparameters for better performance. If necessary, a suitable pre-trained model can be used. The last step involves selecting suitable algorithms and settings.

2.5 Phase V: Evaluation of Results

Model evaluation is critical to ensuring it meets business objectives. This step involves analyzing performance metrics, accuracy, false positive and negative rates, key performance indicators, model quality measures, and evaluating security, risk, and ethics.

Phase V is distributed in five stages, as shown in Figure 7. The first step involves identifying overfitting and underfitting (increase or decrease in the data considered). The second step involves evaluating accuracy and performance metrics. The third step involves evaluating the training, validation, and testing curves. The fourth step involves assessment against established key performance indicators. The last step involves analyzing the impacts on the business, allowing continuous monitoring and iterations of the model.

2.6 Phase VI: Operation

Finally, the operationalization phase places the model in a production environment and requires ongoing management, monitoring, versioning, and iteration to ensure that the model continues to provide value over time.

This phase is organized into five steps, as shown in Figure 8, including implementing the AI system in operational environments and structuring data flow and performance requirements. Next, the versioning and iteration of the AI system are conducted, where the versions of the AI system are managed, and iterations and updates are prepared. These steps make it possible to monitor the AI system continuously.

A productive environment and then evaluate the performance of the project's success about business objectives. Finally, the management and governance of the AI system in production are conducted.

From the above, the proposed methodology provides a comprehensive framework for the effective development of AI projects. She guides teams through the various phases of the project lifecycle, ensuring that all important aspects are considered and that the resulting systems are robust, effective, and aligned with business objectives.

3. USE AND PRACTICAL CASES

In this section, we will explore trends in the use of Artificial Intelligence, highlighting its impact on various sectors and the need for a systematic and integrative approach to implementing AI projects.

3.1 Usage Trends

As presented in the report by (McKinsey, 2023), the potential for productivity growth through AI is estimated to be between $11.0 trillion and $17.7 trillion in economic benefits annually. Around sixty-three generative AI use cases, which were related to sixteen business functions were identified. These cases could deliver a 15 to 40 percent increase if applied across all sectors surveyed.

In another analysis presented in the report (PwC,2017), an increase of 14% in global GDP by 2030 was estimated because of the acceleration of development generated by AI, equivalent to 15.7 trillion dollars. Significant increases are expected for China, North America, Latin America, and Europe.

On the other hand, data analytics and automation startups are helping organizations simplify and streamline the project management office (PMO) function. The most famous case is President Emmanuel Macron's use of the latest technology to maintain up-to-date information on all French public sector projects (Nieto-Rodriguez; Viana, 2023). These intelligent new tools will radically transform the way PMOs operate. In other situations, higher success rates (83% versus 66%) are being achieved in diagnosing head tumors using Artificial Intelligence systems (Boudreau, 2019). Based on the above, advances in AI have the potential to bring significant economic benefits and transform the way organizations operate. However, organizations must be prepared to face the challenges associated with implementing AI and can adapt to rapid changes in the field.

3.2 Practical Cases

The postgraduate course in Artificial Intelligence at SENAC University Center (SENAC, 2023) is an innovative training that seeks to incorporate new disciplinary and transversal skills. With a total workload of 360 hours, the course combines interdisciplinarity, a systemic approach, and practical real-world application. The curricular structure, made up of three thematic blocks, ranges from the fundamentals of Artificial Intelligence to practical projects based on challenges in the professional field.

Aimed at graduates in areas related to computing, the course aims to specialize participants to work in the field of Artificial Intelligence. This course is achieved by training students in intelligent systems management, including necessary technologies, processes, and methodologies. One of the highlights of the course is the subject "Project: Intelligent Systems II – Various Artificial Intelligence Projects". With a workload of 32 hours, this course guides students towards developing an artificial intelligence project, aiming to produce a feasible, simple, quality, and ethical solution to real problems contextualized to the student's daily life or professional interest.

Students are encouraged to experiment and practice using the proposed methodology during the course. In the 2023 academic year, students developed practical projects such as diagnosing COVID-19 through lung exam images; assessing facial expressions as indicators of student engagement during remote classes; and identifying vehicles on carriageways to assist in safety and transport. Using the proposed methodology helped them structure the project planning, seeking to generate value and benefits expected by stakeholders.

These practical cases demonstrate the applicability and effectiveness of the proposed methodology in real-world situations.

4. DISCUSSION ON CURRENT AI DESIGN METHODOLOGIES

This section offers a comprehensive discussion on existing AI design methodologies, comparing traditional and contemporary approaches. It also delves into the challenges and limitations inherent in these methodologies, providing a thorough understanding of the current landscape in AI project development.

4.1 Analysis of Existing AI Design Methodologies

Conducting a critical analysis of AI project methodologies is a crucial stage in understanding the current state of AI project development. This evaluation encompasses a spectrum of methodologies, ranging from conventional to modern approaches, each presenting its own set of advantages and disadvantages. Moreover, this analysis aids in identifying gaps in existing methodologies, providing valuable insights for developing newer approaches. In alignment with the perspective of Richard Socher, former chief scientist at Salesforce, who noted: "AI is a complex field, and I am the first to say that we computer scientists have not progressed as far as many people believe" (Socher, 2018).

The CRISP-DM (Cross-Industry Standard Process for Data Mining) methodology – figure 9, merges as one of the oldest and most widely used in data mining and machine learning methodologies. However, its suitability for projects involving emerging AI technologies, such as deep learning, may need to be revised (IBM, n.d.). More recent methodologies, such as OSEMN (Obtain, Scrub, Explore, Model, and iNterpret) – figure 10, offer a more flexible and adaptable approach. Nonetheless, they may require a steeper learning curve for project teams (DSPA, n.d.).

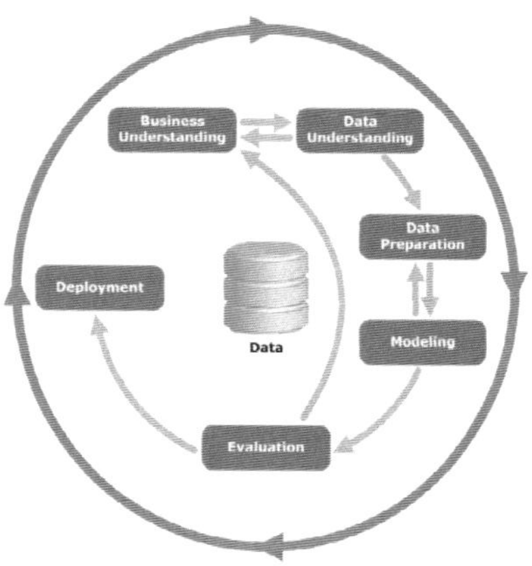

Figure 9. CRISP-DM Framework

Source: (IBM, n.d.)

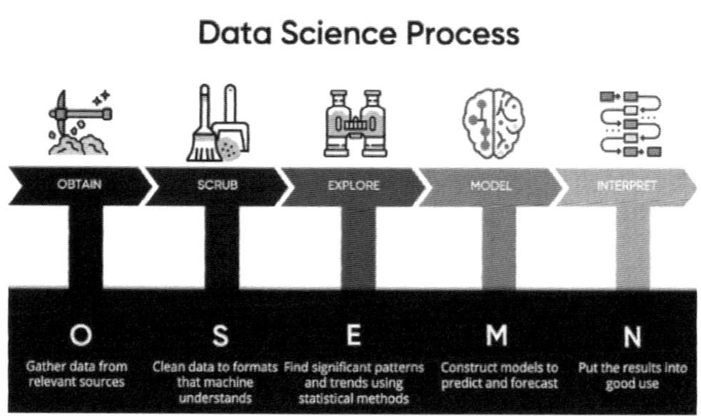

Figure 10. OSEMN Framework

Source: (DSPA, n.d.)

This review of AI project methodologies is a valuable exercise, providing organizations with tools to choose the most appropriate approach for their specific AI projects, highlighting the constant need for innovation and adaptation in the face of the continuous evolution of AI technology.

4.2 Contrasting Traditional and Modern AI Design Methodologies

A comparative analysis between traditional and modern AI design methodologies proves indispensable for understanding the evolution and progress in AI. Traditional methodologies, such as CRISP-DM, have exhibited efficacy in data mining and machine learning projects over several decades. CRISP-DM, although established and effective in many industries, may need to be revised for challenges presented by modern AI technologies such as deep learning.

On the other hand, given the rapid advancement of AI technology, newer approaches such as OSEMN, which align more adaptable to current needs, are emerging. OSEMN offers a flexible and adaptable approach, especially useful for projects that involve large volumes of data and require advanced machine learning techniques.

This comparative analysis underscores the significance of continuous evolution in AI project approaches, emphasizing the need for adaptability and flexibility in selecting the most suitable methodology for each project.

4.3 Challenges and Limitations of AI Methodologies

A critical examination of the challenges and limitations associated with current AI project methodologies is imperative when implementing AI projects. While methodologies such as CRISP-DM and OSEMN have demonstrated effectiveness in numerous projects, they exhibit limitations, ranging from inflexibility in adapting to newer technologies to a lack of guidance on ethical and privacy issues.

CRISP-DM, despite its widespread usage effectiveness, may not be apt for projects involving emerging AI technologies such as deep learning and natural language processing.

Likewise, although OSEMN is a newer and more flexible methodology, it may need to provide more guidance on ethical and privacy issues, which are increasingly relevant in AI.

Despite the strengths of current AI design methodologies, it is crucial to be aware of their limitations, underscoring the necessity to develop newer approaches capable of addressing these challenges and adapting to the rapid changes in the field of AI.

4.4 Insights from Case Studies: Practical Applications

Case studies provide valuable insights into the practical applications of AI design methodologies, facilitating an analysis of how these methodologies are implemented in real-world situations. These studies offer an opportunity to comprehend the challenges and successes associated with these implementations, highlighting the adaptability of these methodologies across diverse sectors.

For instance, a case study might examine the application of the CRISP-DM methodology in a data mining project in the healthcare sector, detailing the various phases of the methodology, from understanding the business objectives to implementing the model. Similarly, another case study could explore using the OSEMN methodology in a machine learning project in the financial sector, highlighting the specific steps for data preparation, model construction, and interpretation of results.

Case studies emerge as a powerful tool for understanding the practical applications of AI design methodologies by providing insights into how these approaches can be adapted and applied in different contexts to address complex problems. From the above, this literature review provides a comprehensive overview of existing methodologies for AI design. It highlights the strengths and limitations of these methodologies and emphasizes the continued need for innovation and adaptation in the face of the rapidly evolving field of AI.

5. FINAL CONSIDERATIONS

The methodology proposed for AI projects in this study aims to fill a crucial gap in the systematic and integrative approach needed to address emerging challenges in this field. The methodology overcomes the limitations of traditional methodologies and stands out for its flexibility and adaptability.

During the literature review, it became evident that traditional methodologies have limitations in the face of recent advances, and the proposal seeks to overcome these limitations, providing an innovative approach to face the complex challenges associated with the development of AI systems.

As a perspective for future work, integrating this methodology with other practices recognized in project management, such as those outlined by the Project Management Body of Knowledge – PMBOK® (PMI, 2021), can be explored to search for best practices. Furthermore, the application of the methodology in broader contexts, such as portfolio and program management (PPM) and operations-related processes (such as DevOps or Machine Learning Ops), can be investigated (Lwakatare et al., 2019; Bradley, 2023).

ACKNOWLEDGEMENT

We are grateful to the SENAC University Center, Santo Amaro campus, for providing a conducive environment and essential support for successfully implementing the proposed methodology in the Artificial Intelligence Projects classes of the postgraduate course in Artificial Intelligence.

Furthermore, we thank the students who dedicated themselves and participated in the experiments applying the methodology proposed in this work. This work shows the spirit of learning and innovation that characterizes our institution but also highlights the dedication and enthusiasm of our students. We will continue to explore the ever-evolving challenges and frontiers in Artificial Intelligence.

REFERENCES

Boudreau, P., 2019. Applying Artificial Intelligence to Project Management. ISBN: 9781687550941.

Bradley, J., Kurlansik, R., Thomson, M., & Turbitt, N.,2023. The Big Book of MLOps (2nd ed.). Databricks. Available at: [https://www.databricks.com/resources/ebook/the-big-book-of-mlops] (Accessed on: Oct 21, 2023).

Dean, J., 2021. AI is not as smart as you think – but it could be. TED Talk, Aug.

DSPA, n.d. OSEMN Data Science Life Cycle. Data Science Process Alliance. Available at: [https://www.datascience-pm.com/osemn/] (Accessed on: Oct 5, 2023).

Gebru, T., 2022. Building Transparency into AI Projects. Harvard Business Review, Jun 20.

IBM, n.d. CRISP-DM Help Overview. IBM Knowledge Center. Available at: [https://www.ibm.com/docs/en/spss-modeler/18.4.0?topic=dm-crisp-help-overview] (Accessed on: Oct 5, 2023).

LeCun, Y., Bengio, Y., & Hinton, G., 2015. Deep learning. Nature, 521 (7553), pp.436–444.

Lwakatare, L. E., Kuvaja, P., & Oivo, M., 2019. Dimensions of DevOps. In Agile Processes in Software Engineering and Extreme Programming – Workshops (pp. 247-255). Springer.

Mckinsey, 2023. The economic potential of generative AI The next productivity frontier. Mckinsey & Company, June 2023 Available at [https://www.mckinsey.com/capabilities/mckinsey-digital/our-insights/the-economic-potential-of-generative-ai-the-next-productivity-frontier#/] (Accessed on: Oct 19, 2023).

Ng, A., 2017. Why AI Is the New Electricity. Stanford Graduate School of Business, Mar 11.

Nieto-Rodriguez, A., Viana, R., 2023. How AI will Transform Project Management. Harvard Business Review, Feb 2.

PMI, Project Management Institute ®. (2021). A Guide to the Project Management Body of Knowledge (PMBOK® Guide). Seventh Edition. Newtown Square: Project Management Institute.

PwC, 2017. "Sizing the prize: What's the real value of AI for your business, and how can you capitalise?" PwC, September 5, 2017. Available at: [https://www.pwc.com/gx/en/issues/data-and-analytics/publications/artificial-intelligence-study.html] (Accessed on: Oct 19, 2023).

SENAC. t.d. Curso de Pós Graduação em Inteligência Artificial. SENAC SP University Center. Available at: [https://www.sp.senac.br/pos-graduacao/pos-em-inteligencia-artificial] (Accessed on: Oct 19, 2023)

Socher, R., 2018. Algorithms, Data, and New Workflows: 3 Concepts Behind AI and Your Future Success. Salesforce. Available at: [https://www.salesforce.com/blog/ai-deep-learning-productivity-blog/] (Accessed on: Oct 5, 2023).

ATTAINING SCIENTIFIC RIGOUR IN SOCIO-TECHNICAL RESEARCH WITH HUSSERL'S DESCRIPTIVE PHENOMENOLOGY

Gianni Jacucci
Department of Information Engineering and Computer Science - DISI - University of Trento
Via Sommarive , 9 I-38123 Povo (TN), Italy

ABSTRACT

Socio-Technical (S-T) research, being a human science, places paramount importance on subjective data, as "facts-in-the-conscience." Husserl's phenomenology presents itself as the fitting philosophical foundation for addressing these "facts-in-the-conscience" across all human sciences. This line of reasoning gives rise to thought-provoking inquiries. How do we appropriately handle these facts-in-the-conscience? How can we effectively harness Husserl's phenomenology? Should we emulate Amedeo Giorgi and adopt his Husserlian Descriptive Phenomenological Method (DPM), a method tailored to establish a scientific foundation for psychological research? Could DPM serve as the pathway to validate "facts-in-the-conscience" as legitimate data for constructing Evidence-Based Proofs? What else do we need to control subjectivity? In Heidegger's words: *"How do we teach each other speak objectively about these subjective things?"* We describe an example that offers insights into "eidetic"[1] responses to these inquiries. Namely, we introduce an approach based on gathering pronunciations of members of a Community of Practice, on their experience of phenomena in their professional field, expressed in the language of their profession: the Query Experiment (QE). This procedure satisfies the requirements for scientific rigour dictated by Descriptive Phenomenology. We conclude that QEs offer the avenue to attain rigorous scientific answers to S-T Research questions.

KEYWORDS

Descriptive Phenomenology, Socio Technical Research, Qualitative Research, Epistemology, Scientific Rigour, Methodology

1. INTRODUCTION

Subjective Experience and Reflection, in Human Sciences

What leads to the potential divergence between facts-in-the-conscience and facts in the real world? As facts-in-the-conscience central to human sciences – perceptions, intuitions, emotions – are not directly accessible to objective verification, non neutral predispositions towards phenomena - prejudices, or a priory positions from prior experience - pose challenges to human sciences. Rectifying perceptual biases necessitates cultivating awareness through routine experience and diligence, as in *professional* training within a *community of practice*.

What are the evidences of interference of consciousness, and subjectivity in general, with the scientific discourse? Let's go back to the very beginning of phenomenology, by recalling Schutz, as done by Bednar and Welch (2006): "When elaborating upon 'meaningfulness' Schutz … questions how it is possible for any mutual understanding or communication between people to take place … He reflects that such possibilities can only be approached via 'sedimentation' of pre-interpreted experiences built up through conscious life. Any justifiable methods for interpreting social interrelationship must then be based on careful description of underlying assumptions and their implications. He goes on to suggest that the methods of the social sciences cannot be regarded as adequate to this task." Note that, at Schutz times, human sciences performed with the objectivist epistemology of natural sciences. Bednar and Welsh then go on: "They require a philosophical analysis. And phenomenology ... has not only opened up an avenue of approach for such an analysis but has in

[1] Eidetic, in Psychology: denoting mental images having unusual vividness and detail, as if actually visible.

addition started the analysis itself. ... This concept of a 'sedimentation' of pre-interpreted, lived experience comes about, for Alfred Schutz, through reflection. ... Thus, meaningfulness can only be attributed in retrospect. ... "

The authors then go on to link these first thoughts on phenomenology to the thoughts on information systems, formed in a Socio-Technical perspective:

"In considering Schutz's view, the authors are reminded of the work of Börje Langefors, in the mid Sixties, with the Infological Equation. Reflecting on the nature of information systems, Langefors suggests that those people who are to interpret data in order to inform themselves must be viewed as part of the system. ... Meaning (information or knowledge) is thus created by each individual. Pre-knowledge ... is considered to be created through the entire lived experience of the individual concerned (cf. Schutz's concept of 'sedimentation'). He observes that communication may be seen to approach success most closely where individuals interpreting the same data belong to a group, definable for example by ...common professional interest, e.g. standardized accounting data among accountants."

From these foundational, phenomenological views, we retain a concept of crucial importance for our perspective on reducing subjective variance: by continuous sharing with professional peers, during their routine professional activities, the members of a community of practice cleanse the meanings they extract from world experiences within their professional field, freeing all meanings from subjective biases and prejudices. As a consequence, the resulting consolidated meanings can be regarded to be as close as they can get to generally accepted - or universal. And even objectively close to reality, or good for science: a basic tenet of the present paper.

Except of course for deformations connected with autopoetic mechanisms generated during evolution by our human specie, for survival (like for example, alterations in the perception of colours or light intensity in human vision, due to a natural negative feed back mechanism, that allow expanding the region of our light sensitivity for security).. (Maturana and Varela 1979, Jacucci 2015). For these affect all human beings in an essentially equivalent way. For example, in front of an image overwhelmed by the red colour, we all perceive white regions in the picture as green, as sensitivity to red is reduced by an equivalent artificial - by nature - 'saturation' of the optical nerve: however, there is no green light there.

As autopoietic mechanisms are not limited to the sensorial domain, we should watch out for mental distortions possibly affecting in the same way all members of a community of practice: as, for example, a cultural bias. These eventual distortions need to be identified and possibly corrected. Sometimes their effects are reduced in 'difference' measurements.

Scientific rigour off subjective data: Our QE and Giorgi's DPM

Back to our goal: how to attain scientific rigour from subjective data. An example: To get an opinion on the efficacy of a certain therapy supporting children with psychosocial emotional differences, one could directly ask the therapists involved in performing that therapy. To obtain a scientific proof of that efficacy, however, one must revert to an empirical method, as opinions are subjective. A mainstream view today, in medical and special education communities. Yet, on second thought, the common opinion of a group of therapists cannot just be disregarded, and it should not be: Researchers need a way out.

One century ago, Edmund Husserl stated that scientists should take phenomenology—not empiricism—as the correct philosophical basis for all sciences, specially those that address facts in the conscience, which lay outside of sensorial experiences and are not accessible to empiric proof. The question about phenomenological investigations then arises: What method yields scientifically valid proofs? In the therapy dilemma above, how should researchers ask therapists about their opinions and how should the researchers treat their answers to obtain scientifically valid proof by following Husserl's suggestion and using phenomenology as a philosophical basis? Furthermore, are the therapists the right subjects to ask? Should researchers prepare them in advance?

We illustrate an answer to these questions with an example from paediatrics, using as litmus colouring matter, guiding design choices of a scientific 'Query Experiment' (QE), the Descriptive Phenomenological Method (DPM) that Giorgi defined for Psychology (1970, 2009).

We shall show that the answer requires the intentional construction of an appropriate 'actor-network', enrolling in it both human, and non human or material actors, and the delegation to that network, of important action elements of the prescribed scientific analysis, while charting child development in the example.Our basic tenet, of reverting to community of practice members, offers to QE the needed key additional success element.

The Query Experiment (QE): Utilising Giorgi's DPM to get direct, scientifically rigorous experimental answers to questions of interest.

To ensure the scientific rigour of results, Husserl's Descriptive Phenomenological Philosophy (DPP) (1982/1913) provides controls while utilising intuition to access facts-in-the-conscience: devoid of references to prior knowledge, unconcerned with matching the real world, and incorporating checks of free imaginative variations. Amedeo Giorgi has extended Edmund Husserl's DPP, defining the methodology of the DPM for scientific research in Psychology. This method holds the potential for extension into other disciplines in the realm of Human Sciences. It presents a way to extract the genuine disciplinary meaning of relevant phenomena.

How can we effectively apply DPM to conduct a scientific Query Experiment (QE), successfully? Let's recall that Giorgi's DPM declaratively entails meticulous descriptions of the observed phenomenon, captured from a natural perspective, and faithfully conveyed by an uninitiated participant. To extract scientifically relevant meanings within the discipline, these descriptions are subjected to analysis by a researcher who adopts a phenomenological attitude, devoid of reliance on prior knowledge (that must be 'bracketed') and unconcerned with congruence to the real world. This process involves verification through various free imaginative variations, serving as stringent controls to ensure scientific rigour in capturing the essence of the phenomenon, expressed in an eidetic form.

In the experiments we intend to conduct, however, it is imperative that those exposed to the phenomenon hold the reference theoretical knowledge structure in their minds. This structure is not to be bracketed but meticulously compared with the phenomenon, structured in uncompromising details, in order to respond to the query. What measures can we employ to achieve this?

We propose an approach implementing DPM requisites directly to the observer, in scientific experiments of this type, by resorting to members of a community of practice. The approach amalgamates observation, description, and reporting, conducted by a conscious, experienced professional, within their professional attitude. It entrusts part of the scientific controls, linked with Husserl's phenomenological perspective, to the fusion of the professional's intuition with their tacit personal knowledge, and the mirrored structure of the reporting artefact. The therapists' personal professional knowledge grants the pure rendition of the object by their immediate intuition in front of the phenomenon, correctly reported because of the alignment, by design, between structure of personal knowledge and structure of reporting artefact. This procedure enforces all advantages of reverting to community of practice members.

Plan of the paper.

The focus of the rest of the present conceptual paper revolves around Amedeo Giorgi's DPM. The initial discussion has delved into some fundamental criteria governing scientific rigour. Succinctly, we now revisit the three foundational philosophies that underpin qualitative research methods: empiricism, hermeneutics, and phenomenology[2]. Within this context, we elucidate the distinct attributes, merits, and susceptibilities inherent in the methods they engender. In this endeavour, we comprehensively introduce Giorgi's critical insight and writings on qualitative research.

The purpose of this presentation is threefold: A) to reflect on epistemology and method in ST research; B) to ensure that the ST Community is well-informed about the merits of the phenomenological approach and explicitly of extending Giorgi's Descriptive Phenomenological Method (DPM) to our Query Experiment (QE) approach, and to furnish an exemplar of our own ST research wherein the the extended DPM and QE assume a critical role; and C) to formally propose our QE as a viable candidate for methodological employment in ST research.

2. THREE QUALITATIVE APPROACHES

Qualitative methods find extensive acceptance and widespread use in Socio-Technical (ST) research for Information Systems (IS). A multitude of methodologies have been introduced over time. Yet, these methodologies are fundamentally underpinned by three distinct philosophies that provide the guiding principles for the scientific approaches stemming from them. To elucidate these philosophies we draw from Amedeo Giorgi's discourse on this subject (2018).

[2] Distinguishing more, and somewhat differently, than usual between hermeneutics, and phenomenology.

2.1 Empiricism

Empiricism, the oldest philosophy of science dating back five centuries, originally designed to support scientific endeavours in the natural sciences, remains dominant across many fields of study. However, during the early 20th century, two other philosophies emerged: phenomenology and hermeneutics. At its core, empiricism asserts that all knowledge must stem from direct experience, with no reliance on a priori truths. Sensory modalities and tangible observations are given prominence. Subsequent verification, particularly by others, plays a crucial role in establishing robust knowledge, failing which information is regarded as provisional.

One of the earliest qualitative methods rooted in empiricism is Grounded Theory (GT), originating within Sociology. GT employs a comparative analysis approach wherein data examination yields hypotheses that form tentative theories, subsequently subject to ongoing data scrutiny. This methodology generates theory from empirical data, dispelling speculative conjecture. Simultaneous involvement in data collection and analysis, coupled with the construction of analytical codes and categories derived directly from data, ensures the development of stringent data-dependent codes and categories. Thus, all formulated concepts and properties must be firmly rooted in the data. Subsequent comparisons and distinctions within the data, viewed from disciplinary lenses such as sociology or psychology, facilitate the potential generation of initial theoretical hypotheses. A note of caution is echoed by Giorgi: "… GT emphasises conceptualisation and not description, abstracting from time, place, and persons in a way that description does not…. the researcher must transform the detected everyday meanings into disciplinary meanings, in order to build a theory. But this could be…" problematic, as the researcher, for example, "could interpret the everyday empirical meanings psychoanalytically, behaviourally, or cognitively and still be justified as a psychological interpreter" (Giorgi 2018, p. 12). Hence, GT is grounded in empirical foundations rather than being purely empirical. Nevertheless, in its practical application, it holds recognition as a scientific method.

2.2 Hermeneutics

To grasp the essence of "understanding," transcending mere methodical approaches for investigating human science phenomena, Heidegger (1962) and Gadamer (1975/1960) established hermeneutics. At its core, hermeneutics asserts that comprehending human phenomena necessitates interpretation. Consequently, knowledge, at its best, embodies a plausible comprehension of a phenomenon, in contrast to the definitive, objective understanding typical of the natural sciences that permits no alternatives. The objective of such research lies in comprehending lived experiences through the meanings conveyed within them. However, texts are products of human creation, infused with perspectives and expressed through language marked by word ambiguity. Additionally, texts introduce context, giving rise to considerations of the author's intentions and the intended audience. The method guiding scientific research into human phenomena stands in stark contrast to that governing natural phenomena, governed by causes and effects. Hermeneutic thinkers contend that subjectivity exerts significant influence on human phenomena. Consequently, there is no independent starting point when dealing with human phenomena. To navigate this, hermeneutic researchers universally engage within the hermeneutic circle, a protocol suited to this situation. Hermeneutic reasoning is circular, though not a self-defeating cycle, as aptly expressed by Palmer (1969): "The whole receives its definition from the parts, and reciprocally, the parts can only be understood in reference to the whole".

The hermeneutic method has two basic elements: "… 1) that the researcher produces the best interpreted meaning … not without other possible understandings … and 2) that the analysis requires the use of the hermeneutic circle with its fore-structure of understanding." (Giorgi 2018, p. 14). It tends, albeit with a different route than empiricism, also to detect and clarify everyday lived meanings, as expressed by humans, and turn them into precise disciplinary meanings. Given the assumptions of the procedures, hermeneutic results are interpretations, theories with a degree of tentativeness.

2.3 Phenomenology

Husserl (1970a, 1970b) phenomenology employs a descriptive approach. For him, intuition is the basis for knowledge acquisition, not interpretation. Intuition is " … how phenomena present themselves to acts of consciousness. The modes of appearance of all objects are meant to be described …" (Giorgi 2018, p. 20).. "…

the phenomenological philosophical method … consists of three basic steps: experience or imagine a concrete phenomenon and carefully describe it; second systematically but freely vary dimensions of the phenomenon in order to ascertain its essential features; and, third describe the essence that has been discovered, once the method of free imaginative variations has been completed. This is also known as the eidetic reduction of the concrete phenomenon. … " (Giorgi 2018, p. 20).

Some adjustments are necessary to transition from philosophy to the realm of science and a human-focused scientific discipline (psychology, sociology, or other). This extension is performed by Giorgi in Psychology with his PDM. "The ultimate outcome of phenomenological analyses are eidetic expressions concerning the meaning of experiential events. What phenomenology adds to normal scientific analyses are the probing into subjective acts that are the correlates of worldly presentations." And how does PDM really work? "Phenomenology … delves into the realm of subjective human consciousness. It seeks to understand the essence of human experiences, the way individuals make sense of their interactions with the world, and how they perceive and interpret phenomena. By examining the subjective acts (thoughts, feelings, perceptions, etc.) that accompany our encounters with the world, phenomenology adds depth and context to our understanding of reality." "(Giorgi, Giorgi, and Morley 2017). What are the specific results of the PDM method? "The result of the application of the scientific phenomenological method are eidetic descriptions that are general and based upon intuitions that are clarified with the help of the procedure of imaginative variations." (Giorgi 2018, p. 22).. But the connection to the real world requires, in principle, further analysis. After solving this vulnerability, in the sequel we shall see how, descriptive phenomenology can lead to the establishment of scientific evidence.

2.4 Respective Approach Vulnerabilities *vis a vis* Scientific Rigour

All three philosophies support methods that " … attempt to come up with a precise disciplinary meaning of data expressed in the language of everyday life." (Giorgi 2018, p. 27). The scientific attitude towards phenomena is quite different from the "natural attitude" exhibited by common people in everyday life, populated by common sense and "horse sense". Phenomenology has the same problem as empiricism, i. e., how to escape the "natural attitude". But " … the solution it tries out is the opposite of the theoretical and the objectifying, where the emotions are barred and the lived experience cleansed. Phenomenology looks for an a-theoretical comportment and interpretation beyond the natural attitude …" (Ciborra 2009/2004)[3].

With respect to the theme of scientific rigour: empiricism contains a remnant of uncertainty in the choice of theory, hermeneutics in the choice of interpretation. Uncertainty can be reduced with objectivist criteria: by being methodic, systematic, general, critical, and by sharing and verification with others. These do not concern theorising or interpreting in particular, and those vulnerabilities remain in part. Descriptive phenomenology, conversely, can attain full scientific precision concerning facts-in-the-conscience, while its connection to the real world necessitates further scrutiny. Addressing, and responding to this vulnerability empowers descriptive phenomenology to establish scientific substantiation. We do it reverting to community of practice members.

3. THE PHENOMENOLOGICAL APPROACH, DELVED AND EXEMPLIFIED

So, we need assume the phenomenological stance.

A century has passed since Husserl's assertion (1982/1913, 1974) regarding Transcendental Phenomenology as the foundational philosophy for all sciences, including human sciences. Husserl's research based on Phenomenology has, indeed, been able to capture the distinctively "human" aspect.

We shall describe Husserl's descriptive phenomenological philosophy in some detail, including Giorgi's modified approach of the DPM method for scientific rigour. Then the example of application of DPM.

Husserl's phenomenology, philosophical foundation of human sciences. The strength of Husserl's innovative philosophy (1982/1913, 1970a, 1070b, 1974, 1977, 1991; Giorgi 1983) is that facts from researcher's conscience, transcending natural objects, are considered just as real as those regarding natural

[3] Note Ciborra's usage in this remark of the word phenomenology: he is implicitly including in it (his own) hermeneutics approach, at variance with our choice of word usage in this paper. Our choice of usage follows Giorgi's.

objects. Husserl's phenomenology concentrates on what is essential of a phenomenon, accurately describing it, clarifying the meaning of its essence: description, not interpretation, not construction, not explanation. Descriptions of the essence of phenomena are taken as real, scientifically sound. When carefully cleaned by phenomenological epoché (no reference to expectations from past experience) and transcendental reduction (no preoccupation of actual reality). Found in their factical details, guided by subject's intention, illuminated by discovery through phenomenological intuition, shared by intersubjective dialogue with participating research community, and subject to free imaginative variations. (Giorgi, Giorgi, and Morley 2017). We shall keep this in mind in the following (Subsection 3.1).

Giorgi's modified approach: the DPM method for scientific rigour. "Since Husserl's method is philosophical, any strict application of this method will produce philosophical results. As psychologists, we desire results that are psychological and scientific, not philosophical; consequently, some modifications were made to Husserl's method in order to produce results that are scientific and psychological, ..." (Giorgi 2018, p.21), transforming the meaning units into phenomenological AND sensitive expressions in the discipline of interest (for Giorgi, psychologically). But the relevance of Giorgi's DPM approach is not limited to Psychology.

3.1 An Example of Application of the DPM Approach into a QE

The example we present for the application of DPM/QE to ST research, employs the DPM method in order to assist in the selection of appropriate design-choices in carrying out a Query Experiment (QE), ensuring that Giorgi's conditions for scientific rigour be in fact met in each experiment detail. The paper in question (Jacucci 2020) examines the utilisation of a tailored scaffolding support within a clinic's information infrastructure. This support facilitates the promotion and documentation of therapists' descriptive data, expressed in their expertly trained professional language, based on their subjective observations, objectively carried out in a professional-psychologist attitude, while intuitively and inseparably merging (part of) the analysis with the observation. This process forms an integral part of a meticulous and precise descriptive phenomenological investigation into a child's behaviour during treatment. Human reporting and (the remaining part of) the analytical functions are executed through the information infrastructure, which solidifies, for analysis automation, select aspects of the intended human actions. Scaffolding structures and functions, particularly the Daily Treatment Notes (DTN), are accurately designed to meticulously capture, record, and restore the original conscious events and meanings. This encompasses both the observation of the phenomenon and the subsequent analysis of the child's behaviour data.

The key strength of this approach, facilitating the application of Giorgi's scientific method (Giorgi, Giorgi, and Morley 2017) by researchers, lies in the utilisation of the conceptual framework employed by therapists within their specific therapeutic practice. Specifically, the Developmental, Individual differences, Relational (DIR)/floortime treatment psychological theory developed by Greenspan and Wieder (1997, 1998, 2006) forms the basis for articulating child development behaviour across distinct Functional Emotional Development Levels (FEDL). Of paramount significance are the particulars of uncompromising details of the FEDL scale, and the structure of the DTN, that suppress subjective biases. These are fully elucidated in the paper (Jacucci 2020). These aspects are communally shared within the proficient therapist community of the clinic, functioning as a cohesive Community of Practice (Lave and Wenger 1991; Wenger 1998) and benefiting from a Web of Shared Understanding (Baskin 1999). This shared framework acts as the dedicated scaffolding support, enabling the accurate encapsulation of therapists' insights using their own conceptual terms, while simultaneously ensuring adherence to Giorgi's stipulations (Giorgi, Giorgi, and Morley 2017). This framework inherently provides a means to control for essential scientific dimensions as prescribed by Giorgi's method: (a) transcending immediate sensory data, (b) disregarding common sense biases, and (c) proactively considering the potential influence of relevant free imaginative variations on the essence of the phenomena. Devoid of the efficacy underpinning the FEDL theoretical framework and DTN, it would all amount to potentially valuable but haphazardly collected and reported opinions.

Summing up the crucial design choices of the experiment: observers-analysts performing in the professional attitude, members of the same community of practice, sharing the understanding of the conceptual structure of their profession as personal knowledge, characterised by uncompromising details, incorporated in the scaffolding information system (IS) that records their notes. We go in depth with a few considerations below.

Let's see the Results of this QE experiment. The analysis aimed to derive overall meaning from DTN data, specifically by summing the differences in Likert scale values for each FEDL level before and after treatment. Statistical averaging helped distill a clear outcome. The average difference of values before and after treatment, calculated across all 75 entries—five therapists, five children per therapist, three FEDL sub-step values per child (5x5x3)—is distinctly positive, with an average value change of +0.33 units; accounting for an error, calculated as the mean square deviation (0.4 units) divided by the square root of 75, of+/-0.05 units. Therapists' reports the validity of the DIR treatment:

"We affirm its reality" (+0.33 +/-0.05 units)

The resultant impact is positive, with a final mean value some seven standard deviations away from the control point (0.0 units). This positive trend is denoted as "significantly above statistical noise," a robust finding in any quantitative inquiry. Therapists' subjective knowledge is firmly grounded in scientific, rigorous, objective foundations. This opens avenues for future experimentation with greater statistical weight over extended timeframes, and larger therapist-child cohorts, and confirmation through comparable, independent experiments (Jacucci 2020).

Free imaginative variations, critically extracting valid results. Three circumstances stand as evident candidates for significative, free imaginative variations: 1) the DIR theory, 2) the FEDL scale, 3) the clinic in which the experiment is conducted. After which, the resulting general meaning of the experiment are robust and stable upon "free imaginative variations" of contextual conditions.

One: Reference theory. Naturally the aligned structures of personal knowledge and mirroring reporting artefact cannot necessarily correspond meticulously to the structure and nature of the real world. And, the rigorously scientific answer of the experiment to the original question might be dependent on them. If the chosen knowledge structure is not too far from reality, the answer will be nonetheless meaningful, thus satisfying the QE question with scientific rigour.

Two: FEDL scale. This holds true for diverse Likert scale selections or even modifications to the DTN structure, within certain confines.

Three: Clinic. Envisioning the experiment conducted in an alternate DIR clinic with different organisational, cultural, and therapist training dynamics prompts a different perspective. Here, we acknowledge a limitation: the QE experiment simultaneously informs us about the efficacy of DIR as well as the proficiency of the specific DIR clinic under scrutiny. If the answer is affirmative, it signifies the effectiveness of DIR treatments, and the quality of the clinic at the same time. Yet it does not guarantee the outcomes of experiments in other clinics.

Consideration #1: Connection to the real world . We anticipated that the connection to the real world requires, in principle, further analysis. In experiment 3.1, this is done through criticality, achieved through A) the utilisation of a well-established developmental scale, universally understood by all therapists in their practice, and B) the participation of therapists from the same community of practice, immersed in the shared (Greenspan's) therapeutic culture. The centrality of critical conditions lies in its capacity of establishing a genuine connection and adherence to the tangible world. This framework leaves no room for preconceptions or illusions in the observations of expert therapists. And, we see no room for cultural bias, in applying the FEDL scale: it details as objective facts children behaviours, in order of appearance during development in our culture.

Consideration #2: FEDL scale in DTN helps respect ethnomethodology. The utilisation of routine conceptual language hold profound importance in ethnomethodology. Therapists convey observations of child behaviour within DTN using the language specific to their therapeutic practice and profession. We cite phenomenologist Harold Garfinkel, the pioneer in ethnomethodology: "The ensuing studies seek to treat practical activities, practical circumstances, and practical sociological reasoning as subjects of empirical study. By bestowing attention on everyday life's most ordinary activities with the same scrutiny reserved for extraordinary events, we endeavor to understand them as phenomena in their own right. The central assertion is that the procedures by which members generate and manage organized daily affairs settings are identical to members' processes for rendering those settings 'account-able'" (Garfinkel 1967, p. 1). In the QE of 5.5, the language, structure, and scale employed to depict child development (accounting) align with the clinical treatment (management) language, structure, and scale. While this fact ensures exact correspondence between observed and described, and absence of alterations in recording, the uncompromising details warrant control of subjective biases.

Consideration #3: The DIR treatment assessed as Evidence Based Practice. This most promising treatment, DIR, based on parent involvement, is not currently supported by public health care in the Western world, as it is not yet declared an Evidence-Based-Practice (EBP), due to the difficulty of scientifically controlling parent behaviour.An EDP declaration can now be claimed by this experimental outcome, using subjective data.

4. THE QUERY EXPERIMENT (QE): WHY DOES IT WORK? WHAT IS ITS USE?

What is the lesson to be learned from the experiment described in section 3.1? To utilise Giorgi's DPM in QE to get direct, scientifically rigorous experimental answers to questions of interest. Let us discuss the merit of this.

Realising a QE requires a situation in which:

A. the Query Experiment field exhibits a dedicated professional Community Of Practice (COP)

B. the COP possesses a theoretical Conceptual Framework (CF), routinely use in their practice

C. the Query can be expressed in the language of that theoretical CF

D. an IS platform can be constructed employing the CF language to capture answers from COP members

In the paediatric example: A. the DIR occupational therapists are the COP, B. their FEDL scale is the CF, C. the level of child development is precisely expressible in the FEDL language, D. the clinic DTN constitute the IS platform. How do these concepts relate to Giorgi's DPM criteria of rigour?

At times, the aim in pursuing the objectives of a human science might not be just to rigorously unveil the genuine nature of a particular phenomenon. Instead, the objective might be to obtain a rigorously scientific answer to a specific question—one that might not be framed in the actual terms of the still-unknown phenomenon. In such cases, one might forego the privilege of phenomenological intuition's ability to meticulously uncover the true nature of the phenomenon, in exchange for the capacity to precisely obtain, with scientific rigour, an answer to the specific question of interest. This question can only be formulated in the context of an approximate, available theory, which can be employed as a point of reference in the experiment. A theory not to be 'bracketed', but used as comparison, while observing and intuiting.

The delineation of roles in data acquisition and experiment analysis, distinguishing between the observer and the researcher, and the shift of phenomenological intuition from the observer to the researcher, are not necessarily the only configurations assumable in scientific experiments. In the instance described in 5.5, for example, it is advantageous to maintain observation and analysis in direct contact, precisely at the juncture of professional intuition. In such a case, directly applying the scientific controls inherent in Giorgi's DPM to the activities of this individual proves to be essential.

Thanks to the affiliation and live and active belonging to a community of practice, the therapists' personal professional knowledge (Polanyi 1964, 1969) grants the pure rendition of the object by their immediate intuition in front of the phenomenon, correctly reported because of the alignment, by design, between structure of personal knowledge and structure of reporting artefact. This framework is distinguished by its explicit meanings, leaving no room for uncertainty. Through their informed expertise, therapists possess a learned personal insight. Their observant and professional depiction of child behaviour is rooted in a conscientious and unbiased approach. This approach, driven by intention and intuition, aligns as phenomenological.

This as an authentic, direct application of the rigid requirements of Giorgi's method, extended to a scenario where truth doesn't emerge within an uncharted realm of consciousness, but instead surfaces within the context of a well-established conceptual framework – a scaffold nurtured by therapists' professional proficiency and shared within their community of practice. Part of data analysis is thus fused with the intuition of the therapist observers adopting a professional attitude, while their personal professional knowledge, structured in uncompromising details, fosters the absence of biases, hallucinations, or the interference of common sense. The rest of the accurate data analysis resorts by design to details of the information infrastructure. In this way, the requisites of DPM, including an attitude sensitive to the phenomenon, parsing descriptions in meaning units while keeping a sense of the whole, transforming meaning units into sensitive expressions within the discipline, resilience against contamination and free imaginative variations, assure the integrity of the scientific inquiry. This approach holds the potential to resonate credibly within the concerned professional communities.

QE is a good candidate to address the issues of method raised in ST research. (Ricciardi 2008, 2009).

5. ECHOES OF HUSSERL'S, HEIDEGGER'S, AND GIORGI'S WORDS

Following Husserl and his phenomenological philosophical principles, Giorgi with DPM has provided the world with a method granted to achieve scientific rigour in human disciplines. The 'Scientific-Subjective View' is a gap in ST research to be filled by DPM's QE. That much said, we are now in a position to enjoy with serenity some flashes of authentic *joy of the truth*, from the founding fathers of phenomenology.

Summing up what Husserl, Heidegger, and Giorgi state: Life must be **"... understood in a primal scientific way as leaping out from its source." "... the conceptuality of the object ... (is) drawn out of the mode *in which the object is originally accessible. ...*" " ... Even though the results are expressed in terms of "lived meanings", they have the solidity of facts."** Let us consider their message in detail:

Descriptive phenomenology is in an advantageous situation for scientificity, because description resides at the beginning of the conscious event: **" ... the conceptuality of the object ... must be drawn out of the mode *in which the object is originally accessible",*** Heidegger declares (1962, p.17).. And, as Giorgi points out (2018, p. 30): Because it is descriptive, phenomenology's claim is epistemologically stronger: it says that this is how things present themselves to acts of consciousness. .... Consequently, while grounded theory comes up with theories and hermeneutics results in interpretations, phenomenology's descriptive psychological approach emphasizes presentational findings. **Even though the results are expressed in terms of "lived meanings", they have the solidity of facts.** The claim is made that the experiences were actually lived in the light of the discovered meanings".

Husserl's 'principle of all principles' says with precision the role of intuition in scientific endeavours: " ... *all philosophical pronouncements must be grounded in something immediately accessible to us*." " ... the logic of the grasp of the object, and the conceptuality of the object ... must be drawn out of the mode *in which the object is originally accessible*. Also decisive for the definition of the life situation in which the object comes to be experienced and, further, the basic intention in which the experience from the outset aims at the object (how the sense of the situation and of the anticipatory intentional grasp (the preconception)) is given 'its due'" (Heidegger 1962, p.17). **Life, thus, must be "understood in a primal scientific way as leaping out from its source"** (Heidegger 2002, p. 82). "The here and now of the situation offers such a primordial insight into life." (Guignon , p.86)

Our task for Heidegger: *"how do we teach each other speak objectively about these subjective things?"*

"'Letting things be' is the theme Heidegger writes a great deal about in his post-World War II writings, but it is only another way of reciting the principal phenomenological slogan from Being and Time, "To the things themselves!" Our work of making social inquiries is not irrelevant, because we have the important descriptive task, Heidegger tells us, of raising "the phenomenal content of disclosure existentially to a conceptual level". ...... That is, our thinking must be kept appropriate to the events we are describing, and we must avoid submerging those events beneath our brilliant plans and theories, but we still need to reflect formally upon them. So now have our most serious task – **how do we teach each other speak objectively about these subjective things?**" (Lieberman *et al.*, 2009).

6. CONCLUSIONS

In the paediatric example, we enforced a standardised, precise, operational, repeatable expression of child behaviour descriptions by participating therapists, with use of descriptive features and meanings familiar to their practice, and translated data and results from qualitative to quantitative language, to allow for seamless comparison and averaging. This path brought scientific value to transcendental phenomenology approaches—enacted with scientific methodology—establishing as objective subjectively perceived facts in the individual conscience of people in a specific group. With Giorgi's DPM and our QE, we turned an information-system-based methodology into a legitimate candidate for assessment studies, acting on an appropriately chosen group of individuals. Providing positive evidence for the effectiveness of a sophisticated treatment approach for special children, based on parent involvement: the DIR-based clinical treatment, supporting this practice as EBP, an Evidence Based Practice. A fact not yet accepted by the professions concerned, as the usual approach to EBP, based on objective monitoring of the treatment arena, fails for the impossibility of scientific control of parent behaviour, during the objectivist EBP test. Not an EBP then, up to now, albeit all involved therapists volunteer positive indications: ***"We affirm its reality"***. Now an EBP, as we correctly collect their opinion turning it into science.

- **QEs: Our path towards scientific rigour**

We have adopted Giorgi's DPM as a litmus test in QEs for obtaining scientific rigour in the acquisition and analysis of facts-in-the-conscience type of subjective data. We design an original path, utilising in QEs the conceptual apparatus for scientific rigour of Giorgi's DPM, while the conscience of the operating professionals hosts the presence of the professional knowledge structure, as scaffold for confronting and comparing the phenomenon; within a modified scheme of play exhibiting coalescence of observation and analysis. With this machinery, reminder of the Actor Network Theory (ANT) (Latour 1999), we encompass the assessment of Evidence Based Practice for an advanced treatment of child developmental differences.

- **QEs: the presence-at-hand, in the subject's conscience, of a tacit knowledge structure, within a changed scheme of play: observe and analyse together**

More than one avenue exists in fact to utilise DPM for science in the making: adhere to using Giorgi's method as defined, or employ it as a guide to construct QE experiments that ensure scientific credibility, as we show. Either way, DPM guarantees scientific rigour. QEs are an authentic application of Giorgi's criteria, extended to a scenario where truth doesn't emerge within an uncharted realm of consciousness, but instead surfaces within the context of a well-established conceptual framework – a scaffold nurtured by therapists' professional proficiency and shared within their community of practice. This enables professionals performing in the professional attitude in QEs, to obtain results phenomenologically and also scientifically correct.

- **Utilising of Giorgi's DPM and QEs for scientific rigour in treating facts-in-the-conscience**

Following Husserl and his phenomenological philosophical principles, Giorgi with DPM has provided the world with a method granted to achieve scientific rigour in human disciplines. The emphasis now is on method: only pairing Giorgi's DPM method and QEs will foster acceptance of phenomenology as an approach to the subjective world of human conscience, granting scientific rigour in investigations and crucial research experiments. The quest for scientifically acceptable qualitative research methods is evident for all to see. Leveraging on aspects of method is the way towards greater acceptance of phenomenology as philosophical basis of S-T Research. A gap exists that requires filling—let's embrace this challenge, using phenomenology, DPM, and QEs.

REFERENCES

Baskin, A. (1999). Preface. In A. Baskin, G. Kovacs, & G. Jacucci G. (Eds.), *Cooperative knowledge processing in engineering design* (pp. xvii–xx). IFIP, Kluxers Academic Publishers.

Bednar, P, and Welch, C. (2006) Second Order Discourse: Critically Informed Research. ECRM2006. https://www.researchgate.net/publication/264057721_Second_order_discourse_critically-informed_research.

Ciborra, C. (2004/2009) *The Mind or the heart? It depends on the (Definition of) Situation. in Bricolage, Care and Information, Claudio Ciborra's Legacy in Information Systems Research*, by Chrisanthi Avgerou, Giovan Francesco Lanzara and Leslie P. Wilcoks, Palgrave, London and New York, 2009, See also *http://projectsfinal.interaction-ivrea.it/web/2004_2005.html*

Gadamer, H.-G. (1975). Truth and method. London: Sheed and Ward (Original publ. in 1960)

Garfinkel, H. (1967). *Studies in Ethnomethodology*. Paradigm Publishers.

Giorgi, A. (1970). *Psychology as a human science: A phenomenologically based approach*. Harper & Row.

Giorgi, A. (1983) *Concerning The Possibility Of Phenomenological Psychological Research*, Journal of Phenomenological Psychology 14(1) 129-169.

Giorgi, A. (2009). *The descriptive phenomenological method in psychology: A modified Husserlian approach*. Duquesne University Press.

Giorgi, A. (2018). *Reflections on certain qualitative and phenomenological psychological methods*. University Professors Press.

Giorgi, A., Giorgi, B, and Morley, J. (2017*). The Descriptive Phenomenological Psychological Method*, BK-SAGE WILIG_STAINTON-170067 CH11 indd 176-192.

Greenspan, S. I., & Wieder, S. (1997). Developmental patterns and outcomes in infants and children with disorders in relating and communicating: A chart review of 200 cases of children with autistic spectrum diagnoses. *The Journal of Developmental and Learning Disorders*, 1, 87–141.

Greenspan, S. I., & Wieder, S. (1998). *The Child with Special Needs*. Da Capo Press.

Greenspan, S. I., & Wieder, S. (2006). *Engaging Autism.* Da Capo Press.

Guignon, C. (2002) Philosophy and Authenticity: Heidegger's Search for a Ground for Philosophising. In M. Wrathall and J. Malpas (eds), Heidegger, Authenticity and Modernity, Vol. 1, The MIT Press 79-101

Heidegger, M. (1962). *Being and Time* (J. Macquarrie & E. Robinson, Trans.). SCM Press.

Heidegger, M. (2002) Gesamtausgabe - Band 18 - Grundbegriffe der Aristotelischen Philosophie (1924) Frankfurt am Main: V. Klostermann.

Husserl, E. (1970a) Logical investigations. Humanities Press.

Husserl, E. (1970b). *The crisis of European sciences and transcendental phenomenology: An introduction to phenomenological philosophy* (D. Carr, Trans.). Northwestern University Press.

Husserl, E. (1974) Kant and the idea of transcenden- tal philosophy. (Trans. T.E. Klein and W.E. Pohl). The Southwestern Journal of Philosophy, 5 (3): 9–56. (German original, 1923/24).

Husserl, E. (1977) Phenomenological psychology. (Trans. J. Scanlon). The Hague: Martinus Nijhoff Publishers. (German original, 1962).

Husserl, E. (1982*). Ideas pertaining to a pure phenomenology and to a phenomenological philosophy: First Book: General introduction to a pure phenomenology* (F. Kersten, Trans.). Kluwer Academic Publishers. (Original work published in 1913)

Husserl, E. (1991) On the phenomenology of the consciousness of internal time (1893–1917). (Trans. J.B. Brough). Dordrecht: Kluwer Academic Publishers. (German original, 1966).

Jacucci, G. (2015). Autopoisis and cognition, an outstanding outcome of phenomenology: What is in it for a physicist? [Seminar]. GBB.60.workshop, Rome, Italy. https://www.academia.edu/12204390/

Jacucci, G. (2020). "We know it is real": harvesting consciousness with a descriptive information system. http://www.itais.org/ITAIS2020_proceedings/pdf/24.pdf

Latour. B. (1999). On recalling ANT. in ANT and after J.Law and J. Hassard eds. Blackwell.

Lave, J., & Wenger, E. (1991). *Situated learning*. Cambridge University Press.

Lieberman, K., Fele, G., D'Andrea, V., Campagnolo, G. M., Curzi, Y., & Viscusi G. (2009). Phenomenology and the social study of information systems: Conversations with Kenneth Liberman. *Università deli Studi di Trento, Dipartimento di Sociologia e Ricerca Sociale, Quaderno*, 46, 11–24. https://www.researchgate.net/publication/38959539_Phenomenology_and_the_Social_Study_of_Information_Systems_Conversations_with_Kenneth_Liberman

Maturana, H., and Varela F. (1979) Autopoiesis and Cognition: The Realization of the Living. Boston Studies in the Philosophy of Science. Paperback.

Palmer, R. E. (1969) Hermeneutics. Northwestern University Press.

Polanyi, M. (1966). *The tacit dimension*. Routledge & Kegan Paul.

Polanyi, M. (1969). *Knowing and being*. Routledge & Kegan Paul.

Ricciardi, F. (2008) The tacking knowledge strategy. Claudio Ciborra, Konrad Lorenz and the ecology of IS, Interdisciplinary Aspects of Information Systems Studies, Springer.

Ricciardi, F. (2009) Epistemology of Information Systems: Time for Something New? Positivism, Interpretivism, and Beyond, in: A. D'Atri & D. Saccà (ed.), IS: People, Organizations, Institutions, and Technologies. Springer. 267-275,.

Wenger, E. (1998). *Communities of Practice*. Cambridge University Press.

UTILIZING STRATIFIED SYSTEMS THEORY TO OPTIMIZE WORKFORCE ALLOCATION FOR SUSTAINABLE QUALITY DELIVERY IN DEVOPS TEAMS: A CASE STUDY

Hanlie Smuts[1], Paul Louw[2], Danie Smit[1,2], Ingo Waechter[2] and Vanessa Sardinha-da Silva[2]
[1]*University of Pretoria, Pretoria, South Africa*
[2]*BMW Group IT ZA Hub, Menlyn Maine, Pretoria, South Africa*

ABSTRACT

Software development, integration, deployment, and operational management require various complex skill sets. Furthermore, organizations are expected to deliver product-based applications and services faster than traditional software development processes, within specific cost, speed, and quality parameters. Given these challenges, information technology (IT) organizations structure their software teams around development and operations (DevOps). As software development for different product lines carries different levels of complexity, the optimal DevOps workforce mix becomes a key consideration. In this case study, we designed a generic DevOps workforce mix profile for product line delivery by applying stratified systems theory as a common language reflecting weighted drivers of workforce mix. We then compared actual workforce data to the generic DevOps workforce mix profile to establish optimal fit. We propose a set of repeatable guidelines to enhance organizations' understanding of the over- and under-representation of DevOps workforce mix allocation. Through an improved understanding, organizations may staff teams with an optimal balance between seniority, quality delivery, and operational costs and inform talent development and allocation strategies.

KEYWORDS

Stratified Systems Theory, Workforce Optimization, Sustainability, DevOps Workforce Allocation

1. INTRODUCTION

Changing technologies and new ways of working are disrupting employees' jobs and current skill sets; consequently, organizations face potential shortages of skills critical to growing their business (Agrawal et al., 2020). As a result, organizations have the challenge of managing talent and staff teams with people with the right skills and skill levels (Wiblen and Marler, 2019, Dery and Sebastian, 2017). Additionally, worldwide economic pressures are forcing organizations to examine their IT team structures and how they are organized (Yu and Zhou, 2021, Larson and DeChurch, 2020). This is also the case for major technology companies such as Twitter (Forbes, 2022) and Meta (Meta, 2023). Organizations that fail to optimize their team allocations within this context are considered inefficient (Barambones et al., 2021).

Given these challenges, IT organizations structure their software teams around development and operations (DevOps), exploiting a combination of practices and tools designed to increase the organization's ability to deliver applications and services faster than traditional software development processes (Senapathi et al., 2018, Lwakatare et al., 2016). Such a DevOps team incorporates developers and IT operations employees working collaboratively throughout a software product's lifecycle. The DevOps team allocation attempts to address organizational structures that hinder cross-functional alignment across different subunits within the IT function (Jabbari et al., 2016, Wiedemann et al., 2020).

According to López-Fernández et al. (2021), how to organize and structure DevOps teams remains a challenge. Hence, for an enhanced understanding of the optimal workforce allocation of such a DevOps team for sustainable quality delivery, the objective of this case study was to investigate the optimal DevOps workforce mix by considering the research question "*What is the optimal workforce allocation to enable sustainable quality delivery in a DevOps team*?". Since the workforce in an organization is not unlimited, the optimal staffing of teams becomes an organizational requirement (Marnewick and Langerman, 2020, López-Fernández et al., 2021). By understanding the optimal workforce allocation, organizations will be able to staff teams with an optimal balance between seniority, quality delivery, and operational costs.

The rest of this paper is structured as follows: In Section 2, we provide the background to this research paper, and in Section 3, we describe the research methodology. The data analysis and findings are discussed in Section 4, the contribution in Section 5, and Section 6 concludes the paper.

2. BACKGROUND

Software development, integration, deployment, and operational management require various and complex skill sets (Alawneh and Abbadi, 2022). Organizations would typically allocate dedicated teams to each of these skill sets and enforce the separation of duties according to the organizational structure. However, this separation of duties introduces several challenges, such as operational performance issues, lack of multiple rapidly timed software releases, and unforeseen security threats (Kuusinen et al., 2018). In this context, DevOps is a change in mindset for disjointed teams, enabling higher resilience, team elasticity, improved performance, and sped-up delivery processes (Alawneh and Abbadi, 2022).

2.1 Optimal Workforce Allocation

Software businesses are redirecting their expansion toward service-oriented business models (Sousa et al., 2015). Developers strive to enhance the systems, while simultaneously focusing their efforts on the fundamental concepts of collaboration, automation, and iteration (Duffy, 2015). While testing the systems, developers and operations teams learn from their previous code failures and problems. Based on the system feedback and recommendations, software developers and operations teams improve their level of performance quickly, which reduces the effort, budget and time required for deployment (Ogala, 2022). These quick cycles have been extended to incorporate a focus on automation and software tools for rapid deployment in lean-agile frameworks. By adopting the agile approach, emphasising software integration, iteration, delivery, and deployment, the automation process enables teams to attend to designing optimal procedures (Ogala, 2022).

Development, deployment, infrastructure, operations, and monitoring team members' work on various items of a software product (Alawneh and Abbadi, 2022). To deliver product-related services, these product-oriented teams must establish dedicated service units interfacing with customers (internal or external) and working closely with them (Dakkak et al., 2023). The optimal approach of control–alignment in product-oriented cross-functional teams is important, as neglecting one control part of interdependent work outputs would lead to misalignment (Wiedemann et al., 2019).

By integrating cross-functional teams, DevOps bridges functional silo software development and operations units accountable for planning, building, and running system processes and delivery lifecycles. Stability and quality of new software features, as well as faster time to market, are achieved by cross-functional teams through the integration of the operations and software planning phases (Wiedemann et al., 2019).

2.2 Sustainable Quality Delivery

DevOps as a concept is associated with both non-technical and technical practices (Lwakatare et al., 2019) and represents a potential answer to quality and time limitations in software development (Wiedemann et al., 2020). The purpose of DevOps is to increase the speed, quality and frequency of software delivery using automated procedures (Jha et al., 2023). Furthermore, product orientation for DevOps teams aims to achieve the balance between innovation and stability and between speed of delivery and quality (Liang, 2021, Sharma, 2017). To understand how DevOps teams achieve a high level of product orientation, the complexity of the product, level of quality delivery required, associated cost, and long-term sustainability of the team must be considered (Ebert et al., 2016). Consequentially, even though a DevOps team is controlled by a team leader, the team members are also required to manage themselves within the team, often supported by technology (Wiedemann et al., 2019).

Creating a DevOps culture poses a challenge due to the substantial adjustments required in work approaches and collaboration amidst contextual variations (Jha et al., 2023). In product organization, vertical divisions that are fully responsible must maintain self-contained operations throughout the entire lifecycle. This entails a diverse skill set accountable from concept to completion (Feijter et al., 2017). The role that encompasses the entire process involves constantly adjusting to evolving circumstances, such as shifts in customer needs, alterations in legislation, and the introduction of new technologies. Within a DevOps culture, there is a notable focus on ongoing enhancements to minimize inefficiencies, optimize speed, cost, and smooth handovers, and consistently elevate the quality of products and services. Consequently, experimentation stands as a crucial endeavor for integrating and fostering a learning-oriented approach by gaining insights from errors (Jha et al., 2023).

2.3 Stratified Systems Theory

This paper aims to identify a mechanism for optimal DevOps workforce allocation, enabling sustainable quality delivery. Scholars have investigated different approaches to optimal DevOps implementation. Hamzane and Khalyly (2021) investigated which IT governance methods informed the deployment of DevOps teams. However, this approach did not take cognizance of the appointed workforce's job roles and capabilities. Others investigated a specific yet narrow focus for DevOps implementation, such as the Internet of Things (López-Peña et al., 2020), cloud computing (Wettinger et al., 2016) or information management systems (Qumer Gill et al., 2018).

For this study, we utilized stratified systems theory (SST), defined by Elliott Jaques, as it provides a common classification system for various occupations (Jaques, 1986). SST offers a framework for understanding human capability and the cognitive processes required for individuals to plan and execute goal-directed activities bound by quality, time, and cost within levels of discretion that require judgment and intuition (Jaques, 2017). The foundation of SST is that, as individuals achieve varying points in cognitive power, they draw from different states of cognitive functioning, such as shaping, reflection, articulation, extrapolation, and transformation (Jaques, 2017). The interrelationship between cognitive power and cognitive functioning is depicted in Table 1 as seven hierarchical strata of increasing complexity of work that require greater abstractive capabilities.

Table 1. Hierarchical strata of increasing complexity of work (reproduced and adapted from ((Jaques, 2017))

Stratum	Work complexity	Cognitive mechanism	Work theme	Capability
1	Perform one task at a time. Daily, weekly, and monthly quotas	Concrete shaping, concrete thinking, linear pathways	Quality	Cost Reduction (Touch and Feel)
2	Direct an aggregate of tasks. Diagnose problems	Reflective articulation, formulate new ideas, handle ambiguity	Service	Cost Control (Accumulation)
3	Direct one operating subsystem. Predict shorter-term needs	Linear extrapolation, alternate pathways	Practice	Cost Efficiency (Connecting)
4	Oversee operating subsystems. Design new methods and policies	Develop alternative systems, abstract from data, parallel processing	Strategic Development	Value Control (Modelling)
5	Command one complex system. Connections to environments	Shape and reshape whole systems, boundaries. Utilize theory	Strategic Intent	Value Creation (Weaving)
6	Oversee complex systems, groups of business units. Plan long-term strategy	Reflective articulation between systems. Higher conceptual approaches	Corporate Citizenship	Organizational viability (Revealing)
7	Construct complex systems. Construct versus predict future	Linear extrapolation. Develop new theories	Corporate Prescience	Industry shaping (Previewing)

Table 1 summarizes the seven strata of work, work complexity, cognitive mechanisms, work themes, and associated capabilities. The SST framework is particularly applicable to organizations with complex and stratified hierarchies through which they manage their workforce (Bezuidenhout et al., 2021, Törnblom et al., 2018).

3. MATERIALS AND METHODS

The organization where the case study was executed is a manufacturer of premium automobiles and a provider of mobility services. The case study organization is a worldwide digital transformation leader transforming its IT into fully agile and its DevOps into becoming more flexible, customer-centric, and value-driven. In addition, the case study organization also moved from projects to products and from bimodal IT to DevOps, ensuring complete collaboration and transparency between IT and the business. It has structured its IT portfolio around products and value streams and introduced new technologies to support microservice and cloud-based architectures to gradually replace its legacy monolithic applications. The case study organization supports open-source technology for its data ecosystem, which is key for portability, interoperability, interconnectivity, and data sovereignty (ARC Advisory Group, 2022).

The main objective of this case study was to identify a mechanism for optimal DevOps workforce allocation, enabling sustainable quality delivery. We achieved this outcome by following a design science research (DSR) approach and, in particular, the approach proposed by Hevner (2007) consisting of three cycles: the relevance cycle (contextual environment of the study presented in Section 2.1), the rigor cycle (extract relevant knowledge base of scientific foundations, experience, and expertise that informs the research project highlighted in Section 2.2) and the design cycle (Hevner, 2007). The design cycle iterates between the core activities of building and evaluating the design artifacts and processes of the research. For the design cycle, we followed the processes suggested by Frey and Osborne (2017) and Bezuidenhout et al. (2021) that combined the classification of occupations based on strata of work with a predictive model. Specifically, we executed two design (build) steps: (1) define drivers of the case organization's occupations and (2) define the case organization's DevOps occupation labels and consequential generic DevOps workforce mix profile. For the evaluation step, we analyzed workforce human resources data (HRD) and compared it to the design. The research approach we followed is visualized in Figure 1.

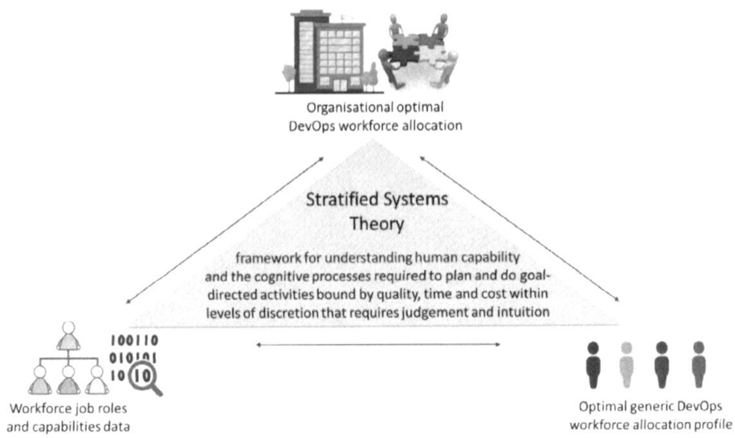

Figure 1. Research approach (Source: authors' visualization)

Figure 1 also emphasizes the interrelationship among optimal DevOps workforce mix allocation, skills, and competencies, as well as job roles to which employees are appointed and the generic DevOps workforce mix profile. The organization wishes to optimize deployment time, budget, and effort and appoint employees in organizational structures and job roles to achieve organizational outcomes. Simultaneously, the organization requires an optimal DevOps workforce mix to achieve the desired organizational outcomes. Finally, employees, together with their job roles and capabilities, are allocated to the optimal generic DevOps workforce mix profiles. For these interrelationships to be made explicit and manageable, the SST is applied, as shown in the center of Figure 1, to create a common language among these three aspects and enable mapping among the entities.

3.1 Drivers of the Case Organization's Workforce Mix

The case study organization applies drivers of the workforce mix. The aim of the workforce mix was to balance cost optimization, skills retention, and high-quality delivery. The drivers of the workforce mix include complexity (the complexity of the product), process knowledge (associated with the product), network (refers to the size of the network required to get the work done), criticality (the unavailability of the DevOps product in time has a severe impact on the organization's performance, e.g., impact on the start of production, sales, finances), and maturity level (high maturity as a product or low maturity). In addition, a particular weight, as determined by the case study organization, was allocated to each driver, summarized in Table 2. The weight allocation aligns with the process executed by Karemera and Ngubiri (2012) and Malik and Bilberg (2019) (human–robot collaborative assembly), whereby allocation is based on tasks and actors that are not necessarily homogeneous, and the allocation ceilings are based on weights rather than numbers.

Table 2. Drivers and associated weighting of workforce mix of DevOps team (Source: case study organization)

Driver	Driver of workforce mix	Associated weighting of drivers per DevOps team
1	complexity	25%
2	process knowledge	20%
3	network	10%
4	criticality	25%
5	maturity level	20%

The complexity and criticality of the product under development carry the highest weight of 25% since the more complex and critical the product is, the more time and resources it would require to design, develop, test, and implement. This investment in time and resources can be a significant challenge for the case study organization as it implements its IT strategy and manages ever-growing customer demands.

3.2 Definition of Case Organization's DevOps Occupation Label

To determine the optimal workforce mix for the DevOps development teams of the case study organization, the SST strata (refer to Section 2.3 and Table 1) were applied to determine the occupation that should form part of a DevOps team, as the SST strata provide a common classification system for various job roles. The advantage of mapping the case study organization occupations to a common classification system is that any job role (e.g., system engineer, solution architect, agile master, product manager, etc.) is associated with a particular SST stratum, and it provides the common ground for job analysis, pay grade association, accountability, and seniority.

The proposed mapping of the SST strata to the case study organization's DevOps team occupations is shown in Table 3.

Table 3. Mapping of case study organization's DevOps occupations to SST strata

SST Stratum	SST Work theme	Case study organizations DevOps team occupation label and years of experience	
1	Quality	Entry level	0–2 years experience
2	Service	Advanced level	3–4 years experience
3	Practice	Senior level	5–10 years experience
4	Strategic Development	Expert level	10+ years experience
5	Strategic Intent	Chief expert	deep level of expertise and knowledge
6	Corporate Citizenship	Not applicable	
7	Corporate Prescience	Not applicable	

In terms of the DevOps team occupation label mapping for the case study organization, the first five SST levels, i.e., cost reduction, cost control, cost efficiency, value control, and value creation, were mapped since these strata aligned to the case study organization's product-based and business line transformation. Strata 6 and 7, i.e., organizational viability and industry-shaping, were not relevant and were marked "Not applicable" for the DevOps team occupation labels of the case study organizations, as the work complexity for these two strata related to long-term planning for a group of business units and prediction of the future.

The associated occupation label assigned to each workforce mix was based on several scenarios considered by the case study organization. If a DevOps team is too junior, then such a team might not have the expertise to deliver high-quality, complex products as opposed to teams that are too senior, pointing to ineffective use of company resources. Furthermore, teams that are too senior might not build enough long-term skills for the team to be sustainable, or having a senior team close to retirement might place long-term product delivery at risk.

To determine typical DevOps workforce mix profiles (i.e., based on DevOps team occupation labels related to SST as defined in Table 3), 32 managers of product lines in the case study organization were invited to rate their product lines using a three-point scale: 1 (low), 2 (medium) and 3 (high). We combined Tables 2 and 3 as data collection instruments shown in Table 4. Each product line manager considered the drivers of the workforce mix for their particular product lines and rated them accordingly.

Table 4. Data collection instrument (Source: case study organization)

Drivers of workforce mix		Entry level	Advanced level	Senior level	Expert level	Chief expert
complexity	25%	1, 2, 3	1, 2, 3	1, 2, 3	1, 2, 3	1, 2, 3
process knowledge	20%	1, 2, 3	1, 2, 3	1, 2, 3	1, 2, 3	1, 2, 3
network	10%	1, 2, 3	1, 2, 3	1, 2, 3	1, 2, 3	1, 2, 3
criticality	25%	1, 2, 3	1, 2, 3	1, 2, 3	1, 2, 3	1, 2, 3
maturity level	20%	1, 2, 3	1, 2, 3	1, 2, 3	1, 2, 3	1, 2, 3

We calculated the score based on the driver weight and the rating captured by the participating managers. The purpose of this data collection was to establish generic profiles of DevOps teams, suggesting an ideal mix of the workforce based on the drivers of the workforce mix. We applied SST to establish an ideal profile mix, and based on the calculated score per DevOps team occupation Level, three generic (ideal) profiles were identified, as shown in Figure 2.

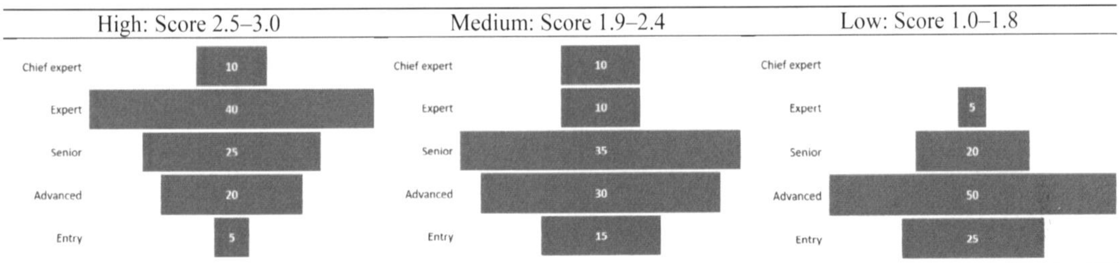

Figure 2. Profiles of DevOps team workforce mix based on SST (Source: authors' visualization)

Scores of 1.0 to 1.8 were denoted a Low DevOps profile, where 25% of the team consisted of entry-level employees, 50% advanced-level employees, 20% senior-level employees, and 5% expert-level employees (Figure 1). For the Low DevOps profile mix, no chief expert-level employees were allocated to the DevOps workforce allocation, as the SST work theme and strategic intent were not relevant in this instance nor required by the complexity of the product line. A Medium DevOps profile was defined for a score of 1.9 to 2.4, where 15% of the team consisted of entry-level employees, 30% advanced-level employees, 35% senior-level employees, and 10% expert and chief expert-level employees, respectively (Figure 1). Finally, for scores of 2.5 to 3.0, a High DevOps profile was defined by combining 5% of entry-level employees, 20% advanced-level employees, 25% senior-level employees, and 40% expert and 10% chief expert-level employees (Figure 1). From the visualization presented in Figure 2, it can be observed that the SST work theme (DevOps team occupation label) increases in importance as the complexity of the drivers of the workforce mix increases.

Therefore, the three DevOps workforce mix profiles depicted in Figure 2 represent generic profiles associated with low, medium, and high complexity product lines and provide a basis for the data analysis phase of this research study, Step 3 in our design process, discussed in the next section.

4. DATA ANALYSIS AND FINDINGS

Employee data and team occupation labels (Table 3) are held in the human resource system (HRS) of the case study organization. DevOps team data were extracted from the HRS and grouped per their allocation to different product lines. For each product line, the actual allocation of the workforce mix could be determined and compared to the generic profiles designed, as shown in Figure 3.

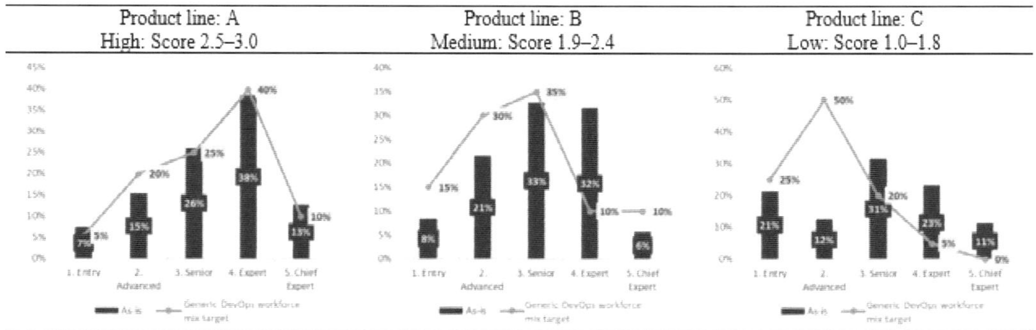

Figure 3. Actual DevOps team workforce mix compared to generic (ideal) profiles designed (Source: authors' visualization)

In Figure 3, the actual DevOps workforce mix extracted from the case study organization's HRS is shown as a bar graph, while the generic profiles designed (Figure 2) are shown as a line graph. The overlayed profiles are presented for a high, medium, and low DevOps workforce mix, and the product lines were coded with alphabetic labels so as not to compromise the case study organization.

By comparing the actual DevOps workforce mix to the desired workforce mix, the DevOps workforce mix for Product Line C indicates that higher SST work theme levels are allocated (senior, 31% actual vs. 20% required; expert, 23% actual vs. 5% required; and chief expert, 11% vs. 0% required) as opposed to the required profile of 50% occupied by 12% of the actual employees. By comparing the actual DevOps workforce mix to the generic (required) DevOps workforce mix, the case study organizations could normalize teams and ensure that the competence and skill required to deliver the particular product line are addressed optimally.

5. GUIDELINES AND CONTRIBUTION

The main aim of this case study was to define a mechanism for optimal DevOps workforce allocation to enable sustainable quality delivery. As organizations have different organizational structures with their associated job profiles, the constitution of DevOps teams will reflect these different views. By applying SST that provides a common classification system for various occupations (Jaques, 1986), thereby creating a common language (Figure 1) between the required DevOps workforce mix and the actual DevOps workforce mix, the gap between the requirement and reality can be determined, and once identified, the gap could be addressed.

This DSR study contributes to both practice (the rigor cycle defined by (Hevner, 2007) in Section 3) and the body of knowledge on the subject of the optimal allocation of the DevOps workforce mix (the relevance cycle defined by (Hevner, 2007) in Section 3).

5.1 Contribution to The Body of Knowledge

We achieved the objective of this DSR study by executing a particular approach (presented in Figure 4) in a case study organization by suggesting particular repeatable guidelines.

STEP 1	STEP 2	STEP 3	STEP 4	STEP 5
Map SST Work theme to the organization's DevOps team occupation labels	Create the generic (ideal) DevOps team workforce mix	Extract HRS data of actual employee allocation	Compare generic to actual DevOps profile mixes	Analyze the gap and implement an action plan to address over- or under-representation

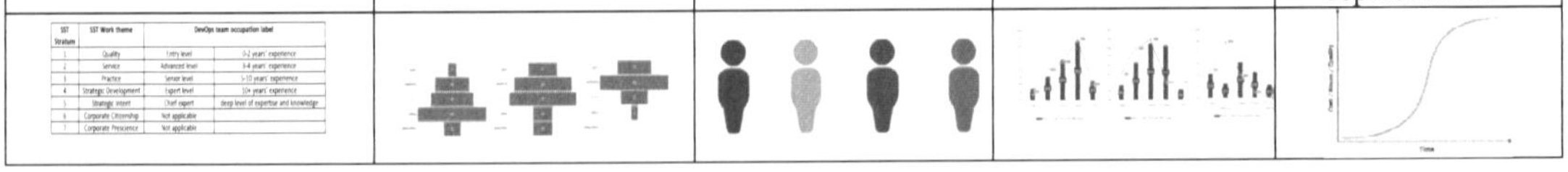

Figure 4. Proposed guidelines for determining and optimizing the DevOPs workforce mix (Source: authors' visualization)

This research study suggested guidelines for determining and optimizing the DevOps workforce mix. This was achieved by creating a common language based on SST to define an organization's requirement for an optimal generic DevOps workforce mix. Organizational roles must be mapped to the SST work themes (Step 1), whereafter, we propose a mechanism to, with input from product and service managers, create the required DevOps workforce mix (Step 2). Once defined, the actual employee data can be extracted from the HRS (Step 3), enabling the comparison of the as-is workforce allocation to the required DevOps workforce mix (Step 4). The difference between the actual and the required DevOps workforce mix profiles can be assessed, and strategies can be implemented to address over- and under-representation toward optimizing time, quality, and cost (Step 5).

5.2 Practical Contribution

From a practical perspective, the guidelines described in Section 5.1 were executed in a case study organization, resulting in key inputs in terms of its DevOps workforce allocation strategy. In particular, it assisted the case study organization (as far as product line ownership is concerned) in managing the increased accountability and responsibility of High DevOps profile product lines with the skills of its employees. Furthermore, the analysis informed cost reprioritization based on product line ownership. Finally, strategic decisions could be made regarding investment in young talent and talent access relationships.

By applying the guidelines for optimal DevOps workforce mix allocation, organizations will be able to allocate employees to product-line delivery with an optimal balance between seniority, complexity, quality delivery, and operational costs (staff and timed delivery).

6. CONCLUSION

The main aim of this case study was to identify a mechanism for optimal DevOps workforce allocation, enabling sustainable quality delivery. This objective was achieved through a DSR research approach, applying SST as a common language to create a generic DevOps workforce mix profile for the case study organization. The DevOps workforce mix profile was established for low-, medium- and high-complexity product lines and incorporated different SST strata related to case study organization DevOps team occupation labels.

With the generic DevOps workforce mix profiles defined, the actual HRM data of employees allocated to the DevOps teams were extracted, mapped to the SST strata, and compared to the generic profile designed. By comparing the desired DevOps workforce mix to the actual workforce mix, the case study organization can manage the DevOps workforce mix as the gap between the desired and actual workforce mix provides a basis for optimization. This optimization informs the talent management and recruitment strategies and optimizes human resources cost. By allocating the DevOps workforce mix according to the desired DevOps workforce mix profiles, the case study organization can ensure that the correct combination of roles can deal with all complexities of the product line development.

We acknowledge that the generic DevOps workforce mix designs are somewhat coarse (high, medium, and low); this could be refined in terms of future research. As the drivers of the workforce mix (Table 1) are context-sensitive, future research could develop guidelines for organizations to define and weigh these drivers as a key input to the generic DevOps workforce mix model. The case study organization has a well-defined organizational structure and job roles, and further research would be required to generalize our proposed guidelines (Figure 4) in an environment where these structures are more fluid.

REFERENCES

Agrawal, S., De Smet, A., Lacroix, S. & Reich, A. (2020). To Emerge Stronger From The COVID-19 Crisis, Companies Should Start Reskilling Their Workforces Now. *Mckinsey Insights (Issue May)*, 1-7.

Alawneh, M. & Abbadi, I. M. Expanding Devops Principles And Best Practices Based On Practical View. (2022) International Arab Conference On Information Technology (ACIT), 2022. IEEE, 1-6.

ARC Advisory Group (2022). Industrial Digital Transformation Top 25. *ARC Special Report. Www.Arcweb.Com.*

Barambones, J., Richoux, F., Imbert, R. & Inoue, K. (2021). Resilient Team Formation With Stabilisability Of Agent Networks For Task Allocation. *ACM Transactions On Autonomous And Adaptive Systems (TAAS),* 15, 1-24.

Bezuidenhout, C., Wocke, A., Plint, N. & Mthombeni, M. (2021). The Impact Of Job Automation On Shifts In Levels Of Work.

Dakkak, A., Bosch, J. & Olsson, H. H. (2023). Devservops: Devops For Product-Oriented Product-Service Systems. *Arxiv Preprint Arxiv:2305.08601.*

Dery, K. & Sebastian, I. M. (2017). Managing Talent For Digital.

Duffy, M. (2015). Devops Automation Cookbook: Over 120 Recipes Covering Essential Automation Techniques. *Birmingham, UK: Packt Publishing.*

Ebert, C., Gallardo, G., Hernantes, J. & Serrano, N. (2016). Devops. *Ieee Software,* 33, 94-100.

Feijter, R., Vliet, R., Jagroep, E., Overbeek, S. & Brinkkemper, S. 2017. Towards The Adoption Of Devops In Software Product Organizations: A Maturity Model Approach. *Technical Report Series.*

Forbes. (2022). *Elon Musk Moves Quickly On Twitter Restructuring [Website], Https://Www.Forbes.Com/Sites/Derekbaine/2022/10/29/Elon-Musk-Moves-Quickly-On-Twitter-Restructuring--Huge-Layoffs-On-Saturday/, (Accessed 11 July 2023)* [Online]. [Accessed].

Frey, C. B. & Osborne, M. A. (2017). The Future Of Employment: How Susceptible Are Jobs To Computerisation? *Technological Forecasting And Social Change,* 114, 254-280.

Hamzane, I. & Khalyly, B. E. Towards An IT Governance Of Devops Metamodel. 2021 International Conference On Decision Aid Sciences And Application (DASA), 2021. IEEE, 824-827.

Hevner, A. R. (2007). A Three Cycle View Of Design Science Research. *Scandinavian Journal Of Information Systems,* 19, 4.

Jabbari, R., Bin Ali, N., Petersen, K. & Tanveer, B. What Is Devops? A Systematic Mapping Study On Definitions And Practices. Proceedings Of The Scientific Workshop Proceedings Of XP2016, 2016. 1-11.

Jaques, E. (1986). The Development Of Intellectual Capability: A Discussion Of Stratified Systems Theory. *The Journal Of Applied Behavioral Science,* 22, 361-383.

Jaques, E. (2017). *Requisite Organization: A Total System For Effective Managerial Organization And Managerial Leadership For The 21st Century*, Routledge.

Jha, A. V., Teri, R., Verma, S., Tarafder, S., Bhowmik, W., Kumar Mishra, S., Appasani, B., Srinivasulu, A. & Philibert, N. (2023). From Theory To Practice: Understanding Devops Culture And Mindset. *Cogent Engineering,* 10, 2251758.

Karemera, C. & Ngubiri, J. Complexity Of The Resource Allocation/Matching Problem With Weight Based Ceilings. Algorithms And Architectures For Parallel Processing: 12th International Conference, ICA3PP 2012, Fukuoka, Japan, September 4-7, 2012, Proceedings, Part II 12, 2012. Springer, 245-254.

Kuusinen, K., Balakumar, V., Jepsen, S. C., Larsen, S. H., Lemqvist, T. A., Muric, A., Nielsen, A. Ø. & Vestergaard, O. A Large Agile Organization On Its Journey Towards Devops. 2018 44th Euromicro Conference On Software Engineering And Advanced Applications (SEAA), 2018. IEEE, 60-63.

Larson, L. & Dechurch, L. A. (2020). Leading Teams In The Digital Age: Four Perspectives On Technology And What They Mean For Leading Teams. *The Leadership Quarterly,* 31, 101377.

Liang, Q. (2021). *Continuous Delivery 2.0: Business-Leading Devops Essentials*, CRC Press.

López-Fernández, D., Díaz, J., García, J., Pérez, J. & González-Prieto, Á. 2021. Devops Team Structures: Characterization And Implications. *IEEE Transactions On Software Engineering,* 48, 3716-3736.

López-Peña, M. A., Díaz, J., Pérez, J. E. & Humanes, H. (2020). Devops For Iot Systems: Fast And Continuous Monitoring Feedback Of System Availability. *IEEE Internet Of Things Journal,* 7, 10695-10707.

Lwakatare, L. E., Kilamo, T., Karvonen, T., Sauvola, T., Heikkilä, V., Itkonen, J., Kuvaja, P., Mikkonen, T., Oivo, M. & Lassenius, C. (2019). Devops In Practice: A Multiple Case Study Of Five Companies. *Information And Software Technology,* 114, 217-230.

Lwakatare, L. E., Kuvaja, P. & Oivo, M. (2016). An Exploratory Study Of Devops Extending The Dimensions Of Devops With Practices. *Icsea,* 104, 2016.

Malik, A. A. & Bilberg, A. (2019). Complexity-Based Task Allocation In Human-Robot Collaborative Assembly. *Industrial Robot: The International Journal Of Robotics Research And Application,* 46, 471-480.

Marnewick, C. & Langerman, J. (2020). Devops And Organizational Performance: The Fallacy Of Chasing Maturity. *IEEE Software,* 38, 48-55.

Meta. 2023. *Update On Meta's Year Of Efficiency [Website], Https://About.Fb.Com/News/2023/03/Mark-Zuckerberg-Meta-Year-Of-Efficiency/, (Accessed 11 July 2023)* [Online]. [Accessed].

Ogala, J. O. (2022). A Complete Guide To Devops Best Practices. *International Journal Of Computer Science And Information Security (IJCSIS),* 20.

Qumer Gill, A., Loumish, A., Riyat, I. & Han, S. (2018). Devops For Information Management Systems. *VINE Journal Of Information And Knowledge Management Systems,* 48, 122-139.

Senapathi, M., Buchan, J. & Osman, H. Devops Capabilities, Practices, And Challenges: Insights From A Case Study. Proceedings Of The 22nd International Conference On Evaluation And Assessment In Software Engineering 2018, 2018. 57-67.

Sharma, S. (2017). *The Devops Adoption Playbook: A Guide To Adopting Devops In A Multi-Speed IT Enterprise*, John Wiley & Sons.

Sousa, T. B., Correia, F. F. & Ferreira, H. S. (2015). Patterns For Software Orchestration On The Cloud. *Proceedings Of The 22nd Conference On Pattern Languages Of Programs.* Pittsburgh, Pennsylvania: The Hillside Group.

Törnblom, O., Stålne, K. & Kjellström, S. (2018). Analyzing Roles And Leadership In Organizations From Cognitive Complexity And Meaning-Making Perspectives. *Behavioral Development,* 23, 63.

Wettinger, J., Breitenbücher, U., Kopp, O. & Leymann, F. (2016). Streamlining Devops Automation For Cloud Applications Using TOSCA As Standardized Metamodel. *Future Generation Computer Systems,* 56, 317-332.

Wiblen, S. & Marler, J. H. (2019). The Human–Technology Interface In Talent Management And The Implications For HRM. *HRM 4.0 For Human-Centered Organizations.* Emerald Publishing Limited.

Wiedemann, A., Wiesche, M., Gewald, H. & Krcmar, H. (2020). Understanding How Devops Aligns Development And Operations: A Tripartite Model Of Intra-IT Alignment. *European Journal Of Information Systems,* 29, 458-473.

Wiedemann, A., Wiesche, M., Thatcher, J. B. & Gewald, H. (2019). A Control-Alignment Model For Product Orientation In Devops Teams–A Multinational Case Study.

Yu, G. & Zhou, X. (2021). The Influence And Countermeasures Of Digital Economy On Cultivating New Driving Force Of High-Quality Economic Development In Henan Province Under The Background Of" Double Circulation". *Annals Of Operations Research*, 1-22.

INCREASING TIME REGISTRATION IN AN AGILE ENVIRONMENT THROUGH NUDGING IN HUMAN-COMPUTER INTERACTION

Max Schrijen[1], Mark van der Pas[1] and Ksenia Podoynitsyna[2]
[1]*European Center for Digital Transformation, Willem II singel 2, 6041HS, Roermond, The Netherlands*
[2]*Jheronimus Academy of Data Science, Sint Janssingel 92, 5211 DA, 's-Hertogenbosch, The Netherlands*

ABSTRACT

This paper examines the impact of nudging in HCI on the time registration in an agile organization. More specifically, two nudges have been implemented, the customized information nudge and the anchoring nudge. Time registration plays a crucial role in increasing the transparency on the resource planning in an agile organization. Admitting the proven potential of nudges, we intend to investigate whether the implementation of nudges could improve the time registration behavior of employees. We conducted a randomized field experiment amongst the employees of an agile organization, where the employees were assigned to any of the implemented nudges. This field experiment consisted of a mixed-design utilizing a within- and between-subjects design. The results show that the implementation of both the nudges do not lead to an significant increase in the amount of registered time. Yet, we do find improvements for the organization of interest in this study. Therefore we encourage future research to repeat this study in an organization that has a larger sample size. These results contribute to existing literature on nudging in a work-related setting, with a specific focus on an agile-based organization.

KEYWORDS

Nudging, HCI, Agile, Time Registration

1. INTRODUCTION

Our society relies heavily on information technology. Processes like same day delivery, online banking or even the efficient supply of power and water are made possible by complex information technology. A total of 4.5 trillion dollars will be spent on IT in 2023, which keeps growing (Gartner, 2023).

For enhancing processes using information technology in organizations, two main methodologies are generally known, waterfall and agile (Thesing et al., 2021). In the waterfall methodology, a linear process is followed (Fagarasan et al., 2021). When using the waterfall methodology, each phase can start after the before going phase has been finished. Waterfall methodology relies heavily on project management. One of the fundamental instruments to measure a project's success is the iron triangle (Bryde, 2008, Ika, 2009). This triangle measures a project based on three constraints. The available budget for the project, the available time for a project, and the delivered quality/scope/performance/requirements of a project (Terry, 2017, Van Wyngaard et al., 2013, Badewi, 2016, Pollack et al., 2018). In the waterfall approach, the scope/quality is often fixed when initiating a project, while the budget and time elements are adjustable (Thesing et al., 2021, Breyter, 2022). In contrast to waterfall, there is agile methodology, which has a cyclical nature rather than linear. Reflecting the iron triangle on the agile methodology shows the opposite of waterfall. The budget and time elements are given in agile, while the quality is flexible (Breyter, 2022). The final product can be delivered in shorter and less meticulous planned steps compared to a waterfall project (Van der Feltz et al., 2020).

Both the waterfall and agile methodologies are instruments to allocate resources to enhance the information technology infrastructure. The resource planning required for both follows a different structure. In the waterfall methodology, the planning of resources is executed by a project manager and normally done before a gate or milestone is requested but at least at the start of a project (Williams, 2005, Breyter, 2022). Upon starting the project, the quality a project needs to achieve is established, and based on this the required budget and time is planned. While for agile, the resource planning is done by team members who are given a fixed amount of budget and time. Which should be divided over separate sprints and user stories. This process of resource planning is an iterative and flexible approach (Breyter, 2022). That adapts to the progress of the deliverables. The plan is continuously reviewed and adjusted when new information on the deliverables becomes available making the accuracy of initial estimates in agile less easily verifiable compared to waterfall. So, improving the verifiability of estimate accuracy could have benefits for the value of estimates made as accuracy is a key driver in forecasting (Van der Pas and Furneaux, 2015).

From these two methodologies, this study focuses on improving the time registration process, which is a part of resource planning, in the agile methodology. Time registration is also called time allocation, but in this paper, the term time registration more accurately describes the process. Registering time is the process of capturing the worked hours by employees, which can eventually be used in other parts of the resource planning. For waterfall projects, it is well known that a lot of projects experience budget and schedule overrun (Alami et al., 2022, Budzier and Flyvbjerg, 2011, Molokken and Jorgensen, 2003). In agile this is less likely, as the time and budget elements are fixed (Breyter, 2022). What could happen in agile, however, is that the promised resources are not delivered, leading to fewer colleagues in the team than expected. This is something that accurately registering time can solve by making the colleagues' availability more transparent. Yet from practice, we know that time registration is not a beloved process and may not happen accurately. Due to laziness, an overwhelming time registration tool or because the time registration task is too demanding. For that reason, improving the time registration process is relevant in agile methodology.

Improving the time registration can be done in several ways. One possibility of doing this is via the use of nudges. Nudges have been shown to improve decisions made in the work environment (Bammert et al., 2020). Examples of nudges are setting a default, providing reminders or altering the salience of specific options. To the best of our knowledge, little is known about nudging in time registration in agile environments. We therefore propose nudges as possible improvement in this research. They are integrated into the time registration tool to improve the human-computer interaction (HCI) and eventually the time registration process. Human-computer interaction is a discipline regarding the interaction between users and computers (Brey and Søraker, 2009). Optimizing the interaction between users and computers could bring several benefits, such as improving user experience and ensuring the functionality of the system (Liu et al., 2021, Mirsch et al., 2017). Capturing the worked hours by employees requires human input. It is therefore essential that the system is usable and user friendly. By applying a human centered design the goals of HCI can be achieved as well as the final purpose. Which is a match between the information system and the user's needs and requirements (Issa and Isaias, 2022). So, to better understand how to increase the registered time in an agile world, via an optimized human-computer interaction. We get to the following research question:

How to increase the registered time in an agile environment through the exploitation of nudges in human-computer interaction?

The organization of interest in this study is a European software organization. They are using a project and portfolio management (PPM) tool to manage their portfolios, that contains a time registration module. In this time registration module, the organization's employees interact with the software and are required to register the hours they have worked for customers. The organization works according to an agile manner and performs their time registration on a high level in agile, the initiatives. They use program increments to manage their deliverables, combined with cross-functional-teams, initiatives and user stories to define requirements. It mostly resembles the Scale Agile Framework (SAFe). Despite their Agile structure, time registration is not done on a daily basis, but rather weekly or monthly. Which is mainly due to the fact that the Agile components are not all handled in the same tool, causing people to only access the time registration tool weekly. This paper discusses the theoretical framework including the hypotheses in the following section. The methodology and the results are outlined in the sections thereafter. Finally, the conclusion and any limitations are highlighted in the final section of the paper.

2. THEORETICAL FRAMEWORK

This paper focuses on the use of nudges in the HCI to improve the process of registering time. These areas are related as nudges are commonly used in HCI (Caraban et al., 2019), and nudging can be applied in improving the time registration process while using HCI principles. In this paper we view time registration as a decision making process. Initially, when people hear the term decision-making in a project environment, they think of investment decisions, project cancellation decisions, or any decisions that have a significant impact on the organization. However, it is essential to note that decision-making happens at all levels in an organization. The process of decision-making refers to the cognitive process of selecting an action from multiple alternatives. Applying this definition to the time registration process we can consider that time registration is a form of decision-making carried out by people of an organization. An employee must evaluate multiple factors and is influenced by bounded rationality. This theory states that individuals make decisions based on information available to them, in which they are limited by their cognitive minds (Simon, 1997, Hernandez and Ortega, 2019). In the context of time registration, they might use heuristics, or mental shortcuts to estimate the hours worked, given that limited information about their exact working schedule or tasks is available. Alternatively, too much work, procrastination or even laziness could invoke bounded rationality as people don't take any effort to register their time correctly.

Besides this, it is known that people are not rational in their decision-making (Kahneman, 2017, Thaler and Sunstein, 2008). This irrationality is often systematic and consistent, resulting from cognitive bias (Blanco, 2017). Important here is the Dual Process theory of decision-making. To properly understand the human behavior of decision making there exists the Dual Process theories about system 1 and system 2 thinking. In his book, Kahnemann distinguishes two types of systematic thinking. System 1 thinking, which is fast, based on your intuition and automated. At the same time system 2 thinking is based on reasoning, slow, effortful, and controlled (Kahneman, 2017). In time registration, system 1 thinking would be immediately filling out 8 hours for a whole day. In contrast, system 2 would be used when considering the exact activities and estimating the time spent per activity. Because system 1 thinking is fast and automated, it is the most prone to cognitive biases.

Common examples of cognitive biases that affect our private or work lives are the halo effect, optimism bias, or anchoring bias (Helweg-Larsen and Shepperd, 2001, Kahneman, 2017, Sharot, 2011). In time registration, the optimism bias can, for example, sneak in when people are overconfident in their skills. Many of these cognitive biases are created by heuristics that people taught themselves to overcome the cognitive load. Well-known heuristics are the status quo, the availability heuristic, and the representativeness heuristic (Blanco, 2017). To leverage these cognitive biases and steer people towards better decisions, a technique called nudging can be used (Battaglio Jr et al., 2019). A nudge is a change in how choices are presented that influences behavior without limiting options or altering economic incentives. It must also be easy to opt out of and not costly (Thaler and Sunstein, 2008). Nudging has been proven efficient at influencing behavior on different occasions, such as the creation of healthy eating habits or improving diabetes control (Arno and Thomas, 2016, Kwan et al., 2020, Bucher et al., 2016, Cadario and Chandon, 2020).

Several years after the introduction of nudging by Thaler and Sunstein, the term "digital nudging" made its rise. Digital nudging is the use of design elements within digital platforms, to steer people's behavior when making choices in a digital setting (Schneider et al., 2018, Weinmann et al., 2016). Some examples of digital nudges are positioning, placebo, hiding, and deceptive visualizations. Digital nudges can be used in HCI to improve the usability of a system. (Caraban et al., 2019, Mirsch et al., 2017). In a paper published by Jesse & Jannach, 87 digital nudges are divided into four categories explaining the types of nudges. They categorize the nudges into "Decision Information", "Decision Structure", "Decision Assistance", and "Social Decision Appeal" nudge (Jesse and Jannach, 2021). One of the nudges they highlight is the "customized information" nudge. This nudge is part of the "Decision Information" category and tailors the available information to the user's needs to decrease the cognitive load of a decision. The nudge has been tested in several different settings and provided promising results (Sagara, 2009, Peters et al., 2006, Hardisty et al., 2010, Boogen et al., 2022).

In the current time registration process, the employees receive a list of all the initiatives available in the organization. From this list, the employee must identify the initiatives they have worked on, to register the amount of worked hours. An advantage of this is that the user can easily start registering time on new initiatives. But this list has the drawback of showing more initiatives than an employee is working on. Employees can work on one or several initiatives simultaneously meaning that most of the initiatives in the list are irrelevant to the corresponding user. Besides this, searching for the correct initiative to register your time on becomes burdensome and time-consuming. That is error-prone, as an employee can accidentally write time on the wrong initiatives. Which eventually increases the difficulty for the resource planning team.

We could ease the process of finding initiatives and registering time by applying the customized information nudge, to improve the HCI of the time registration module. In the context of time registration, we will do this by narrowing down the list an employee has to choose from. The new list will be personalized to the user by only showing initiatives a user registered the latest time on. As most initiatives have a duration of months or years, the list will often show the correct initiatives. If the process of registering the time becomes easier, we think that the number of hours that will be written increases and therefore hypothesize the following:

H1: providing the user with a personalized list of projects in the time registration tool increases the amount of registered time.

Another nudge mentioned by Jesse & Jannach is the anchoring-and-adjustment nudge (2021). This nudge is based on the anchoring effect, which influences the decisions of an individual based on earlier information (Furnham and Boo, 2011). The anchoring-and-adjustment nudge has received a lot of attention in research and has been tested in various domains. Such as the tourism and political industry (Kim and Hyun, 2021, Cho et al., 2017).

The underlying mechanisms of the anchoring effects can be explained by two main models. Anchoring-and-adjustment is a two-stage process in which people start from an initial value, adjusted to a final value. So, different starting values lead to different final estimates biased towards the initial values (Tversky and Kahneman, 1974). This is also called insufficient adjustment because people tend to stop adjusting when they reach a plausible estimate. Alternatively, there is the selective accessibility model. Which explains anchoring based on confirmatory hypothesis testing. During the estimation process, knowledge consistent with the anchor gets triggered affecting the final judgment. The individuals then test the hypothesis that the anchor is the correct value (Furnham and Boo, 2011). From both these two models, it is shown in the literature that the insufficient adjustment process is used when the anchors are generated by the individuals themselves. Whereas selective accessibility is often utilized when the anchors are created by external parties such as experimenters (Furnham and Boo, 2011).

In the time registration tools known by the author, no anchors are presented to the users, which could lead to fewer registered hours than worked hours. To test the effect of anchoring, we will add arbitrary anchors in the tool according to the following logic. For full time employees working 40 hours in 5 days it can be expected that 8 hours per day is the standard. So, anchors with a value of 8 will be shown as arbitrary anchors for each workday of an employee. To test if the introduction of arbitrary anchors affects the hours registered by an employee, we hypothesize the following:

H2.1: using arbitrary anchors in the time registration tool increases the amount of registered time.

According to the insufficient adjustment theory by Tversky and Kahnemann users are insufficiently adjusting the anchor downward or upward leading to their final estimate (Tversky and Kahneman, 1974). This would mean that users who are presented with a higher anchor tend to give higher estimates accordingly. However, the anchors should still be in a plausible range. Studies have shown that when the anchors reach extremity or implausibility, they do not have the desired anchoring effect (Mussweiler and Strack, 2001, Wegener et al., 2001). This holds for the adjustment mechanism, in which people adjust the estimates within a plausible range (Wegener et al., 2010). The same is true for the theory of selective accessibility. Literature has proven that under this theory, higher anchors lead to higher estimates, but this is also limited to anchors that are plausible rather than implausible or extreme (Furnham and Boo, 2011).

Drawing upon the theories above, it would be credible to increase the registered time by utilizing higher anchors, provided they fall within a plausible range. To find the effect of more advanced anchors we test the use of personalized anchors in hypothesis 2.2. As these anchors are created by a third party, we expect that the selective accessibility model will be triggered. The individuals will thus judge the suggestions that the provided hours (anchors) are their actual worked hours or not, and decide based on their judgement on an adjustment. For a typical workday, the plausible range is between 0 and 8 hours. Nevertheless, in the scenario where an employee's registered time is currently 3 hours per day, an anchor value of 8 would still be deemed implausible for the user. As such, it is proposed that the use of higher anchors should be tailored to the employee. Consequently, hypothesis 2.2 is formulated to assess the efficacy of the anchoring nudge as stated below:

H2.2: using personalized higher anchors (within a plausible range) increases the registered time by employees.

3. METHODOLOGY

The three hypotheses above were examined using two main experiments, consisting of several sub-experiments. All of them were carried out in the same European software organization. This organization initiated the process of registering time by their employees at the beginning of 2022. The time registration entails sending out an email each Friday morning requesting that employees submit their worked hours. There are approximately 150 employees in the organization who are expected to complete this task on a weekly basis. In this section, we will dive deeper into the experimental design, the participants selection, the data collection, and the data analysis.

3.1 Expt. 1: The Effect of a Personalized List on the Amount of Registered Time

In experiment 1, we designed a study that aimed to observe the number of hours subjects recorded while being presented with a personalized list of projects. This experiment has been conducted prior to the second experiment over a three-and-a-half-week timespan. The rationale for conducting the experiments in this sequence was that the second set of hypotheses (2.1 and 2.2) required all subjects to work with the personalized list. We opted for a three-and-a-half-week timeframe as we anticipated observing quick outcomes from the first intervention. The experiment was carried out on half of the subjects. The other half of the population already customized their project list, making them irrelevant for hypothesis 1.

Experimental design The experiment was conducted as a field experiment in which we assessed the impact of the personalized list in the real world. Prior to the experiment, participants were used to receiving a list with all existing projects. The personalized list, however, only presented projects a subject registered the latest time on for subjects who registered time this year. For subjects who did not register time during the current year, the personalized list displayed projects in which they actively participated. The experiment utilized a mixed design of between and within-subjects designs. During the first week, half of the subjects received the treatment with the personalized list (treatment group). While the other half of the subjects received the complete list of all projects (control group). In the second week of the experiment, the control group received the personalized list. Enabling a between-subjects design in the first week, and a within-subjects design afterwards.

The experiment was performed on 76 participants randomly assigned to two groups from a pool of 150, excluding the 74 who already personalized their list.

Data collection The data for this experiment was collected based on the subject's input. Although the email asking to register time is sent each Friday, the exact moment of time registration varies heavily amongst the subjects. A subject can register her hours once a month for the whole month while others register every week for the same week. This leads to inconsistent time registration interval moments within the organization.

For each time registration made by a subject, we collected the date for which the time has been registered (called "Registered Date"), the date on which the subjects registered the time (called "Registered On"), the value registered by the subject (called "Value), and the identifier of the subject (called "UserId"). A record for a subject could thus look as follows (2023-03-06, 2023-03-10, 7, 4404). In the example case in the paragraph above, both subjects would thus have 20 rows of data for 20 working days. However, the subject writing for one month at a time has for each of the 20 rows the same "Registered On" date, while the other subject has 4 different "Registered On" dates. This difference in time registration moments complicated the statistics used for the data analysis.

Data analysis For the data analysis, we conducted a quantitative analysis consisting of two types of t-tests: a paired t-test for the within-subjects design, and an independent-samples t-test for the between-subjects design. In the within-subjects design, we compared the number of registered hours per day before and after the intervention. To ensure a fair comparison, we made the assumption that subjects register their time at regular intervals (e.g. every two weeks). To account for this trend, we analyzed the same number of days before the intervention and after the intervention. For instance, if a subject registered time for 10 days after the intervention, we compared this with the last known 10 days before the intervention. Assuring an apples-to-apples assessment of the time intervals before and after the intervention. In the between-subjects design, we compared the group that received the personalized list with those that did not receive it during the first week of the experiment. We applied the same comparison logic as in the paired t-test, unless we had significantly more responses from one specific group. In such cases we compared the average number of hours per day instead of analyzing the hours for each individual day. To account for the varying number of days with responses, ensuring a fair comparison between the groups. Besides the t-tests we also executed an OLS regression on our data to find the possible effects of control variables. The OLS regression included four control variables: the subject's category (internal or external), the number of days since the subject was created in the system as this is an indication of how long the subject is already registering time, the total number of teams the subject is part of and the number of days between each time registration moment. The dependent variable was the sum of all registered hours per subject within each experiment.

Subjects not registering time after the intervention were left out of the data analysis.

3.2 Expt. 2: The Effect of Anchor Types on the Amount of Registered Hours

In the second experiment, we studied the effect of anchors and anchor types on the time registered by the subjects. In total we tested two hypotheses spread over a time span of four weeks. In the first two weeks we tested the effect of the higher personalized anchors on the amount of registered time. In the second two weeks, we implemented arbitrary anchors and examined the effects of arbitrary anchors.

Experimental design The second experiment was also conducted as a field experiment, where we tested the impact of two different types of anchors on the amount of registered time. The subjects were divided into two groups: one group received the higher personalized anchor, while another received the arbitrary anchor. Both groups consisted of 75 people, drawn from the total population. This experimental setup allowed us to determine the general impact of anchoring on time registration, as well as the effect of personalized anchors against arbitrary anchors. The arbitrary anchor was presented to half of the participants and was an anchor of 8 hours. The higher personalized anchors were calculated by adding 10 per cent to the participant's latest registration value, with a maximum of 40 hours, and a minimum of 2 additional hours per week, to see if this would increase their registered time. This algorithm was chosen since we expected that a difference less than 2 would not be enough to push the time registration and 40 hours is the standard somebody works a week, so larger anchors would not be plausible. We used a mixed design of within- and between-subjects design to analyze the data. The within-subjects design compared each participant's performance in the group receiving personalized anchors and arbitrary anchors with their performance in the weeks before the experiment. The between-subjects design was used to compare the group receiving the personalized anchors, the groups receiving no anchors and the group receiving arbitrary anchors.

A randomized table was used to divide the total pool of 150 in two groups of 75 people per group.

Data collection The data for experiment two has been collected in the same way as in experiment one, in the same table with the following columns: Registered Date, Registered On, Value, UserId.

Data analysis The data analysis for experiment two involved a quantitative analysis which included two types of t-tests: the paired t-test and the independent-samples t-test. The purpose of the paired t-test was to analyze the improvements within the groups receiving personalized and the arbitrary anchors. Specifically, we compared the number of hours registered per day before and after the anchor intervention, using the same number of days in the comparison to account for trends in the time registration of subjects. To measure the performance of the personalized anchors against the other groups, we used two independent-samples t-tests. One test compares the group receiving personalized anchors with a group receiving no anchors. Another test to compare the group receiving personalized anchors with the group receiving the arbitrary anchors. Each of the t-tests was conducted over a two week period, following the same data analysis logic as in the independent samples t-test mentioned in 3.1. Additionally, we performed the OLS regression in the second experiment as well. Here we used the same dependent and independent variables as mentioned above.

4. RESULTS

In total we received 995 responses during our experiment, with most of the responses (694) during the second experiment. Additionally the response ratio between the two groups in H1 was heavily skewed towards the treatment group, probably affecting the between analysis. In the sections below, we analyze exactly how these responses lead to the acceptance or rejection of our hypotheses.

4.1 Testing the Customized Information Nudge (H1)

In H1, we investigated the impact of the personalized list on the amount of time registered by users, using a within- and between-subjects design. Specifically, we hypothesized that the implementation of the personalized list would lead to an increase in registered hours. To test this hypothesis, we performed a paired t-test. In our test, we found a statistically significant difference with $t(290) = 4.94$ and $p < 0.01$ between the before ($M = 5.13$, $SD = 4.88$), and after ($M = 5.76$, $SD = 2.21$) groups. This is an increase of 12%.

During the first test also the total number of hours registered by all employees increased with 42%. Indicating the possible presence of confounding factors. To address this, we conducted an independent-samples t-test on the control and treatment groups. This test indicated no significant difference with a p-value of 0.35. The insignificance of the t-test can be explained by the few responses we received during the between-design of H1. As a robustness check, we also performed two Wilcoxon tests on the within- and between-subjects design. Both tests showed the same significance level as the t-tests and confirmed our findings.

Additionally, we executed an OLS regression on the results from the within- and between-subjects design to find the effect of the mentioned control variables which turned out to be insignificant.

Based on these findings, we reject H1, that the implementation of a personalized list increases the number of registered hours. This conclusion is supported by the significant increase in registered hours observed after the implementation of the personalized list, but also by the absence of a significant difference between the treatment and control groups in the independent-samples t-test. Overall, the results suggest that other factors played a role in the increased hours and that the increase is not solely coming from the personalized list.

4.2 Testing the Anchoring Nudges (H2.1 & H2.2)

The initial anchoring effect of arbitrary anchors on the time registration behavior of users was tested using a within-subjects design. We performed a paired t-test to compare the number of hours registered per day by the subjects before and after receiving an arbitrary anchor. In the test, we found no significant difference between the before ($M = 5.61$, $SD = 2.25$) and after ($M = 5.56$, $SD = 2.37$) groups; $t(233) = -0.34$ and $p = 0.74$. Additionally, we executed a Wilcoxon test as a robustness check, returning the same insignificant result. To test if the addition of control variables had any effect on the relationship we also ran an OLS regression test. This test showed no significant results.

Despite literature finding that arbitrary anchors should already show the anchoring effect. We found no significant difference in the effect of arbitrary anchors on the number of registered hours. Therefore we reject H2.1, indicating there is no relationship between arbitrary anchors and the amount of time registered by a user.

The third hypothesis, the effect of higher personalized anchors on the amount of registered time has been tested with a paired t-test and independent-samples t-tests. For the paired t-test we found no significant difference; $t(109) = 0.68$, $p = 0.49$ between the hours per day before ($M = 5,79$, $SD = 2.37$) and after receiving the personalized anchors ($M = 5.91$, $SD = 2.22$). Then we performed two independent-samples t-tests. First, we compared the control group that did not receive any anchors with a treatment group receiving the higher personalized anchors. The difference between the control group ($M = 4.11$,$SD = 2.08$) and the treatment group ($M = 5.91$,$SD = 2.22$) was highly significant; $t(220) = 6,3$, $p < 0.01$. Indicating an increase in registered hours by the introduction of the personalized anchors. Second, we compared the effect of personalized anchors against arbitrary anchors. In this test we found an insignificant difference; $t(469) = 1,31$, $p = 0.19$, between the group receiving arbitrary anchors ($M = 5.53$, $SD = 5.69$) and the group receiving the personalized anchors ($M = 5.80$, $SD = 4.48$). As a robustness check, we also executed the Wilcoxon test for each of the three test in H2.2. The Wilcoxon tests returned the same significance levels for each t-test, confirming our findings.

Besides the t-tests, we performed three OLS regressions including the four control variables. Resulting in one significant OLS regression for the second between test with $p < 0.05$.

Due to the small sample sizes most of the t-tests and OLS regressions turned out to be insignificant. We therefore executed an additional robustness check to see if a longer duration of the experiment, with more responses, would lead to significant results. Performing an independent-samples t-test on the data resulted in a significant difference; $t(695) = 4.438$, $p < 0.01$, between the group receiving no/arbitrary anchors ($M = 5.08$, $SD = 2.38$) and the group receiving personalized anchors ($M = 5.83$, $SD = 2.15$). Insinuating that a longer duration of the experiment, with more responses, could lead to more significant results than we found now.

Looking at the findings from the t-tests we find a higher number of hours registered per person in the group receiving the personalized anchors in each t-test. This difference is however only significant for one t-test. Based on the fact that we find support for H2.2 in one of the three tests, we partially support the hypothesis. As the results are partially in line with the expected hypothesis. Indicating that the usage of higher personalized anchors in a time registration tool could lead to an increase in the number of hours registered by users.

5. DISCUSSION AND CONCLUSION

In this study, we conducted a field experiment to analyze the effect of two nudges on the amount of registered time in an agile organization. The motivation for conducting this study was the need to improve the time registration. Improved time registration was required to better understand the actual allocation of resources as well as to enhance resource planning. With the chosen experimental set-up we were able to test a set of interventions that shed light on the use of nudges in time registration in agile. Based on the outcomes of our experiments we made the following observations.

The results of the first hypothesis test indicate that introducing a personalized list, based on the customized information nudge, has a positive effect on the number of registered hours. This initial result implies the same as the hypothesized association and is in line with the findings from Sagara, 2009, Peters et al., 2006, Hardisty et al., 2010, and Boogen et al., 2022. In each of their studies, they all found positive effects of the customized information nudge. At the same time, we found that the overall number of registered hours also increased. This could imply that the significant increase in our experiment was not solely caused by implementing the personalized list. It appeared that management in the participating organization was additionally informing people to register their time. Which is another form of nudging called reminding. The additional reminders of management performed as an extra trigger for employees to register more time. The fact that an additional nudge was applied besides the customized information nudge leads us to not support H1, as the findings cannot be wholly contributed to the personalized list. One possible way to improve this in the future is by properly analyzing the possible nudges that could have an effect and separating them.

Second, implementing arbitrary anchors does not significantly increase the amount of registered time. The findings in the results section are contrary to the hypothesized association and even contradict claims in earlier literature by Furnham and Boo, 2011 that is based on the selective accessibility model. One possible explanation is that the interval of time registration for the users did not allow them to retrieve the judgment-relevant knowledge properly, and therefore hampered the confirmatory hypothesis testing. This judgment-relevant knowledge is important for confirmatory hypothesis testing in the selective accessibility model (Mussweiler and Strack, 1999). It could for example be that, due to the long/irregular intervals, users were not able to retrieve the correct knowledge upon deciding what time to fill out. Therefore the selective accessibility model was not triggered and the anchoring effect did not work. Another possible explanation for this difference could be that the 8 hours is too arbitrary for these specific users. According to findings from Furnham and Boo, 2011 the anchor should be in a plausible range to have effect. In case the 8 hours is not plausible in the organization we tested the anchor, e.g. their work day is 6 hours, the 8-hour anchor is seen as an "implausible" anchor. Removing the anchoring effect, causing people to not utilize the given anchor in registering their time.

Third, the results of the final hypothesis indicate that personalized anchors increase the number of registered hours. This difference was only not significant enough to accept the second hypothesis. Therefore we partially support hypothesis 2.2. Not completely accepting the hypothesis is in contrast with earlier studies from Tversky and Kahneman, 1974, Furnham and Boo, 2011, and Wegener et al., 2010. It is surprising nonetheless that the difference, in registered hours between the groups, in the second between test (0.27) is so small compared to the first between test (1.8). We believe that the time registration habit of the users could have played a major role in this. The second between test ran in the last and first week of a month. From previous time registration behavior, we know that people are registering more hours at the end of the month. So, therefore it is likely the case that the users registered the most and a higher number of hours during the second between test. In this way, they compensate for the small number of hours registered in the first weeks of the month. Leading to a smaller and therefore insignificant difference in the second between test.

Besides the theoretical implications for the nudging literature, our study provides new insights into nudging in HCI. Recent studies into nudging in HCI have mainly focused on the security, marketing, and social media domain using social experiments (Bergram et al., 2022). This knowledge is extended by us with a study into the effect of nudges in HCI in the work domain using a field experiment. Specifically, we explained how the customized information nudge did not solely lead to a change in employee behavior. For the anchoring nudge, we explained that the anchor needs to be personalized to the behavior of the employee to have any effect. We also found that designing a nudge in an information system is a complex task. Especially understanding the employee behavior that should be changed by the nudge. A person's behavior can be explained according to the theory of planned behavior by intention and can be predicted by three concepts: their attitude towards a behavior, the belief others have about the behavior (subjective norm), and their perceived behavioral control (Ajzen, 1991, van der Pas and Walczuch, 2019). While running experiment one, colleagues and management of the participating organization appeared to be reminding employees of their time registration tasks. This form of real-life nudging, via reminders, taps the subjective norm of people and affects their behavior. It implies that when designing a nudge, researchers should be aware of the effect the nudge has on each of the concepts defined in the theory of planned behavior. As different nudges can affect different behavioral concepts.

Our study also suggests implications for the agile literature. Applying the iron triangle (Bryde, 2008, Ika, 2009) on agile methodology showed that the time and budget constraints are fixed (Breyter, 2022). Our work, however, suggests that the given time in agile is not fixed. We found that employees registered more time when management asked this of them. Although the findings are insignificant, the time registration did improve on average with 18% for the specific organization after implementing the nudges. Both these findings indicate that the given time in agile is not a fixed facet, but rather an input that can change. Moreover, a key concept of agile methodology is the teams (Wińska and Dąbrowski, 2020). Agile organizations consist of several cross functional teams that work together to achieve a common goal. Our findings implicate that within these teams communication is an important aspect that should not be overlooked by the individuals in a team. The effect the real-life reminder nudge had on the registered time was larger than the effect of the implemented digital nudges. This implies that face-to-face communication is more effective in agile than digital communication.

The results of this study indicate two important findings. Initially, we found no significant support for hypotheses 1 and 2.1, but found partially support for hypothesis 2.2. We also saw that the combination of a real-life reminder nudge and the customized information nudge led to an increase in registered hours. Which indicates that the registered time in an agile environment cannot be increased solely through the usage of customized information and arbitrary anchoring nudges in the human-technology interaction. While at the same time, the results for hypothesis 1, and hypothesis 2.2 were still showing positive increases in the amount of registered time. Meaning that although the findings were insignificant, the organization still benefitted from the implementations. Combining this with the proven effects of nudging in previous literature we believe that further research is required in the field of nudging in an agile environment.

6. LIMITATIONS AND SUGGESTIONS FOR FUTURE RESEARCH

Firstly, our findings indicate an improvement in the total amount of registered time for the participating organization. Nevertheless, the findings in this study were not statistically significant, which limits the generalizability of our findings. Based on existing literature finding promising results, we strongly believe that future research could find results that are generalizable across the agile environment. Therefore, we would recommend future research to build upon this study to find generalizable effects of nudging on time registration in agile environments. Besides this, we also see the potential of other nudging techniques in an agile environment. Agile is an upcoming and well-established management style that has already proven to be very powerful. More specifically, future research should examine the effect of other nudges in agile environments that have not been tested in this study. For example, the gamification nudge, which incentives people to perform a certain action that could, for example, spark better behavior and decision making.

The influence of extraneous variables due to the set-up of this study is raising an additional limitation. This study has been executed in the form of a field experiment. Field experiments are executed in the real-world and resemble situations encountered in our daily lives. The benefit of this is that field experiments have high external validity. Meaning that the findings can be generalized to settings outside the experiment. However, the control over the influence of extraneous variables is limited, which weakens the strength of the relationship found between the variables of interest. To overcome this, randomization is applied. Additionally, a field experiment is hardly replicable due to it being executed in the real world. To control the effect of extraneous variables researchers often use controlled experiments. The strength of this setup is that the researchers have control over the extraneous variables, leading to a high internal validity of the outcomes. While at the same time the set-up lacks external validity, limiting the generalizability of a controlled study.

Another limitation is the time registration level of the organization in this study. In agile, a goal can be broken down into multiple levels, where the exact levels depend on the model used. The organization in this study registered their time on a higher level. While you could also register time on the levels below. The benefit of registering time on the lower levels is that the levels are more accurate. We believe that registering time on the more precise levels could therefore also increase the amount and accuracy of the registered time. Any future research could thus examine how the different levels in agile affect the amount and accuracy of registered time.

During our research we also found evidence for effects of precise anchors and the usage of machine learning (ML) in anchoring (Janiszewski and Uy, 2008, Wang et al., 2018, Vaccaro and Waldo, 2019). ML models could be used to create more accurate and precise anchors for an even larger anchoring effect. Therefore, we would recommend future research to examine the effect of ML based anchors in an agile environment. We also suggest that resource planning is used as an input for the ML model to determine anchor. This could improve the anchor and push the relevance of accurate resource planning.

Additionally, we suggest that more moderating variables are considered in future research. In this study little was known about the subjects that participated in the experiments. At the same time, character traits of the subjects can function as moderating variables. For example, the technological literacy of subjects could affect the response to the nudges. Or the motivation of a subject could be taken into account. Motivated subjects could have a stronger orientation towards accurately registering their time. Next to personal traits, other moderating variables could be considered, such as the team dynamics, task complexity or the time pressure the subject is experiencing.

Finally, we acknowledge that the available sample size for this study was relatively small. This led to most of the tests being insignificant. For the insignificant t-tests, we found that we would need between two and over twenty times the amount of responses received during this study in order for them to be significant with the differences found. Any future research is thus encouraged to perform a study like ours on a larger scale, in this case a longer time period. Which we believe will lead to better and generalizable results for this context.

REFERENCES

Ajzen, 1991. Ajzen, I. (1991). The theory of planned behavior. Organizational behavior and human decision processes, 50(2):179–211.

Alami, A., Østergaard Madsen, C., and Krancher, O. (2022). Government it projects: Current evidence of cost and schedule overrun and their antecedents. Advances in Information Systems Development: Crossing Boundaries Between Development and Operations in Information Systems, pages 109–125.

Arno, A. and Thomas, S. (2016). The efficacy of nudge theory strategies in influencing adult dietary behaviour: a systematic review and metaanalysis. BMC public health, 16(1):1–11.

Badewi, A. (2016). The impact of project management (pm) and benefits management (bm) practices on project success: Towards developing a project benefits governance framework. International Journal of Project Management, 34(4):761– 778.

Bammert, S., König, U. M., Roeglinger, M., and Wruck, T. (2020). Exploring potentials of digital nudging for business processes. Business Process Management Journal.

Battaglio Jr, R. P., Belardinelli, P., Bellé, N., and Cantarelli, P. (2019). Behavioral public administration ad fontes: A synthesis of research on bounded rationality, cognitive biases, and nudging in public organizations. Public Administration Review, 79(3):304–320.

Bergram, K., Djokovic, M., Bezençon, V., and Holzer, A. (2022). The digital landscape of nudging: A systematic literature review of empirical research on digital nudges. In Proceedings of the 2022 CHI Conference on Human Factors in Computing Systems, pages 1–16.

Blanco, F. (2017). Cognitive bias. Encyclopedia of animal cognition and behavior, 1(6).

Boogen, N., Daminato, C., Filippini, M., and Obrist, A. (2022). Can information about energy costs affect consumers' choices? evidence from a field experiment. Journal of Economic Behavior & Organization, 196:568–588.

Brey, P. and Søraker, J. H. (2009). Philosophy of computing and information technology. In Philosophy of technology and engineering sciences, pages 1341–1407. Elsevier.

Breyter, M. (2022). Waterfall, agile, and hybrid delivery frameworks. In Agile Product and Project Management: A Step-by-Step Guide to Building the Right Products Right, pages 127–160. Springer.

Bryde, D. (2008). Perceptions of the impact of project sponsorship practices on project success. International journal of project management, 26(8):800–809.

Bucher, T., Collins, C., Rollo, M. E., McCaffrey, T. A., De Vlieger, N., Van der Bend, D., Truby, H., and Perez-Cueto, F. J. (2016). Nudging consumers towards healthier choices: a systematic review of positional influences on food choice. British Journal of Nutrition, 115(12):2252–2263.

Budzier, A. and Flyvbjerg, B. (2011). Why your it project might be riskier than you think. Harvard Business Review, 89(9).

Cadario, R. and Chandon, P. (2020). Which healthy eating nudges work best? a meta-analysis of field experiments. Marketing Science, 39(3):465–486.

Caraban, A., Karapanos, E., Gonçalves, D., and Campos, P. (2019). 23 ways to nudge: A review of technology-mediated nudging in humancomputer interaction. In Proceedings of the 2019 CHI Conference on Human Factors in Computing Systems, pages 1–15.

Cho, I., Wesslen, R., Karduni, A., Santhanam, S., Shaikh, S., and Dou, W. (2017). The anchoring effect in decision-making with visual analytics. In 2017 IEEE Conference on Visual Analytics Science and Technology (VAST), pages 116–126. IEEE.

Fagarasan, C., Popa, O., Pisla, A., and Cristea, C. (2021). Agile, waterfall and iterative approach in information technology projects. In IOP Conference Series: Materials Science and Engineering, volume 1169, page 012025. IOP Publishing.

Furnham, A. and Boo, H. C. (2011). A literature review of the anchoring effect. The journal of socio-economics, 40(1):35–42. Gartner, 2023. Gartner (January 18th, 2023). Gartner forecasts worldwide it spending to grow 2.4% in 2023.

Hardisty, D. J., Johnson, E. J., and Weber, E. U. (2010). A dirty word or a dirty world? attribute framing, political affiliation, and query theory. Psychological science, 21(1):86–92.

Helweg-Larsen, M. and Shepperd, J. A. (2001). Do moderators of the optimistic bias affect personal or target risk estimates? a review of the literature. Personality and social psychology review, 5(1):74–95.

Hernandez, J. G. V. and Ortega, R. P. (2019). Bounded rationality in decision–making. MOJ Research Review, 2(1):1–8.

Ika, L. A. (2009). Project success as a topic in project management journals. Project management journal, 40(4):6–19.

Issa, T. and Isaias, P. (2022). Usability and human–computer interaction (hci). In Sustainable Design: HCI, Usability and Environmental Concerns, pages 23–40. Springer.

Janiszewski, C. and Uy, D. (2008). Precision of the anchor influences the amount of adjustment. Psychological Science, 19(2):121–127.

Jesse, M. and Jannach, D. (2021). Digital nudging with recommender systems: Survey and future directions. Computers in Human Behavior Reports, 3:100052.

Kahneman, D. (2017). Thinking, fast and slow.

Kim, H. L. and Hyun, S. S. (2021). The anchoring effect of aviation green tax for sustainable tourism, based on the nudge theory. Journal of Sustainable Tourism, 29(7):1082–1097.

Kwan, Y., Cheng, T., Yoon, S., Ho, L., Huang, C., Chew, E., Thum-boo, J., Østbye, T., and Low, L. (2020). A systematic review of nudge theories and strategies used to influence adult health behaviour and outcome in diabetes management. Diabetes & Metabolism, 46(6):450–460.

Liu, Y., Sivaparthipan, C., and Shankar, A. (2021). Human–computer interaction based visual feedback system for augmentative and alternative communication. International Journal of Speech Technology, pages 1–10.

Mirsch, T., Lehrer, C., and Jung, R. (2017). Digital nudging: Altering user behavior in digital environments. Proceedings der 13. Internationalen Tagung Wirtschaftsinformatik (WI 2017), pages 634–648.

Molokken, K. and Jorgensen, M. (2003). A review of software surveys on software effort estimation. In 2003 International Symposium on Empirical Software Engineering, 2003. ISESE 2003. Proceedings., pages 223–230. IEEE.

Mussweiler, T. and Strack, F. (1999). Comparing is believing: A selective accessibility model of judgmental anchoring. European review of social psychology, 10(1):135–167.

Mussweiler, T. and Strack, F. (2001). Considering the impossible: Explaining the effects of implausible anchors. Social Cognition, 19(2):145– 160.

Peters, E., Västfjäll, D., Slovic, P., Mertz, C., Mazzocco, K., and Dickert, S. (2006). Numeracy and decision making. Psychological science, 17(5):407– 413.

Pollack, J., Helm, J., and Adler, D. (2018). What is the iron triangle, and how has it changed? International journal of managing projects in business.

SAFe. Safe framework. https://scaledagileframework.com.

Sagara, N. (2009). Consumer understanding and use of numeric information in product claims. University of Oregon.

Schneider, C., Weinmann, M., and Vom Brocke, J. (2018). Digital nudging: guiding online user choices through interface design. Communications of the ACM, 61(7):67–73.

Sharot, T. (2011). The optimism bias. Current biology, 21(23):R941– R945.

Simon, H. A. (1997). Models of bounded rationality: Empirically grounded economic reason, volume 3. MIT press.

Terry, N. P. (2017). Appification, ai, and healthcare's new iron triangle. J. Health Care L. & Pol'y, 20:117.

Thaler, R. H. and Sunstein, C. R. (2008). Nudge: Improving decisions about health, wealth, and happiness. Penguin.

Thesing, T., Feldmann, C., and Burchardt, M. (2021). Agile versus waterfall project management: decision model for selecting the appropriate approach to a project. Procedia Computer Science, 181:746–756.

Tversky, A. and Kahneman, D. (1974). Judgment under uncertainty: Heuristics and biases: Biases in judgments reveal some heuristics of thinking under uncertainty. science, 185(4157):1124–1131.

Vaccaro, M. and Waldo, J. (2019). The effects of mixing machine learning and human judgment. Communications of the ACM, 62(11):104– 110.

Van der Feltz, W., Van der Pas, N., Van der Pas, M., (2020). Time estimation improvement in agile development.

Van der pas, M. and Furneaux, B. (2015). Improving the predictability of IT investment business value.

Van der Pas, M. and Walczuch, R. (2019). Behavior of organizational agents on managing information technology. In Intelligent Computing: Proceedings of the 2018 Computing Conference, Volume 2, pages 774–788. Springer.

Van Wyngaard, C., Pretorius, J., and Pretorius, L. (2013). Deliberating the triple constraint trade-offs as polarities to manage—a refreshed perspective. In 2013 IEEE International Conference on Industrial Engineering and Engineering Management, pages 1265–1272. IEEE.

Wang, X., An, X., Luo, H., Xu, S., Yu, X., Hu, S., and Wang, Y. (2018). Anchoring effect as a nudge on improving public health: Two field experiments. Acta Psychologica Sinica, 50(8):848.

Wegener, D. T., Petty, R. E., Blankenship, K. L., and Detweiler-Bedell, B. (2010). Elaboration and numerical anchoring: Implications of attitude theories for consumer judgment and decision making. Journal of consumer psychology, 20(1):5–16.

Wegener, D. T., Petty, R. E., Detweiler-Bedell, B. T., and Jarvis, W. B. G. (2001). Implications of attitude change theories for numerical anchoring: Anchor plausibility and the limits of anchor effectiveness. Journal of Experimental Social Psychology, 37(1):62–69.

Weinmann, M., Schneider, C., and Brocke, J. v. (2016). Digital nudging. Business & Information Systems Engineering, 58(6):433–436.

Williams, T. (2005). Assessing and moving on from the dominant project management discourse in the light of project overruns. IEEE Transactions on engineering management, 52(4):497–508.

Wińska, E. and Dąbrowski, W. (2020). Software development artifacts in large agile organizations: a comparison of scaling agile methods. Data-Centric Business and Applications: Towards Software Development (Volume 4), pages 101-116. Springer.

Short Papers

INVESTIGATING SOFTWARE DEVELOPMENT BUSINESS PROCESSES USING SOFT SYSTEMS METHODOLOGY

Gökçe Günaydın and Sevgi Özkan Yıldırım
Information Systems Dept., Middle East Technical University
Üniversiteler Mah, Dumlupınar Bulv. No:1 06800, Ankara/Turkey

ABSTRACT

Organizations continually strive for operational excellence by refining their processes, streamlining workflows, and minimizing employee turnover to enlarge operational efficiency, enhance productivity, decrease wastage, and improve overall performance. The journey towards process improvement commences with a comprehensive understanding of existing operations which requires a thorough analysis of data and active engagement with stakeholders. In this endeavor, Soft System Methodology (SSM) emerges as a highly effective problem-solving approach, well-suited for analyzing complex processes and identifying appropriate enhancements.

This paper is dedicated to the application of SSM in software development process (SDP) across two interlinked organizations. In this study, SSM is leveraged to implement various problem-solving techniques such as systems thinking, rich picture drawings, root definition and related systems construction, conceptual model creations and action planning, all aimed at providing continuous process improvement.

Within the context of this research, the study is formed by four sub-processes of SDP, namely Design Management, Technical Development, Testing, and Training processes. These individual sub-processes undergo the rigorous application of a seven-staged SSM methodology to uplift system performance. Notably, the final stage of SSM, which involves actual action implementations that are outlined in the research and some feasible ones are developed.

The findings of this study underscore the efficacy of SSM while investigating poorly structured issues within the SDP. Notably, it underscores the importance of real-world activities, while proposing necessary actions to overcome challenges within the SDP landscape.

KEYWORDS

Soft Systems Methodology, Software Development Process, Process Improvement, Systems Thinking

1. INTRODUCTION

Enterprise Resource Planning (ERP) is a vital software system for organizations, enabling data tracking and process monitoring by integrating business operations. Software development is consequently crucial for ERP, necessitating a comprehensive approach involving human relations, hardware, software, effective project management, and a commitment to continuous enhancement. In accordance with Checkland and Scholes' (1999) system definition, SDP can be seen as a system with sub-processes, each with designated boundaries and components generating outputs, potentially leading to feedback loops. Recognizing SDP's emergent behavior, SSM is used to enhance SDP, emphasizing stakeholder participation and sustaining continuous improvement, fitting its iterative nature. This research aims to define SDP enhancements, using SSM to propose changes for a more effective process. It also serves as a model for stakeholders, illustrating continuous improvement and effective communication channel establishment within organizations.

1.1 Research Methodology

The study, using interpretive research, aims to improve the SDP through qualitative methods. Adopting Stake's (1995) case study approach, it focuses on a unique half-private, half-state-owned company with complex processes in the context of an ERP software development project.

Data collection involves semi-structured interviews, observations, document examination, and focus group studies, managed and analyzed by the researcher within a subcontractor company. Four case studies for sub-processes are selected. SSM (Waring, A., 1996) guides problem exploration, collecting stakeholder perspectives and conducting interviews. SSM analyzes using rich pictures, BPMN system demonstrations, and process explanations. The CATWOE rule and root definition is defined, and conceptual models illustrate potential improvements. Comparisons with real-world applications identify needed changes and they are proposed and implemented by the subcontractor organization.

2. EMPIRICAL FINDINGS: CASE STUDY APPLICATION

SDP starts with a customer's need, involving process design, code development, testing, and deployment on the ERP system. Two organizations are involved: the customer (employer) initiates the need, while the subcontractor firm handles the process design, code development, testing, and deployment. Due to confidentiality issues, the study predominantly focuses on the subcontractor firm.

2.1 Stage 1-2: Finding Out About Problem Situation and Analysis

To define problematic issues in the process, data are collected from semi-structured interviews, focus group meetings, observations that involves stakeholders of the SDP which have roles as developers, designers and customers. (For meeting notes refer to Günaydın, G., 2023).

As a result of data collection phase, issues and primary task related areas are constructed. Encountered issues are lack of know-how, managerial competence, customer relations, morale and motivation, authority and power. Primary task related areas are defined as design management, technical development and testing. According to analysis, SDP composes of three main sub-processes which are 'Design Management', 'Technical Development' and 'Testing' process respectively and one supporting sub-process which is 'Training Process'. In this paper, only 3 main sub-processes are depicted, for training process refer to Günaydın, G.,2023. Regarding to data, rich pictures and BPMN diagrams of the processes are drawn below.

2.1.1 Design Management Process

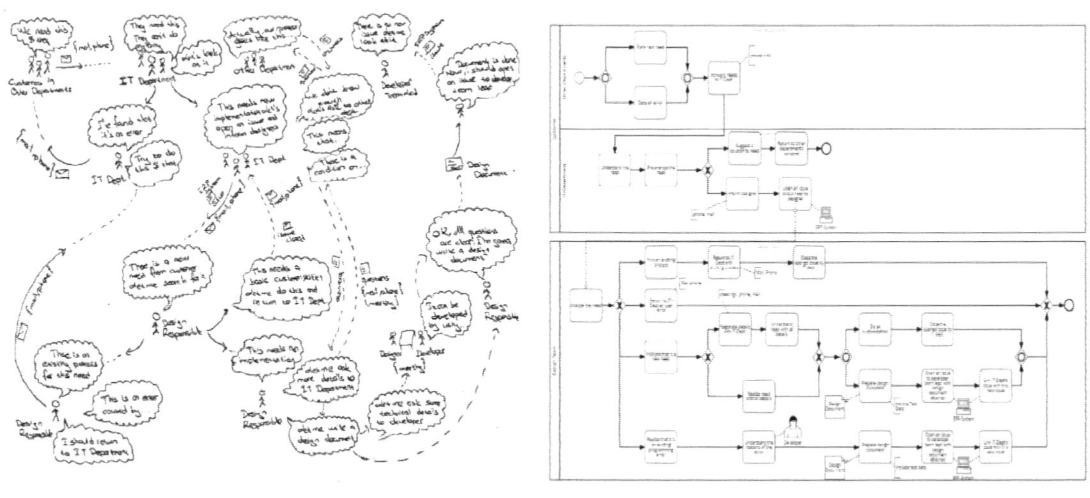

Figure 1. (a) Rich picture (b) BPMN of Design Management Process

2.1.2 Technical Development Process

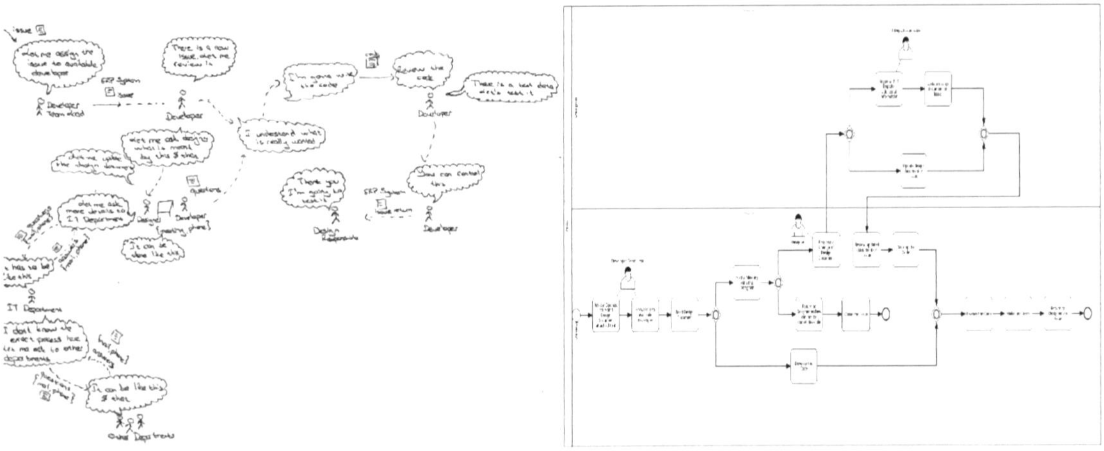

Figure 2. (a) Rich picture (b) BPMN of Technical Development Process

2.1.3 Testing Process

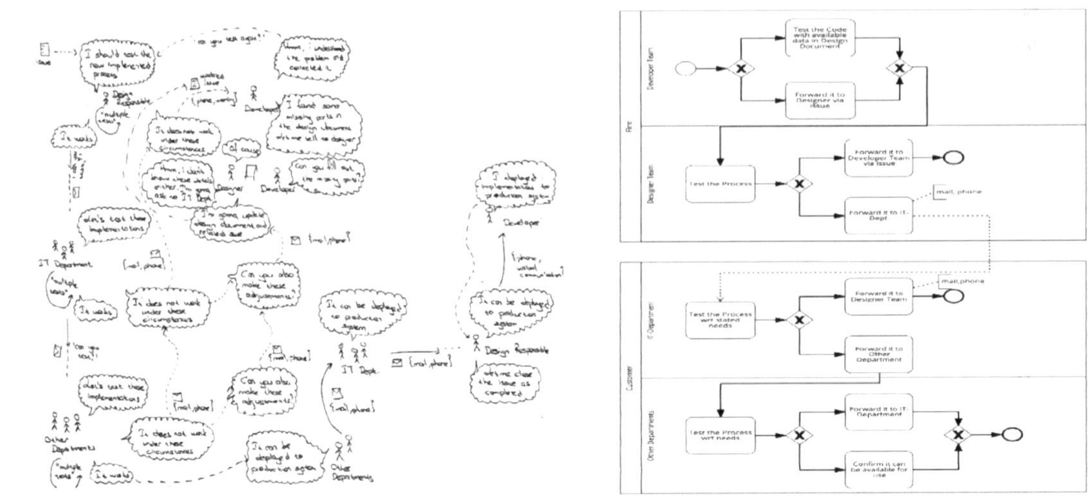

Figure 3. (a) Rich picture (b) BPMN of Testing Process

2.2 Stage 3: Root Definition of Relevant System

Root definition is applied to all sub-processes in order to improve overall software development process. To achieve this, CATWOE rule is defined and applied.

Table 1. Root Definition

Customers	Actors	Transformation	Worldview	Owners	Environment
Designers, developers, managers,department's ERP responsibles and end users.	Employees of SDP such as designers, developers, IT-department and departments' ERP responsibles	Reconstructing some sub-process steps in order to achieve more efficient software development process.	Designers and developers have the most influential view to achieve the most effective improvement	ERP system that is currently in use by, managers, customers and employees	Office, work area, infrastructure and ERP system

Root Definition: A system (SDP) owned and operated by stakeholders to monitor operations, make improvements and provide reliable data by using ERP tools and human resources in order to achieve an efficient software development.

2.3 Stage 4-5: Constructing Conceptual Model and Comparing with Real-World Activities

In stage 4-5, conceptual models of all sub-processes are constructed and compared with real world activities. Below figures depict the comparisons of each sub-process with real world activities.

2.3.1 Comparison of Conceptual Model of Design Management Process with Real World Activities

Conceptual Model	Real World Activities	Change	Roles	Conceptual Model Cont'd	Real World Cont'd	Change	Roles	Conceptual Model Cont'd	Real World Cont'd	Change	Roles
Understand the need and identify customers	End users' needs aren't considered, the designer primarily engages with IT	All stakeholders should be identified	Designer	Define criteria(s) to prioritize requirements	Lack of defined criteria for prioritization due to undefined requirements	New requirements document creation	Designer	Finalize design document	Design document is written	New design document creation	Designer
Define goals and objectives	Goals and objectives are determined through meetings, calls, or emails for improvement	No change	Designer	Conduct a focus group meeting to prioritize requirements and to make relations between them	Focus group meeting are aimed to understand processes better rather than review requirements; outcomes are not documented	New requirements document creation	Designer, IT and other dept.	Prepare a test document according to design document	No test document due to absence of template; test data, if any, are added to the design document	New test document creation	Designer
Conduct research and find alternatives	Limited research due to the designer's lack of knowledge; alternatives are not consistently explored	Extensive research	Designer	Create a requirements document	No defined requirements template	New requirements document creation	Designer	Review design document and define test objectives	This step is not valid due to absence of test document	Include in new test document	Designer
Make a detailed conceptual document	No standardized conceptual document	New conceptual document creation	Designer	Send requirements document to customers for verification	Lack of requirements document makes this step invalid	New requirements document creation	Designer	Identify test scenarios and send to IT-Dept. for verification	This step is not valid due to absence of test document	Include in new test document	Designer
Send conceptual document to all customers for verification	Inadequacies in verification arise	New conceptual document creation	Designer, IT and other dept.	Start to prepare design document with approved requirements	Design documents are not consistently based on requirements; reliance on customer-stated needs	New design document creation	Designer, IT and other dept.	Create and prioritize test cases	This step is not valid due to absence of test document	Include in new test document	Designer
From approved conceptual document, create functional decompositions of processes	Processes lack detailed decomposition; often not documented	Write in conceptual document	Designer	Model requirements by using modeling techniques such as use case diagrams, activity diagrams and class diagrams	Minimal use of modeling techniques; technical ERP language prevails over use cases	Include in new design document	Designer	Design test data	Limited inclusion if test data in the design document, if available.	Include in new test document	Designer
Identify requirements with respect to functional decompositions	Requirements are not systemically identified, prioritized or grouped	New requirements document creation	Designer	Develop a prototype for user reviews and feedback mechanism	Prototypes are barely utilized, despite ERP capabilities for their creation	Do prototypes and include in design document	Designer, IT and other dept.	Define test environment	The test environment is primarily defined, leveraging the ERP software mentioned.	Include in new test document	Designer
Group requirements as functional, non-functional and business	Requirements are not systemically identified, prioritized or grouped	New requirements document creation	Designer	Revise and update requirements and design document with respect to feedbacks.	Feedbacks provided verbally by customers; instructions to developers are also verbal	Include in new design document by tracking versions.	Designer	Finalize test document	This step is not valid due to absence of test document	New test document creation	Designer

Figure 5. Comparison of conceptual model of design management process with real world activities

2.3.2 Comparison of Conceptual Model of Technical Development Process with Real World Activities

Conceptual Model	Real World Activities	Change	Roles	Conceptual Model Cont'd	Real World Cont'd	Change	Roles
Review opened issue and attached documents	Opened issue is reviewed by both technical manager and developer.	No change	Developer	Execute test cases	Absence of test document makes this step invalid. However, if there are test data in design document, they are executed.	Test document	Developer
Ask designer for incomprehensible parts (review with designer)	Developer mostly asks designer for incomprehensible parts by phone, teleconference or face-to-face meetings.	No change	Developer	Record test results	Absence of test document makes this step invalid. Moreover, results of test data are not recorded.	Test document	Developer
Write code	When everything is understood, code is written.	No change	Developer	Log defects	Absence of test document makes this step invalid.Moreover, there is not any defect logging.	Test document	Developer
Show interim designs to designer and get feedback	Designs are shown at the end of the coding. This causes reworks most of the time.	Interim protoypes should be discussed	Developer, Designer	Verify Fixes	Absence of test document makes this step invalid.However, test data can be used to verify fixes.	Test document	Developer
Review code	Code review is done but sometimes not accurately which is also causes reworks.	No change	Developer	Retest	Retest is done.	No change	Developer
Finalize coding	Code is finalized	No change	Developer	Finalize testing	Testing is finalized by developer.	No change	Developer
Review test document	Absence of test document makes this step invalid. However, if there are test data in design document, they are reviewed.	Test document	Developer	Return to designer and change opened issue's status as development can be tested	Developer returns to designer to test the developments via issue.	No change	Developer

Figure 6. Comparison of conceptual model of technical development process with real world activities

2.3.3 Comparison of Conceptual Model of Testing Process with Real World Activities

Conceptual Model	Real World Activities	Change	Roles	Conceptual Model Cont'd	Real World Cont'd	Change	Roles
Test the process according to test scenarios	There is not any formed test scenarios, however, implemented process is tested.	Test document review	Designer	If test is successful, request testing from other departments	Test request is asked via mail or phone	No change	Other Departments
Record test results	Test results are not documented.	Include in test document	Designer	Test the process	There is not any formed test scenarios, however, implemented process is tested.	Test document review	Other Departments
If test is not successful, return to developer with test results and developer modifies the code	Test results are not documented, but it is told to developer verbally or short notes are forwarded to developer	Test document update	Designer, Developer	If test is not successful, return to IT Department with test results	Test results and sample data are returned to IT Department via mail or phone.	Test document update	Other Departments
If test is successful, request testing from IT Department	Test request is asked via mail or phone	No change	Designer, IT dept.	If test is successful, request for deployment	Deployment request is asked via mail or phone.	No change	IT, other departments
Test the process according to scenarios	There is not any formed test scenarios, however, implemented process is tested.	Test document review	IT Dept.	Deploy the improvements after everything is approved	Designer asks for deployment to developer	No change	Designer, Developer
If test is not successful, return to designer with test results	Test results and sample data are returned to designer via mail or phone	Test document update	Designer, IT dept.	Close the issues	After deployment is done, all issues are closed by designer	No change	Designer

Figure 7. Comparison of conceptual model of testing process with real world activities

2.4 Stage 6: Debate

In this part, main suggested process changes or variations are specified These suggestions are discussed with related focus groups. (Detailed explanations for parts 2.4 and 2.5 can be found in Günaydın, G., 2023).

1. System goals and objectives should be established through a conceptual document.
2. Process should be broken down into sub-processes, documented into the conceptual document.
3. An extensive requirements process is essential.
4. Design document should include requirements, modeling techniques, and prototypes for the process.
5. A comprehensive test document is indispensable.
6. Identifying test management activities is essential.

2.5 Stage 7: Take Action

Findings and proposed changes are shared with subcontractor. Some feasible changes are implemented like new templates (conceptual, requirements, design, test) within the organization. Company started to use these documents, and upload them to the ERP system for issue tracking.

3. CONCLUSION

Results highlight design management as the most challenging process, with testing process facing issues. Mass collaboration aids change investigation, emphasizing shared knowledge. Conflict resolution involves one-to-one dialogues, ERP issue examination, and on-site observations. SSM is valued for flexibility in socio-cultural contexts, supporting continuous improvement through process monitoring. Future improvements can be measured with key performance indicators, acknowledging confidentiality limits in stakeholder and organization name disclosure and potential process omissions in interviews.

REFERENCES

Checkland, P., & Scholes, J. (1999). *Soft systems methodology in action*. John Wiley & Sons.

Günaydın, G. (2023). *Seven Stage Model Of The Soft System Methodology For Software Development Process,* Middle East Technical University, Ankara.

Stake, R.E. (1995). *The Art of Case Study Research*, Sage.

Waring, A. (1996). *Practical Systems Thinking*, Thomson.

SUSTAINABILITY TRACING FOR COMPANIES: GOVERNANCE, REGULATION, ECONOMICAL AND ETHICAL CONSIDERATIONS

Galena Pisoni[1], Bálint Molnár[2], Szabolcs Korba[2] and Maria Moloney[3*]
[1]York business School, York St John University, Lord Mayor's Walk, YO31 7EX, York, UK
[2]Information Systems Department, Eötvös Loránd University~(ELTE), Budapest, Hungary
[3]University College Dublin, Belfield, Dublin 4, Ireland

ABSTRACT

The proliferation of big data has led to a data explosion, which has surpassed enterprises' ability to appropriately analyse the multitude of data types that now exist. Arguably, one such data type that is challenging for companies to currently exploit but that would benefit greatly from big data analytics is tracing their sustainability performance. Currently, there is consensus in the literature that sustainability tracing based on big data analytics can have a considerable impact in achieving improved organizational sustainability. In a previous paper, we proposed an AI-based framework which uses ESG data to predict and forecast the sustainability performance of companies, and we reflected on how companies could use our framework to implement their enterprise architectures. In this paper, we reflect how our framework can be transformed into a platform solution for ESG data analysis. Our paper contributes to the literature in two ways, firstly by analysing, the regulatory, ethical, and legal opportunities and challenges associated with such am AI platform implementation scenario and secondly by leveraging this platform implementation to outline how companies can use data as a strategic asset for sustainability decision-making.

KEYWORDS

Sustainability, Enterprise Architectures, Business Intelligence Reporting, Data Analytics, Data-driven Decision Making, ESG

1. INTRODUCTION

Sustainability management has increased in popularity in recent years. At the societal level, it is essential to manage the increased risks arising from accelerated change (climate change, the shift from a linear to a circular economy, growing inequality) and to find a balance between economic and social needs. Investors, regulators, consumers and employees increasingly expect companies to be good stewards not only of financial capital but also of natural and social capital, and to ensure that they have the right governance conditions to maintain it. Companies care more about being sustainable in how they do business to meet increased expectations and the legal requirements that reflect them, and indeed to increase and maintain their market competitiveness. Paying attention to the media makes businesses feel more pressure to be sustainable. This leads to questions about how to see if they are making progress towards their sustainability goals.

Businesses use ESG guidelines to check how environmentally friendly, socially responsible, and well-run their companies are. These guidelines inform environmental, social, and governance policy in company decisions. In fact, recent research shows that companies with an ESG agenda not only have better financial sustainability and performance, but they also have higher valuations. Companies that care about environmental, social, and governance issues are seen as more trustworthy, and they do a better job of managing risks and making sure they are prepared for long-term challenges (Xie, 2019; Pedersen, 2020). In addition to reporting, ESG can also become a competitive tool: in addition to the mandatory data, companies can also demonstrate their commitment to sustainability by publishing other corporate data.

[*]Corresponding author: maria.moloney@ucd.ie

At the same time, Artificial Intelligence (AI) has changed the way businesses use data and operate. AI, along with Machine Learning (ML), and automation, is now pervasive and has become increasingly important for how organizations work. In the last few years, AI has been helpful for companies to analyze and better understand their own organization. Prior to this, businesses used to do their search and selection tasks manually. They used information from self-disclosure and annual business operations, which often contained and led to errors and inaccuracies.

Present methods of using AI to track sustainability aspects of companies are limited in scope (Ebinger & Omondi, 2020; Lee et al., 2021; Hofmann & Langner, 2020). Using ML and AI for analysing ESG big data is still in its infancy and many companies have not yet been successful in their attempts (Macpherson, et al, 2021). We posit, however, that big data can help companies measure how well they follow sustainability rules by leveraging their existing data to yield more precise results, leading to more informed decision-making. At the same time, the effective use of big data requires compliance with the existing rules on the processing of personal data and a rethinking of the relationship framework.

In a previous paper, we used a multi-industry approach to analyze and create a decision support platform that can be used across to various industries and types of businesses. This approach uses technology to gather data from across companies, study it to assess the company's level of sustainability and if necessary, assist them in making smarter decisions to improve their sustainability. In this paper we reflect on:

- possible governance approaches for such platforms, and how they affect working conditions, sustainability, and growth. We reflect on the involvement of people and community, and the different ways people can work together and make decisions with such platforms,
- analyze ethical aspects of such platforms, i.e. fairness, data protection, and making sure that all citizens are involved.
- existing policies and regulatory challenges and opportunities around sustainability collaboration.
- economic value potential such platform can provide, and their impact on social and open innovation.

Future platforms must be open, inclusive, and adaptable for everyone by design. This includes involving people in the process and ensuring the systems support diverse users' needs in their daily activities. In Europe, open infrastructures like open-source projects are getting a lot of attention because of their importance in the digital world and the government's focus on digital independence. However, being open has challenges, as we outlined above from the perspective of governance, ethics, regulation, and economics. In this paper, we analyze the literature on the above-mentioned aspects and propose suitable solutions.

2. SUSTAINABILITY TRACING OF COMPANIES

Sustainability tracing of companies can be captured by Supply Chain Management (SCM) and Information Logistics (IL) and Production Logistics (PL) procedures. Information Logistics embraces documents, and any data format, that can flow through the business processes and the workflows of firms. The trustworthiness of information can be guaranteed by appropriate blockchain technology. Additionally, conformance to reporting requirement, either internal or external, can be demonstrated by following approved standards of accounting methods (European Parliament and of the Council (2024)). A typical property of an ESG Information System (ESG IS) is that the stakeholders involved are numerous, and the input data originates from a vast number of resources. The Triple Bottom Line notion (TBL) is embedded in business management to support sustainability, the three dimensions being economic, environmental, and social (Elkington, J. (1998)). The IL plays a crucial role in ensuring traceability, and in assisting addressing uncertainty and complexity within companies and in the intercompany information exchange. Companies are discovering blockchain's potential to improve external reports through smart contracts, validation, consensus algorithms, and third-party verifications. Blockchain technology through the distributed ledger that provides data integrity and immutability gives trustworthiness to models that are processed by AI, Data Science and Machine Learning. More reliable data means augmented modelling abilities, and new qualitative data may have resulted in the creation of entirely new models.

2.1 AI-Based Architecture Solution

Companies use various types of data to achieve sustainable practices. This data comes from their operations, company records and external sources, such as the internet, and audio and image files. Some companies use Data Warehouses to store and integrate data from different sources, while others use Lakehouses for similar purposes (Haelen, B. 2024).

This practice of data collection and analysis helps companies make decisions using the data (Golfarelli and Rizzi 2009; Kimball 2010). The data warehouses contain static information that remains unchanged. Its purpose is to help the company quickly find answers. Initially, unstructured data from various sources is organized and cleaned. The same data ingestion process is carried out in the case of Lakehouse, however, the gathering of meta-data and creating indexes and links happens through an intelligent data dictionary. Subsequently, a dependable source of information is created for predicting and prescribing different ESG components. By integrating different types of data, an effective data system is established that allows for gradual modification and utilization of the data.

The diagram in Figure 1 shows the kind of data a company can use for ESG rules detection and application.

A data lake is a different type of storage system that should for such situations. The data warehouse deals with organized data, while the data lake has unstructured data that needs to be organized before it can be used. In our architectural solution (Figure 1), we have a data warehouse for making big decisions over a long period of time, and a data lake for making smaller, daily decisions. The data lake has a smaller version of the data and is separate from the data warehouse for long-term reporting and data retrieval.

Companies choose the KPIs they want to monitor for the different ESG areas. Dashboards make it easier to see how a company is performing in areas such as environment, society and governance. The dashboard can help the company make better decisions.

In the data lake, we need to make sure that the data is kept secure and follows the rules for data protection and GDPR. A list of different ML and AI tools should be kept for use by the data lake and data warehouse. Advanced access control methods should be used to protect the integrity, confidentiality and availability of the data. This includes using strong passwords and multi-factor authentication.

2.2 Governance, Legal, Economical and Ethical Consideration

- Governance considerations. Selecting an optimal level of openness is crucial. Managers should carefully consider the governance aspects and the sustainability considerations for their individual company. Just letting different stakeholders use a platform may not be enough for them to truly commit (Halckenhaeusser, Foerderer & Heinzl, 2020). Open access does not necessarily encourage more people to get involved, especially if it is not clear who oversees the platform and why. When a more structured governance approach is in place, relevant and diverse stakeholders can become more involved in using and consulting the data (Schreieck, Wiesche & Krcmar, 2016).
- Legal requirements will mandate the types of information companies share and its level of detail. Such sustainability platforms would need to define and balance companies' obligations in relation to protection of personal data, transparency, prevention and enforcement procedures (antitrust infringements). These are in addition to defining both platform stakeholder roles and their criteria and liability regimens (Eisenmann, Parker & Van Alstyne 2009).
- Economic aspects, in a broader sense, open innovation refers to companies, people and institutions working together to create innovative products. In a world of distributed knowledge, it is imperative that companies rely not only on data from their own products / services, because in general companies have lots to gain if they combine knowledge from diverse sources. This approach can set the basis for the construction of new business models that are yet to be tapped, in terms of both, value creation and value capture (Vanhaverbeke & Chesbrough 2014).
- Ethical considerations. Solid ethical foundations should guide how the platform is designed, implemented and managed over time. Design by itself cannot ensure good implementation. Data privacy, fairness, accountability and transparency are critical ethical aspects to embed from the start. In addition, such platforms should consider inclusion, and how people with different abilities levels can access the information. Consideration should be given to whether a non-expert consumer of a complex and sophisticated product/service can actually obtain useful, meaningful information from a

professional business, or whether mandatory expert qualifications (standards, peer reviews, sandboxes) may be necessary. Such platforms should be good-for-all and prevent any opportunistic behavior (Seth, 2019).

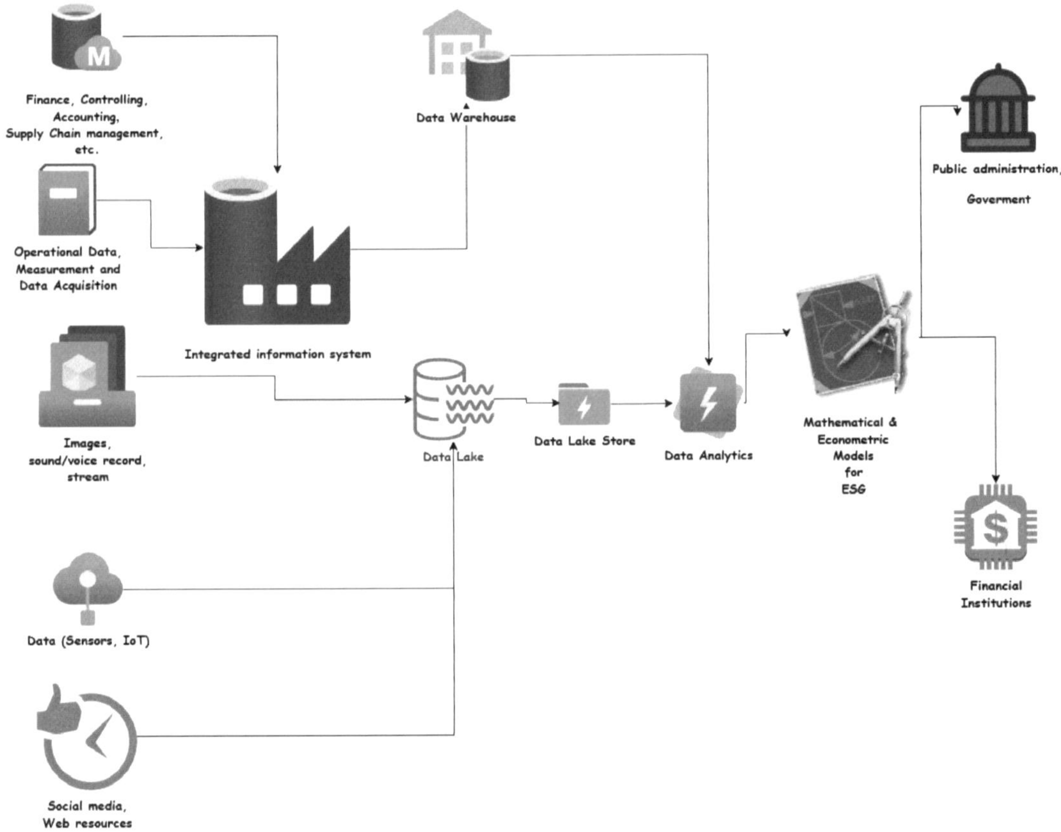

Figure 1. Data sources and their utilization for analysis and prediction of ESG-rules adherence for companies

3. DISCUSSIONS AND FUTURE STEPS

To our knowledge, our research is the first to look at how to create a platform that helps companies track their environmental, social, and governance criteria and offers services to help them improve their performance. This can be a great tool for businesses to help them see how well they are doing in the areas of environmental, social, and governance criteria. They can then work on improving the areas where they are not doing well

Our work and previous research show that looking at how companies handle environmental, social, and governance issues using big data is important for studying sustainability. In general, people are starting to care more about sustainability, but we still need to do more research to find out how artificial intelligence can help finance sustainability in the future. Many companies are working together to study how they make decisions to be more sustainable. This is also getting a lot of attention and money from the EU for research projects.

ACKNOWLEDGEMENT

This research was supported the Thematic Excellence Programme TKP2021-NVA-29 (National Challenges Subprogramme) funding scheme and by the COST Action CA19130 - "Fintech and Artificial Intelligence in Finance Towards a transparent financial industry" (FinAI)."

REFERENCES

Crona, B. (2021). Sweet Spots or Dark Corners? An environmental sustainability examination of Big Data and AI in ESG. Big Data Analytics, AI, ML for Environmental, Social and Governance (ESG) Control, Performance and Risk Management, in Handbook of Big Data and Analytics in Accounting and Auditing. http://dx.doi.org/10.2139/ssrn.4037299

Ebinger, F.; Omondi, B. (2020) Leveraging digital approaches for transparency in sustainable supply chains: A conceptual paper. Sustainability, 12, 6129. https://doi.org/10.3390/su12156129

Eisenmann, T. R., Parker, G., & Van Alstyne, M. (2009). Opening platforms: How, when and why. *Platforms, markets and innovation*, *6*, 131-162.

Elkington, J. (1998). Partnerships from cannibals with forks: The triple bottom line of 21st-century business. *Environmental Quality Management*, 8: 37–51. https://doi.org/10.1002/tqem.3310080106

European Parliament and of the Council (2024). REGULATION (EU) 2020/852 OF THE EUROPEAN PARLIAMENT AND OF THE COUNCIL of 18 June 2020 on the establishment of a framework to facilitate sustainable investment, and amending Regulation (EU) 2019/2088. https://eur-lex.europa.eu/legal-content/EN/TXT/?uri=CELEX%3A32020R0852.

Golfarelli, M., & Rizzi, S. (2009). A survey on temporal data warehousing. International Journal of Data Warehousing and Mining (IJDWM), 5(1), 1-17.

Haelen, B. (2024). *DELTA LAKE up & running*. D. Davis (ed.). [Sebastopol, California]: O'Reilly Media, Inc.

Hofmann, E.; Langner, D. (2020) The Rise of Supply Chain Viability–Digital Solutions as a Boosting Role, [https://www.alexandria.unisg.ch/publications/261668].

Kimball, R., & Ross, M. (2010). The Kimball group reader: relentlessly practical tools for data warehousing and business intelligence. John Wiley & Sons.

Lee, C.; Kim, Y.; Shin, Y. (2021) Data Usage and the Legal Stability of Transactions for the Commercial Operation of Autonomous Vessels Based on Digital Ownership in Korean Civil Law. Sustainability, 13, 8134. https://doi.org/10.3390/su13158134

Macpherson, M.; Gasperini, A.; Bosco, M. (2021) Artificial Intelligence and FinTech Technologies for ESG Data and Analysis. Available at SSRN 3790774.

Pedersen, L.H.; Fitzgibbons, S.; Pomorski, L. (2020) Responsible investing: The ESG-efficient frontier. Journal of Financial Economics. https://doi.org/10.1016/j.jfineco.2020.11.001

Schreieck, M., Wiesche, M., & Krcmar, H. (2016, June). Design and Governance of Platform Ecosystems-Key Concepts and Issues for Future Research. In *Ecis* (Vol. 16, pp. 12-15).

Seth, A. (2019). A new paradigm to accommodate ethical foundations in the design and management of digital platforms. *Manuscript, IIT Delhi*.

Tang, B. W. (2020). Independent AI Ethics Committees and ESG Corporate Reporting on AI as Emerging Corporate and AI Governance Trends. The AI Book: The Artificial Intelligence Handbook for Investors, Entrepreneurs and FinTech Visionaries, 180-185.

Vanhaverbeke, W., & Chesbrough, H. (2014). A classification of open innovation and open business models. *New frontiers in open innovation*, *6*, 50-68.

Xie, J.; Nozawa, W.; Yagi, M.; Fujii, H.; Managi, S. (2019) Do environmental, social, and governance activities improve corporate financial performance? Business Strategy and the Environment, 28, 286–300. https://doi.org/10.1002/bse.2224

TOWARD INTEGRATED DISASTER PREVENTION AND MITIGATION SYSTEM LINKING DISASTER INFORMATION COLLECTION AND PROPERTY DAMAGE SIMULATION

Toshihiro Osaragi, Noriaki Hirokawa and Maki Kishimoto
Tokyo Institute of Technology
2-12-1-M4-1 Ookayama, Meguro, Tokyo 152-8550, Japan

ABSTRACT

In this research, we will build an integrated disaster prevention and mitigation system on the same platform that enables the rational use of early disaster information. For this purpose, we will integrate the models and systems that have been developed in disaster prevention/mitigation simulation research by organizing input/output information and assumptions relating to several disaster scenarios. Simulation analyses that have previously been performed under uncertain conditions and assumptions will now be repeatedly executed using the disaster information collected and accumulated through the disaster information collection and sharing system as constraints. By replacing some of the uncertain information or assumptions with actual observation data, it becomes possible to obtain more precise simulation results at any time, and we can expect even greater disaster mitigation support effects. This system will be used to conduct disaster prevention drills and field experiments to detect risks and issues that have been overlooked in the past, and at the same time consider ways to provide disaster prevention and mitigation support to overcome these.

KEYWORDS

Disaster Prevention/Mitigation, Disaster Information, Cloud Server, Uncertain Information, Simulation System

1. INTRODUCTION

Simulation research on disaster prevention and mitigation is highly dependent on how to handle the existing countless uncertainties. For example,

- Detailed analysis is possible if we could know the date, time, location, and scale of a disaster, but in reality, it is impossible to obtain beforehand even these types of basic information.
- The spatial distribution of people staying in a city changes from moment to moment (Ratti et al., 2006; Calabrese et al., 2011; Iqbal et al., 2014; Deville et al., 2014), hence there are limitations to human damage estimation based on the population distribution over a specific time section (Osaragi, 2016).
- How people's disaster-relating activities (disaster information collection, firefighting activity, rescue operations, etc.) can mitigate damages has not been sufficiently analyzed.

Thus, past disaster prevention and mitigation simulation research has facilitated discussion by focusing on a specific event by assuming environments and conditions (Oki and Osaragi, 2018). Although setting simple assumptions is effective in reducing the number of scenarios (combinations of conditions), there is a large discrepancy between reality and assumptions, and it is difficult to grasp the overall picture of disasters that occur as a result of a chain of diverse conditions. Furthermore, the discrepancy with reality has not been discussed in depth due to the reasons for the difficulty in setting assumptions.

In order to address these limitations of conventional disaster prevention and mitigation simulation research, this research examines them from the following viewpoints.

- Clarify the assumptions, and input/output information of the models/systems that have been proposed and developed with a proven track record, and organize the dependencies between the models/systems.

- Integrate each model/system by interconnecting them on the same platform, and by implementing it in an environment that can operate even in the event of an actual disaster, and estimate an overall picture of a disaster that occurs in a chain of various events. Namely, we build an integrated disaster prevention/mitigation system that can capture disasters.
- Perform integrated simulations in real time assuming immediately after a disaster occurs, and re-execute, update, and synchronize the simulation results.
- Verify the effectiveness of integrated disaster prevention and mitigation systems through various field experiments, and comprehensively verify efficient and effective disaster prevention and mitigation measures from a scientific perspective.

2. CONCEPT OF INTEGRATED SYSTEM TO BE DEVELOPED

As shown in Figure 1, we have developed a "property damage estimation system" that estimates property damage under limited information that can be obtained in earlier phases (Hirokawa and Osaragi, 2016), and a "disaster information collection and sharing system" that was expected to be used by disaster volunteers (Osaragi and Niwa, 2018). Tokyo Metropolitan GIS data were mainly used for these systems. By integrating these two systems in the same cloud computing server, we will develop a simulation system that is constantly synchronized with disaster information. First, in Phase 1, building collapse simulations and street blockage simulations are automatically executed using earthquake early warnings obtained from an external API server as trigger information. In addition, fire spread simulations are automatically executed based on fire outbreak information obtained from high-altitude cameras or drones. Using these simulation results, even immediately after a disaster occurs, when no damage information for each location is available, it is possible to provide information based on simulation results for preparing initial responses. In Phase 2, the various simulations performed in Phase 1 are simultaneously repeated using the disaster information as a given constraint, which is accumulated on the server from moment to moment. By replacing some of the uncertain information with actual observed data and recalculating using the certain information as constraints, it is expected we will be able to obtain more accurate simulation results.

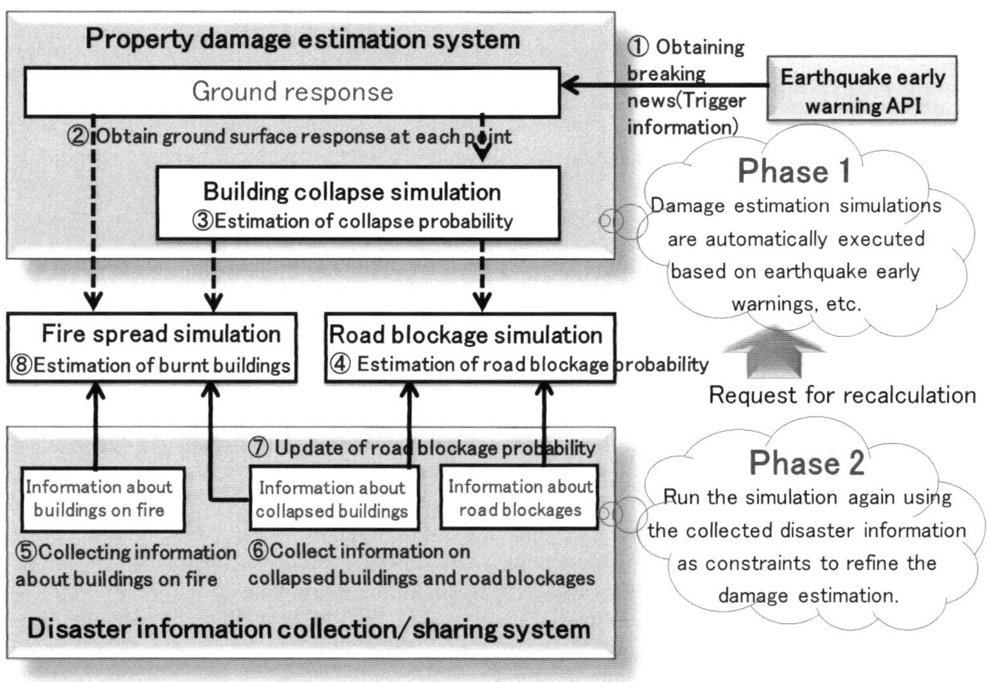

Figure 1. Linkage of property damage estimation system and disaster information collection and sharing system.

3. RELATED RESEARCH

Since natural disasters are extremely complex phenomena, they have often been partially analyzed by focusing only on specific events or making many assumptions (Mordvintsev et al., 2014; Mas et al., 2013). However, there are significant limitations when comprehensively considering actual natural disasters that are composed of a variety kind of phenomena. In order to assess disasters from wider viewpoints, it is necessary to interconnect individual models/systems and operate them in an integrated manner. In addition, the importance of updating simulation results by repeating calculations is significantly high, since disaster phenomena that are actually occurring can provide concrete information on unknown assumptions or conditions.

In the previous research, there are problems that the disaster prevention and mitigation simulations that have been developed so far are scattered and independent, and there is a lack of perspective on how to utilize observation data in simulation. In the process of social implementation of various simulation models and systems, we encounter these problems and come up with the idea for this research.

There are countless simulation studies related to disaster prevention and mitigation from various viewpoints (Ertugay and Duzgun, 2006; Claes et al., 2011; Oskarsson et al., 2020; Osaragi et al., 2020; Pradhan et al., 2022). In particular, in Japan, which is a country prone to earthquakes, many sophisticated simulation models have been proposed and validated using data obtained from damage surveys of past actual disasters. Empirical data, technical details, and case studies validating the proposed systems are described in the previous research (Osaragi and Hirokawa, 2017a; Osaragi and Hirokawa, 2019; Osaragi et al., 2018). However, many simulation models have been proposed independently, and no system has been proposed that comprehensively captures and describes the complex aspects of disasters.

There is a lot of research on developing disaster prevention and mitigation systems overseas, but due to differences in building structures and street widths, it is difficult to find anything that can be directly applied to Japan. Furthermore, concerning fire spread models, most overseas studies focus on fires inside buildings or forest fires, and there are very few models that describe the spread of fire in areas with a high density of wooden houses (Osaragi and Hirokawa, 2017b). Therefore, especially concerning earthquake disasters, there is a need to develop a model unique to Japan that takes into account the characteristics of earthquakes, ground characteristics, building characteristics, regional characteristics, etc. in Japan.

4. SYSTEM CONFIGURATION TO BE CONSTRUCTED

We will develop an integrated disaster prevention and mitigation system using a platform built on a cloud server by integrating models/systems that have been developed individually. Furthermore, we will verify the performance of this system through disaster prevention drills and demonstration experiments in practical operations, and attempt to evaluate its performance with a view to social implementation. The system configuration to be constructed in this research is shown in Figure 2. The outline of each part of Figure 2 (1) to (9) is as follows.

(1) Build an interface for the application server to obtain information such as the epicenter, earthquake intensity, wind direction/speed, and fire outbreak locations from high-altitude cameras and external API servers such as government agencies. We have already started exchanging information on data formats, etc. with the people in charge of the Disaster Prevention Science Research Institute. We are also preparing to collaborate with other research institutions to obtain information on fire outbreak locations using high-altitude cameras and drones.

(2) Information from the external API server is transferred from the application server to the simulation server, and a building collapse model, a street blockage model, a fire spread model, and an evacuation/rescue/firefighting model are automatically executed (Hirokawa and Osaragi, 2016; Kishimoto and Osaragi, 2018). Some of these models have been verified (Osaragi and Hirokawa, 2017a, 2017b). In this research, a series of models are linked together on a cloud server so that they can be automatically executed using only trigger information from an external server.

(3) Build a disaster information collection and sharing system for use by disaster prevention volunteers (Stuart et al., 2014; Petersen et al., 2017; Ngamassi et al., 2017). Posted information about street blockages greatly contributes to the prompt arrival of the fire brigade to the fire scene (Osaragi and Hirokawa, 2019).

In addition, by sharing and utilizing posted information about building collapses, the possibility of rescuing more trapped people increases (Oki et al., 2019). Furthermore, by sharing information with local residents, safe and smooth evacuation can be achieved (Osaragi et al., 2019; Osaragi and Niwa, 2018). In this research, we will conduct a field experiment in which disaster prevention volunteers utilize this system to collect and share disaster information, and attempt system verification. Furthermore, the disaster information collection and sharing system being targeted at "things" will be extended to a system that targets "humans" such as seriously injured people, trapped people, and people requiring assistance. It will be shown that using it not only in emergencies but also in normal times, can contribute to daily mental care (creating a sense of safety and security). In this research, we will conduct field experiments on the normal use of the system to verify the continuity, updateability, and expandability of the system.

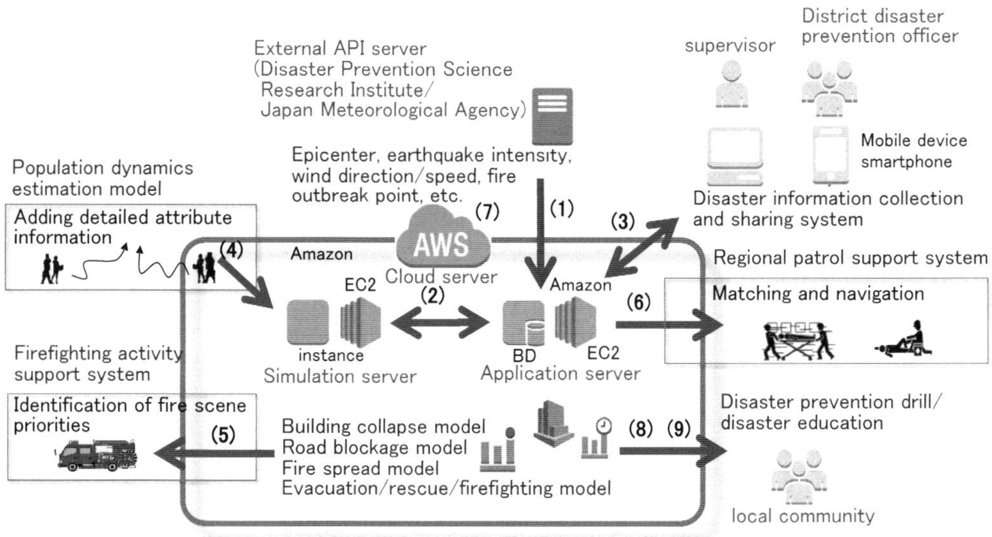

Figure 2. Integrated disaster prevention and mitigation system based on physical damage simulation linked with disaster information collection

(4) Human damage greatly depends on the fundamental problem of "How do we envision the spatiotemporal distribution of people staying and moving in the city, which changes from moment to moment" (Osaragi and Hayasaka, 2020). In other words, it depends on "What kind of people (age, gender, occupation) are doing when (month, day of the week, time), where (location, facility), and what (purpose of stay/movement) are they doing? (Osaragi and Kudo, 2019) " Hence, it is necessary to estimate detailed demographic trends of human movements and conduct analysis based on its estimates. To this end, we developed a method for estimating demographic data with detailed attribute information in near-real time by utilizing multiple demographic data (Osaragi and Hayasaka, 2020). In this research, we aim to generalize this method and incorporate it into a system.

(5) Build a system that supports firefighting activities immediately after a major earthquake based on property damage estimated by the simulation server (building collapse, street blockage, fire spread). If this system supports firefighting efforts, it is possible that the scale of fire spread damage could be reduced to about one-third (Osaragi and Hirokawa, 2017b). In this research, we will apply the firefighting support function to actual firefighting training and examine new problems and issues in detail through field experiments.

(6) Build a regional travel support system that matches "demanders" who need help in the event of a disaster with "responders" who can respond to these requests, making the best use of limited personnel, supplies, and time. Here, the demanders and responders are matched based on real-time information about where and what kind of requests are being made, and where and with what skills personnel are on standby. We will examine the effectiveness of sharing various information about the demanders and the responders while referring to the previous research (Osaragi and Niwa, 2018; Osaragi et al., 2019).

(7) The integrated disaster prevention and mitigation system will be implemented on an overseas cloud server that has excellent disaster resistance and shareability. Developed as a Web application that does not require pre-installation to improve usability. By making the system server event-driven, the number of simultaneous connections can be dramatically increased, making it possible to provide high-speed responses to each user.

(8) Consider ways to utilize damage estimation results to support initial response activities, and attempt to implement the system in society. By customizing the type and number of events to be posted, it can be easily applied to disasters other than earthquake disasters (floods, landslides, etc.) (Mordvintsev et al., 2014). We will also try to apply this technology to flood disasters such as inland water flooding and external water flooding, which are causing major damage in various places these days.

5. CONCLUSION

Simulation research on disaster prevention and mitigation relies heavily on how to handle the myriad uncertainties. Hence, simulation systems developed so far have had to base their calculations on a large number of assumptions. These assumptions may be far removed from real disaster situations, and this has led to large differences between simulation results and actual damage. In order to overcome this problem, this research organizes the dependencies among the myriad of different conditions and, at the same time, constructs a system in which some condition settings are reflected in all modules by integrating various simulations on a cloud computer. In addition, we discussed concrete points to construct a simulation system that can obtain simulation results closer to the real situation by inputting early disaster information obtained from time to time as given conditions into the system.

ACKNOWLEDGEMENT

This work is part of the research outcomes funded by KAKENHI (Grant Number 23H01653).

REFERENCES

Calabrese, F., et al., (2011). Estimating Origin-Destination Flows Using Opportunistically Collected Mobile Phone Location Data from One Million Users in Boston Metropolitan Area, *IEEE Pervasive Computing*, Vol. 10, No. 4, pp. 36-44.

Claes, R. et al., (2011). A Decentralized Approach for Anticipatory Vehicle Routing Using Delegate Multiagent Systems, *IEEE Transactions on Intelligent Transportation Systems*, Vol. 12, No. 2, pp. 364-373.

Deville, P., et al., (2014). Dynamic Population Mapping Using Mobile Phone Data, *Proceedings of the National Academy of Sciences of the United States of America*, Vol. 111, No. 45, pp. 15888-15893.

Ertugay, K., and Duzgun, S., (2006). Integrating Physical Accessibility of Emergency Establishments into Earthquake Risk Assessment, *Proceedings Geohazards, Engineering Conferences International*, ECI Digital Archives.

Hirokawa, N. and Osaragi, T., (2016). Earthquake Disaster Simulation System: Integration of Models for Building Collapse, Road Blockage, and Fire Spread, *Journal of Disaster Research* (Special Issue on Disaster and Big Data 1), Fuji Technology Press Ltd., Vol. 11, No. 2, pp. 175-187.

Iqbal, Md. S., et al., (2014). Development of Origin-Destination Matrices Using Mobile Phone Call Data: A Simulation Based Approach, *Transportation Research Part C: Emwrging Technologies*, Vol. 40, pp. 63-74.

Kishimoto, M. and Osaragi, T., (2018). Accessibility Assessment of Emergency Vehicles in Tokyo Metropolitan Area after a Large Earthquake, *3D Spatial Information Science - The Engine of Change*, ISPRS, Vol. XLII-4, pp. 303-308.

Mas, E., et al., (2013). An integrated simulation of tsunami hazard and human evacuation in La Punta, Peru, *Journal of Disaster Research*, Vol. 8, No. 2, pp. 285-295.

Mordvintsev, A. S., et al., (2014). Simulation of city evacuation coupled to flood dynamics, *Pedestrian and Evacuation Dynamics 2012*, Springer, pp. 485-499.

Ngamassi, L. et al., (2017). Social media visual analytic toolkits for disaster management: a review of the literature, *Proceedings of the 14th international conference on information systems for crisis response and management (ISCRAM)*, Albi, France.

Oki, T., et al., (2019). Quick Estimation Method of Property Damage and Human Casualty in the Event of a Large Earthquake, *Journal of Disaster Research*, Vol. 14, No. 3, pp. 478-488.

Oki, T. and Osaragi, T., (2018). Effects of Firefighting Activities Performed by Local Residents to Mitigate Fire Destruction Damage and Human Casualties in Large Earthquakes, *Journal of Disaster Research*, Vol. 13, No. 2, pp. 272-280.

Osaragi, T., (2016). Estimation of Transient Occupants on Weekdays and Weekends for Risk Exposure Analysis, *Proceedings of the 13th international conference on information systems for crisis response and management (ISCRAM)*, Rio de Janeiro, Brazil.

Osaragi, T., et al., (2018). Assessment of Street Network Accessibility in Tokyo Metropolitan Area after a Large Earthquake, *Journal of Disaster Research*, Vol. 13, No. 2, pp. 262-271.

Osaragi, T., et al., (2019). Efficient Regional Travel for Rescue and Relief Activities in a Disaster, *Computational Urban Planning and Management for Smart Cities*, Springer, pp. 425-441.

Osaragi, T., et al., (2020). Estimate of the Number of People Walking Home after Compliance with Metropolitan Tokyo Ordinance on Measures Concerning Stranded Persons, *Advances and New Trends in Environmental Informatics*, Springer Nature Switzerland AG, pp. 17-35.

Osaragi, T., and Hayasaka, Ryo., (2020). Prediction of Spatiotemporal Distributions of Transient Urban Populations with Statistics Gathered by Cell Phones, *Proceedings of the 6th International Conference on Geographical Information Systems Theory*, Vol. 1, pp. 33-44.

Osaragi, T. and Hirokawa, N., (2017a). Simulation Analysis of Fire Brigade Action Strategies During Multiple Simultaneous Fires, *Journal of Disaster Research*, Vol. 12, No. 2, pp. 311-319.

Osaragi, T. and Hirokawa, N., (2017b). A Decision Support System for Fighting Multiple Fires in Urban Areas Caused by Large Earthquakes, *Lecture Notes in Geoinformation and Cartography*, Springer, Vol. Part I, pp. 77-93.

Osaragi, T. and Hirokawa, N., (2019). Simulation Analysis of Fire Hydrant Usability Levels after Large Earthquake, *Proceedings of the 16th international conference on information systems for crisis response and management (ISCRAM)*, Valencia, Spain, pp. 22-35.

Osaragi, T., and Kudo, R., (2019). Enhancing the Use of Population Statistics Derived from Mobile Phone Users by Considering Building-Use Dependent Purpose of Stay, *Geospatial Technologies for Local and Regional Development*, Springer, pp. 185-203.

Osaragi, T. and Niwa, I., (2018). Development of System for Real-Time Collection, Sharing, and Use of Disaster Information, *Lecture Notes in Geoinformation and Cartography*, Springer, pp. 211-229.

Oskarsson, P.A., et al., (2020). Enhancing resilient response in inter-organizational contexts: Learning from experience, *Proceedings of the 17th international conference on information systems for crisis response and management (ISCRAM)*, Blacksburg, VA, USA.

Petersen, L., et al., (2017). Public expectations of social media use by critical infrastructure operators in crisis communication, *Proceedings of the 14th international conference on information systems for crisis response and management (ISCRAM)*, Albi, France.

Pradhan, S., et al., (2022). ICT Adoption for Tourism Disaster Management: A Systematic Review, *Proceedings of the ISCRAM Asia Pacific Conference.*

Ratti, C., et al., (2006). Mobile Landscapes: Using Location Data from Cell-Phones for Urban Analysis, *Environment and Planning B: Planning and Design*, Vol. 33, No. 5, pp. 727-748.

Stuart, M., et al., (2014). Real-time crisis mapping of natural disasters using social media. *IEEE Intell Syst*, Vol 29, No. 2, pp. 9–17.

RETHINKING THE CENTRALIZATION OF IT GOVERNANCE: VOICES OF SENIORS FROM A LARGE TECHNOLOGY ORGANIZATION

Burcin Sari[1] and Sevgi Özkan Yıldırım[2]
[1]*Middle East Technical University (METU), ASELSAN*
Ankara, Turkiye
[2]*Prof. Dr., Middle East Technical University (METU)*
Ankara, Turkiye

ABSTRACT

As some organizations become larger and grow with respect to size, they aim to centralize their IT governance to improve relevant effectiveness and efficiency. However, it is still not fully clear whether this kind of transaction and transformation is firmly meaningful or not. In our research, we questioned the realized benefits of centralization of IT governance. For this purpose, we conducted semi-structured interviews with 11 senior people in a large technology organization. The collected data were analyzed via quasi-statistics, and the findings were elaborated. Our initial results showed that categorical complete centralization and decentralization are not a good solution. High-level centralization with some tailoring options for each business unit, the hybrid way, seems to be better with respect to the views of the senior professionals. Managerial implications and future steps for our initial exploration are also discussed in the paper. This paper is going to be beneficial for professionals and scholars interested in IT governance.

KEYWORDS

Centralized, Decentralized, IT Governance

1. INTRODUCTION

IT governance is defined as a constituent part of enterprise governance, which includes organizational structures, processes and the leadership that provide assurance that the organization's IT supports the organization's objectives and strategies and considered as the responsibility of executive management and board of directors by IT Governance Institute. (ITGI, 2003). In the same content, IT governance is defined as to create decision rights and accountability standards to promote proper behavior in using IT. (Weill and Ross, 2004). It is well understood that IT governance is a framework that provides tool to utilize IT resources to meet business objectives.

In the sense of how IT decision mechanisms are placed in the organizations, centralization and decentralization of IT governance structures have been discuss in the IT governance literature. In the paper of Weill and Ross (2005), it is stated that centralized IT governance enhance standardization to achieve low business costs while some organizations seek to meet local customer needs by applying decentralized It governance.

In the middle of centralized and decentralized IT governance discussion, a moderate way of govern IT has emerged, federal IT governance model. It would be a bridge between centralized and decentralized IT governance which enables to take advantage of value of both ways. It is introduced to comfort the tension between distinctly-seemed IT governance decision making models. (Weill and Ross, 2005)

As the discussions have been focusing on how to place IT governance decision making mechanisms across business units, our goal of the study have been shaped around to seek advantage and opportunity to improve side of centralization of IT governance. So, we define our research question as follow:

- What are the benefits of centralization of IT governance?
- Which aspects are emerged to be improved to enhance centralization of IT governance?

2. RELATED WORKS

Centralization and decentralization of IT governance have been widely discussed in the IT governance literature as business processes becomes to relies on IT systems in organizations.

Historically, Bloomfield (1992) introduces centralization or decentralization of IT in terms of the use of computers in organizations. Soon, Sambamurthy and Zmud (1999) discusses the three modes of IT governance as centralized, decentralized, and the federal mode by utilizing multiple contingencies theory. They suggest reinforcing and dominating contingencies leads to centralized or decentralized IT governance, while conflicting contingencies lead to federal mode of IT governance.

To enhance more practical view of centralization of IT governance, impact of mode of IT governance have been also discussed in the literature. According to the study of Tanrıverdi (2006), it is found that centralized, decentralized or federal mode of IT governance has no significant impact on IT synergy and firm performance. As Brown and Grant (2005) discuss, it is crucial to explore IT governance concept to figure out to find right mechanisms to govern IT decisions. In their study, it could be understood that is it commonly accepted that a centralized governance enables a greater control over IT standards and a greater opportunity to benefit from economies of scale, while a decentralized governance enables customization of solutions for each business unit. (Brown and Grant, 2005)

Adams, Larson and Xia (2007) have discussed the concepts of IT governance with CIOs to figure out which mode would be appropriate approach to govern IT throughout multi-business unit enterprises. Surprisingly, in contrast to the studies that propose federal IT governance model is ideal, CIOs of larger organizations promotes centralized IT governance. In recent study of Merge (2019) introduces digital services teams (DST) which are formed in the purpose of handling large-scale IT projects which couldn't be managed by centralized CIO's office. DSTs extends the theory of centralized and decentralized IT departments by introducing space between two distinct approaches.

Addition to discussion around cost-efficiency and responsiveness to local needs, Xue, Ray and Gu (2011) challenges the views by claiming that firms tend to decentralized IT governance in more unpredictable environments. Firstly, organizations tend to decentralize IT infrastructure to be more responsive to the local needs; however, as uncertainty increases, they centralize IT infrastructure to make decisions and take actions in shorter period. (Xue, Ray and Gu, 2011)

Recent discussions show that centralized or decentralized approaches doesn't have to be selected as a separated approach. Magnusson (2013) states that decentralization and centralization could be managed in parallel; in the similar content, Bianchi et al. (2017) claims that it would enhance IT governance across the faculties if the IT infrastructure is centralized and the IT operations are decentralized.

Lastly, Liu, Huang and Lucas (2020) extends the discussion of centralization or decentralization of IT governance by introducing the approach how centralized IT decision making affects the probability of cybersecurity breaches. The authors found out that centralized IT governance has impact on the probability of cybersecurity incidents and decreases the number of them by enforcing standardized, organization-wide security protocols.

3. METHODOLOGY

Our study follows a qualitative approach by interviewing the senior employees who have at least 10 years' experience and have plenty knowledge about IT governance. All participants work in the same technology firm that is selected for this study. The firm has centralized and decentralized IT governance functions which serve 10.000+ employees' technological needs. The participants were selected based on their role in the organization as their roles require to understand the needs of IT governance.

Five questions are asked to the participants to get their insight about how IT decision making mechanisms should be placed in the firm that they work at. They responded to the questions not only based on their experience in that firm but also based on their previous experience and their knowledge.

Table 1. Questions to the Interviewees

Number	Questions
1	May you give us some information about your roles, responsibilities, and experiences in your organization?
2	According to your experiences, which way is the best to provide or get IT services (either fully centralized, fully decentralized, or hybrid based on the needs)?
3	Regarding your experiences, what is the most significant benefit of centralizing IT services?
4	Regarding your experiences, what is the biggest problem of centralizing IT services?

Table 2. Responses to "According to your experiences, which way is the best to provide or get IT services (either fully centralized, fully decentralized, or hybrid based on the needs)?"

Respondent	Responses	Centralized/ Decentralized/ Hybrid
R1	Providing IT services in a fully centralized topology is the best option regarding to my experience.	Centralized
R2	A hybrid approach to providing IT services is the most effective. While some services can be centralized for standardized and efficient delivery, certain business units or regions may require localized or decentralized IT services to provide to their specific needs and regulations. Finding the right balance between centralization and decentralization ensures agility, flexibility, and responsiveness.	Hybrid
R3	Fully centralized but a strong IT department is the best way to provide efficient and effective solutions to problems.	Centralized
R4	Getting IT services with fully centralized systems could lead to push business processes to adapt standardized IT Infrastructure. If company had enough sources, fully decentralized systems would be more productive in terms of utilizing IT Infrastructure.	Decentralized
R5	There is no best way, there is optimum way in IT solutions based on requirements. In that point, hybrid model can be optimum.	Hybrid
R6	Hybrid based on the needs is the best way.	Hybrid
R7	It is hybrid based on the needs. Because requirement analysis is important phase to determine whether the service is centralized or hybrid. While it may be centralized if capability is enough in view of knowhow or resource, I strongly believe that it should be hybrid even if capacity is not enough due to any reason or the needs are fully new trend issues.	Hybrid
R8	Hybrid based IT services may be more efficient and a better way of serving IT services for a company. Centralized IT networks/services may cause a lack of flexibility for the IT employees with respect to fully decentralized ones. Centralized IT services may cause reduction in the costs for the hardware expenses for the company but decrease the flexibility and the freedom of configuration of the IT teams according to their needs and also increases the vulnerability of the systems regarding to have a one central location-based configuration of the systems. It is therefore, a hybrid system providing both cost efficient and a flexible/non-vulnerable may be the most efficient way in my own way of thinking.	Hybrid
R9	Until now, all of the companies that I worked at have provided IT services by a centralized IT organization. However, I cannot say their IT organizations are fully centralized because in order to satisfy the different units' needs, different sub-units like financial affairs resolution, supplier relations resolution, project management resolution have been established and been in contact with those units closely. According to my experiences, both satisfying these needs and being agile while doing this requires hybrid IT structures.	Hybrid
R10	IT management should be structured in a hybrid way. Central IT management I continue to conduct personal visits to determine the company's IT policy and standards, as well as IT services distributed across business units, in accordance with centrally registered policies.	Hybrid
R11	According to my experiences and when advantages and disadvantages of each method is considered hybrid based seems to be the best way.	Hybrid

Based on the discussion around which way is the best to provide or get IT services (either fully centralized, fully decentralized, or hybrid based on the business needs, majority of the respondents suggest that hybrid model would be the best option.

Table 3. Responses to "Regarding your experiences, what is the most significant benefit of centralizing IT services?"

Respondents	Responses	Benefits
R1	The sustainability of solutions, ensuring compliance with company standards, and information security.	Sustainability of IT solutions
R2	Reducing expenses (data center, hardware, software, personnel, energy, time and operational costs) seems to be the most significant benefit of centralizing IT services.	Reducing expenses
R3	The most significant benefit of centralizing IT services is the ability to achieve economies of scale and operational efficiencies. By consolidating resources, technologies, and expertise, organizations can streamline processes, reduce costs, enhance service quality, and improve consistency across the entire IT landscape.	Achieving economies of scale and operational efficiencies
R4	Central IT department provides common solutions to problems which at the end is easier to manage and have a standard way of working.	Common solutions to problems
R5	It would reduce the software development cost and purchasing IT hardware.	Reducing IT costs
R6	First advantage is always standardization in tools, applications and reports and also other dominant advantage is cost optimizations.	Standardization in IT applications, cost optimization
R7	Cost efficiency and standardization of processes are the most significant benefit.	Standardization of processes, cost efficiency
R8	I think it is the ease of management and support based on visibility.	Ease of management of IT applications
R9	Reducing the costs of hardware expenses, office and administrative costs.	Reducing IT costs
R10	Centralized IT structures can be more standardized; thus, it will be easy to manage provided services and achieve a consistent quality.	Standardization to support quality
R11	I believe that the implementation of basic policies and standards will be easier, good practices determined by feedback from sub-teams will be easily disseminated, efficiency in software license management and use will increase, and corporate cyber security studies can be implemented more easily by centralized IT management.	Standardization of IT policies and standards

The participants of the interviews discuss the benefits of centralizing IT services and suggest that it would provide sustainability of IT solutions, reducing cost of IT investments, achieving economies of scale and operational efficiencies, common solutions to IT problems, standardization in IT policies, applications and processes, ease of management of IT applications.

Table 4. Responses to "Regarding your experiences, what is the biggest problem of centralizing IT services?"

Respondents	Responses	Problems
R1	Today, the expectations from IT, IT demands, the impact of IT on business and its potential to add value have possibly reached the highest level to date. We are experiencing this in an environment where IT is mostly centralized. When we look at the outcomes of this intense demand and centralized IT environment, a study conducted among Gartner members reveals that speed to complete initiatives are 59% behind expectations, and speed to realize value is 52% behind expectations. Therefore, we can say that strictly centralized IT structures are struggling to fulfill the expectations and meet the speed requirements of the day.	Struggling to fulfill the expectations and meet the speed requirements
R2	Organizational structure conflicts, lack of qualified IT personnel, need for IT budget seems to be the problems of centralizing IT services.	Organizational structure conflicts, lack of qualified IT personnel

R3	One of the challenges of centralizing IT services is striking the right balance between standardization and customization. While centralization promotes consistency and cost savings, it may limit the flexibility and agility needed to address unique business requirements or local regulations. Finding the optimal balance is crucial to avoid hindering business operations or innovation.	Limiting the flexibility and agility needed to address unique business requirements
R4	When the company is too big for the IT department to handle (a weak IT department), then each department tends to solve their own problem regardless of a central IT. That means, shadow IT's start to appear in the organization which is the biggest problem of centralized IT.	Emerging of shadow IT
R5	In some cases, it forces processes to adapt to the central IT Infrastructure such as software and hardware.	Forcing business process to adopt standardization
R6	Slow reaction time to solve problems could occur.	Slow reaction time to IT issues
R7	Speed of problem solving is the biggest problem.	Low speed of problem solving
R8	It could lead to lose of control. If the centralized IT support team is unable to resolve an issue, it can lead to a loss of control over the enterprise's IT infrastructure and applications.	Loss of control over the enterprise's IT infrastructure and applications
R9	Increasing the vulnerability of the system regarding the failures, accidents regarding the one and only central location-based hardware, servers and etc.	Increasing the vulnerability of the system
R10	Easy management and consistent quality can be seen as an advantage at first, however attaining efficiency and internal customer satisfaction is beyond this. Centralizing IT services and being strict about that could lead to inefficient processes and unsatisfied internal customers.	Inefficient processes and unsatisfied internal customers
R11	I estimate that the biggest problem that will arise would be bulkiness. This situation can hinder today's agile digital transformation.	Hindering today's agile digital transformation

The participants of the interviews discuss the drawbacks of centralizing IT services and provide insights which could be listed as struggling to fulfill the expectations, meet the speed requirements, organizational structure conflicts, lack of qualified IT personnel, limiting the flexibility and agility needed to address unique business requirements, emerging of shadow IT, forcing business process to adopt standardization, slow reaction time to IT issues and low speed of problem solving, loss of control over the enterprise's IT infrastructure and applications, increasing the vulnerability of the system, inefficient processes and unsatisfied internal customers and hindering today's agile digital transformation.

4. DISCUSSION AND CONCLUSION

As business process dependency on information systems, the organizations' concern about how to place IT governance functions arises. Centralization and decentralization of IT governance have been widely discussed in IT governance literature from the beginning of use of computers. As the organizations start to operate their business functions across worldwide, the discussion how to meet business technological needs have emerged in terms of placing It decision making functions throughout the organization.

To explore the optimum solution to centralization or decentralization IT governance functions, the papers that focus on "centralization" and "IT governance" concepts have been analyzed. Recent studies show that the third approach to the centralization discussion have been emerged as federal or hybrid solution.

In our study, an interview series have been conducted in a large technology firm that has complex IT projects and infrastructure. The interviewees have plenty knowledge about IT governance and 10+ years of working experience in various departments such as IT, manufacturing and digitalization departments.

Based on the interview results, it is concluded hybrid IT governance model could be the best solution to meet business units' needs by not centralization of whole IT functions. As the interviewees discuss centralizing IT services, and they suggest that this approach would provide sustainability of IT solutions, reducing cost of IT investments, achieving economies of scale and operational efficiencies, common solutions to IT problems, standardization in IT policies, applications and processes, ease of management of IT applications. Consequently the interviewees introduce the drawbacks of centralizing IT services as struggling to fulfill the expectations, meet the speed requirements, organizational structure conflicts, lack of qualified IT personnel, limiting the flexibility and agility needed to address unique business requirements, emerging of shadow IT, forcing business process to adopt standardization, slow reaction time to IT issues and low speed of problem solving, loss of control over the enterprise's IT infrastructure and applications, increasing the vulnerability of the system, inefficient processes and unsatisfied internal customers and hindering today's agile digital transformation. During the discussion of centralization of IT governance functions, it is introduced that IT quality and response time have the highest importance over usefulness, accessibility and ease of use.

For further studies, it is suggested to study on which IT governance functions should be centralized or decentralized by considering IT concerns that have been discussed in this study.

REFERENCES

Adams, C., Larson, E., & Xia, W. (2007). A trend toward more centralized information technology (IT) management.

Bianchi, I. S., Sousa, R. D., Pereira, R., & Luciano, E. (2017). IT governance structures in Brazilian, Dutch and Portuguese universities. *Procedia Computer Science*, *121*, 927-933.

Bloomfield, B. P., & Coombs, R. (1992). Information technology, control and power: The centralization and decentralization debate revisited. *Journal of management studies*, 29(4), 459-459.

Brown, A. E., & Grant, G. G. (2005). Framing the frameworks: A review of IT governance research. *Communications of the Association for Information Systems*, *15*(1), 38.

ITGI. (2003). *Board Briefing for IT Governance* (2nd ed.). Information Systems Audit and Control Association.

Liu, C. W., Huang, P., & Lucas Jr, H. C. (2020). Centralized IT decision making and cybersecurity breaches: Evidence from US higher education institutions. *Journal of Management Information Systems*, *37*(3), 758-787.

Magnusson, J. (2013). Intentional decentralization and instinctive centralization: a revelatory case study of the ideographic organization of it. *Information Resources Management Journal (IRMJ)*, 26(4), 1-17.

Mergel, I. (2019). Digital service teams in government. *Government Information Quarterly*, 36(4), 101389.

Sambamurthy, V., & Zmud, R. W. (1999). Arrangements for information technology governance: A theory of multiple contingencies. *MIS quarterly*, 261-290.

Schwarz, A., & Hirschheim, R. (2003). An extended platform logic perspective of IT governance: managing perceptions and activities of IT. *The journal of strategic information systems*, *12*(2), 129-166.

Tanriverdi, H. (2006). Performance effects of information technology synergies in multibusiness firms. *MIS quarterly*, 57-77.

Weill, P., & Ross, J. W. (2004). IT Governance: How Top Performers Manage IT Decision Rights for Superior Results. *Harvard Business Press.*

Weill, P., & Ross, J. W. (2005). A matrixed approach to designing IT governance. *MIT Sloan management review.*

Xue, L., Ray, G., & Gu, B. (2011). Environmental uncertainty and IT infrastructure governance: A curvilinear relationship. *Information Systems Research*, 22(2), 389-399.

IMPACTS OF DIGITAL–HEALTH LITERACY AND HELPING BEHAVIORS ON SPORTS AND RECREATION-RELATED INJURY PREVENTION IN SENIOR CITIZENS

Terence Kam-Ho Chau, Ron Chi-Wai Kwok and Jessica Choi-Fung Cheung
City University of Hong Kong, Hong Kong, China

ABSTRACT

This research-in-progress study is one of the first empirical studies to shed light on the effects of seniors' digital and health literacies on their sports and recreation-related injury (SRI) prevention behaviors. It draws on the outcome expectancy theory to investigate the mechanism by which digital–health literacy increases the awareness of SRI prevention in seniors and encourages their purchases of SRI prevention tools. It also suggests that various helping behaviors can be regarded as moderators of the aforementioned relationships. A quantitative survey and follow-up focus group sessions will be conducted in Hong Kong. The findings of this study may hint at the behaviors of senior populations in other aging societies and inspire public policy and marketing strategies. Preliminary data collection and analysis results will be presented at the conference.

KEYWORDS

Digital Literacy, Health Literacy, Helping Behavior, Outcome Expectancy Theory, Sports Injury Prevention, Senior Citizens

1. INTRODUCTION

Thanks to the rapid development of Information and Communication Technology (ICT), citizens are able to access various healthcare resources from the Internet. Seeking online healthcare information is not limited to younger generations who grew up along with the Internet (Gesser-Edelsburg, 2021). This is also popular among elderly (e.g., Abbaspur-Behbahani et al., 2022). Creating and viewing online media content of healthcare knowledge and experiences were found to be beneficial to the wellbeing of elderly creators and viewers (e.g., Liang et al., 2022). Having said so, studies have rarely evaluated senior citizens' digital and health literacy levels which may have significant implications for their wellbeing (Chen and Chan, 2014).

Engaging in active lifestyles is one of the healthcare-related phenomena on social media as more people realize the various benefits of sports and recreational physical activities in relation to longevity and noncommunicable diseases (e.g., Liang et al., 2022). Studies have shown that participation in sports and recreational physical activities among the senior population – that is, those aged 55 years or older – increased by 5% following the COVID-19 outbreak (Kim et al., 2022). Unfortunately, sports and recreation-related injury (SRI), refers to the physical injuries that occur due to participating in sports or recreational physical activities (Falvey et al., 2009), also increased over the same period. The number of hospital cases pertaining to seniors' SRI has recorded a 2.4-fold increase (Chu et al., 2021). This finding prompted us to consider SRI prevention as equally important to adopting active lifestyles among the senior populations.

The SRI issue in seniors is also evident in the vast volume of SRI prevention tips and tools available online. On one hand, the supply of online SRI resources may be attracted by the purchasing power of senior citizens. In the US, for instance, senior citizens controlled 70% of disposable income in 2015 and are expected to inherit $15 trillion over the next 15 years (Totty, 2023). On the other hand, the plenty of online SRI prevention resources may be driven by seniors' substantial demands. In the US, the annual online spending of seniors was recorded at US$7 billion in the recent decade, primarily for the health and preventive care (Gitnux, 2023). Ironically, among the numerous studies on injuries in seniors, the few explicitly related SRI are generally stocktake reports (e.g., Chu et al., 2021; Sang, 2023) with limited implications for academics, senior wellbeing, and society as a whole.

Against this background, this study poses a core research question to guide the development of its analysis: To what extent do digital and health literacies in seniors affect their SRI prevention behaviors? This study draws on the outcome expectancy theory (Behling and Starke, 1973; Vroom, 1964) to investigate the mechanism by which seniors' digital–health literacy (expectancy) impacts their awareness of SRI prevention (valence), which encourages their purchases of SRI prevention tools (targeted behavior). Furthermore, we hypothesize that various helping behaviors can be regarded as rewarding features (instrumentality) that moderate the aforementioned relationships. The hypothesized relationships between the purchases of SRI prevention tools and the predictors are elaborated in the following sections.

2. OUTCOME EXPECTANCY THEORY IN THE CONTEXT OF SPORTS AND RECREATION-RELATED INJURY PREVENTION IN SENIORS

The outcome expectancy theory posits that a performing behavior is the result of positive expectations of the outcomes of that behavior (Vroom, 1964). This relationship comprises three components: 1) expectancy, one's belief in the efficacy of achieving the expected reward by performing the targeted behavior; 2) instrumentality, one's expected reward for performing that behavior; and 3) valence, one's perceived value of that reward (Behling and Starke, 1973). The outcome expectancy theory has been widely adopted in healthcare research in the context of psychology and social science, as behavioral motivations represent the principal intervention target in this field (Jones et al., 2001).

Applying the outcome expectancy theory to the context of SRI prevention in seniors, we hypothesize that the targeted behavior can be operationalized as seniors' purchases of SRI prevention tools. This behavior results from digital–health literacy (expectancy) and the awareness of SRI prevention (valence). Furthermore, we posit that various helping behaviors are rewards (instrumentality) that moderate the aforementioned relationships. Figure 1 illustrates the proposed research model.

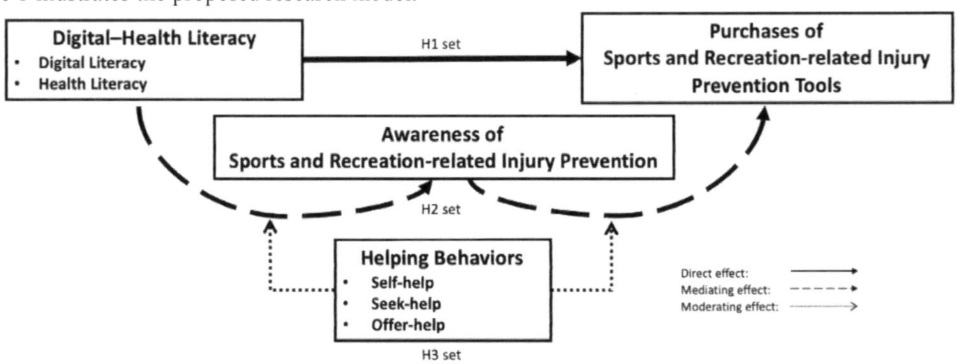

Figure 1. Proposed research model

2.1 Digital–Health Literacy as Expectancy

Digital literacy is defined as the ability to find, evaluate, utilize, share, and create information and ideas responsibly and ethically using the ICT (Reddy et al., 2022). It functions as an essential component for surviving and thriving in the digital era because it manipulates the dissemination of information that can reshape the world into a better one (Ng, 2012). Besides, health literacy refers to the capacity to obtain, process, and apply health information and services to make appropriate health decisions (Epstein, 2021). Low health literacy is associated with increased hospitalization and an impaired ability to self-manage (Nutbeam, 2000). Furthermore, it is a hurdle for patients to interpret healthcare systems and communicate with healthcare providers, depriving them of their deserved protection (Edward et al., 2018).

Digital literacy and health literacy are often interwoven as eHealth literacy (Norman and Skinner, 2006). eHealth literacy is a hybridized measure of digital and health literacies widely employed in academic research owing to its simplicity and reliability. Nevertheless, this approach cannot distinguish between individual and collective effects of digital and health literacies, which may direct and influence different cognitions and behaviors (Neter and Brainin, 2012). We argue that a sufficient clarification of these effects is necessary to obtain meaningful predictions and nuances of subsequent behaviors with the objectives of enriching academic research, designing interventions, and inspiring marketing strategies in related industries.

We therefore propose that digital–health literacy can be combined, without neglecting their individual effects, to represent seniors' beliefs in their digital–health knowledge that yields the expected benefits of SRI prevention. According to the outcome expectancy theory, we hypothesize that seniors with higher digital–health literacy (expectancy) are more capable and efficient in accessing and applying resources for SRI prevention using the ICT, and are therefore more likely to purchase the tools required to facilitate SRI prevention. Thus, it is ideal for seniors to be digital- and health-literate; lacking either literacy may hinder the best outcomes. This leads to the following hypothesis:

H1 set: *Digital–health literacy individually and collectively increases purchases of SRI prevention tools.*

2.2 Awareness of Sports and Recreation-Related Injury Prevention as Valence

Sports injury prevention is a sequential cycle that comprises the following stages: 1) identification of problems, 2) understanding of factors and mechanisms associated with said problems, 3) recognition of preventive measures, and 4) application and evaluation of said measures (Van Mechelen et al., 1992). An awareness of SRI risks and prevention in seniors represents the first target of development in intervention projects (Chu et al., 2021; Sang, 2023). This aligns with the assumption of the outcome expectancy theory that an appreciation of positive outcomes (valance) determines one's behavior. In other words, physically active seniors are less likely to prevent SRI if they are unaware of the issue, even though they have access to relevant resources.

We therefore posit that as the direct cause of purchases of SRI prevention tools, awareness of SRI prevention positively mediates the relationships between digital–health literacy and purchases of SRI prevention tools.

H2 set: *Awareness of SRI prevention mediates the relationship between digital–health literacy and purchases of SRI prevention tools.*

2.3 Helping Behaviors as Instrumentality

Helping behaviors refer to actions intended to alleviate a situation for oneself or others in need (Rickwood and Thomas, 2012). These behaviors can be categorized as follows: 1) seek-help, wherein one interacts with other people to solicit external assistance to improve their situation; 2) offer-help, wherein one takes appropriate actions to improve the situation of others in need; and 3) self-help, wherein one uses available resources to improve their situation without communicating or interacting with others in person. The last of these is not a new notion, yet it has become increasingly popular owing to the ubiquity and versatility of the ICT (Rickwood and Thomas, 2012).

The present study regards helping behaviors as the actions of seniors that solicit external help or facilitate others to achieve SRI prevention goals. By performing the right helping behaviors, senior citizens can be rewarded as their needs are satisfied. The rewarding attribute of different helping behaviors can be justified by Maslow's hierarchy of needs (Maslow, 1954; Yount, 2008) which explains the rationale for performing different helping behaviors. Physically active senior citizens may attempt to use available resources to ensure their own safety when playing sports and recreational physical activities, that is, self-help for safety needs. They may solicit help from other resourceful individuals because their experiences resonate, that is, seek-help for social needs. They may also apply their resources to help others prevent SRI, that is, offer-help for self-actualization needs.

Overall, we posit that helping behaviors are a rewarding feature (instrumentality) of the outcome expectancy theory. Senior citizens anticipate rewards (fulfilling needs) if they possess adequate resources that allow them to help or seek help, motivating them to make relevant purchases. Specifically, we hypothesize that helping behavior driven by a higher level of need has a stronger effect. In other words, offer-help can trigger the most significant change in the direction and strength of the effect of digital–health literacy on the awareness of SRI prevention and the effect of the awareness of SRI prevention on purchases of SRI prevention tools, compared to the effects of self-help and seek-help. Hence,

H3 set: *Helping behaviors moderate the relationships between digital–health literacy, awareness of SRI prevention, and purchases of SRI prevention tools.*

3. METHODOLOGY

A quantitative survey and follow-up focus group sessions will be conducted in Hong Kong targeting senior citizens, or "silver-age individuals", aged 55 or older. According to the Hong Kong Government, senior citizens represent more than 2.9 million, or 38.4%, of its total population. To proactively minimize the social healthcare burden, the government has encouraged seniors to engage in regular sports or recreational physical activities. Consequently, SRI cases have increased along with the number of physically active seniors. This indicates that Hong Kong seniors are frequently exposed to the risk of SRI.

In this study, participation is voluntary and anonymous. Participants will be recruited via different channels, such as social media communities of senior populations, advertisements on social media sites, professional associations, and clinics. Asian Academy for Sports & Fitness Professionals (www.aasfp.hk), a world-recognized training provider for registered exercise professionals, has agreed to collaborate on the present project for data collection. Around 1,000 responses will be captured. Follow-up focus group sessions will be conducted to gather qualitative data and enrich the quantitative results. Only respondents who agree to participate in the focus group sessions will be invited. Preliminarily, 50 individuals, or 5% of the total number of survey respondents, are expected to participate.

Data collected will solely be used for the purposes of this study. This research proposal will be submitted to the University Research Ethical Review Committee to ensure that there are no potential ethical issues.

The questionnaire will be developed by adapting the measurements established in prior literature (e.g., Epstein, 2021; Ng, 2012). Considering the potential effects of personal factors on the dependent variables, demographic factors such as gender, age, education, and health conditions will also be captured and controlled for in the data analysis. As the senior populations in Hong Kong may have different native tongues, both English and Chinese versions of the questionnaire will be prepared. The original English questionnaire will be translated into Chinese using the back-translation method. A sample questionnaire will be presented at the conference.

All multi-item scales with the proposed constructs will be tested to confirm the data reliability and validity. A multiple regression analysis will be conducted to test the proposed research model based on the testing procedures suggested by Hair (2017) using SmartPLS. Moreover, measuring parameters – namely proactive/reluctant for helping behaviors and high/low for all other constructs – will be applied to obtain continuum effects of the constructs for comparative purposes. Thus, deeper and broader results are expected to be obtained.

4. CONCLUSION

This research-in-progress study represents one of the first empirical studies to elucidate the effects of seniors' digital and health literacies on their SRI prevention behaviors. Drawing on the outcome expectancy theory, this study rationalizes the mechanism by which SRI prevention awareness in seniors mediates the causal relationship between digital–health literacy and purchases of SRI prevention tools. It examines the moderating role of helping behaviors in the aforementioned relationships. It also critically revisits the operationalization of digital–health literacy to discover their individual and collective effects, supplementing previous findings that rely on the simplified hybrid scale of eHealth literacy. The application of measurement parameters may reveal the continuum effects of the constructs for comparative purposes. Practically, the findings of this study will inspire software engineers to develop SRI prevention gerontechnology based on the digital–health proficiency and needs of seniors. This may enable practitioners to tailor marketing strategies, guide seniors in making informed purchasing decisions, and allow policymakers to design appropriate interventions that meet seniors' goals. Preliminary data collection and analysis results will be presented at the conference.

REFERENCES

Abbaspur-Behbahani, S., Monaghesh, E., Hajizadeh, A. and Fehresti, S. (2022). "Application of mobile health to support the elderly during the covid-19 outbreak: A systematic review." *Health Policy and Technology,* Vol.11 No.1, pp.100595.

Behling, O. and Starke, F.A. (1973). "The postulates of expectancy theory." *The Academy of Management Journal,* Vol.16 No.3, pp.373-388.

Chen, K. and Chan, A.H.S. (2014). "Gerontechnology acceptance by elderly hong kong chinese: A senior technology acceptance model (stam)." *Ergonomics,* Vol.57 No.5, pp.635-652.

Chu, W.Y.C., Chong, Y.C. and Mok, W.Y. (2021). "Hiking-related orthopaedic injuries: Another epidemic during the covid-19 pandemic." *Journal of Orthopaedics, Trauma and Rehabilitation,* Vol.28 pp.22104917211059543.

Edward, J., Carreon, L.Y., Williams, M.V., Glassman, S. and Li, J. (2018). "The importance and impact of patients' health literacy on low back pain management: A systematic review of literature." *The Spine Journal,* Vol.18 No.2, pp.370-376.

Epstein, H.-a.B. (2021). "The health literacy questionnaire." *Journal of Consumer Health on the Internet,* Vol.25 No.3, pp.303-309.

Falvey, E., Eustace, J., Whelan, B., Molloy, M., Cusack, S., Shanahan, F. and Molloy, M.G. (2009). "Sport and recreation-related injuries and fracture occurrence among emergency department attendees: Implications for exercise prescription and injury prevention." *Emergency Medicine Journal,* Vol.26 No.8, pp.590-595.

Gesser-Edelsburg, A. (2021). "Using narrative evidence to convey health information on social media: The case of covid-19." *Journal of medical Internet research,* Vol.23 No.3, pp.e24948.

Gitnux. (2023). "*Baby boomer spending trends worth watching in 2023* [Online]." Gitnux. available at: https://blog.gitnux.com/baby-boomer-spending-trends/ [accessed].

Hair, J.F. (2017). "*A primer on partial least squares structural equation modeling (pls-sem),*" Sage, Los Angeles.

Jones, B.T., Corbin, W. and Fromme, K. (2001). "A review of expectancy theory and alcohol consumption." *Addiction,* Vol.96 No.1, pp.57-72.

Kim, E.J., Park, S.M. and Kang, H.W. (2022) "Changes in leisure activities of the elderly due to the covid-19 in korea." *Frontiers in Public Health,* Vol.10 pp.966989.

Liang, Y.-W., Wang, J., Yu, S.-P., Lin, J.-K. and Chung, A. (2022). "Creating a healthy life for the elderly through participation in self-media: A study on the demands of the elderly in self-media." *International Journal of Environmental Research and Public Health,* Vol.19 No.19, pp.12774.

Maslow, A. (1954). "*Motivation and personality,*" Harper & Row, New York, USA.

Neter, E. and Brainin, E. (2012)."Ehealth literacy: Extending the digital divide to the realm of health information." *Journal of medical Internet research,* Vol.14 No.1, pp.e19.

Ng, W. (2012). "Can we teach digital natives digital literacy?" *Computers & Education,* Vol.59 No.3, pp.1065-1078.

Norman, C.D. and Skinner, H.A. (2006). "Eheals: The ehealth literacy scale." *Journal of medical Internet research,* Vol.8 No.4, pp.e507.

Nutbeam, D. (2000). "Health literacy as a public health goal: A challenge for contemporary health education and communication strategies into the 21st century." *Health promotion international,* Vol.15 No.3, pp.259-267.

Reddy, P., Sharma, B. and Chaudhary, K. (2022). "Digital literacy: A review in the south pacific." *Journal of Computing in Higher Education,* Vol.34 No.1, pp.83-108.

Rickwood, D. and Thomas, K. (2012). "Conceptual measurement framework for help-seeking for mental health problems." *Psychology research and behavior management,* pp.173-183.

Sang, X. (2023). "Common sports injuries and health services in the elderly." *Rev. bras. med. esporte,* pp.e2022_0471-e2022_0471.

Totty, K. (2023). "*Millennials vs baby boomers: Which is the most valuable generation?* [Online]." Hallmark. available at: https://www.hallmarkbusiness.com/insights/article/millennials-vs-baby-boomers-which-is-the-most-valuable-generation/ [accessed 2023].

Van Mechelen, W., Hlobil, H. and Kemper, H.C. (1992). "Incidence, severity, aetiology and prevention of sports injuries: A review of concepts." *Sports medicine,* Vol.14 pp.82-99.

Vroom, V.H. (1964). "Work and motivation."

Yount, W.R. (2008). "Transcendence and aging: The secular insights of erikson and maslow." *Journal of Religion, Spirituality & Aging,* Vol.21 No.1-2, pp.73-87.

ORGANIZATIONAL CULTURE AND DIGITAL RESILIENCE: COMPETING VALUES PERSPECTIVE

Anita Neumannova
WU Vienna University of Economics and Business,
Welthandelspl. 1, Vienna, Austria

ABSTRACT

The increased number of information and communication technologies (ICTs) streamlining the core business processes of organizations leads to benefits as well as risks, which need to be managed in face of disruptions. To do so, organizations need to achieve digital resilience (DR). Organizational culture (OC) can foster resilience capabilities through enabling knowledge flow within organizations, however, its connection to DR is yet to be explicated. OC aspects stand on three levels, with values being the most accessible one. The OC values connected to DR capabilities appear to be of both flexible and control basis. This short paper applies the lens of competing values framework (CVF) to indicate which types of OCs are suited to foster DR capabilities. The preliminary findings of a scale-up case study indicate a seamless shift between contrasting values enables organizations to portray higher levels of DR capabilities during crisis situations.

KEYWORDS

Digital Resilience, Organizational Culture, Competing Values Framework, Intellectual Capital, Case Study

1. INTRODUCTION

The number of turbulent events affecting the information and communication technologies (ICTs) ingrained in firms' core processes, such as the Covid-19 pandemic, has been increasing in recent times (e.g., Sarkar et al., 2021). To successfully overcome and bounce forward from such disruptions, organizations need to portray higher levels of digital resilience (DR) capabilities which can, for instance, be fostered through specific organizational cultures (OC) (Boh et al., 2023). OC serves as a source of sustained competitive advantage and leads to the creation and perseverance of intangible assets (Alavi et al., 2005; Ferreira, 2014), which are imperative to overcome crisis situations (Cheng et al., 2023; Mubarik et al., 2022). Albeit OC has been connected to the presence of resilience (Coldwell, 2010; Weick, 1987), its effect on fostering DR capabilities is yet to be fully explicated among information systems (IS) scholars.

DR is a rather novel concept defined as the "*capabilities developed through the use of digital technologies to absorb major shocks, adapt to disruptions, and transform to a new stable state*" (Boh et al., 2023, p. 344). Nowadays, given the speed and enhanced numbers of digital transformations, organization increasingly focus on digitizing their operations which leads to benefits as well as risks that need to be managed – for instance through DR (Neumannova et al., 2023). OC is the "glue" that ensures the cohesion among employees within organizations (Schein, 1985), and that enables knowledge flow (Alavi et al., 2005; Attar et al., 2019). OC can be explicated into three levels encompassing its aspects (Schein, 1985). The most studied one has been connected to values (Gong et al., 2022; Gregory et al., 2009).

In order to study OC through the lens of its values, Cameron and Quinn (2006) defined the competing values framework (CVF) standing on the dimensions of flexibility vs. control, and internal vs. external focus. The values of OC discussed in relation to DR have been connected to openness and flexibility (Boh et al., 2023; Morisse & Prigge, 2017) as well as control and reputation (Marotta & Pearlson, 2019; Sarkar et al., 2020; Sarkar et al., 2021) portraying ambiguity in terms of values that denote the type of OC needed to foster higher levels of DR capabilities. In addition, researchers rather addressed these values as by-products as opposed to key aspects of DR. The following research question shall guide the efforts of clarifying this ambiguity: ***What is the role of OC values in fostering DR capabilities?***

In this short paper I am presenting preliminary findings of a qualitative data collected from a late-stage scale-up located in the e-commerce industry. Scale-ups offer a rich contextual setting due to competing forces between adaptability and control in crisis situations (Neumannova et al., 2023). The theoretical contributions of this paper are embedded in taking the value-centric approach to understanding the role of OC in developing DR capabilities, and showcasing that shifts among values enable the presence of DR. In the next section I describe the conceptual background, followed by the description of applied and envisioned methods. Next I discuss the preliminary findings, and conclude the paper by explicating initial contributions, limitations and next steps.

2. CONCEPTUAL BACKGROUND

Organizational culture (OC) is an elusive term that is hard to grasp due to its complex nature. Scholars have postulated specific aspects of OC lead to higher effectiveness of organizations (Denison & Mishra, 1995; Gregory et al., 2009), aid in managing change (Gong et al., 2022; Hartl, 2019), or help with deployment of systems development methodologies (Iivari & Huisman, 2007; Leidner & Kayworth, 2006). The understanding of OC is fundamental to discerns the knowledge flow within an organization and its subsequent transformation to organization-wide knowledge (Kannan & Aulbur, 2004; Wang et al., 2011). Organization-wide knowledge is an element of intellectual capital (Bollen et al., 2005) and a known driver of resilience behavior (Cheng et al., 2023).

In relation to resilience, Parsons (2010) have argued organizational unity driven by OC enables firms to withstand unprecedented times and Weick (1987) has postulated OC is a source of high reliability. When delving into the effect of OC on digital resilience (DR), the extant articles appear to be rather scarce and address the relationship as a by-product. DR is built on three sub-capabilities of absorb, adapt, and transform, where OC is interlinked with the adapt sub-capability (Boh et al., 2023). However, Morisse and Prigge (2017) propose innovation focused culture creates the needed "know-what" to cope with crises and Marotta and Pearlson (2019) denoted security-oriented culture creates resilience plans aiding organizations to absorb unprecedented times. Further scholarly works denote OC based on decision making aspects fosters higher levels of resilience capabilities (Sarkar et al., 2020; Sarkar et al., 2021). Consequently, the lacking unity among information systems (IS) scholars leads to open question towards the types of OC needed to create organization-wide knowledge and foster DR capabilities.

2.1 Competing Values Framework

OC can be described through three levels, with each one denoted by its complex manifestations (i.e., artifacts, values, and assumptions) (Schein, 1985). Assumptions, the deepest level of OC, are the internal belief systems of individuals which shape their behaviors or relationships (Leidner & Kayworth, 2006). At the surface level, OC is denoted through artifacts which are the observable patterns of behaviors (Iivari & Huisman, 2007). In the mid-level, OC is manifested through values. Values portray deep levels stemming from OC assumptions, however, which are visible enough to grasp (e.g., Shih & Huang, 2010). Consequently, the focus on understanding OC through its values has been prevalent among researchers, where the lens of competing values framework is applied (Cameron & Quinn, 2006).

The competing values framework (CVF) is a comprehensive model applied by scholars to study the effect and impact of OC across organizations (e.g., Hartl & Hess, 2017; Shih & Huang, 2010). CVF enables the assessment of OC along fours dimensions on two axes (Cameron & Quinn, 2006). The first axis focuses on the dimensions of flexibility vs. control, while the second one is dealing with internal vs. external focus. The dimensions of internal vs. external focus are connected to market orientation, and flexibility vs. control focus on internal processes within organizations. Together the axes create four quadrants that denote clan (stands on internal focus and flexibility), adhocracy (stands on external focus and flexibility), hierarchy (stands on internal focus and control), and market (stands on external focus and control) cultures. Nevertheless, Ferreira (2014) uncovered not every type of OC denoted through CVF can be linked to organizations' intellectual capital. This implies certain cultures would not enable the presence of DR capabilities. However, it is imperative to note, organizations are not likely to showcase values of only one type of OC as each can be seen as an ideal type that organizations should strive for (Hartl & Hess, 2017; Shih & Huang, 2010).

Scholars addressing the aspects of OC in relation to DR have to date uncovered contrasting types of OC were needed to gain DR capabilities. One stream of research states OC based on openness, flexibility, and knowledge creation ensures organizations can adapt to unforeseen events (e.g., Boh et al., 2023). Nevertheless, the second stream rather proposes OC based on reputation, secureness and controlled decision-making enables resilience behavior (e.g., Marotta & Pearlson, 2019).

3. METHODOLOGY

To gain a comprehensive understanding on the role of OC in relation to DR capabilities, I have focused on interpretive case study methodology. Case selection is an integral part of case studies and ensures the richness of findings (Eisenhardt, 1989). I postulate scale-ups offer a comprehensive study setting. Scale-ups are organizations focusing on rapid growth targets (Neumannova et al., 2023; Tippmann et al., 2023), while balancing the presence of flexible structures and the need for higher levels of internal control (Demir et al., 2016). According to OECD (2007), scale-ups are firms portraying a growth of at least 20% over a three year period in terms of turnover or employees. Company Artemis (a pseudonym to achieve anonymity) is a European scale-up located in the e-commerce industry. Artemis has been founded in 1994, and in 2004 has transformed into a holding company. Since the offset of the Covid-19 pandemic Artemis nearly doubled its profit on a yearly basis, offering an appropriate study setting to answer the research question.

3.1 Data Collection and Analysis

To gather the data, I have conducted 5 pilot semi-structured interviews ranging from 47-59 minutes with people directly involved in IT decisions during Covid-19 pandemic, and who could shape OC within the company (*ex-Vice-Board Director, CTO, ex-CTO, Head of IT, and Head of IT Architecture).* Three of the interviews were conducted in English, and two in the native language of the interviewees. I ensured both the anonymity and the comfortability of participants. The main research instrument used to facilitate the interviews was a questionnaire constructed through the overview of DR literature. Each interview was recorded (upon consent from participants), transcribed and enriched through notes taken during the interviews. As a next step, the gathered data will be analyzed through guidelines determined by Gioia et al. (2013) using NVivo software. Following Gioia (2021), I understand interviewees as "knowledge agents" who possess the knowledge and perceptions of the discussed situations. The coding process of Gioia method is based on iterative process steps which compare codes to theoretical underpinnings in order to arrive at aggregate dimensions rooted in a grounded model (Lehmann & Recker, 2022). In the following, I illustrate in a narrative descriptive manner the preliminary results of the pilot interviews.

4. PRELIMINARY FINDINGS

Company Artemis appears to possess a deeply ingrained organizational culture (OC) which influences its knowledge flow, knowledge retention as well as crisis responses. During the interviews, one interviewee underlined "*when you join [Artemis], you need to go through five mandatory tests or exams that you have to pass so you understand at least the basics of how the company works".* The preliminary findings further indicate Company Artemis has been accustomed to overcoming crisis situations on a routine basis due to the specificities of the e-commerce industry. An interviewee mentioned that "*[Artemis] is already battle hardened, because of something that we call the season, which is obviously the Christmas season*". The e-commerce industry changes based on "seasons" and as a consequence, Artemis creates a crisis management team as a first line of response to navigate the situation. Nevertheless, the subsequent steps of managing the crisis situation then rather happen in a dynamic and agile manner. Consequently, Artemis portrays the presence of contrasting values deeply ingrained in its OC in order to overcome crises, such as the Covid-19 pandemic.

Company Artemis had to overcome two challenges connected to the Covid-19 pandemic. Firstly, it had to expand its remote control focus to allow for home enterprise resource planning (ERP) software access. Secondly, it had to expand its SQL servers to account for an increased number of customers. When delving deeper into the aspects of OC Artemis draw on, at first Artemis focused on planning and controlling aspects. During the interviews an interviewee stated that "*as soon as we [Artemis] saw that, there's a crisis,..., we started to write down plans, because I think that you always have to have at least some plan of the battle*" and that "*if you have some protocols you can stick to, it's always better*". Furthermore, Artemis also structured its crisis team to handle diverse issues. One interviewee especially mentioned "*in the crisis mode, we [Artemis] have some, the head of the crisis has a resource team that are specialists in the area that needs to be solved*".

Nevertheless, in the subsequent steps of handling the Covid-19 pandemic challenges, Artemis draw on its "*start-up attitude*". One interviewee purported "*we [Artemis] are corporates already and I would say, but we are still able in crisis situations to work really agile and in startup attitude*" and that in "*in [Artemis] DNA, there is improvisation*". All such portrays that albeit at the beginning of Covid-19 pandemic Artemis rather drew from the planning and controlling aspects of its OC to cope with the crisis, within the next steps it rather focused on improvisation and flexibility to adjust to the situations at hand. This has been further underline with the focus on solving Covid driven challenges as an interviewee stated "*we don't have planned for for moving the whole company to the home office, so it was improvisation*". Another interviewee further mentioned, "*the crisis [Covid 19 pandemic] is a project that needs a lot of different rules, and you need to be really agile, and you need to do a lot of decisions on the go*", which strengthens the preliminary findings of shifting values.

5. CONCLUSION, LIMITATIONS AND NEXT STEPS

In this short paper I have focused on the role of organizational culture in the development of digital resilience (DR). The preliminary findings imply firms should draw on contrasting values within their OC to effectuate DR capabilities. Furthermore, it can be inferred certain values can be connected to fostering specific types of DR sub-capabilities (i.e., absorb, adapt, and transform). However, given the focus on a narrative case-study description within this short paper, it is arduous to stipulate specific propositions and draw explicit conclusions. The preliminary findings expand on Hartl and Hess (2017), and Shih and Huang (2010) who showcase organizations do not portray only one OC depicted by the competing values framework, however, can rather draw on contrasting ones due to contextual aspects. This research thus contributes to the body of IS literature aiming to understand how knowledge created through OC enables the presence of DR capabilities.

This short paper, however, is not without limitations. Firstly, the number of interviewees does not offer a complete case understanding. OC is a complex concept that can be subjectively described among interviewees. To fully understand the intricacies within one case study, multiple interviews need to be conducted to cross-validate the findings. Furthermore, observations should be implemented to gain a richer understanding. Secondly, the limitations of this paper stand on the preliminary stages of the data analysis. Consequently, it is arduous to draw precise conclusions that require concrete analysis steps to be enacted. Therefore, as a next steps to expand on this short paper, I will focus on analyzing the data based on steps proposed by Gioia et al. (2013) to ground findings and conducting further interviews to cross-validate propositions.

REFERENCES

Alavi, M., Kayworth, T. R., & Leidner, D. E. (2005). An Empirical Examination of the Influence of Organizational Culture on Knowledge Management Practices. *Journal of Management Information Systems*, Vol. 22, No. 3, pp. 191-224.

Attar, M., Kang, K., & Sohaib, O. (2019). Knowledge sharing practices, intellectual capital and organizational performance. *Proceedings of the 52nd Hawaii International Conference on System Sciences*. Hawaii, USA, pp. 5578-5587.

Boh, W., Constantinides, P., Padmanabhan, B., & Viswanathan, S. (2023). Building digital resilience against major shocks. *MIS Quarterly*, Vol. 47, No. 1, pp. 343-360.

Bollen, L., Vergauwen, P., & Schnieders, S. (2005). Linking intellectual capital and intellectual property to company performance. *Management Decision*, Vol. 43, No. 9, pp. 1161-1185.

Cameron, K. S., & Quinn, R. E. (2006). *Diagnosing and Changing Organizational Culture: Based on the Competing Values Framework*. Wiley.

Cheng, K.-T., Hsu, J. S.-C., Li, Y., & Brading, R. (2023). Intellectual capital and team resilience capability of information system development project teams. *Information & Management*. Vol. 60, No. 1, 103722.

Coldwell, T. S. (2010). *Bricolage culture: A study of the effects on organizational resilience.* University of Maryland University College, USA.

Demir, R., Wennberg, K., & McKelvie, A. (2016). The Strategic Management of High-Growth Firms: A Review and Theoretical Conceptualization. *Long Range Planning,* Vol. 50, No.4, pp. 431–456.

Denison, D. R., & Mishra, A. K. (1995). Toward a theory of organizational culture and effectiveness. *Organization Science*. Vol. 6, No. 2, pp. 204-223.

Eisenhardt, K. M. (1989). Building theories from case study research. *Academy of Management Review,* Vo. 14, No. 4, pp. 532-550.

Ferreira, A. I. (2014). Competing Values Framework and its impact on the intellectual capital dimensions: evidence from different Portuguese organizational sectors. *Knowledge Management Research & Practice*, Vol. 12, pp. 86-96.

Gioia, D. (2021). A systematic methodology for doing qualitative research. *The Journal of Applied Behavioral Science*, Vol. 57, No. 1, pp. 20-29.

Gioia, D. A., Corley, K. G., & Hamilton, A. L. (2013). Seeking Qualitative Rigor in Inductive Research. *Organizational Research Methods*, Vol. 16, No. 1, pp. 15-31.

Gong, L., Jiang, S., & Liang, X. (2022). Competing value framework-based culture transformation. *Journal of Business Research,* Vol. 145, pp. 853-863.

Gregory, B. T., Harris, S. G., Armenakis, A. A., & Shook, C. L. (2009). Organizational culture and effectiveness: A study of values, attitudes, and organizational outcomes. *Journal of Business Research*, Vol. 62, No. 7, pp. 673-679.

Hartl, E. (2019). A Characterization of Culture Change in the Context of Digital Transformation. *AMCIS 2019 Proceedings*. Cancun, Mexico.

Hartl, E., & Hess, T. (2017). The role of cultural values for digital transformation: Insights from a Delphi study. *AMCIS 2017 Proceedings*. Boston, USA.

Iivari, J., & Huisman, M. (2007). The relationship between organizational culture and the deployment of systems development methodologies. *MIS Quarterly*, Vol. 31, No. 1, pp. 35-58.

Kannan, G., & Aulbur, W. G. (2004). Intellectual capital: Measurement effectiveness. *Journal of Intellectual Capital*, Vol. 5, No. 3, pp. 389-413.

Lehmann, J., & Recker, J. (2022). Offerings That are "Ever-in-the-Making". *Business & Information Systems Engineering*, Vol. 64, No. 1, pp. 69-89.

Leidner, D. E., & Kayworth, T. (2006). A review of culture in information systems research: Toward a theory of information technology culture conflict. *MIS Quarterly*, Vol. 30., No.2, pp. 357-399.

Marotta, A., & Pearlson, K. (2019). A culture of cybersecurity at Banca Popolare di Sondrio. *AMCIS 2019 Proceedings*. Cancun, Mexico.

Morisse, M., & Prigge, C. (2017). Design of a business resilience model for Industry 4.0 manufacturers. *AMCIS 2017 Proceedings*. Boston, USA.

Mubarik, M. S., Bontis, N., Mubarik, M., & Mahmood, T. (2022). Intellectual capital and supply chain resilience. *Journal of Intellectual Capital*, Vol. 23, No. 3, pp. 713-738.

Neumannova, A., Bernroider, E. W. N., & Obwegeser, N. (2023). Digital Operational Resilience: The Role of Non-routine Responses in Crisis Situations. *ECIS 2023 Research-in-Progress Papers*. Kristiansand, Norway.

OECD. (2007). *Eurostat-OECD manual on business demography statistics*. Paris. OECD.

Parsons, D. (2010). Organisational resilience. *Australian Journal of Emergency Management,* Vol. 25, No. 2, pp. 18-20.

Sarkar, A., Wingreen, S., & Ascroft, J. (2020). Towards a practice-based view of Information Systems Resilience Using the Lens of Critical Realism. *Proceedings of the 53rd Hawaii International Conference on System Sciences*. Hawaii, USA, pp. 6184-6193.

Sarkar, A., Wingreen, S., Ascroft, J., & Sharma, R. (2021). Bouncing Back after a Crisis: Lessons from Senior Management Team to Drive IS Resilience. *Proceedings of the 54th Hawaii International Conference on System Sciences*. Hawaii, USA, pp. 6712-6721.

Schein, E. H. (1985). *Organizational Culture and Leadership*. Jossey-Bass, San Francisco.

Shih, C.-C., & Huang, S.-J. (2010). Exploring the relationship between organizational culture and software process improvement deployment. *Information & Management*, Vol. 47, No. 5-6, pp. 271-281.

Tippmann, E., Ambos, T. C., Del Giudice, M., Monaghan, S., & Ringov, D. (2023). Scale-ups and scaling in an international business context. *Journal of World Business*, Vol. 58, No. 1, 101397.

Wang, D., Su, Z., & Yang, D. (2011). Organizational culture and knowledge creation capability. *Journal of Knowledge Management*, Vol. 15, No. 3, pp. 363-373.

Weick, K. E. (1987). Organizational culture as a source of high reliability. *California Management Review*, Vol. 29, No. 2, pp. 112-127.

AGILE IT MANAGEMENT: DEVOPS ADOPTION IN THE FINANCE INDUSTRY

Lars Günthardt, Rehmil Sabani, Simon Bärtschi and Mike Krey
Zurich University of Applied Sciences, School of Management and Law
St. Georgen-Platz 2, 8401 Winterthur, Switzerland

ABSTRACT

DevOps is the modern organizational approach to unite the agile project world with the most cost-effective and stable IT operations. Swiss financial institutions tend to have numerous legacy systems, as well as specific regulatory requirements that make the shift to DevOps particularly challenging. In this paper, we created a new DevOps method specifically designed to address the outlined requirements. In order to verify the benefits of the method, a survey of 53 employees was conducted within a Swiss financial institution. It was found that the existing elements of the new method provide the basis, but the description of the instantiation of the method, as well as the exact room for interpretation of the legal requirements, provides the additional value desired.

KEYWORDS

DevOps, Development and IT Operations, Swiss Banks, Swiss Banking Industry, Method Engineering

1. INTRODUCTION

While agile methods primarily address the earliest delivery of functional increments from agile sprints to the customer to generate customer benefits quickly, the operational aspect is less emphasized. As an extension of agile project-specific methods, the DevOps (development & operation) approach is becoming increasingly widespread. More importantly, DevOps is a paradigm which aims at bridging this gap and improving performance within the teams to meet rapidly changing customer demands (Bucena & Kirikova 2017).

DevOps is the widely adopted approach for IT organizations seeking to encompass the entire software lifecycle. It proves valuable not only for expediting software releases to market but also for ensuring cost-effectiveness and sustainability in its operation. While classic universal banks have dominated Switzerland, this landscape could change with increasing digitalization. The shift away from direct customer contact to digital services eliminates the need for expensive branch networks, removing barriers to market entry.

In the Swiss financial market, authorities and regulators play a crucial role and exert significant influence on business activities. For example, while it is relatively easy to open an account in the UK with a passport photo scan, in Switzerland the Swiss Financial Market Supervisory Authority (FINMA) requires video identification, significantly impacting the customer experience (FINAM 2008). Alongside FINMA, the Swiss National Bank, as an independent central bank, establishes basic conditions for economic development, particularly in the financial sector. Other stakeholders in the Swiss financial center, such as Esisuisse (self-regulatory organization for banks in Switzerland), the Banking Ombudsman, and SIX Group, must also be considered in decision-making.

2. PROBLEM STATEMENT AND OBJECTIVES

To facilitate the introduction of DevOps, various frameworks, methods, and checklists have been proposed by academia and practice to successfully implement DevOps and minimize risks (Soellner, 2017). Various scholars point to this scarcity in literature, noting that implementation in practice creates a level of uncertainty (Leite et al. 2019). Lwakatare et al. (2015) further point out that the implementation of DevOps is particularly challenging in banking, where strong regulations must be considered, and organizational boundaries exist. In this paper, we address the issue that banks in Switzerland currently lack clear guidelines on how to successfully implement DevOps. Furthermore, there are no clear guidelines on how to overcome the challenges they currently face.

Based on the objectives discussed above, the following research questions were derived:

- **RQ: What are the core components of a DevOps methodology that take into account the special characteristics of the Swiss financial market?**

The focus of this paper is on a practical DevOps method for large and medium-sized Swiss financial service providers. Newly founded, currently relatively small financial companies, which may not be the focus of FINMA and typically have an IT system landscape built from scratch, are not considered.

3. RESEARCH METHODOLOGY

This paper follows the tradition of business informatics, which sees itself as an applied science and draws on instruments from real, formal, and engineering science perspectives. On this basis, theory-practice integrating research approaches are used, with the aim of presenting practice-relevant results and recommendations, but also creating transparency in order to evaluate the scientific contribution of the paper. In the upcoming section a literature review provides the most recent state of DevOps research, leading to a concluding discussion on challenges and barriers to DevOps for organizations. A literature review was conducted investigating contributions ranging from 2014 until 2023. In order to classify existing approaches and identify their relevance for the identified problem, the taxonomy framework by Cooper (1984) is applied.

Following this approach the following databases were searched, using *"DevOps"*, *"Bank"* AND *"Method"*, *"DevOps Adoption"* as search terms in titles and abstracts: (1) ACM Digital Library, (2) IEEE Xplore Digital Library to explore sources with a technology perspective such as the development and implementation of DevOps systems, (3) AIS Electronic Library (AISeL) to locate core DevOps topics such as the use of DevOps in organizations or in management.

The intended DevOps adoption model is created using the tools of design science, which aims to improve human and organizational capabilities by designing new artifacts. The paper follows the Design Science Research (DSR) methodology based on Hevner (2004). The next part focuses on establishing the theoretical foundation for creating a DevOps method.

4. DEVOPS – STATE OF THE ART

The drive for faster time-to-market has prompted a paradigm shift toward a development philosophy known as DevOps. Across the papers reviewed on the subject, it is evident that companies anticipate significant advantages from adopting this organizational model.

Gundelsby (2018) underscores the crucial aspect of team autonomy, emphasizing the need to consolidate competencies throughout the entire life cycle within the DevOps team. Following the principle 'if you build it, you run it,' Gundelsby argues that competencies for implementation, testing, and deployment must be unified within the same DevOps team. This requires appropriate autonomy. The author further elaborates that architectural guidelines play a pivotal role in enabling this autonomy. With this approach, legacy systems that are built as monoliths can also be split over time. This architectural requirement allows for scaling and is therefore also applicable to larger companies.

The goal of the DevOps approach is to foster more efficient and effective collaboration among the areas of development, IT operations, and quality assurance. There are various interpretations of DevOps, but in general, it involves unifying the realms of software development and IT operations through culture, practices, and tools (Augsten 2020). Different methods exist to support this approach, with some aiming to expedite and automate specific phases of the application lifecycle, while others focus on process creation and productivity enhancement (Microsoft 2020). Drawing from methods, tools, and best practices, various models have been developed, serving as frameworks that companies can utilize. Following a literature review, we identified four methods as the most relevant for developing a dedicated DevOps approach. Table 1 provides a summary of these four methods.

Table 1. Methods of DevOps

Model	Description	Source
Google Accelerate State of DevOps 2019	- Six years of research - data from 31'000 professionals - Practical - Correlation between elements	Forsgren et al. 2019
SAFe DevOps CALMR	- Integration in SAFe Framework - CALMR Values	SAFe 2023
DevOps Institute Blueprint	- Certification authority - CALMS Values - Three Ways: Continuous Flow, Feedback, Continuous Improvement	DevOpsInst 2021
Conceptual framework characterizing the DevOps phenomenon	- Abstract - 22 papers analyzed -Key elements: Collaboration, Automation, Measurement, Monitoring	Lwakatar et al. 2015

The analysis of the four methods showed that there is no universal DevOps method. It turns out that DevOps can be applied in traditional banks despite various legacy systems and has a positive impact on the speed of software development. The most important process-related aspects, in addition to the classic setup for agile methods, are automation and team autonomy. Desired team autonomy can be primarily achieved through architectural specifications such as a microservice architecture with managed API.

5. A METHOD FOR ADOPTION OF DEVOPS IN THE BANKING INDUSTRY

In business informatics, a problem is defined as the gap between the current state, which is well-defined, and a final state, also well-defined. Consequently, a method refers to a systematic approach, algorithm, or guidance presented as a process to resolve this problem and attain the desired end state.

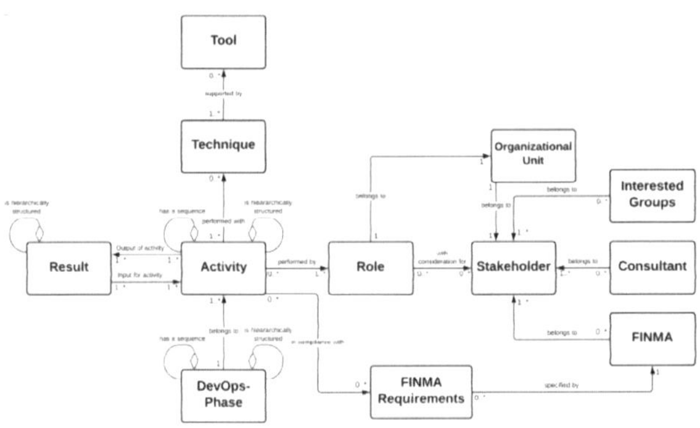

Figure 1. Meta-model of DevOps Method

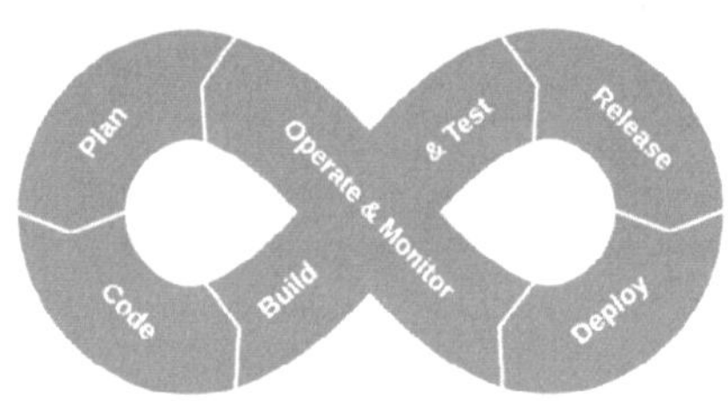

Figure 2. DevOps Lifecycle

The concluding aspect of Method Engineering, as per Gutzwiller, is the meta-model (1994). This meta-model serves as the construction plan of the method, outlining the relationships among the individual elements. Figure 1 illustrates the meta-model for the developed method tailored to the Swiss banking industry. As the meta-model illustrates, the results, activities, and DevOps phases are hierarchically structured. Additionally, the DevOps phases and activities have a sequence and are thus described in a procedural model. The meta-model was expanded to include relevant stakeholders and FINMA requirements that have a direct influence on the activities.

In practical applications, regardless of the industry, there are typically eight phases that encompass DevOps (cf. Table 1). However, in this paper, some phases have been combined, resulting in a total of six phases. This consolidation aims to enhance efficiency and reduce error rates. Figure 2 illustrates the six main activities, which are performed through an iterative process.

The elements of Gutzwiller described were used to design the method for the Swiss banking industry (1994). These elements are described below for all six main activities.

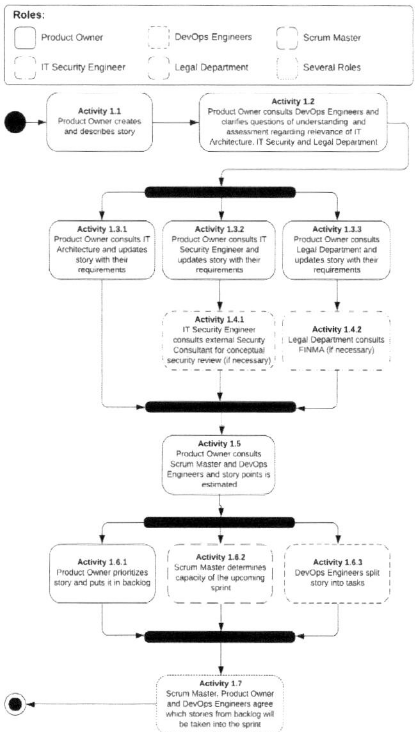

Figure 3. Activity 1 - Plan

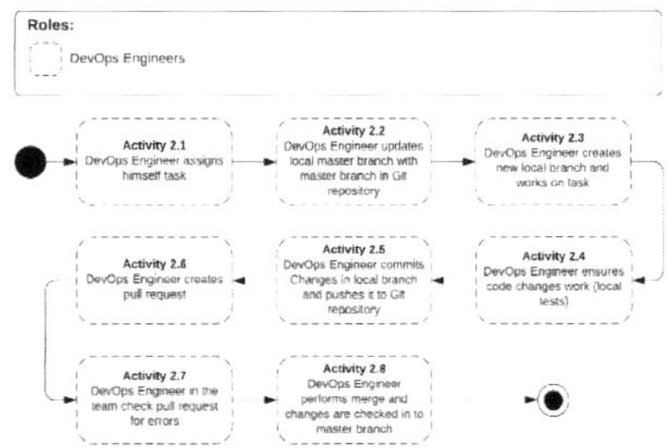

Figure 4. Activity 2 - Code

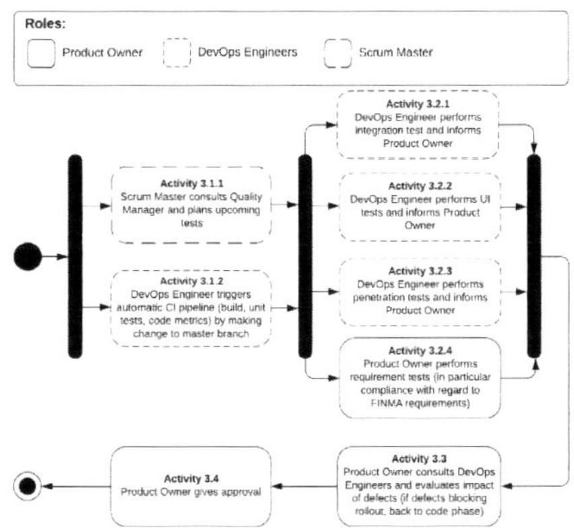

Figure 5. Activity 3 – Build & Test

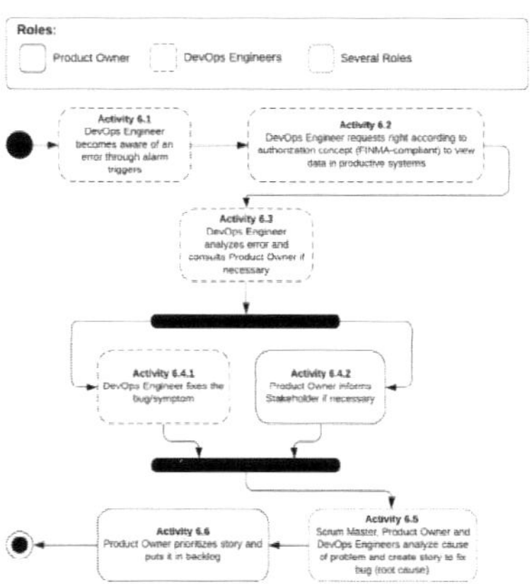

Figure 6. Activity 4 – Release

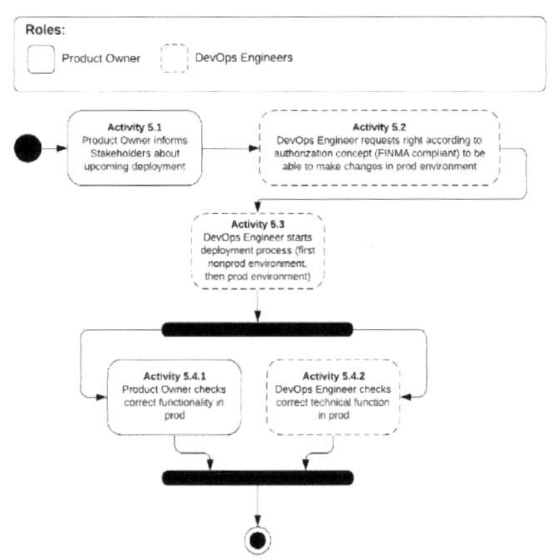

Figure 7. Activity 5 – Deploy

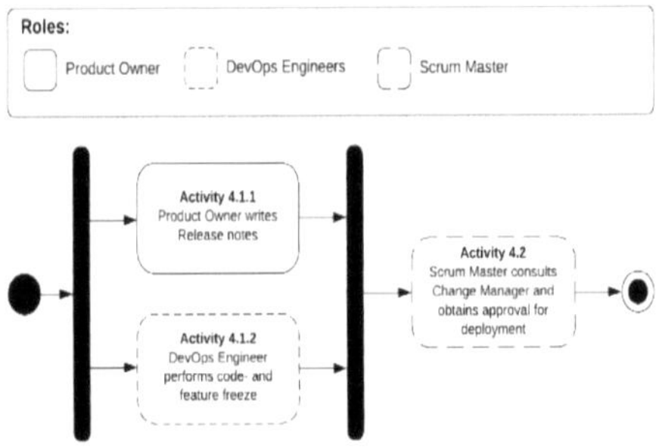

Figure 8. Activity 6 - Operate & Monitor

Table 2. Techniques and Tools of Activity 1 – Plan

Technique	Tool
Requirements Catalogue	Atlassian Jira, Confluence
Evaluation Planning	Atlassian Jira, Confluence
Plan Scope Management	Atlassian Jira, Confluence
SMART Goals	-
Skill Radar	Atlassian Add-on
Project Communication Plan	Atlassian Confluence, MS Office
Stakeholder Expectation Management	Atlassian Confluence, MS Office
Stakeholder Influence Matrix	Atlassian Confluence, MS Office

Table 3. Roles of Activity 6 - Operate & Monitor

Activity	Product Owner	DevOps Engineer	Scrum Master	IT Architect	Security Engineer	Legal Department	Quality Manager	Change Manager	Stakeholders	FINMA
6.1	I	R	I							
6.2		R								
6.3	C	R								
6.4.1		R								
6.4.2	R								I	
6.5	R	R	R							
6.6	R	I	I							

6. EVALUATION OF THE METHOD

This section focuses on the survey and interviews conducted in order to gain a deeper understanding of the DevOps implementation processes. The evaluation process ensures the applicability of the meta-model under real-world conditions. Interviews were conducted including two banks that have not yet implemented DevOps and two that have already adopted DevOps into their software engineering process.

First, we introduced the questionnaire as well as the meta-model. A walkthrough of the meta-model was conducted as part of a workshop with experts and executives.

The results were obtained as follows: A Swiss financial institution that transitioned to DevOps in 2023 was selected as the basis for reviewing the method. The institution is currently in the midst of the transformation phase. Within this financial institution where the review was conducted, the existing DevOps teams were visited during their daily meetings. The methodology was presented, followed by a questionnaire and evaluation process. This allowed for the collection of opinions from 53 employees working with DevOps, including those fulfilling the roles of Product Owners, Scrum Masters, and DevOps Engineers. Overall, the following three topic areas were covered:

- **Understandability and usefulness of the presented method:** In addition, general suggestions for improvement were obtained. 92.45% found the method basically understandable, understandable, or very understandable.
- **Assessment of the DevOps method introduced in the financial institution:** 79.25% of those surveyed felt a need for action, especially in the area of automation. Of these, 64.15% rate the need for action as very great, 22.64% as great.

The most relevant insights were as follows: The key lies in the implementation. If, through the created method, every employee gets involved in the implementation process and has the same information and therefore the same understanding of the method, collaboration would become clearer. There is enough information available about DevOps. The only valuable thing about a company-wide defined DevOps method is that everyone, including management and the infrastructure department, understands that everyone in the DevOps team needs to be able to access anywhere if required. Otherwise, it is just a DevThird-Level-Support instead of DevOps.

7. CONCLUSION

The survey results made it clear that the method is not particularly value-adding at this point. However, the general consensus was that the created method could serve as a foundation. With certain additions, the method could become a valuable asset for companies aiming to make the transformation to DevOps more cost-effective.

Specific elements identified by the participants that would enhance the method's value include the following:

- Not only should the method be transparent, but also the implementation steps and roadmap should be made clear to all affected employees from the beginning. This ensures that everyone has access to the same information and reduces the likelihood of encountering a fait accompli.
- The most valuable aspect of the created method is its precise interpretation of legislative requirements and those of FINMA. It is crucial to explore how existing laws can be interpreted to the fullest extent in support of the DevOps culture. For instance, if the defined method outlines how the need-to-know principle can be interpreted to maximize access by DevOps engineers to required environments, it adds significant value. This would enable DevOps teams to operate as autonomously as possible without infringing any laws.

The newly designed method comprising the meta-model, the ten roles, and the six associated activities with their techniques and tools, is fundamentally sound. The vast majority of survey participants found no issues with the existing elements and found them understandable.

REFERENCES

Augsten S. Was ist DevOps? [Internet] [cited 2020 Oct 27]. Available from: https://www.dev-insider.de/was-ist-devops-a-570286/.

Bucena, I., & Kirikova, M. (2017). Simplifying the DevOps Adoption Process. BIR Workshops. 1-15.

Cooper HM. The integrative research review: A systematic approach. Beverly Hills, Calif.: Sage Publications; 1984.

DevOps Institute. DevOps Foundation Blueprint [Internet] [cited 2021 Jan 10]. Available from: https://devopsinstitute.com/certifications/devops-foundation/.

FINMA. Rundschreiben 2008/21: Operationelle Risiken - Banken. 2008.

Forsgren, N., Smith, D., Humble, J. & Frazelle, J. Accelerate State of DevOps 2019 [Internet] [cited 2021 Jan 10]. Available from: https://services.google.com/fh/files/misc/state-of-devops-2019.pdf.

Gundelsby JH. Enabling autonomous teams in large-scale agile through architectural principles. In: Aguiar A, editor Proceedings of the 19th International Conference on Agile Software Development Companion

Hevner, A. R., March, S. T., Park, J., & Ram, S. (2004). Design science in information systems research. MIS quarterly.

Leite, L., Rocha, C., Kon, F., Milojicic, D., & Meirelles, P. (2019). A survey of DevOps concepts and challenges. ACM Computing Surveys (CSUR). 52(6). 1-35.

Lwakatare, L. E., Kuvaja, P. & Oivo, M., editor. Dimensions of DevOps. Cham: Springer International Publishing; 2015. (Agile Processes in Software Engineering and Extreme Programming; vol. 212).

Mircosoft. Was ist DevOps? [Internet] [cited 2020 Oct 27]. Available from: https://azure.microsoft.com/de-de/overview/what-is-devops/.

SAFe. DevOps [Internet]. Available from: https://www.scaledagileframework.com/devops.

Soellner, D. (2017). DevOps in der Praxis - Handlungsfelder für eine erfolgreiche Zusammenarbeit von Entwicklung und Betrieb. Wiesenbaden: CrossMark.

DATA LITERACY MEASUREMENTS: A SYSTEMATIC LITERATURE REVIEW

Aleksa Komosar[1], Sara Koprivica[1], Davide Taibi[2], Aleksandar Ivic[1], Darko Stefanovic[1] and Sara Kijanovic[1]
[1]*Faculty of Technical Sciences, University of Novi Sad, Trg Dositeja Obradovica 6, Novi Sad, Serbia*
[2]*Institute for Educational Technology, National Research Council of Italy, Via Ugo la Malfa, Palermo, Italy*

ABSTRACT

Data literacy is a complex concept that includes the skills necessary for an individual's success in the digital age. By measuring the level of data literacy, concept improvements, and greater success are realized. The goal of this research is to observe the trends when the word is about the measurement of data literacy with respect to the method, the population, and the countries in which the measurements were carried out. The PRISMA approach was used in the paper, and the Scopus and Web of Science databases were searched. Inclusion and exclusion criteria led to 22 papers to be analyzed. The results show surveys as the most frequent measurement tool in the fields of education, among students and teachers. When it comes to countries, China and Indonesia have the largest number of conducted investigations.

KEYWORDS

Data Literacy, Data Skills, Data Competencies, Measurements, Assessments, Literature Review

1. INTRODUCTION

The essential understanding of data, its storage, processing, presentation, and extraction are very important both for humans and for the aspect of Industry 4.0, where data is the basis for creating knowledge and value (Leon-Urrutia et al., 2022). Today's world is characterized by the rapid development of information technologies, where large amounts of data are created, which opens the door to the need to understand how to use data and the need for data literacy. According to Gartner's report from 2018 (Logan, 2018), the weak development of an individual's data literacy is the second major obstacle to achieving success in the digital age (Marjanovic et al., 2022).

Furthermore, the European Commission presents a plan (*Digital Education Action Plan (2021-2027) | European Education Area*, 2020), where the eighth point of the second priority refers to the development of digital competencies and skills in the area of the data literacy concept. Due to its complexity, the concept of data literacy can be approached in different ways. Ying Cui et al. (Cui et al., 2023) distinguish between the definition of data literacy among students, citizens, and teachers. They noticed differences in the way data literacy is measured for different age categories in different areas.

On the other hand, Bahareh Ghodoosi et al. (Ghodoosi et al., 2023) focused on data literacy in education. Additionally, the development of data literacy competencies in a university context was explored in (Taibi et al., 2021). They found a discrepancy in the understanding of the competencies that make up the concept of data literacy in different fields. The existence of generally standardized metrics and criteria for measuring data literacy provides a better basis for further development and monitoring. The concept of data literacy overlaps with the concept of digital literacy, as well as other related literacies - information, visualization, and statistics literacy (Vuorikari et al., 2022). In the study of Lin et al. (Lin et al., 2023) was shown that data literacy affects digital competencies, but also that ICT skills significantly affect the degree of data literacy. For the data literacy concept to be fully understood and developed, it is necessary to constitutionalize the measurement methods. Also, to obtain the quantification of different levels of data literacy with the tendency of further development.

The aim of this paper is to provide insight into the most frequently used methods, according to the target groups by generalizing the measurement of data literacy at different levels. To address our research objective, we designed and conducted a systematic literature review using PRISMA flowchart with defined inclusion and exclusion criteria. The paper is organized as follows. Section 2 is related to the definition and background of the data literacy concept. Section 3 presents the used methodology, as well as the inclusion and exclusion criteria. In section 4 the results and discussion are presented. Section 5 refers to the conclusion of results with a tendency for future investigation and development.

2. BACKGROUND OF DATA LITERACY CONCEPT

The data literacy concept is based on the ability to understand, use, and process data, solving real-world problems using practical and creative skills to make decisions including an ethical component (Mandinach & Gummer, 2013). Based on DigiComp II (Vuorikari et al., 2022) data competencies for citizens are divided into four groups: data collection, data management, data evaluation, and data application. Every group of data literacy competencies is characterized by data skills that are necessary to develop a competence. On the other hand, data literacy competencies from DigiComp II can be expanded by additional defined competencies (Ridsdale et al., 2015; Vuorikari et al., 2022). Furthermore, some authors defined conceptual, core, and advanced competencies. Regarding Ridsdale (Ridsdale et al., 2015), data conversion, metadata use and creation, data curation, security, data preservation, and evaluating decisions based on data are advanced competencies. The main conceptualizing trend of data literacy competence is data management and visualization to create better value in the process of data decision-making (Ridsdale et al., 2015). Different approaches to measuring the level of data literacy require the observation of data literacy concepts at different levels.

3. METHODOLOGY

To make a comprehensive review of the state-of-the-art in the area of data literacy level measurement, Preferred Reporting Items for Systematic Reviews and Meta-Analyses (PRISMA) framework was used. According to PRISMA, there are three phases of reviewing: 1. identification, 2. screening, and 3. including. For this literature review, the databases Scopus and Web of Science were searched. Due to the different uses of the term data literacy, the search string was expanded with terms such as "data skills" and "data competencies" using operator OR. On the other hand, "assessment" and "empirical study" terms were used to expand the possibility of papers that include measurement methods. The final search string was: ("data literacy" OR "data skills" OR "data competencies") AND ("measurements" OR "assessment" OR "empirical study").

Developed research questions for this comprehensive review are the following:

RQ1: How is measured the level of data literacy?

RQ2: Which target groups is addressed by the measurement activity?

RQ3: In which countries the studies concerning the measure of data literacy level have been conducted?

Inclusion criteria: IC1 - The main objective of the paper must be related to data literacy, data literacy competencies, and data skills and assessment methods. IC2 - The study must be an article or conference paper published between 2018 and 2023. IC3 - The paper must be written in English. IC4 – Only papers that authors managed to access should be accepted. IC5 - There must be the study/research with the participants. IC6 - There must be a defined population of the research and geographical location.

Exclusion criteria: EC1 - Papers that are not related to the research questions. EC2 - Duplicate papers. EC3 - Demonstrations, preliminary studies, position papers, technical reports, posters, and proof-of-concept and theoretical papers were excluded. Figure 1 shows the PRISMA workflow conducted by the authors. The data extracted from each paper will be title, abstract, keywords, country, year of publication, publisher, and type of paper.

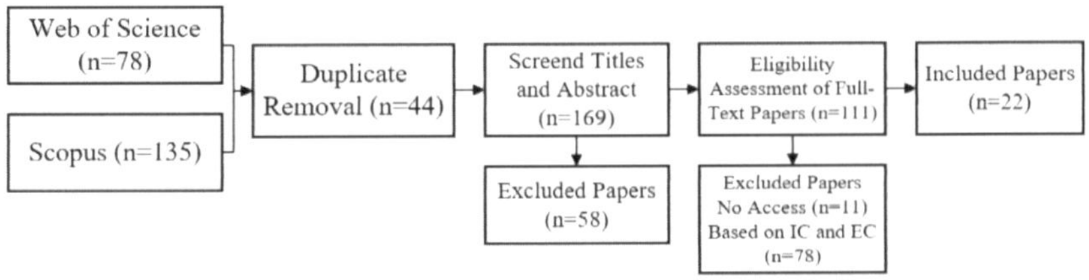

Figure 1. PRISMA workflow

4. RESULTS AND DISCUSSION

Based on the search string used on Scopus and Web of Science, there were 213 papers. 44 duplicate papers were removed. After extracted data defined in Section 3, all papers were screened by title and abstract. In that phase, 58 papers were excluded. In the next step, all full-text papers were assessed. Due to no access, 11 papers were excluded, and 78 papers were excluded based on inclusion and exclusion criteria. In the end, 22 papers were included in this study. One of the main obstacles during this systematic review was the different approaches – educational or general to the data literacy concept by the authors and different definitions. Based on research in 2018 were no papers, in 2019 there is 1 paper. In 2020 the number increased to 2, and in 2021 to 6. The biggest number of papers is in 2022. Currently, in 2023 there are 5 papers. The number of papers that have data literacy for the field is increasing year by year. Only two papers are conference paper and the rest represents articles. To answer the first and second questions, Table 1 was created.

Table 1. Review of measurements and target group

Measurement	Field	Population	Papers
Survey	Education	In-service teachers	(Freddano & Pandolfini 2022), (Luo et al., 2022), (Zhao et al., 2021)
		Students	(Duc et al., 2022), (Burress, 2022), (Saddiqa et al., 2021)
		Professionals	(Rafiq & Ameen, 2022)
	General	Professionals	(Ongena, 2023), (Kröplin et al., 2022), (Kouts-Klemm, 2019)
Test	Education	Pre-service teachers	(Wurster et al., 2023), (Wu et al., 2023)
		Students	(Suryadi et al., 2021), (Rahmawati et al., 2020)
	General	Citizens	(Tabak & Dubovi, 2023)
		Professionals	(Palsa & Mertala, 2023)
Observational study	Education	Students	(Li et al., 2022), (Saddiqa et al., 2021)
Interview	Education	Pre-service or in-service teachers	(Conn et al., 2022), (McDowall et al., 2021), (McDowall et al., 2021)
		Students	(Saddiqa et al., 2021)
	General	Professionals	(Kouts-Klemm, 2019)
OTTO model	Education	Pre-service teachers	(Kennedy-Clark et al., 2021)
Mirecal model	Education	Student	(Lusiyana, 2020)

The percentage of 68,1% refers to included papers are in the field of education. Concerning the target group, there are different categories as in-service, pre-service teachers, and professionals. Professionals in the field of education are all staff that work in educational institutions. On the other hand, professionals represent medical staff, sports, and journalists. (RQ1): The main measurement tool was a survey – of 10 papers, followed by a test – of 6 papers. Some of the papers include mixed methods or approaches (Kennedy-Clark et al., 2021; Kouts-Klemm, 2019; Saddiqa et al., 2021). (RQ2): Pre-service teachers are the main focus group of investigation based on those results. Also, focus groups are students, in-service teachers, and professionals. (RQ3): Based on the geographical location of the research, three papers refer to China, but also Indonesia.

Larger studies in the field of education were conducted in several locations, within schools and universities, to compare the results. Data literacy affects the development of digital competencies, which can be closely related to the degree of digitization of a country (Lin et al., 2023).

5. CONCLUSION

This paper presents a systematic literature review in the field of data literacy concept. The research clearly shows the need for standardized tools and metrics in this area to improve the data literacy concept but also compares the obtained results. To get better results, the data literacy concept needs to be viewed through the field in which the target group operates. By separating the data literacy concept into competencies, a more detailed presentation of the skills of an individual is achieved, which results in better measurement results. In the future, one of the possible focuses may be comparing the level of data literacy of students of different majors, but also of different age groups in the general target group. Additionally, measurement methods should include specific parts for other relevant literacies, such as digital. By using standardized methods of measurement at the global level, the results can contribute to development and comparison.

REFERENCES

Burress, T. (2022). Data Literacy Practices of Students Conducting Undergraduate Research. *College & Research Libraries*, *83*(3). https://doi.org/10.5860/crl.83.3.434

Conn, C. A., Bohan, K. J., Bies-Hernandez, N. J., Powell, P. J., Sweeny, S. P., Persinger, L. L., & Persinger, J. D. (2022). Expected data literacy knowledge and skills for early career teachers: Perspectives from school and district personnel. *Teaching and Teacher Education*, *111*, 103607. https://doi.org/10.1016/j.tate.2021.103607

Cui, Y., Chen, F., Lutsyk, A., Leighton, J. P., & Cutumisu, M. (2023). Data literacy assessments: A systematic literature review. *Assessment in Education: Principles, Policy & Practice*, *30*(1), 76–96. https://doi.org/10.1080/0969594X.2023.2182737

Digital Education Action Plan (2021-2027) | European Education Area. (2020). https://education.ec.europa.eu/focus-topics/digital-education/action-plan

Duc, N. T. M., Viet, K. H., & Lan, V. T. N. (2022). Impact of Scholarly Project on students' perception of research skills: A quasi-experimental study. *The Asia Pacific Scholar*, *7*(4), 50–58. https://doi.org/10.29060/TAPS.2022-7-4/OA2748

Freddano, M., & Pandolfini, V. (2022). Teacher Training on Data Literacy for School Evaluation and Improvement: A Teacher Professional Development Experience in Italy. *Education and Self Development*, *17*(1), 89–98. https://doi.org/10.26907/esd.17.1.08

Ghodoosi, B., West, T., Li, Q., Torrisi-Steele, G., & Dey, S. (2023). A systematic literature review of data literacy education. *Journal of Business & Finance Librarianship*, *28*(2), 112–127. https://doi.org/10.1080/08963568.2023.2171552

Kennedy-Clark, S., Galstaun, V., & Reimann, P. (2021). Preparing pre-service teachers for Teaching Performance Assessments using the OTTO Model. *Teachers and Teaching*, *27*(1–4), 164–180. https://doi.org/10.1080/13540602.2021.1933420

Kouts-Klemm, R. (2019). Data literacy among journalists: A skills-assessment based approach. *Central European Journal of Communication*, *12*(3), 299–315. https://doi.org/10.19195/1899-5101.12.3(24).2

Kröplin, J., Huber, T., Geis, C., Braun, B., & Fritz, T. (2022). eSurgery—digital transformation in surgery, surgical education and training: Survey analysis of the status quo in Germany. *European Surgery*, *54*(5), 249–258. https://doi.org/10.1007/s10353-022-00747-x

Leon-Urrutia, M., Taibi, D., Pospelova, V., Splendore, S., Urbsiene, L., & Marjanovic, U. (2022). Data Literacy: An Essential Skill for the Industry. In B. Lalic, D. Gracanin, N. Tasic, & N. Simeunović (Eds.), *Proceedings on 18th International Conference on Industrial Systems – IS'20* (pp. 326–331). Springer International Publishing. https://doi.org/10.1007/978-3-030-97947-8_43

Li, A. W., Sinnamon, L. S., & Kopak, R. (2022). Exploring learning opportunities for students in open data portal use across data literacy levels. *Information and Learning Sciences*, *123*(9/10), 601–620. https://doi.org/10.1108/ILS-01-2022-0003

Lin, R., Yang, J., Jiang, F., & Li, J. (2023). Does teacher's data literacy and digital teaching competence influence empowering students in the classroom? Evidence from China. *Education and Information Technologies*, *28*(3), 2845–2867. https://doi.org/10.1007/s10639-022-11274-3

Logan, V. (2018). *Fostering Data Literacy and Information as a Second Language: A Gartner Trend Insight Report*.

Luo, J., Wang, M., & Yu, S. (2022). Exploring the factors influencing teachers' instructional data use with electronic data systems. *Computers & Education*, *191*, 104631. https://doi.org/10.1016/j.compedu.2022.104631

Lusiyana, A. (2020). *Measuring The Physics Students' Data Literacy Skill In The Era Of Industry 4.0 By Using Mirecal Learning Model*. *9*(01).

Mandinach, E. B., & Gummer, E. S. (2013). A Systemic View of Implementing Data Literacy in Educator Preparation. *Educational Researcher*, *42*(1), 30–37. https://doi.org/10.3102/0013189X12459803

Marjanovic, U., Taibi, D., Cabral, P., Urbsiene, L., Kasaj, A., & Marques, S. M. (2022). Digital Transformation Missing Ingredients: Data Literacy. In B. Lalic, D. Gracanin, N. Tasic, & N. Simeunović (Eds.), *Proceedings on 18th International Conference on Industrial Systems – IS'20* (pp. 340–344). Springer International Publishing. https://doi.org/10.1007/978-3-030-97947-8_45

McDowall, A., Mills, C., Cawte, K., & Miller, J. (2021). Data use as the heart of data literacy: An exploration of pre-service teachers' data literacy practices in a teaching performance assessment. *Asia-Pacific Journal of Teacher Education*, *49*(5), 487–502. https://doi.org/10.1080/1359866X.2020.1777529

Ongena, G. (2023). Data literacy for improving governmental performance: A competence-based approach and multidimensional operationalization. *Digital Business*, *3*(1), 100050. https://doi.org/10.1016/j.digbus.2022.100050

Palsa, L., & Mertala, P. (2023). Contextualizing Everyday Data Literacies: The Case of Recreational Runners. *International Journal of Human–Computer Interaction*, 1–12. https://doi.org/10.1080/10447318.2023.2241612

Rafiq, M., & Ameen, K. (2022). Research data management and sharing awareness, attitude, and behavior of academic researchers. *Information Development*, *38*(3), 391–405. https://doi.org/10.1177/02666669211048491

Rahmawati, L., Wilujeng, I., & Satriana, A. (2020). Application of STEM learning approach through simple technology to increase data literacy. *Journal of Physics: Conference Series*, *1440*(1), 012047. https://doi.org/10.1088/1742-6596/1440/1/012047

Ridsdale, C., Rothwell, J., Smit, M., Bliemel, M., Irvine, D., Kelley, D., Matwin, S., Wuetherick, B., & Ali-Hassan, H. (2015). *Strategies and Best Practices for Data Literacy Education Knowledge Synthesis Report*. https://doi.org/10.13140/RG.2.1.1922.5044

Saddiqa, M., Magnussen, R., Larsen, B., & Pedersen, J. M. (2021). Open Data Interface (ODI) for secondary school education. *Computers & Education*, *174*, 104294. https://doi.org/10.1016/j.compedu.2021.104294

Suryadi, Mahardika, I. K., Supeno, & Sudarti. (2021). Data literacy of high school students on physics learning. *Journal of Physics: Conference Series*, *1839*(1), 012025. https://doi.org/10.1088/1742-6596/1839/1/012025

Tabak, I., & Dubovi, I. (2023). What drives the public's use of data? The mediating role of trust in science and data literacy in functional scientific reasoning concerning COVID-19. *Science Education*, *107*(5), 1071–1100. https://doi.org/10.1002/sce.21789

Taibi, D., Fernandez-Sanz, L., Pospelova, V., Leon-Urrutia, M., Marjanovic, U., Splendore, S., & Urbsiene, L. (2021). Developing Data Literacy Competences at University: The experience of the DEDALUS project. *2021 1st Conference on Online Teaching for Mobile Education (OT4ME)*, 112–113. https://doi.org/10.1109/OT4ME53559.2021.9638912

Vuorikari, R., Kluzer, S., & Punie, Y. (2022). *DigComp 2.2, The Digital Competence framework for citizens: With new examples of knowledge, skills and attitudes*. Publications Office of the European Union.

Wu, X., Xu, T., & Zhang, Y. (2023). Research on the data analysis knowledge assessment of pre-service teachers from China based on cognitive diagnostic assessment. *Current Psychology*, *42*(6), 4885–4899. https://doi.org/10.1007/s12144-021-01836-y

Wurster, S., Bez, S., & Merk, S. (2023). Does learning how to use data mean being motivated to use it? Effects of a data use intervention on data literacy and motivational beliefs of pre-service teachers. *Learning and Instruction*, *88*, 101806. https://doi.org/10.1016/j.learninstruc.2023.101806

Zhao, Y., Pinto Llorente, A. M., Sánchez Gómez, M. C., & Zhao, L. (2021). The Impact of Gender and Years of Teaching Experience on College Teachers' Digital Competence: An Empirical Study on Teachers in Gansu Agricultural University. *Sustainability*, *13*(8), 4163. https://doi.org/10.3390/su13084163

REDUCING COMPLEXITY BY USING LINGUISTIC SUMMARIES FOR BUSINESS INTELLIGENCE REPORTING

Galena Pisoni[1], Erika Mináriková[2], Miroslav Hudec[3], Hanna Kristin Skaftadottir[4], Bálint Molnár[5], Miljan Vučetić[6,7] and Denisa Sedláková[3]

[1]York business School, York St John University, Lord Mayor's Walk, YO31 7EX, York, UK
[2]Faculty of Economic Informatics, University of Economics in Bratislava, Bratislava, Slovakia
[3]Faculty of Economics, VSB–Technical University of Ostrava, Ostrava, Czech Republic
[4]Department of Business, Bifröst University, Reykjavík, Iceland
[5]Information Systems Department, Eötvös Loránd University~(ELTE), Budapest, Hungary
[6]Vlatacom Institute of High Technologies, Belgrade, Serbia
[7]Singidunum University, Belgrade, Serbia

ABSTRACT

Because of the competitive economy, organizations today seek to rationalize, innovate and adapt to changing environments and circumstances as part of their efforts. We discuss in particular the use of linguistic summaries for business intelligence reporting, and the strength of this approach to enhance the support in efficiency and effectiveness of business execution. The strength of linguistic summaries approach lies in its possibility to provide explanation to the business managers, in a humanly understandable way, regarding the actual state of business execution, insights to support better decisions and provisions regarding future activities, therefore providing transparent way to analyze and use data in their possession. Solid business intelligence reporting is essential to control and assure organizational evolution. Therefore, the objective of this paper is to present a reference enterprise architecture for data collection and mining of summaries, applicable to companies. Additionally, it aims to analyze the challenges and opportunities associated with the implementation of linguistic summaries in business intelligence reporting, particularly considering diverse data types and amounts of data.

KEYWORDS

Linguistic Summaries, Enterprise Architectures, Business Intelligence Reporting, Data Analytics, Data-driven Decision Making

1. INTRODUCTION

Firms see the potential of utilizing different types of data in their possession to gain valuable insights and improve their decision-making processes. Overall, the ability to handle existing and new data types opens up new possibilities for businesses to further leverage their data assets and gain a competitive edge.

As we move to the higher level in a company, i.e., tactic or strategic, the granulation should be less-detailed and interpreted in an understandable way. The candidate is linguistic summaries. Sentence such as *the most of elderly customers have low level of financial literacy, or the most of young customers have very negative opinion regarding waiting time* are understandable at first glance. A usual business intelligence reporting at this level is by dashboards which provide a quick overview and do not require real-time data (Vaisman & Zimányi, 2022). This visualization includes tables, graphs, statistical figures and the Key Performance Indicators (KPI). However, it is not an easy task to visualize the aforementioned summarizing sentences by tables, graphs or statistical figures.

By analyzing a larger data set, a retail bank can gain valuable insights into its multi-channel customer interactions. Log files contain detailed information about customer inter- actions, such as the channels used (e. g, online banking, mobile app, call center, the duration of each interaction, the actions taken by the customer, and any errors or issues encountered). Transnational data contain information related to loans statuses, opinions in internal surveys, records about payment behaviour (like interest rate paid on time, debts, etc.). Analyzing these data can help the bank understand how customers are using different channels, identify pain points in the customer journey, and make data-driven decisions to improve customer experience and satisfaction across all channels. Providing summarized knowledge in the form of linguistic summaries (to decision makers) about e.g., the multi-channel customer interactions support optimizing bank's channels and security of customer transactions (Shao et al, 2022).

Another possible application in finance, can be the insurance subdomain, and this kind of analysis allows the insurer to identify patterns and trends in customer interactions that may indicate dissatisfaction. By converting the speech in call center recordings into written text, the insurer could use various techniques such as natural language processing and sentiment analysis to summarize customers sentiment and identify potential issues or concerns. By surveys and the other channels, insurance companies and government receive valuable insight about the weaknesses and how to improve, for instance, financial literacy, especially when the recognized weaknesses are interpreted by flexible functional dependencies and linguistic summaries (Vučetić et al, 2022). Next, through this analysis, the insurer can gain valuable insights into the common rea- sons for customer dissatisfaction, such as a long waiting time, denied claims, or confusing policy information. They might also identify specific keywords or phrases that are frequently associated with dissatisfaction, enabling them to take proactive measures to address these concerns and improve customer experience. By understanding customer dissatisfaction more accurately, the insurer can implement targeted strategies to improve customer satisfaction and loyalty. Linguistic summaries could help in this respect by providing an easy way to interpret observed patters in a simplified way when usual reporting approaches like maps, graphs or statistical figures are not suitable (Pisoni, 2021), or when linguistic summaries provide an explainable add-on to the existing visualization techniques (Hudec, Bednárová & Holzinger, 2018). In this contribution, we explore the concept known as linguistic summaries (see, e.g., (Boran, Akay & Yager, 2016), (Lesot, Moyse & Bouchon-Meunier, 2016)) to reveal, whether these summaries are beneficial and how we can improve business intelligence reporting with the linguistic summaries supporting the usual business intelligence goals.

2. ENTERPRISE ARCHITECTURE FOR DATA COLLECTION AND MINING SUMMARIES

Recently, the efficient and effective utilization of data became an essential issue. Transformation of data collection from simple substantiated data to data that originate from large-scale monitoring led to the requirement of disciplined data analytic. Data can be listed as a traditional data coming from the business operation, and operational data originating from different sources. The latter data are usually unstructured and heterogeneous; either we consider their structure or their content. Data should be accompanied by meta-data that describes the essential information about the content and can be utilized to categorize and organize data to exploit them for advanced data mining (Arnott, 2008).

By combining unstructured and structured data, companies can gain a more comprehensive understanding of their customers and operations. Unstructured data refers to information that does not fit into a traditional database, such as social media posts, customer reviews, or text documents. On the other hand, structured data is organized and easily searchable, typically stored in databases or spreadsheets. Even in databases (e.g., fuzzy databases) or spreadsheets, we might expect mixed data types for a single attribute like numeric values, hesitant or fuzzy numbers, and neighbouring categorical values, when uncertainty should not be neglected. When these data types are brought together, companies can uncover deep insights that may have been overlooked if they only focused on one type of data (Qihai, Tao & Tao, 2008).

Previous research has shown that analysis of data that originated from structured databases and external sources is relatively straightforward with the use of data warehouses (Kimball, 2011). The main function of the data warehouse is to integrate data and transform them into the confirmed structure, relevant for the domain of interest. However, more than 80% of the data of enterprises are in semi-structured and unstructured format since the Data Lakes solutions in tandem with data warehouses are the viable options. The methods of data science (DS), machine learning (ML), and Natural Language Processing (NLP) should fit the Data Lake properties to achieve meaningful results (Pisoni, Molnár & Tarcsi, 2021).

When data are collected and stored, various data analysis is possible. Beneficially, KPI for the stakeholders should be expressed in a clear visual way like traffic light (red, yellow, green) or indicated by arrows (Vaisman & Zimányi, 2022) especially when require immediate reaction. The reporting with linguistic summaries gives another view, for instance a relation among KPIs or relation to other data like *the most of the weeks in considered period values are in the yellow area close to the red area*. These interpretations provide the basis for supporting effective decision-making from operational to strategic levels. In order to generate the linguistic insights as afore discussed, the relevant "data ingestion" framework, or the way the data are fed to the data warehouse, should be set in place. Relevant levels of security should be treated in line with existing regulations (foremost GDPR) for data management and governance. Even though linguistic summaries provide a summarized overview, when we cope with the rare loans or behaviour, then it might reveal which people contribute to the summarized sentences.

The benefit of developing and implementing a robust approach capable of collecting, transforming, storing and reporting by diverse approaches including linguistic summaries is that the business can, if of interest, extend the reporting of the collected data by the other internal and external data and adjust reporting to diverse user categories. For instance, citizens and users with disabilities benefit from linguistic summaries, which provide an easy way to communicate mined patterns from data (Hudec, Bednárová & Holzinger, 2018). For advanced business users, external data covering, e.g., social and economic aspects of people in targeted areas, weather conditions, and organized events can reveal how these parameters influence the flux of customers in the different branches, e.g., whether *at least half of rainy days the extensive use of credit cards in region R is recorded*. With an approach as is under development in this work, regulatory authorities would have a better overview of all activities in different banks.

3. LINGUISTIC SUMMARIES IN BRIEF AND THEIR RELATION TO BUSINESS INTELLIGENCE DASHBOARDS

Linguistic summaries rely on the theories of fuzzy sets and fuzzy logic, where belonging to concepts like *high revenue*, and to quantifiers like *most of* is a matter of degree. The concept of linguistic summaries and their application is explored in e.g., (Hudec, Bednárová & Holzinger, 2018; Boran, Akay & Yager, 2016; Lesot, Moyse & Bouchon-Meunier, 2016). While the other prototype forms are also promising and could be examined and applied in a similar manner, this preliminary is focused on the classic prototype forms.

The classic form of lingustic summary is *Q entities in a data set have S*. Quantifier *Q* and summarizer *S* are usually formalized by fuzzy sets, i.e. *most of customers have medium loans*. The proportion of elements in a data set X that fully and partially satisfies the predicate S is defined as

$$y_B(\mathbf{x}) = \frac{1}{n}\sum_i^n \mu_S(x_i) \tag{1}$$

where n is the number of elements in a data set and the membership function μ formalizes summarizer S. The validity (truth value) of the summary is calculated as

$$v_B(\mathbf{x}) = \mu_Q(y_B(\mathbf{x})) \tag{2}$$

where the function μ formalizes relative quantifier Q. Both y_B and v_B assume values in the unit interval.

The classic form of linguistic summary with restrictions is *QR entities in database have S*, where restriction R focuses on a part of data set relevant for the summarization, i.e., *most of the middle-aged customers have medium loans*. The proportion ofrecords that satisfies summary is defined as

$$y_R(\mathbf{x}) = \frac{\sum_{i=1}^n(\mu_S(x_i)\wedge\mu_R(x_i))}{\sum_{i=1}^n\mu_R(x_i)} \tag{3}$$

where n is the number of elements in a data set and the mem-bership function μ formalizes, both S and R. Analogously to (2) we calculate the validity for (3)

$$v_R(\mathbf{x}) = \mu_Q(y_R(\mathbf{x})) \tag{4}$$

The other quality criteria should be applied like data coverage and quality of fuzzy sets (Lesot, Moyse & Bouchon-Meunier, 2016) to avoid summarieson outliers and isolated entities, which do not reflect entities correctly. For instance, when data set consists of a very few middle-aged customers, then any conclusion about the behaviour of these entities is not valid.

4. DISCUSSION

The idea, as we outlined in this paper, positions the challenge of summarizing data in relation to the efficient use of linguistic summaries for creating insights for financial companies. Our paper aims to incite encourage a deeper discussion in this direction. In this section, we reflect on the future challenges and opportunities for research in this domain, and we define unexplored or underexplored research opportunities in the domain.

Generally, linguistic summaries are applicable for any data type. When considering documents, we can explore whether *the majority of annual reports documents contain phrases related to recession or issues with paying dept* (basic form), or *whether the majority of annual reports documents in agricultural domain contain phrases related to recession or issues with paying dept* (form with restriction). The next example are surveys or social media posts, where a summary *like about half of young bank clients express strong hesitance in asking for loans* reveals the opinion and expected actions of a considered category of potential customers.

Visualization is conveyed by diverse types. Concerning graphs, a large variety of them exist. For instance, pie chart are suitable for percentages, while bar graphs for comparing different departments and their development. Mosaic graphs are suitable for drill-down considering two attributes, while radar graphs express comparable satisfaction of each category of provided service (Vaisman & Zimányi, 2022). Statistical figures like correlation express, whether two attributes are correlated. But, when correlation is high only on parts of considered attributes domains, statistical figures or graphs are not convenient way. For this kind of information, linguistic summaries are suitable option. Linguistic summaries are also a convenient alternative for several other types like expressing proportions. An illustrative example of dashboard is in Figure 1.

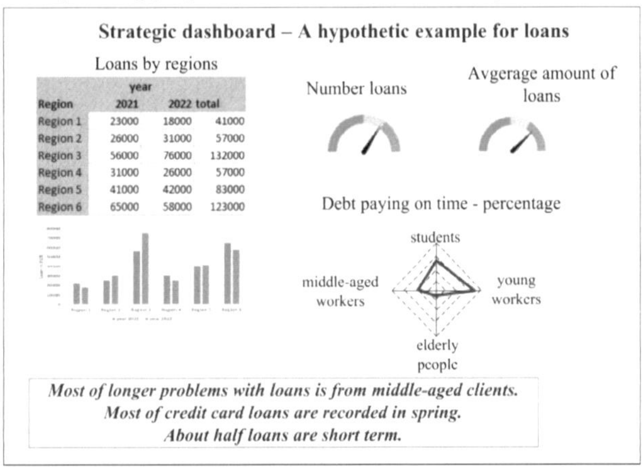

Figure 1. The proposed dashboard augmented by linguistic summaries

The illustrated dashboard in Figure 1 contains three summarized sentences. The challenge is to recognize all the relevant sentences. If domain experts declare in advance which attributes are of the upmost importance, then it is not a hard task to compute all related validities and quality measures. The situation differs when the most relevant sentences should be mined from a larger set of attributes. It is an optimization task for future work.

Further research needs to investigate the feasibility of incorporating human oversight into the processes of generating linguistic summaries, to ensure the results do not go unchecked and whatever errors that may be produced by the system are caught before error is propagated to dashboards and damage is done. In this way, the system is corrected for future use. A possible addition is the study of flexible interfaces like phenotropic interaction (aims to enable artificial systems to understand and adapt to user requirements) (Colombo, 2023) that is, use communication with data warehouse that includes methods for understanding human perceptions expressed as natural language to better reply to people's real desires and needs rather than applying traditional interfaces which require precise statements.

Another interesting research direction is the applicability of linguistic summaries for financial regulation. Would such application help and bring benefits for financial decision-makers in terms of understanding the data provided by different banks for regulatory scrutiny? In this way decision makers should consider, whether a particular summary is specific for one bank is spread among majority of banks. Recently applied quality measure (van der Heide & Triviño, 2009) might be helpful in this direction.

How ethical issues impact such analysis is always a consideration for companies, especially in the financial industry. Societal or any type of harm should be minimized. Any novel application and analysis of data opens various ways for companies to generate profit, however, this may come for instance at the cost of privacy, or irresponsible or illegal use of data. These issues are intensified and should be seriously considered. Generally, linguistic summaries provide a summarized information about the relation between subdomains of considered attributes. Thus, when a large amount of data is available, then it is a hard task to recognize particular person. However, summaries might recognize a vulnerable sub group of people. On the other hand, public institutions could create targeted education programs for such a sub group of people.

5. CONCLUSION

The research explores the linguistic summaries approach as an efficient way for reducing complexity in business intelligence reporting in general for decision making support. A short- quantified sentence of natural language is understandable at first glance and therefore should be considered for dashboards. We emphasize that linguistic summaries should not be considered as a competitor to existing business intelligence dashboards, but rather as a complementary visualization to well-established approaches.

ACKNOWLEDGEMENT

This research was supported the Thematic Excellence Programme TKP2021-NVA-29 (National Challenges Subprogramme) funding scheme and by the COST Action CA19130 - "Fintech and Artificial Intelligence in Finance Towards a transparent financial industry" (FinAI)." The partial support of the SGS project No. SP2024/083 of the Ministry of Education, Youth and Sports of the Czech Republic is kindly appreciated.

REFERENCES

Arnott, D. (2008). Success factors for data warehouse and business intelligence systems.

Boran, F. E., Akay, D., & Yager, R. R. (2016). An overview of methods for linguistic summarization with fuzzy sets. *Expert Systems with Applications*, *61*, 356-377.

Colombo, M. (2023). Phenotropic Interaction. In *Phenotropic Interaction: Improving Interfaces with Computing with Words and Perceptions* (pp. 21-32). Cham: Springer Nature Switzerland.

Hudec, M., Bednárová, E., & Holzinger, A. (2018). Augmenting statistical data dissemination by short quantified sentences of natural language. *Journal of Official Statistics*, *34*(4), 981-1010.

Kimball, R. (2011). The evolving role of the enterprise data warehouse in the era of big data analytics. *Kimball Gr.*

Lesot, M. J., Moyse, G., & Bouchon-Meunier, B. (2016). Interpretability of fuzzy linguistic summaries. *Fuzzy Sets and Systems*, *292*, 307-317.

Pisoni, G. (2021). Going digital: case study of an Italian insurance company. *Journal of Business Strategy*, *42*(2)

Pisoni, G., Molnár, B., & Tarcsi, Á. (2021). Data science for finance: Best-suited methods and enterprise architectures. *Applied System Innovation*, *4*(3), 69.

Qihai, Z., Tao, H., & Tao, W. (2008, August). Analysis of business intelligence and its derivative-financial intelligence. In *2008 International Symposium on Electronic Commerce and Security* (pp. 997-1000). IEEE.

Shao, C., Yang, Y., Juneja, S., & GSeetharam, T. (2022). IoT data visualization for business intelligence in corporate finance. *Information Processing & Management*, *59*(1), 102736.

Vaisman, A., & Zimányi, E. (2022). Data warehouse systems. Design and Implementation. *2nd Edition, Springer, Berlin*

van der Heide, A., & Triviño, G. (2009, November). Automatically generated linguistic summaries of energy consumption data. In *2009 Ninth international conference on intelligent systems design and applications* IEEE.

Vučetić, M., Brokešová, Z., Hudec, M., & Pastoráková, E. (2022). Financial literacy and psychological disaster preparedness: applicability of approach based on fuzzy functional dependencies. *Information Processing & Management*, *59*(2), 102848.

OVERVIEW OF USAGE OF OPEN GOVERNMENT DATA IN BUILDING MACHINE LEARNING AND AI SOLUTIONS: A SYSTEMATIC LITERATURE REVIEW

Sara Kijanovic[1], Sara Koprivica[1], Davide Taibi[2], Aleksandar Ivic[1], Darko Stefanovic[1] and Aleksa Komosar[1]

[1]*Faculty of Technical Sciences, University of Novi Sad, Trg Dositeja Obradovica 6, Novi Sad, Serbia*

[2] *Institute for Education Technology, National Research Council of Italy, Palermo, Italy*

ABSTRACT

This paper provides a systematic literature review on integrating Open Government Data (OGD) with machine learning (ML) and artificial intelligence (AI) solutions. OGD refers to publicly accessible data produced or collected by governmental entities, promoting transparency and citizen engagement. The paper explores the application of OGD in various social development domains, highlighting its potential impact. It also highlights the difficulties and challenges that researchers face. The findings suggest that leveraging OGD in ML and AI has the potential to drive innovation, improve decision-making, and foster inclusive development across sectors. The review emphasizes the importance of responsible practices in utilizing OGD for ML and AI purposes.

KEYWORDS

Open Government Data, Open Data, Artificial Intelligence, Machine Learning, Literature Review

1. INTRODUCTION

Open Government Data (OGD) constitutes both a philosophical underpinning and a progressively evolving set of policies. Its core mission is to advance transparency, accountability, and the generation of value by facilitating universal access to government data for all (*Open Government Data - OECD*, n.d.). The core goal of OGD is that the citizens have the right to access data and information generated by governments in order to create common value and trust in the government (Fleiner, 2018).

In the context of our swiftly advancing digital environment, the fusion of data-driven technologies with principles of government transparency has opened up a promising frontier for innovation. The contemporary world is witnessing an unprecedented creation of data, a substantial share of which is administered by governmental institutions worldwide. In the development of advanced technologies such as machine learning (ML) and artificial intelligence (AI), new and innovative solutions are being created that can contribute to the community. As OGD is accessible to everyone, using advanced technologies makes it possible to create solutions that are for the common good of the community (Gao & Janssen, 2020).

Harnessing large data with advanced tech can create smart solutions, improving global lives. Recognizing tech's potential for sustainable development and optimizing existing systems through reengineering is vital. This paper, through systematic literature review (SLR) results, gives insight into the proposed solutions by researchers based on OGD, ML and AI. The aim of this paper is to identify fields that have been the focus of research so far, such as health or economy, and to assess the solutions proposed. Lastly, it provides insights into less developed fields. In order to fulfill our research goal, we designed and conducted a systematic literature review using Preferred Reporting Items for Systematic Reviews and Meta-Analyses (PRISMA) flowchart. We set research questions, as well as inclusion and exclusion criteria.

The rest of the paper is organized as follows. Section 2 provides an overview of the concept of Open Government Data, machine learning and artificial intelligence. Section 3 presents Methodology, and in Section 4 are presented results and discussion. Lastly, in Section 5, we gave Conclusion about this SLR.

2. OPEN GOVERNMENT DATA

OGD stands for Open Government Data, which represents information created using public funds and offered for use or distribution according to licenses that allow derivative work and commercial use (Janssen et al., 2012). Open government initiatives promote transparency and engagement to enable effective oversight, and in doing so, they also foster trust in the government from the citizens. The data must be available in formats that can be used without payment of fees or other restrictions, and at least one tool must be accessible for their processing (*Почетна - Отворени подаци*, n.d.). Data formats are diverse, with a prevalence of not proprietary and machine-readable file formats, such as CSV and JSON.

Open Data, especially OGD, offers diverse benefits, including improved public administration efficiency, private sector economic growth, and broader social welfare. It enhances performance, leading to more efficient public services and reduced unnecessary spending through cross-sector data sharing. Easy access to information and knowledge benefits the economy by fostering innovation and new business models. Society benefits from increased transparency and accessibility, promoting collaboration, participation, and social innovation (*What Is Open Data | Data.Europa.Eu*, n.d.) By signing the Open Government Directive at the White House in 2009 (*Open Government Directive*, 2009), the expansion and development of open data began.

It's important to emphasize that Open Data and Open Government Data are not the same concept. Data can be opened by non-governmental organizations and institutions that are not part of the government. OGD refers specifically to data that the government opens to all interested parties.

3. METHODOLOGY

The main focus of a systematic literature review (SLR) is to provide a comprehensive summary of the existing research and evidence on a specific research question or topic. For this SLR Preferred Reporting Items for Systematic Reviews and Meta-Analyses (PRISMA) framework was used. The aim of the PRISMA statement is to help authors improve the reporting of SLR, and PRISMA consists of a four-phase flow: 1. Identification, 2. Screening, 3. Eligibility and 4. Included (Moher et al., 2009). We used two databases for this literature review – Scopus and Web of Science. For searching papers, we used string: ("Open government data" or "OGD") AND ("machine learning" or "artificial intelligence").

Two research questions has been posed:

RQ1. What are the primary domains or sectors where Open Government Data is predominantly used for ML and AI solutions?

RQ2. What challenges and barriers do researchers face when integrating Open Government Data into ML and AI solutions?

The strategy for identifying primary studies for this literature review was established based on five inclusion and three exclusion criteria outlined below.

Inclusion criteria:

IC1. The main objective of the paper must be related to ML and AI solutions based on OGD primarily.

IC2. If there are additional data sources besides OGD, they must be in the form of Open Data.

IC3. The paper must describe ML/AI solutions over data.

IC4. The paper must be written in English.

IC5. Papers published between 2017 and 2023.

Exclusion criteria:

EC1. Papers that are not related to research questions.

EC2. Duplicate papers.

EC3. Exclude papers that discuss OGD but do not relate it to ML or AI.

Figure 1 presents PRISMA workflow for SLR. The primary data considered for the papers primarily included the title, abstract, keywords, year, and document type. Subsequently, the exclusion of papers was carried out through a thorough examination of the complete paper, within the scope of the third part of the PRISMA statement regarding eligibility.

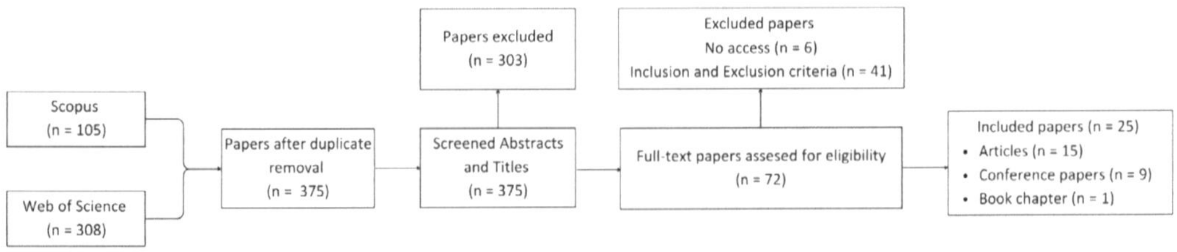

Figure 1. PRISMA workflow

4. RESULTS AND DISSCUSION

After defining the search string, 105 papers were obtained from the Scopus database, and 308 papers from Web of Science. Initially, it was necessary to remove duplicates, which totaled 38. This left 375 papers for the next screening phase. Titles and abstracts of the papers were reviewed, resulting in the exclusion of 303 papers deemed unsuitable for further research. This left 72 papers for the third-part, eligibility assessment. Access was not granted for 6 papers, leading to their exclusion, while 41 papers were rejected based on the defined inclusion and exclusion criteria mentioned in Section 3. In the end, a total of 25 papers were included in the literature review, consisting of 15 articles, 9 conference papers, and one book chapter.

Based on the IC5, papers from the period of 2017 to 2023 were reviewed. One relevant paper from 2017 and 2018 was included, as well as four papers from 2021 and 2023 until August. Additionally, five papers from 2019, 2020, and 2022 each were included in the literature review.

Table 1. Review of the domains that the papers address

Domain	Doman definition	Papers
Economy	Finance	(Mashkova et al., 2017)
	Taxes	(Cha, 2020)
	Real estate	(Karamanou et al., 2022), (Tchuente & Nyawa, 2022)
	Business	(Hopf & Riechel, 2018)
Environment	Agriculture	(Colombo-Mendoza et al., 2022), (Amani et al., 2020)
	Human-elephant conflict	(Gunawansa et al., 2023)
	Temperature maps	(Zumwald et al., 2021)
	Wave height	(Ahmad & Mansurova, 2021)
Policy	Public procurements	(Niessen et al., 2020), (García Rodríguez et al., 2020)
	Public discussions	(Kim et al., 2019)
Traffic	Traffic injuries	(Boonserm & Wiwatwattana, 2021)
	Traffic jam	(Brimos et al., 2023)
Health	Air pollution	(Avvari et al., 2023), (Sethi & Thakur, 2021)
General	Missing persons	(Gomes et al., 2023)
	Urbanism	(Milojevic-Dupont et al., 2020)
	Simplifying OGD based on ML/AI	(Gazzaz & Rao, 2019), (Guberović et al., 2022), (Chen et al., 2019), (Metsker et al., 2019), (Ronzhin et al., 2019), (Stylianou et al., 2022)

Table 1 summarizes the domains with the highest number of papers. Governments globally share datasets on various portals, and selected domains cover specific subfields. For instance, under economics, solutions address finance, taxes, business, and real estate. Other domains are similarly divided, including general ones like missing persons and urbanism, along with solutions applicable to OGD, such as smart searches.

RQ1: It can be clearly concluded that the most attention is currently devoted to creating solutions in the field of environmental preservation and economics. It is concluded that structured data, as mandated by OGD, are effectively used for predictions and statistics, and all proposed solutions can contribute to the community on a daily basis. Though other areas are touched upon, there's a lack of studies on OGD-based smart solutions in education.

RQ2. The majority of authors emphasize that their main obstacles in developing such solutions are poorly structured data, complex, outdated, or unusable, despite being fundamental concepts of open data. (Gazzaz & Rao, 2019), (Mashkova et al., 2017) say that one of the biggest challenges for implementing a solution is the lack of shared data models, even when it comes to OGD at the level of a single state. Authors in (Gomes et al., 2023) highlight issues of data duplication and completeness, emphasizing the need for consistent updates by the government to foster value-added solutions (Brimos et al., 2023). Other authors didn't pinpoint data issues, but prep work for combining datasets is inevitable for effective algorithm application.

5. CONCLUSION

Through a SLR, we explored current solutions created using OGD worldwide. It is evident that increasing attention is being given to developing solutions using OGD for the benefit of communities, as reflected in the growing number of published papers each year, as mentioned in Section 4.

However, there are still domains, such as open education, where solutions need further development. Researchers also frequently encounter issues related to data obtained from official portals. There is a need for data standardization for publication, as well as ensuring the timeliness, accuracy, and reliability of the data. Raising awareness about the contributions of OGD to the community and promoting solutions for the common good based on advanced technologies is essential. With existing knowledge, ideas, and solutions, it is possible to enhance existing information systems with added value using ML and AI in context of OGD. The continuation of the research involves further analysis of concepts and the application of technologies on OGD, deeper examinations, and comprehensive insights into its multifaceted utilization.

REFERENCES

Ahmad, Z., & Mansurova, M. (2021). Machine learning approach to predict significant wave height. *Journal of Mathematics, Mechanics and Computer Science*, *110*(2). https://doi.org/10.26577/JMMCS.2021.v110.i2.08

Amani, M., Kakooei, M., Moghimi, A., Ghorbanian, A., Ranjgar, B., Mahdavi, S., Davidson, A., Fisette, T., Rollin, P., Brisco, B., & Mohammadzadeh, A. (2020). Application of Google Earth Engine Cloud Computing Platform, Sentinel Imagery, and Neural Networks for Crop Mapping in Canada. *Remote Sensing*, *12*(21), 3561. https://doi.org/10.3390/rs12213561

Avvari, P., Nacham, P., Sasanapuri, S., Mankena, S. R., Kudipudi, P., & Madapati, A. (2023). Air Quality Index Prediction. *E3S Web of Conferences*, *391*, 01103. https://doi.org/10.1051/e3sconf/202339101103

Boonserm, E., & Wiwatwattana, N. (2021). Using Machine Learning to Predict Injury Severity of Road Traffic Accidents During New Year Festivals From Thailand's Open Government Data. *2021 9th International Electrical Engineering Congress (iEECON)*, 464–467. https://doi.org/10.1109/iEECON51072.2021.9440287

Brimos, P., Karamanou, A., Kalampokis, E., & Tarabanis, K. (2023). Graph Neural Networks and Open-Government Data to Forecast Traffic Flow. *Information*, *14*(4), 228. https://doi.org/10.3390/info14040228

Cha, T. (2020). Open Government Data for Machine Learning Tax Recommendation. *The 21st Annual International Conference on Digital Government Research*, 331–333. https://doi.org/10.1145/3396956.3397002

Chen, W.-Y., Lu, P. J., & Shiau, S. (2019). IPGOD: An Integrated Visualization Platform Based on Big Data Mining and Cloud Computing. *Proceedings of the 2019 4th International Conference on Big Data and Computing - ICBDC 2019*, 11–16. https://doi.org/10.1145/3335484.3335494

Colombo-Mendoza, L. O., Paredes-Valverde, M. A., Salas-Zárate, M. D. P., & Valencia-García, R. (2022). Internet of Things-Driven Data Mining for Smart Crop Production Prediction in the Peasant Farming Domain. *Applied Sciences*, *12*(4), 1940. https://doi.org/10.3390/app12041940

Fleiner, R. (2018). Linking of Open Government Data. *2018 IEEE 12th International Symposium on Applied Computational Intelligence and Informatics (SACI)*, 1–5. https://doi.org/10.1109/SACI.2018.8441014

Gao, Y., & Janssen, M. (2020). Generating Value from Government Data Using AI: An Exploratory Study. In G. Viale Pereira, M. Janssen, H. Lee, I. Lindgren, M. P. Rodríguez Bolívar, H. J. Scholl, & A. Zuiderwijk (Eds.), *Electronic Government* (Vol. 12219, pp. 319–331). Springer International Publishing. https://doi.org/10.1007/978-3-030-57599-1_24

García Rodríguez, M. J., Rodríguez Montequín, V., Ortega Fernández, F., & Villanueva Balsera, J. M. (2020). Bidders Recommender for Public Procurement Auctions Using Machine Learning: Data Analysis, Algorithm, and Case Study with Tenders from Spain. *Complexity*, *2020*, 1–20. https://doi.org/10.1155/2020/8858258

Gazzaz, S., & Rao, P. (2019). Extracting Meaningful Insights on City and Zone Levels Utilizing US Open Government Data. *Companion Proceedings of The 2019 World Wide Web Conference*, 1279–1285. https://doi.org/10.1145/3308560.3316470

Gomes, J., Bernardino, H. S., De Souza, J. F., & Rajabi, E. (2023). Indexing, enriching, and understanding Brazilian missing person cases from data of distributed repositories on the web. *AI & SOCIETY*, *38*(2), 565–579. https://doi.org/10.1007/s00146-022-01456-5

Guberović, E., Alexopoulos, C., Bosnić, I., & Čavrak, I. (2022). Framework for Federated Learning Open Models in e-Government Applications. *Interdisciplinary Description of Complex Systems*, *20*(2), 162–178. https://doi.org/10.7906/indecs.20.2.8

Gunawansa, T. D., Perera, K., Apan, A., Hettiarachchi, N. K., & Bandara, D. Y. (2023). Greenery change and its impact on human-elephant conflict in Sri Lanka: A model-based assessment using Sentinel-2 imagery. *International Journal of Remote Sensing*, *44*(16), 5121–5146. https://doi.org/10.1080/01431161.2023.2244644

Hopf, K., & Riechel, S. (2018). *Predictive Customer Data Analytics – The Value of Public Statistical Data and the Geographic Model Transferability*.

Janssen, M., Charalabidis, Y., & Zuiderwijk, A. (2012). Benefits, Adoption Barriers and Myths of Open Data and Open Government. *Information Systems Management*, *29*(4), 258–268. https://doi.org/10.1080/10580530.2012.716740

Karamanou, A., Kalampokis, E., & Tarabanis, K. (2022). Linked Open Government Data to Predict and Explain House Prices: The Case of Scottish Statistics Portal. *Big Data Research*, *30*, 100355. https://doi.org/10.1016/j.bdr.2022.100355

Kim, H., Ahn, S.-J., & Jung, W.-S. (2019). Horizon scanning in policy research database with a probabilistic topic model. *Technological Forecasting and Social Change*, *146*, 588–594. https://doi.org/10.1016/j.techfore.2018.02.007

Mashkova, A. L., Demidov, A. V., Savina, O. A., Koskin, A. V., & Mashkov, E. A. (2017). Developing a complex model of experimental economy based on agent approach and open government data in distributed information-computational environment. *Proceedings of the Internationsl Conference on Electronic Governance and Open Society: Challenges in Eurasia*, 27–31. https://doi.org/10.1145/3129757.3129763

Metsker, O., Trofimov, E., Sikorsky, S., & Kovalchuk, S. (2019). Text and Data Mining Techniques in Judgment Open Data Analysis for Administrative Practice Control. In A. Chugunov, Y. Misnikov, E. Roshchin, & D. Trutnev (Eds.), *Electronic Governance and Open Society: Challenges in Eurasia* (Vol. 947, pp. 169–180). Springer International Publishing. https://doi.org/10.1007/978-3-030-13283-5_13

Milojevic-Dupont, N., Hans, N., Kaack, L. H., Zumwald, M., Andrieux, F., De Barros Soares, D., Lohrey, S., Pichler, P.-P., & Creutzig, F. (2020). Learning from urban form to predict building heights. *PLOS ONE*, *15*(12), e0242010. https://doi.org/10.1371/journal.pone.0242010

Moher, D., Liberati, A., Tetzlaff, J., & Altman, D. G. (2009). Preferred reporting items for systematic reviews and meta-analyses: The PRISMA statement. *BMJ*, *339*, b2535. https://doi.org/10.1136/bmj.b2535

Niessen, M. E. K., Paciello, J. M., & Fernandez, J. I. P. (2020). Anomaly Detection in Public Procurements using the Open Contracting Data Standard. *2020 Seventh International Conference on eDemocracy & eGovernment (ICEDEG)*, 127–134. https://doi.org/10.1109/ICEDEG48599.2020.9096674

Open Government Data—OECD. (n.d.). Retrieved September 11, 2023, from https://www.oecd.org/gov/digital-government/open-government-data.htm

Open Government Directive. (2009). The White House. https://obamawhitehouse.archives.gov/node/7011

Ronzhin, Folmer, Maria, Brattinga, Beek, Lemmens, & Van'T Veer. (2019). Kadaster Knowledge Graph: Beyond the Fifth Star of Open Data. *Information*, *10*(10), 310. https://doi.org/10.3390/info10100310

Sethi, T., & Thakur, R. C. (2021). Comparison of Machine Learning Algorithms for Air Pollution Monitoring System. In A. K. Dubey, A. Kumar, S. R. Kumar, N. Gayathri, & P. Das (Eds.), *AI and IoT-Based Intelligent Automation in Robotics* (1st ed., pp. 305–322). Wiley. https://doi.org/10.1002/9781119711230.ch19

Stylianou, N., Vlachava, D., Konstantinidis, I., Bassiliades, N., & Peristeras, V. (2022). Doc2KG: Transforming Document Repositories to Knowledge Graphs. *International Journal on Semantic Web and Information Systems*, *18*(1), 1–20. https://doi.org/10.4018/IJSWIS.295552

Tchuente, D., & Nyawa, S. (2022). Real estate price estimation in French cities using geocoding and machine learning. *Annals of Operations Research*, *308*(1–2), 571–608. https://doi.org/10.1007/s10479-021-03932-5

What is open data | data.europa.eu. (n.d.). Retrieved September 12, 2023, from https://data.europa.eu/en/dataeuropa-academy/what-open-data

Zumwald, M., Knüsel, B., Bresch, D. N., & Knutti, R. (2021). Mapping urban temperature using crowd-sensing data and machine learning. *Urban Climate*, *35*, 100739. https://doi.org/10.1016/j.uclim.2020.100739

Почетна—Отворени подаци. (n.d.). Retrieved September 12, 2023, from https://data.gov.rs/sr/discover/

IS CAPABILITY DRIVEN BUSINESS VALUE FOR SOUTH AFRICAN FINANCIAL SERVICE PROVIDERS FROM DIGITAL TRANSFORMATION PERSPECTIVE IN EMERGING ECONOMIES

Michael Makgale Modiba[1] and Raymond Mompoloki Kekwaletswe[2]
[1]*Financial Services Provider, Johannesburg, South Africa*
[2]*Department of Business Management, University of Johannesburg, South Africa*

ABSTRACT

The dynamic advent of technology and innovation are compelling financial service providers in South Africa to rethink and possess a requisite level of Information Systems (IS) capabilities. Frequently, these modifications result in significant disturbances within the service providers. This paper provides insights into the role of IS capability on the process of digital transformation in financial service providers, operating within the context of South Africa as an emerging economy. The paper employs IS capability model and the Technological, Organizational, and Environmental (TOE) framework as theoretical lenses. Interpretive research philosophy is followed in conjunction with a case study as a research strategy. The study findings underscore the significance of robust IS capabilities in generating corporate business value. The paper further highlights that the existing financial service providers' IS capabilities can either facilitate or impede the process of digital transformation. Additionally, the technological, organizational, and environmental contexts of financial service provider as well as those related to resource dependency, play a pivotal role in the successful and the desired digital transformation. This paper argues for the importance of context sensitivity in the realization of IS capability driven business value and the digital transformation within the South African financial service providers.

KEYWORDS

Digital Transformation, Emerging Economies, Financial Service Provider, IS Capability, TOE, South Africa

1. INTRODUCTION

The discourse surrounding the causal relationship between technology and business, namely whether technology drives business or business drives technology, is a subject of considerable intellectual interest. The inherent usefulness of IS capability for organizations is well acknowledged. However, a comprehensive understanding of the specific mechanisms via which it enhances corporate performance remains a subject of inquiry (Crook et al., 2008; Fink, 2011). There is a divergence of viewpoints about the relationship between IS capabilities and business performance (Modiba et al, 2020). Certain studies posit that IS capabilities exert a significant influence on business outcomes whereas others contend that it is business objectives that shape the development and utilization of IS capabilities (Chae et al., 2014; Oliveira et al., 2015). This paper posits that the relationship between business and technology tend to be mutually reliant, with both exerting effect on the other. When examining the correlation between IS capability and business success, it is crucial to take into account the three fundamental components of every organization namely individuals, processes, and technology. In order to achieve success in the process of digital transformation, it is imperative for South African financial service providers to accurately define the fundamental pillars involved and thereafter formulate a strategic plan to effectively propel them forward. Nevertheless, studies conducted on the value of IS capability has produced conflicting findings, which could be attributed to the lack of alignment between IS capabilities and the broader performance metrics of organizations.

2. CONTEXT OF SOUTH AFRICA

South Africa is classified as a developing country although it fares well relative to other developing countries. The country is unique in that it has, for example, eleven official languages and cultural diversity, which ought to be recognized by the financial service providers during their digital transformation journey. To this point, efficacy of strategies implemented in other nations, particularly those in the developed world, may not necessarily align with anticipated outcomes in South Africa, at least not in the current context (Modiba et al, 2020). For example, a significant portion of the South African population resides in rural and semi-urban regions characterized by limited access to contemporary technological resources (*Ibid.*, 2020). However, the adoption of digital technologies has resulted in an enhanced accessibility to financial service provisions. Significant advancements have been made in the realm of digital transformation in the 'Civilized Countries' over the last two decades. Modiba et al, (2020) posit that digital transformation process in emerging economies, specifically in South Africa, faces challenges due to language barriers, cultural diversity, and political influences. Despite the steady rise in economic growth, the technological and capability advancements in infrastructure and connectivity have not kept pace with the rapidly growing digital society. As a result of these circumstances, financial service providers in South Africa have specific challenges that necessitate tailored approaches rather than a universally applicable IS capability and digital transformation strategy and process. Digital inclusion efforts in emerging economies may fail if Internet connectivity is not afforded to all inhabitants. Access to the Internet must be affordable in order for the value of these digital technological innovations to reach every digital society. While there may be additional motivations behind IS capability and technological advancements, solving human financial banking problems, for example, through digital transformation should remain the emerging economy FSPs' primary goal.

3. SURVEY OF SCHOLARSHIP

This section gives a brief overview of prior research undertaken on digital business and digital transformation, which offers valuable foundation and insights into the current key issue addressed by this paper.

3.1 Digital Transformation and IS Capability on Financial Service Providers

In order to facilitate the digital transformation, it is imperative to convert business operations, products, and procedures. However, it is important to note that this is not the sole metric of success. Furthermore, it is imperative for organizations to establish and implement organizational structures that can effectively manage and supervise complex transitions within their operations (Matt et al., 2015). The rapid and substantial advancements in digital technology have had a profound impact on both individuals and markets, resulting in the alteration of various aspects of people's life (Ebert & Duarte, 2016). In order to maintain their viability and competitive advantage, numerous firms and government entities face the imperative to expeditiously transition to digital platforms (Westerman et al., 2011). The aforementioned pressure arises as a consequence of the rapid pace at which technological advancements are generated.

This paper acknowledges an extensive literature pertaining to the descriptions and explorations of digital transformation. According to Modiba and Kekwaletswe (2020), digital transformation refers to the restructuring of corporate processes, business models, and procedures from the perspective of customers, utilizing advanced digital technologies. The concept comprises a range of elements including business processes, models, technology, individuals, and cultural and organizational variables. Modiba and Kekwaletswe (2020) claim that it is imperative for transformational leaders to recognize that the absence of suitable personnel and a conducive organizational culture would result in the failure or limited success of their digital transformation endeavors. Nevertheless, the significance of culture in an organization's achievement cannot be overstated since the absence of an appropriate culture will result in a diminished return on investment for any undertaking. The efficacy of a digital transformation within an organization is contingent upon the individuals engaged in the process, as the involvement of humans is crucial for the realization of such a transition (Kane, 2019). In a dynamic global environment characterized by ongoing change, the culture of a company plays a significant role in determining its propensity to either embrace or oppose change. The achievement of fundamental transformation inside an organization is contingent upon the alignment of its people and the culture (Kane, 2019; Modiba & Kekwaletswe, 2020).

Financial service providers have been significantly altered as a result of the digital transformation, with the introduction of new technology creating potential for business expansion, innovation, and enhancement of the consumer experience. Bruesch and Pareja-Ros (2019) analyzed previously published material as well as case studies to provide insights into the opportunities and problems presented by digital transformation in the financial industry. Accenture (2021) posits that three significant trends that are transforming the landscape of the financial services industry are data-driven insights, tailored customer experiences, and seamless omnichannel interactions. The findings suggest that financial service providers who place a priority on these trends are in a better position to achieve success in a world that is becoming increasingly digital. In a nutshell, the indication is that digital transformation brings opportunities as well as obstacles for the companies that provide financial services. Businesses that place a strong emphasis on their customers, internal culture, and innovative practices are in a stronger position to thrive in today's continuously evolving market. Financial service providers have the opportunity to boost efficiency, improve the overall client experience, and drive revenue growth by adopting digital transformation.

IS Capability for financial service providers in emerging economies such as South Africa is being developed with the intention of assisting with the digital transformation journey. Zehnder (2019) says that digital transformation has the potential to improve customer experience as well as operational efficiency and business models, which can ultimately lead to greater revenue and market share. Zehnder framework supports digital innovation, analytics, and automation as means to improve the quality of service provided to customers. Different techniques can be used by suppliers of financial services, depending on the strengths and weaknesses of the providers, as well as the requirements of the clients. According to the findings of that study, suppliers of financial services in emerging countries confront a number of hurdles, including restrictions on infrastructure, problems with regulations, and a shortage of qualified workers. It can be inferred that if financial service providers in developing nations adhere to the framework for digital technical capabilities, they will be able to conquer these obstacles and increase the consumers' financial well-being.

4. THEORETICAL FRAMEWORKS

Theoretical frameworks are what guide and define the scope of studies. Borgatti (1999) showed that both deductive and inductive research rely heavily on the fundamentals of a theoretical framework. So, this section provides a quick review of theoretical lenses that underpin the rest of the work.

4.1 Model of the IS Capability

Ward and Peppard (1996), provide a Model of Information Systems Capability. The model emphasizes the importance of IS management, technology, organization, and strategy. From the vantage point of developing countries, the model sheds light on the obstacles and possibilities inherent in establishing and capitalizing on IS capabilities. Chua and Yang (2019) suggest that management, organization, and strategy all play important roles in the maturation of emerging nations' IS capacities. Technology is less of a factor because mature technologies are readily available, and prices are lower in developing countries.

Collaborations between businesses, governments, and educational institutions are emphasized as crucial to the development of IS in developing countries. In order to achieve sustainable development in the face of resource restrictions, insufficient digital infrastructure and skill shortages, emerging economies must work together. Overall, Ward and Peppard's IS capability model is a helpful framework for comprehending the elements that determine IS capacities in emerging economies. According to Chua and Yang (1996), there should be a concerted effort on the side of a wide variety of parties to work together in order to successfully construct IS capabilities. The model highlights the importance of information systems capability to a financial service provider (FSP). That is, this model provides a lens that may help FSPs learn more about IS capability and the ways in which they may use their technological resources to advance their digital transformation.

4.2 Technology, Organizational, and Environmental Framework (TOE)

Technology-Organization-Environment (TOE) framework is commonly employed in information systems research. Depietro et al. (1990), argue that a company's strategy for incorporating technical advancements is based on three fundamental factors: technological, organizational, and environmental contexts. Three fundamental pillars exert influence on a corporation's perception, exploration, and assimilation of novel technologies. Furthermore, Depietro et al. (1990) illustrate that technology commonly consists of both internally and externally compatible technologies. Arpaci et al. (2012) examine the development of the TOE framework for organizational technology adoption, which is rooted on the Contingency Theory of Organizations (Tornatzky et al., 1990).

All in all, TOE framework components exhibit interdependencies and exert mutual influence on one another, thereby molding the broader technological environment within a company. Comprehending and effectively handling these contexts is imperative for enhancing productivity, efficiency, and adaptability in the contemporary dynamic digital landscape.

5. DISCUSSION AND INTERPRETATION OF FINDINGS

This section discusses and interprets findings from the interpretive case study of a South African financial service provider, with respect to IS capability and Digital transformation endeavors.

5.1 Organizational Context

The study findings indicated that the FSP business activities included transactional banking, serving business clients, offering various products and services, utilizing different distribution channels, accessing the market, assessing risk, and conducting trade in goods. These activities resulted in revenue generation from core businesses. The strategy focused on capitalizing on opportunities in the African financial markets. The primary concentration areas collaborated to ensure that customers received quick and effective solutions. In terms of delivering IS business value, the strategic value drivers directed their efforts and monitored progress. Partnerships were formed to fulfil customer requirements, with alliances involving resource providers and other entities. Research findings have shown that in South African financial service providers, change management is crucial for leading organizations through transitions and digital transformation processes. The use of digital technologies is essential in ensuring a smooth transition for both employees and technology. Employees are considered the driving force behind the digital transformation of financial service providers, emphasizing the importance of competent management and hardworking staff members for maximum productivity and successful transformation. Leadership plays a significant role in instilling trust among stakeholders and fostering a culture of ethics and risk awareness within the institution. Due to the nature of their business, financial service providers in South Africa face heavy regulations, including strong data protection and privacy controls mandated by the authorities. Financial supervision, technical innovation, and conduct continue to be major drivers for regulating digital transformation in the industry.

5.2 Technological Context

The study findings indicate that the financial service providers have made significant advancements in digitization. Self-service options, human resource management tools, and interoperable technology have been implemented to make banking easier for customers. Additionally, efforts have been made to improve connectivity and collaboration for employees through digital tools. Training and education programs have been put in place to ensure employees are prepared for future jobs that require digital capabilities. The financial service provider has invested in advanced banking platforms with digital capabilities to meet the needs and preferences of customers. These platforms have increased access to banking services for South Africans. The effective management of artificial intelligence (AI) has become increasingly important as resources become scarce and digital initiatives are implemented. Institutions need to invest in personnel with technical proficiency and encourage complex thinking, problem-solving, flexibility, and creativity to successfully implement AI.

Policies and regulations are being developed to address concerns over data privacy and security. These measures aim to safeguard client data, ensure ethical use of data, and protect customer privacy. The adoption of technology within the South African financial service provider involves accepting, incorporating, and utilizing digital banking technologies. Procedures are being broken down into manageable components and coordinated by relevant technological business departments.

5.3 Environmental Context

The study findings indicated that competition within the financial industry in South Africa has intensified due to the emergence of new entrants, particularly digital service providers. These providers offer services that are more convenient, transparent, and customizable, posing a significant threat to traditional banks. To remain competitive, traditional banks must invest in customer-centric technologies to meet evolving consumer needs and preferences. Furthermore, the political landscape in South Africa has had an impact on financial service providers, as politics, factionalism, policy instability, corruption, and mismanagement have disrupted institutional cooperation and economic partnerships. These political changes and instabilities have influenced the digital transformation efforts of financial service providers. Governance and risk frameworks have been implemented across the operations of financial service providers to enhance accountability, effective risk management, performance management, transparency, and leadership. The research also revealed that financial service providers prioritize a culture of caring, growing, learning, and innovation, as well as constructive relations and constant communication with governments and regulatory agencies. This fosters a risk-aware, ethical, and compliant culture, leading to robust internal control mechanisms and risk and compliance frameworks. Compliance with market laws and regulations, as well as maintaining strong relationships with regulatory bodies, minimizes physical security risks for financial service providers. Thus, the ability to effectively mitigate these risks through robust information technology capabilities is crucial in the process of digital transformation.

6. CONCLUSION

This paper highlighted the importance of a strong IS capability driven business value as a prerequisite for successful digital transformation, in the context of emerging economy's financial service providers. The egression of digital government is becoming more relevant and affecting operations transformations in financial service providers. This paper employed IS capability model and the technological, organizational, and environmental framework as theoretical lenses to gain a comprehensive understanding of the experiences of South African financial service providers in the context of the digital transformation in the emerging economy. The key issue at hand is the overall discourse surrounding IS capabilities, which typically lacks specificity when considering their use inside financial service providers operating in emerging economies. This paper argued that the right digital transformation culture and appropriate technological skills should be developed with an awareness of the technological, organizational, and environmental contexts of the financial service provider. The paper concludes that IS capability necessary for a sound Digital transformation journey ought to be cognizant of the country context and cultural diversity.

ACKNOWLEDGEMENT

Mabule Patrick Modiba and Elphinah Adelaide Modiba, Thank you for your unwavering support and encouragement throughout my academic journey.

REFERENCES

Accenture. (2021). The future of digital transformation in financial services. Retrieved from https://www.accenture.com/_acnmedia/PDF-147/Accenture-Future-Digital-Transformation-Financial-Services.pdf.

Arpaci, I., Yardimci, Y. C., Ozkan, S., & Turetken, O. (2012). Organizational adoption of information technologies: A literature review. *International Journal of ebusiness and egovernment Studies*, *4*(2), 37-50.

Borgatti, s. J. R. A. 1999. Elements of research. 11: 2013.

Brüesch, F., and Pareja-Ríos, A. (2019). Digital transformation in financial services: Insights from scholarship and practice. *Journal of Business Research, 98, 365-380.*

Chae, H.-C., Koh, C. E., & Prybutok, V. R. (2014). Information technology capability and firm performance: contradictory findings and their possible causes. *MIS quarterly*, *38*(1), 305-326.

Chua, C. E. H., and Yang, Q. (2019). The dynamics of IS capability development in emerging economies: A longitudinal study. *Information Systems Journal, 29(3), 546-574.*

Crook, T. R., Ketchen Jr, D. J., Combs, J. G., & Todd, S. Y.(2008). Strategic resources and performance: a meta-analysis. *Strategic management journal*, *29*(11), 1141-1154.

Depietro, R., Wiarda, E., and Fleischer, M. (1990). The context for change: Organization, technology and environment. *The processes of technological innovation*, *199*(0), 151-175.

Ebert, C., and Duarte, C. H. C. (2016). Requirements engineering for the digital transformation: Industry panel. *2016 IEEE 24th International Requirements Engineering Conference (RE).*

Egon Zehnder. (2019). Digital Technological Capability Framework for Financial Service Providers in Emerging Markets. Retrieved from https://www.egonzehnder.com/content/dam/atf/north_america/en/articles/Financial_Services_Tech/Digital%20Technological%20Capability%20Framework%20-%20Egon%20Zehnder.pdf

Fink, L. (2011). How do IT capabilities create strategic value? Toward greater integration of insights from reductionistic and holistic approaches. *European Journal of Information Systems*, *20*(1), 16-33.

Kane, G. (2019). The technology fallacy: people are the real key to digital transformation. *Research-Technology Management*, *62*(6), 44-49.

Matt, C., Hess, T., and Benlian, A. (2015). Digital transformation strategies. *Business & information systems engineering*, *57*, 339-343.

Michael Makgale Modiba, Prof Ray M Kekwaletswe, Moroka Dominic Komati. (2020). IT Capability Framework for Digital Transformation in South African Financial Service Providers. *International Journal of Engineering Trends and Technology, 10(2), 24-39.*

Modiba, M. M., and Kekwaletswe, R. M. (2020). Resource dependency framework for digital transformation in South African financial service providers. *International Journal of Computer Trends and Technology*, *68*(4), 107-125.

Oliveira, D. d. L., Maçada, A. C. G., & Oliveira, G. D. (2015). Valor da tecnologia da informação na firma: estudo com empresas brasileiras. *Revista de Administração Contemporânea*, *19*, 170-192.

Tornatzky, L. G., Fleischer, M., & Chakrabarti, A. K. (1990). *Processes of technological innovation*. Lexington books.

Ward, J., and Peppard, J. (1996). *Strategic planning for information systems*. John Wiley & Sons.

Westerman, G., Calméjane, C., Bonnet, D., Ferraris, P., & McAfee, A. (2011). Digital Transformation: A roadmap for billion-dollar organizations. *MIT Center for digital business and capgemini consulting*, *1*, 1-68.

Reflection Papers

DEBUNKING THE MYTH OF CRYPTO ASSETS AS FINANCIAL INNOVATION: UNPACKING THE FALLOUT FROM THE CRYPTO WINTER

Wendy L. Currie[1,2] and Jonathan J. M. Seddon[1]
[1]*Audencia Business School*
8 Route de la Jonelière BP 31222 - 44312, Nantes Cedex 3, France
[2]*Faculty of Management, Law & Social Sciences*
University of Bradford, Richmond Rd, Bradford BD7 1DP, UK

ABSTRACT

Following the Great Recession of 2007/8, bank behavior and government control were viewed in a negative light. The use of blockchain for decentralized financial tokens has been embraced by those seeking an alternative to the existing fiat system. Technology enabled the quick purchase of crypto assets, allowing millions of investors all over the world to access the perceived benefits of decentralized investment. And just as new types of unregulated investments had helped to create the Great Recession, unregulated crypto assets drove the crypto winter of 2021-23. There are strong arguments on both sides as to the benefits and costs created by crypto assets, and the contributions that they make to society.

KEYWORDS

Crypto Assets, Crypto Winter, Derivatives, Financial Regulation

1. INTRODUCTION

The market capitalisation of crypto assets decreased from around €2.68 trillion on 10 November 2021 to €801 billion on 2 July 2022. By 14 June 2023 it was €978 billion, (CoinMarketCap, 2023). An estimated three-quarters of bitcoin users suffered losses on their initial investments at this time. The fall in the price of crypto assets saw millions of investors suffer significant losses. The fallout from the crypto market, described as the *Crypto Winter*, focused attention on balancing the drive for financial innovation to nurture new markets, and the need for governance to protect investors. This research examines the intersection of financial technology and regulatory policy and practice in the context of the U.S. The debate in the U.S. is whether jurisdiction should be controlled by the Commodity Futures Trading Commission (CFTC) or the U.S. Securities and Exchange Commission (SEC). In March 2022, an Executive Order 14067 was signed calling for all agencies to coordinate regulatory efforts (The White House, 2022). So far, it is estimated that 16 percent (40 million) adult Americans have invested in, traded, or used crypto assets. Worldwide, some 300 million people own some form of crypto asset (Chohan, 2022) with the figure only expected to rise.

The structure of this short overview paper is as follows: First, we consider how the two regulatory bodies responsible for oversight of the financial system obfuscates policy development and implementation of crypto asset oversight. Unlike other countries, with only one regulator, the allocation of responsibility between the two bodies is unclear and confusing. Second, the development of blockchain is discussed, and how this technology and associated products (such as Bitcoin) share many similarities with over-the-counter (OTC) derivatives. These instruments fueled the 2008 Global financial crisis (FCIC, 2011). Parallels are drawn with the crypto winter which saw over $2tn wiped off the global market value of crypto assets. Third, interview data is presented, showing respondent quotes in favor and against crypto assets. Finally, we conclude by highlighting the complexity in reconciling two competing narratives on crypto asset regulation and offer suggestions for future research.

2. SIMILARITIES BETWEEN FINANCIAL PRODUCTS

To understand how and why crypto assets were created, it is important to appreciate the driving forces behind their development.

2.1 OTC Instruments and the Great Recession

The U.S. has not always had two regulatory bodies. In the aftermath of the 1929 financial crisis, regulations and laws were created to restore confidence to the U.S. financial markets. In 1934 the SEC was enacted, tasked with executing these acts to protect investors, maintain efficient markets and enable capital formation. The global economy struggled following the Great Depression and World War 2, but by the 1960's, economic growth and the influence of technology shaped the markets.

The SEC's Commodity Futures Trading Commission Act of 1974 proposed sweeping changes to the Commodity Exchange Act (CEA) of 1936. However, the SEC's Chairman declined jurisdiction over the commodity futures industry, which led to the creation of the Commodity Futures Trading Commission (CFTC). Its changes to the CEA of 1974 were '*...to strengthen the regulation of futures trading, to bring all agricultural and other commodities traded on exchanges under regulation, and for other purposes*' (GPO, 1974, p.1389). Now two separate bodies regulated the US financial market.

Much work has been done in trying to understand the causes of the 2008 Great Recession. In the US, following the dot com's bubble burst, low interest rates encouraged the development of new products which could offer high yields (Mohan, 2009). These products were OTC derivatives and fueled the development of mortgage finance and the rapid growth of the subprime mortgage sector. In 1992 the CFTC had been given authority to exempt OTC derivatives from a wide range of transactions (The Futures Trading Practices Act of 1992). Changes made in 2000 to the Commodity Futures Modernization Act represented the most significant reform to the CEA since the creation of the CFTC. Whilst it eliminated any overlapping jurisdiction between the SEC and the CFTC, excluded from regulatory oversight were OTC derivatives executed on electronic platforms. Such justification was supported by arguments which stated that the '*...creation of a regulatory system for such systems in anticipation of problems was inappropriate...the vast majority of OTC derivatives simply are not susceptible to manipulation*' (Greenspan, 2000). By removing government control on how such markets could operate would ensure that innovation in new OTC products would not be lost. Not all were supporters. In the 2002 Berkshire Hathaway report, Warren Buffet wrote '*derivatives are financial weapons of mass destruction, carrying dangers that, while now latent, are potentially lethal*' (Buffet, 2002, p.15).

The quality of the underlying instrument referenced by OTC derivatives (e.g., mortgage-backed securities, credit default swaps) was never questioned, and when the U.S. housing market crashed, the global economy quickly followed. OTC instruments are opaque, making it hard for regulators to see who is buying and who is selling. And when big OTC contact holders collapsed (e.g., Lehman Brothers, AIG), government became worried over contagion. The value of these leveraged contracts was worth $600trillion, over 10 times the words economic output.

2.2 Crypto Instruments and the Crypto Winter

The financial collapse coincided with the release of a paper which presented a peer-to-peer electronic cash system, offering the solution to an '*...electronic payment system based on cryptographic proof instead of trust, allowing any two willing parties to transact directly with each other without the need for a trusted third party*' (Nakamoto, 2008: 1). The need for a new financial system is nothing new, but views such as those opined by von Hayek that fiat currency '*...has the defects of all monopolies: one must use their product even if it is unsatisfactory, and, above all, it prevents the discovery of better methods of satisfying a need for which a monopolist has no incentive*' (von Hayek, 1976, pp 28) had never been realised. Earlier work had edged electronic systems closer to this end goal (Mazieres and Shasha, 2002; Szabo, 2005) but Nakamoto's paper offered a new solution preventing electronic holdings being spent twice. If a database is centrally located, then it is easy to lock a record and prevent its value from being changed, however using a distributed database, no single entity has overall control. Nakamoto's solution was to use a consensus between computers (nodes) which managed the blockchain which recorded every event (Bamakan et al., 2020).

The 2008 financial crisis and an alternative payment system fueled the techno-libertarian dream. Trust in banks and governments had been lost as the scale of the financial disaster was to unfold. Crypto currency offered transactional freedom, security, and ease of making transactions. Privacy was retained as individuals could control their own finance, with pseudo-anonymity. The unbanked would be helped as the goal of financial inclusion would open payment systems to anybody who used a thrustless distributed ledger technology - the blockchain.

Within only a year, the value of crypto assets fell by over 70%. This rapid decline in cryptocurrencies was dubbed the 'Crypto Winter'. Leading up to the first quarter of 2023, a series of events triggered a domino effect of financial losses that led to a disintegration of investor confidence in crypto assets. Crypto firms invested in each other or borrowed from competitor firms in an attempt to support their eco-system. The first problems were seen as the stable coin and token issued by Terraform Labs crashed. Now effectively worthless, it once had a market value of $40bn. Over the next week the global market value dropped by $0.5tn. Between July 2022 and February 2023, eight crypto firms collapsed, all but one filing for either Chapter 11 or Chapter 15 bankruptcy. Chapter 11 allows a company to continue commercial operations whilst restructuring its business. Chapter 15 is used with a foreign bankruptcy, promoting cooperation between US and foreign courts as the business is financially rescued. What was seen was the amount of credit or debt which had exchanged between these private entities. Much compromising of the crypto-tokens generated by themselves.

3. CRYPTO AS AN ILLUSORY INNOVATIVE PAYMENT SYSTEM

Interviews were granted by regulators, software developers, investors, and influencers, and followed a grounded research method. Interviews took place on site visits during July 2022 and June 2023, with on-line follow up calls to check the accuracy on what had been recorded. Table 1. presents a summary of informant responses. Full disclosure on the numbers of people spoken with, sector, analysis methods and supporting literature will be given in a full paper.

Table 1. Interviewee arguments both for and against the use of crypto assets

Arguments for crypto assets (*innovation narrative*)	Arguments against crypto assets (*governance narrative*)
'Need a clear policy for the entrepreneurs, developers, and users of the crypto industry, with congress passing bipartisan legislation to create a sensible regulatory framework for digital stablecoins backed by the US$'.	*'Crypto should not be regulated like banking products because that would give crypto support to the government services afforded to banking'. 'Controls for centralized governance should not be simply applied to decentralized entities'. 'Even if DeFi is decentralized it is not economically decentralized'.*
'Innovative software development that will become stifled as regulation will stop investment'.	*'Crypto industry is built on misinformation, hype, and fraud'. 'It's just lines of code called tokens or coins stored on blockchains to convey legitimacy and technological sophistication'.*
'Crypto assets are software and there is nothing intrinsically good or evil with code, rather it is what people do with it'. 'The code did not commit the crime'. 'Typing computer code is a form of protected speech, supported by the constitution'.	*'Software is only a tool and blockchain is an immature technology, damaging to the environment'. 'Real money has been used to purchase some of the 20k crypto's in existence'. 'Fraud and threats to national security. It finances terrorists, human traffickers, cyber criminals, blackmail, and sanctions evasion'.*
'BTC is a store of value. If backed by US$ and other high quality liquid assets can become the default payment system'. '20m Americans have invested in crypto as an investment'.	*'Marketing driving citizens fear of missing out'. 'Money serves 3 functions: medium of exchange; unit of account; and store of value. None of which crypto does well. At best, a vehicle for speculation – a zero sum game of chance'.*
'Crypto assets are open sourced, decentralized, and transparent'.	*'Assets which offer no products, services or revenue streams and add no overall value to the economy'.*

'Crypto assets can protect against inflation when governments irresponsibly manage their own currencies'.	*'Blockchain and crypto assets are not a solution to fix underlying and structural problems which limit access to financial services'. 'Could cause financial crisis if integrated with a fiat system'.*
'Can provide useful services without the need for a company or a middleman'.	*'It is gambling and speculation'. 'Inflation of the crypto eco system by investing in and borrowing from each other'.*
'Disrupt the existing financial services with faster, more efficient, more productive, and more secure ways of investing, paying transferring and tracking'. 'Entrenched business abhor competition'.	*'Speed at which quantity of crypto assets can be created because they are virtual assets. This gives rise to leverage making the system more at risk to boom and bust. Without any productive capacity, it is impossible to check on the valuation of an asset'. 'Attestation for proof of reserve is no substitute for the rigor of an audit'.*
'BTC has no corporation that controls or issues, no individual or committee because it is decentralized. It is hard to establish there is a common enterprise when there is no controlling central authority'.	*'Crypto is an investment contract. A security, which passes the Howie test: an investment of money, in a common enterprise, with the expectation of profit, to be derived from the efforts of others'.*

4. CONCLUSION

The SEC and CFTC have started prosecutions against numerous crypto companies (e.g., FTX, Celsius, Coinbase, Binance, and Terraform Labs). They have also fined traditional banks, exchanges, fund managers and investment firms – organizations that are fundamental to today's economy. The collapse of the 'bad apples' in the crypto space is seen by all as a necessary activity. Those pro-crypto say this as helping to develop rigor whilst those against say that it is inevitable. Further research will unpack the crypto eco-system to understand more about the market structure and, in particular, the interconnectivity among crypto firms, and how they operate under the radar of global regulatory bodies and institutions to maximize profits.

REFERENCES

Bamakan, S. M. H., Motavali, A., and Bondarti, A.B. (2020). A survey of blockchain consensus algorithms performance evaluation criteria, *Expert Systems with Applications*, 154, https://doi.org/10.1016/j.eswa.2020.113385.

Beck, K. and Ralph, J. (1994). Patterns Generates Architectures. *Proceedings of European Conference of Object-Oriented Programming.* Bologna, Italy, pp. 139-149.

Buffet, W. (2002) Berkshire Hathaway Inc. Annual Report. https://www.berkshirehathaway.com/2002ar/2002ar.pdf.

Coinmarketcap.com (2023) https://coinmarketcap.com/

Financial Crisis Inquiry Commission (2011) The Financial Crisis Inquiry Report. Pacific Publishing Studio, U.S.

Greenspan, A. (2000). Over-the-counter derivatives. Before the Committee on Agriculture, Nutrition and Forestry, United States Senate February 10, 2000. https://www.federalreserve.gov/boarddocs/testimony/2000/20000210.htm.

Mazieres, D. and Shasha, D. (2002). Building secure file systems out of byzantine storage. *Proceedings of the twenty-first annual symposium on Principles of distributed computing*, July, 108–117. https://doi.org/10.1145/571825.571840.

Mohan, R. (2009). Global Financial Crisis: Causes, Impact, Policy Responses and Lessons, Working Paper No. 407. Stanford. https://kingcenter.stanford.edu/sites/g/files/sbiybj16611/files/media/file/407wp_0.pdf.

Nakamoto, S. (2008) Bitcoin: A Peer-to-Peer Electronic Cash System. Retrieved 27 April 2022. https://www.ussc.gov/sites/default/files/pdf/training/annual-national-training-seminar/2018/Emerging_Tech_Bitcoin_Crypto.pdf.

Rossi, M., Mueller-Bloch, C., Thatcher, J. B., and Beck, R. (2019). Blockchain Research in Information Systems: Current Trends and an Inclusive Future Research Agenda. 2009): 13-1405.

Szabo, N. (2005). Bit Gold, December 29. https://nakamotoinstitute.org/bit-gold/.

U.S. Government Information (GPO). (1974). Title I – Commodity Futures Trading Commission. October 23. 1389-1416. https://www.govinfo.gov/content/pkg/STATUTE-88/pdf/STATUTE-88-Pg1389.pdf.

von Hayek, F. A. (1976). *Denationalization of Money: The argument redefined.* London: The Institute of Economic Affairs. First Ed.

WHAT ARE WE TALKING ABOUT WHEN WE TALK ABOUT DIGITAL RESILIENCE?

Everist Limaj
Vienna University of Economics and Business (WU)
Institute for Information Management and Control
Welthandelsplatz 1, 1020 Vienna, Austria

ABSTRACT

Digital resilience has emerged as a critical concept, experiencing lately a surge in research publications. However, the term is being used inconsistently and the current body of studies on the topic is creating a conceptual confusion. In this reflection paper, I present a semantic analysis contrasting how different studies refer to and use digital resilience. A distinction is made between the various meanings of digital resilience through the lenses of polysemy, homonymy, and synonymy. By offering a more nuanced understanding of digital resilience and its usages, this reflection paper contributes to enhance effective communication and comprehension among scholars, thereby helping to advance academic discourse on digital resilience.

KEYWORDS

Digital Resilience, Semantic Analysis, Resilience Meanings, Terminology, Definitions, Reflection Paper

1. INTRODUCTION

In recent years, arguably due to the emergence of several crises (notably the COVID-19 pandemic or different cyber-attacks), the usage of terms related to resilience in scientific literature has grown (Heeks and Ospina, 2019). One of the forms of resilience is digital resilience, which has particularly gained a lot of attention among researchers across disciplines (Boh et al., 2023). Indeed, current research on digital resilience spans from individuals, organizations, communities and societal levels, including diverse domains, amongst others, education, mental health, innovation, cybersecurity, emergency response, or business continuity. The broad and increasing usage of the term has generated many interpretations leading to semantic variations of digital resilience. This diversity in meaning can lead to confusion and misconception among scholars, for instance when they are trying to position or discuss their work within the digital resilience realm. Another issue arises when studies use identical terminology as the query but fail to address the underlying concept scholars are seeking (Krovetz, 1997). Such ambiguity could impede effective communication and advancement of research findings and potentially related theoretical developments (Feldman, 2004). Thus, scholars have called for more research aimed at increasing clarity, refining and standardizing the resilience concepts (Boh et al., 2023, Heeks and Ospina, 2019).

Previous work focusing on clarifying the digital resilience concept is scarce. While there is an emerging focus on enhancing clarity of terms related to resilience, conceptual clarifications specifically on digital resilience are uncommon. To illustrate, Hillmann and Guenther (2021) conduct a thorough review on the concept of *organizational resilience* elucidating both conceptual and operational aspects. Ahmadi-Assalemi et al. (2020) undertake a similar exploration on the concept of *cyber resilience* within the context of cyber-physical systems in smart cities. Further, Righi et al. (2015) review the concept of *resilience engineering* offering a better understanding how to design and evaluate resilient systems in complex socio-technical environments. Furthermore, Biddle et al. (2020) provide an extensive examination of *health system resilience* literature, which seem to predominantly focus on absorptive and adaptive capacities, while overlooking aspects like institutional legitimacy and transformative resilience. Collectively, these studies contribute to a broader comprehension of resilience related concepts, yet emphasize the need for more focused conceptual work for digital resilience.

In this reflection paper, I aim to increase clarity on the concept of digital resilience by analyzing its usages across research studies. However, I do not mean to make normative assertions. The contribution of this article is at best its nuanced descriptive analysis. The central claim posited here is the existence of various semantics of digital resilience. Below, I delineate the relationships among the meanings of digital resilience through the lenses of polysemy, homonymy and synonymy.

2. A SEMANTIC ANALYSIS OF DIGITAL RESILIENCE

The fact that digital resilience is a concept associated with a multitude of meanings, varying widely across studies, presents a source of ambiguity among scholars. Indeed, in several studies, digital resilience is vaguely referenced, often merely in titles or sporadically within the content, without clear definition (e.g. Gray-Denson, 2015, Andersen-Cooke, 2018, Park et al., 2021). Furthermore, those studies that provide a definition typically restrict their explanation to their specific research setting, failing to link it to established theories or other studies, thereby complicating the understanding due to varying interpretations. To clarify these ambiguities, I draw upon methods from linguistic, specifically adopting polysemy, homonymy, and synonymy as an analytical tool. I use the context prism to highlight particular interpretations (Risjord, 2009).

2.1 Polysemy in Digital Resilience

Polysemy is used to describe semantic variations where a term or phrase conveys multiple related meanings, depending on the context in which it is used (Weinreich, 1964). Polysemy is particularly useful in exploring digital resilience as it allows to capture the breadth of meanings a single concept can hold (Klepousniotou et al., 2012). Both across various academic domains and even within individual fields, terms often develop to have layered meanings. Polysemy helps to map out the various interpretations, offering insights into how digital resilience is being used in different scenarios. To illustrate the polysemy (P) of digital resilience, in the following I present six different uses of the term and its related but varied meanings across different contexts. However, additional meanings beyond these might exist.

(P1) **Context: urban planning and development.** In this context, digital resilience is the capacity of individuals and organizations in smart cities to adapt to digital change flexibly (Veglianti et al., 2021). It focuses on integrating ICT and human capital to enhance the balance between competitiveness and sustainability.

(P2) **Context: health sector response to crises.** From this point of view, digital resilience refers to the ability of individuals, organizations, and society to use digital technology effectively in responding to challenges, like COVID-19, emphasizing continuous evolution and transformation in a sustainable manner within the health sector (Magutshwa and Radianti, 2022).

(P3) **Context: higher education sector response to crises.** From this perspective, digital resilience is conceptualized as a process of surviving major exogenous crises, like COVID-19, using digital means in the context of higher education (Bera and Kim, 2021).

(P4) **Context: personal response to crises.** Here, digital resilience is seen as the implementation of information technologies by individuals to adapt, rebound, and recover in the face of challenges and disruptions, particularly during the COVID-19 pandemic (Al-Abdulghani et al., 2021).

(P5) **Context: organizational and employee response to crises.** In this context, digital resilience is defined as the IS-supported adaptation and recovery of employees from short-term and long-term disruptions, like the shift to remote work during COVID-19 (Kohn, 2020b).

(P6) **Context: response capabilities to crises.** A more generalized yet still polysemic interpretation has been given recently from Boh et al. (2023) who define digital resilience as the capabilities that different entities develop to absorb and adapt to major shocks, and to transform into a new, more stable state better prepared for future shocks. The focus is on how digital technologies facilitate overcoming challenges like COVID-19, financial crises or climate change.

2.2 Homonymy in Digital Resilience

Homonymy occurs when a term or phrase has two or more distinct and unrelated semantic meanings, often leading to potential confusion in different contexts (Weinreich, 1964). Homonymy comes into play when the term digital resilience is used in various studies but it has different meanings in different contexts. Particularly in interdisciplinary studies (such as in information systems research), where diverse fields of research intersect, the same term can mean different things. Homonymy allows for the identification and clarification of these differences, reducing potential misunderstandings. To illustrate homonymy (H) of digital resilience, in the following I present three distinctive meanings of the same term used in different contexts.

(H1) **Context: information systems (IS) in business**. Here, digital resilience refers to the ability of an IS to enhance resilience in its output systems while maintaining sufficient resilience in sub-systems, in response to external shocks like financial crises or pandemics (Schemmer et al., 2021). It views digital resilience as a property that mitigates vulnerability and complexity, emphasizing a holistic design approach of IS.

(H2) **Context: fake news.** A divergent homonymic interpretation alludes to digital resilience as a mechanism to mitigate the negative effects of and reduce individual susceptibility to fake news. It involves educating the public and integrating strategies at individual, institutional, and platform levels to combat misinformation (Rodrigo et al., 2022).

(H3) **Context: country strategy response to crises**. Another distinct interpretation of digital resilience refers to the capabilities of agility, diversity, and plurality, which are fostered through engagement of various digital actors including citizen participation, public-private partnerships, and research and development governance (Park et al., 2021).

2.3 Synonymy in Digital Resilience

Synonymy is used to describe the occurrence of different terms or phrases that have similar or identical semantic meanings, allowing them to be used interchangeably in various contexts. Synonymy is important for understanding the interchangeable nature of digital resilience with other terms. It enables shedding light on other terms that are used in place of digital resilience across different disciplines. It is also helpful to identify shared meanings in interdisciplinary fields, where terms from one domain are frequently used in another. To illustrate the synonymy (S) of digital resilience, in the following I present cases of different terms pointing to the same meaning.

In one case, *e-resilience* and *digital resilience* are used as synonyms.

(S1a *digital resilience*) **Context: digital innovation for rural development.** Here, digital resilience refers to the empowerment of rural communities through digital technologies (e.g. e-commerce) (Tim et al., 2020).

(S1b *e-resilience)* **Context: digital IS for developing country.** In this context, *e-resilience* embodies the enhancement of community resilience through digital information systems (e.g. ICT) (Heeks and Ospina, 2019), which reflects a synonymous meaning with digital resilience as used in S1a.

In another case, *cyber resilience*, and *digital (security) resilience* are used as synonyms.

(S2a *digital resilience*) **Context: employee behavior and information security.** *Digital resilience* or *digital security resilience* is described as the "ability to continuously deliver intended outcomes despite adverse cyber events" (Kohn, 2020a). The term refers to employees' ability to respond to security challenges.

(S2b *cyber resilience*) **Context: concept examination.** *Cyber resilience* is defined as "ability to continuously deliver intended outcomes despite adverse cyber events" (Björck et al., 2015). The term refers to the systems and processes that enable an organization to withstand and recover from cyber threats.

3. CONCLUSION

The semantic analysis of digital resilience reveals the complex and multifaceted nature of this concept. The polysemy interpretations emphasize the adaptability and versatility of the term 'digital resilience' across different context and scenarios. The homonymous interpretations indicate the potential for confusion and misinterpretation among scholars. Highlighting synonymous usages contributes to unify understanding of digital resilience concepts, enabling a more effective communication among scholars. In terms of limitations, the analysis does not consider compound digital resilience concepts and is confined to studies selected through convenience sampling, and, thus may not cover all possible interpretations or contexts. Further, there is a risk of subjective categorizations of digital resilience as polysemy, homonymy or synonymy – these are relative concepts themselves. Still, I hope this reflection paper brings more clarity to the digital resilience concept and helps scholars in the future to better navigate the complexity and diversity of meanings associated with this term in various research and practical contexts.

REFERENCES

Ahmadi-Assalemi, G., Al-Khateeb, H., Epiphaniou, G. & Maple, C. (2020). Cyber Resilience and Incident Response in Smart Cities: A Systematic Literature Review. Smart Cities, 3, 894-927.

Al-Abdulghani, Y., Vatanasakdakul, S., Mellon, C. & Aoun, C. (2021). Tough as Nails? An Individual Perspective to Digital Resilience During a Pandemic. AMCIS. Virtual.

Andersen-Cooke, S. (2018). Young & eSafe: Teaching digital resilience. Scan 37, 272-277.

Bera, D. & Kim, D. (2021). Digital Resilience Formation During Covid and Before Covid- A Thematic Analysis in Higher Education Context. Proceedings of the 2021 Pre-ICIS SIGDSA Symposium.

Biddle, L., Wahedi, K. & Bozorgmehr, K. (2020). Health system resilience: a literature review of empirical research. Health Policy and Planning, 35, 1084-1109.

Björck, F., Henkel, M., Stirna, J. & Zdravkovic, J. (2015). Cyber Resilience – Fundamentals for a Definition. In: Rocha, A., Correia, A., Costanzo, S. & Reis, L. (eds.) New Contributions in Information Systems and Technologies. Advances in Intelligent Systems and Computing. Springer, Cham.

Boh, W., Constantinides, P., Padmanabhan, B. & Viswanathan, S. (2023). Building Digital Resilience Against Major Shocks. MIS Quarterly, 47, 343-360.

Feldman, D. C. (2004). What are We Talking About When We Talk About Theory? J. of Management, 30, 565-567.

Gray-Denson, K. L. (2015). Cultural production and digital resilience: Examining female gamers' use of social media to participate in video game culture. In: TRIER-BIENIEK, A. (ed.) Fan Girls and the Media: Creating Characters, Consuming Culture. Rowman & Littlefield.

Heeks, R. & Ospina, A. V. (2019). Conceptualising the link between information systems and resilience: A developing country field study. Information Systems Journal, 29, 70-96.

Hillmann, J. & Guenther, E. (2021). Organizational Resilience: A Valuable Construct for Management Research? International Journal of Management Reviews, 23, 7-44.

Klepousniotou, E., Pike, G. B., Steinhauer, K. & GRACCO, V. (2012). Not all ambiguous words are created equal: An EEG investigation of homonymy and polysemy. Brain & Language, 123, 11-21.

Kohn, V. (2020a). How Employees' Digital Resilience Makes Organizations More Secure. PACIS. Dubai.

Kohn, V. (2020b). How the Coronavirus Pandemic Affects the Digital Resilience of Employees. ICIS. India.

Krovetz, R. (1997). Homonymy and Polysemy in Information Retrieval. Association for Computational Linguistics, 72-79.

Magutshwa, S. & Radianti, J. (2022). Is this Digital Resilience? Insights from Adaptation and Exaptation of a Cyber-Physical-Social System. Proceedings of the 55th HICSS, 2022 Hawaii.

Park, K. R., Sahay, S., Braa, J. & Amarakoon, P. (2021). Digital resilience for what? Case study of South Korea. Proceedings of the Conference on Implications of Information and Digital Technologies for Development, 2021. Virtual.

Righi, A. W., Saurin, T. A. & Wachs, P. (2015). A systematic literature review of resilience engineering: Research areas and a research agenda proposal. Reliability Engineering & System Safety, 141, 142-152.

Risjord, M. (2009). Rethinking concept analysis. Journal of Advanced Nursing, 65, 684-691.

Rodrigo, P., Arakpogun, E. O., Mai Chi Vu, F. O. & Djafarova, E. (2022). Can you be Mindful? The Effectiveness of Mindfulness-Driven Interventions in Enhancing the Digital Resilience to Fake News on COVID-19. Information Systems Frontiers.

Schemmer, M., Heinz, D., Baier, L., Vössing, M. & Kühl, N. (2021). Conceptualizing Digital Resilience for AI-based Information Systems. ECIS. Marrakech: Research-in-Progress Papers, 44.

Tim, Y., Cui, L. & Sheng, Z. (2020). Digital resilience: How rural communities leapfrogged into sustainable development. Info Systems Journal, 31, 323-345.

Veglianti, E., Sidani, D. & De Marco, M. (2021). Digital Resilience for Cities' Smartness. Annual conference of the Italian Chapter of AIS (ITAIS 2021) Proceedings. Trento, Italy.

Weinreich, U. (1964). Webster's third: A critique of its semantics. International J of American Linguistics, 405-409.

INTEGRATING CHATGPT DEVELOPMENT WITH JSON IN INFORMATION SYSTEMS EDUCATION

Ming Wang
Professor, Department of Information Systems, California State University, Los Angeles, 5151 State University Drive, Los Angeles, CA 90032, USA

ABSTRACT

The recent development of artificial intelligence (AI) ChatGPT applications has been rapidly changing the world. ChatGPT, a language model developed by OpenAI, can play an important role in public health, medicine, education, and many other fields. With its ability to generate human-like text based on large amounts of data, ChatGPT also has the great potential to support individuals and communities in making informed business decisions. To catch the industrial trend, information systems (IS) educators must integrate AI ChatGPT technology into the IS curriculum. The study investigates teaching insight of AI Chatbot with JSON development on the cloud platform in a pedagogical approach. The paper presents the importance of integrating ChatGPT with JSON case projects into the IS curriculum, project framework, and delivery modules. Unlike most ChatGPT teaching in IS courses, the study of the projects will reveal the insight of AI Chatbot and adequately teach the next digital generations of students to develop them and prepare them for the challenges they will face in their enterprise career development. In the projects, learners gain hands-on experience in developing AI interactive chatbots on the SAP Conversational AI platform. The significant impacts of such research will benefit IS academic researchers, IS educators, and IS students. The presentation will include a demonstration of JSON code utilization in Chatbot development on the SAP Conversational AI platform and a discussion on the important features of business process Chatbot development.

KEYWORDS

IS Education, IS Curriculum, Pedagogy, ChatGPT, ChatBot, JSON

1. INTRODUCTION

The rapid development of artificial intelligence (AI) applications raises awareness among information systems (IS) educators about the importance of bringing technology into the IS curriculum. To meet the challenge, information systems (IS) educators must think creatively about applying changes to their course content and the skills they give (and they want to give) their students and consider AI chatbot development on cloud platforms into the IS curriculum to help students learn more and work smarter and faster.

The study will investigate ChatGPT AI chatbot development on the SAP Business Technology Platform in a pedagogical approach. ChatGPT, which stands for Chat Generative Pre-trained Transformer, is a large language model–based chatbot developed by OpenAI. Chatbot (Chatter + Robot) is an application with an interface to conduct a chat conversation between a human and an AI agent and automate tasks and workflows. ChatGPT is a powerful tool for creating chatbots to generate artificial intelligence (AI) text and interactively engage in user conversations.

Chatbot replaces or aids a live human agent, providing a human-realistic intelligent response. after receiving text or text-to-speech as input from users, chatbots can converse, supply answers, entertain, and provide customer service. JSON (JavaScript Object Notation) is a data format with diverse uses in electronic data interchange like XML.JSON is related to ChatGPT because ChatGPT can use JSON as an input or output format for various processes. For example, ChatGPT can take a JSON object as an input or intent and generate a natural language description of its contents, or vice versa. ChatGPT can also update or generate JSON data based on a given schema or model or modify existing JSON data based on some rules or criteria specified. ChatGPT can also use JSON to store and retrieve information from its memory or knowledge base. JSON is a versatile and flexible format that can be used for ChatGPT applications.

The general usability of the study of the projects is evident. The paper develops best practices for delivering AI Chatbot fundamental concepts and skills and case study projects in the related courses: cloud application development, business intelligence, and data science courses in different instructional modalities. The projects will significantly contribute to the IS education discipline. By adopting the development steps and innovative algorithms in the projects, students can learn the insight of AI chatbots with JSON and make business process development with solid confidence in their enterprise career development. Learning SAP Conversational AI helps students understand the fundamentals of ChatGPT technology. This AI technology and skills will help students to be hired in large organizations and promote their social mobility and has enormous potential for student internships and placement. The proposed projects will also promote students' learning motivation.

The dissemination of pedagogy will create awareness and exposure to AI technology for IS professionals and educators, build faculty research collaboration and professional network, and develop guidelines for IS educators to teach ChatGPT skills in IS courses and build the bridge between Academia and the AI ChatGPT industry.

The study, although practical, is yet to improve. The projects should be tested on other AI ChatGPT Platforms. The author plans to collect quantitative data and qualitative narratives from instructors who have adopted this approach in their teaching and research. With constructive feedback, positive experiences, and lessons learned, the author hopes to improve the project study and make it more effective in IS education.

2. PROJECT FRAMEWORK

Learning by doing enterprise systems is important in teaching the next generation of digital business leaders. The project focuses on teaching AI chatbot development on the interactive cloud platform with hands-on experience. Student engagement with hands-on case activities is vital to this project. The pedagogical approach will help students optimize their learning outcomes to ensure a better learning experience in learning e-business process integration. The projects will adapt ChatGPT AI Text Generators in favor of the student to achieve their learning outcomes in the integrated business processes. Specific project modules are listed in the following table.

Table 1. Teaching Modules for the development of an interactive AI Chatbot with JSON

Module	Content
Module 1	AI and ChatGPT Concepts Introduction
Module 2	ChatBot Modeling
Module 3	ChatBot Building with JSON
Module 4	ChatBot Training
Module 5	ChatBot Testing
Module 6	ChatBot Deployment

2.1 Student Learning Objectives

- Understand concepts and skills of AI ChatBot.
- Evaluate and compare different AI ChatBot platforms.
- Model the ChatBot for business processes.
- Build the ChatBot with JSON to provide business processes.
- Train ChatBot for business processes.
- Add Entity, Intents, and Skills to the Chatbot.
- Test ChatBot on the conversational AI platform.
- Deploy ChatBot on the Website.

3. PROJECT ACTIVITIES

Conversational Bot Projects on SAP Conversational AI uses its interface to conduct a chat conversation between a human and an AI agent that automates tasks and workflows. Chatbot replaces or aids a live human agent, providing a human-realistic intelligent response. after receiving text or text-to-speech as input from users, chatbots can converse, supply answers, entertain, and provide customer service. The projects focus on developing an interactive AI Chatbot with JSON to support bots on SAP Open Conversational AI and OpenAI platforms. For illustration purposes, the project is currently deployed on SAP Conversational AI Cloud https://cai.tools.sap/. SAP Conversational AI is a part of SAP Business Technology Platform (SAP BTP), an innovation platform optimized for SAP applications in the cloud. SAP BTP combines application development and automation, data and analytics, integration, and AI capabilities in one unified environment.

Different institutions can certainly choose other AI ChatGPT Platforms, such as:

- OpenAI for ChatGPT: https://openai.com/dall-e-2/
- Google Bard: https://bard.google.com/
- Microsoft Bing/Copilot: https://www.bing.com/

Learning outcomes will be reflected in the answers to the following questions after project implementation. 1). What is your chatbot capable of answering? 2). What skills does your chatbot have? 3). How is JSON related to Chat GPT? 4). Run the chatbot. How does it respond to your questions? 5). How would you improve the accuracy and capabilities of your chatbot?

3.1 Project 1: Greeting ChatBot Development

Description: A conversational bot that can greet and tell a joke. The project will be deployed onto the SAP Business Technology Platform and used as a webhook to be called by an SAP Conversational AI chatbot. The five steps of development are as follows.

1. Create an SAP Conversational AI account and a new greeting bot project.
2. Develop the greeting bot in Train, Build, Connect, and Monitor. A). Train: Teach your bot what it needs to understand by creating intents. B). Build: Create your conversational flow with our Bot Builder tool by giving bot skills it can perform. C). Connect: Ship your bot to one or several messaging platforms. D). Monitor: See how users are communicating with your bot, check if the bot is understanding users correctly, and make updates to the bot's intents/entities.
3. Create new intents and add expressions. Fork intent: intents are what people want to tell our bot. Within an intent, we indicate the possible expressions a person might use to communicate that intent.
4. Manage conversation flow with skills.
5. Test by chatting with the bot using Chat Preview.

3.2 Project 2: Customers Shipping ChatBot Development

Description: Students created a Customer Shipping Chatbot in SAP Conversational AI. Customer Shipping Chatbot enables customers to track packages. Students will add features to the chatbot to answer customer questions about pricing a package, require customers to include a size and location, validate the location, show a Google map when a location is validated, and display a message with data from the memory. The customer will indicate that they want to track a parcel. The customer will provide the package number. The customer will confirm that they want to track the package. The Chatbot will call an API to retrieve package info and display it. The customer will indicate they want to price a package. The customer will provide the address and the size of the package. The bot will check the address, and then call an API to retrieve a location map. The bot will display the map and provide a price for the package based on its size. The ten steps of development are as follows.

1. Create a Shipping Bot Skelton in SAP Conversational AI.
2. Create a Particle Number Entity for shipping to be extracted from a conversation AI in Train.
3. Add Intents for Boolean expressions "yes" and "no" by Forking Yes or NO defined in pre-defined Intents since users must indicate whether they accept or reject specific requests from the bot. Forking is simply copying a relationship between your bot and the source of what you forked.
4. Add intents for Boolean expressions "yes" and "no" Customers to indicate if they want information on a parcel by Forking Yes or NO defined in pre-defined Intents.
5. Create a skill for users to track a parcel in Build as a trigger.

6. Add Requirements to Skill (parcel number) in Build so the bot knows whether to complete tracking the parcel. Update the Conversation by assigning particle numbers to JSON objects in the Memory Field.
7. Add Requirement to Skill (yes/no) using Python to send messages to call JSON objects in Memory management.
8. Add action to send a message for skill.
9. Call API to connect Google Maps for the shipping address by calling Webhook.
10. Test the shipping bot with a tracking number in Chat Preview.

4. CONCLUSION

The paper integrates the development of AI Chatbots with JSON in the IS Curriculum. The author provides a comprehensive framework to introduce the development of an AI Chatbot with JSON project in IS education. By adopting this approach, IS educators can integrate AI fundamental concepts and skills and case study projects in the related courses but are not limited to cloud application development, business intelligence, and data science courses. More important is that the study provides practical guidelines to teach the development of ChatGPT with JSON with hands-on experiences. This project prepares students to meet the IT professionals in the digital business world. The significant impacts will be on students' recruitment, job placement, and career development.

Overall, the projects provide hands-on activities on SAP Conversational AI – a low-code chatbot platform.

- Chatbot building to provide customer service shopping bot.
- ChatBot testing on specific tasks such as parcel tracking, address tracking, and shipping quotes.
- Natural Language Processing (NLP) for Expression Analysis on JSON as formatted ChatGPT input
- ChatBot training by creating, adding, updating, and managing intents or entities. Human beings need to retrain the shopping bot on any update made on it.

JSON is important to the ChatBot development in SAP conversational AI and Open AI. Datasets for conversational response selection are from JSON. When you add an Entity or update Entity, you will add a JSON object or update a JSON object. When you open up the ChatGPT UI and ask for some JSON you will get a response from GetFunction ( ) call with a JSON object. You can customize this JSON using SetFunction ( ). The Object includes properties and its values. An intent represents a mapping between what a user says and what action should be taken by the chatbot. Actions correspond to the steps the chatbot will take when specific intents are triggered by user inputs and may have parameters for specifying detailed information about it. Intent detection is typically formulated as sentence classification in which single or multiple intent labels are predicted for each sentence. An entity is in a dataset for extracting parameter values from natural language inputs (Adamopoulou, E. and Moussiades, L., 2020).

ACKNOWLEDGEMENT

The author thanks the SAP University Alliances (UA) for providing the SAP Conversational AI platform and curriculum materials. The author thanks Wroblewski, D. (2021), and Margo, J. (2023) for their tutorials.

REFERENCES

Adamopoulou, E. and Moussiades, L. (2020). An Overview of Chatbot Technology, *Proceedings of IFIP International Conference on Artificial Intelligence Applications and Innovations*, pp 373–383.

Margo, J. (2023). https://developers.sap.com/tutorial-navigator.html

Pearson, B. L. (2021). The Complete Guide to Working With JSON, https://www.nylas.com/blog/the-complete-guide-to-working-with-json/

Wroblewski, D. (2021). Web URL: https://developers.sap.com/tutorials/cai-bot-getting-started.html#d7afb8eb-abda-4b89-9505-2e5beef7dad2

AUTHOR INDEX

Bärtschi, S. ... 163
Bosbach, J. ... 37
Chau, T. ... 153
Cheung, J. ... 153
Cueva, R. ... 61
Currie, W. ... 193
Edwards, M. ... 11
Gebbing, P. ... 29, 37
Günaydın, G. ... 131
Günthardt, L. ... 163
Helms, M. ... 37
Hirokawa, N. ... 141
Hirvonen, M. ... 69
Hudec, M. ... 174
Ivic, A. ... 169, 179
Jacucci, G. ... 95
Jiang, Z. ... 21
Kekwaletswe, R. ... 184
Kijanovic, S. ... 53, 169, 179
Kishimoto, M. ... 141
Komosar, A. ... 53, 169, 179
Koprivica, S. ... 169, 179
Korba, S. ... 136
Krey, M. ... 163
Kwok, R. ... 153
Lattemann, C. ... 29, 37
Leckebusch, J. ... 45
Limaj, E. ... 197
Louw, P. ... 106
Mandic, V. ... 53
Mariano, H. ... 87
Mináriková, E. ... 174
Modiba, M. ... 184
Molnár, B. ... 136, 174
Moloney, M. ... 136
Néto, J. ... 87
Neumannova, A. ... 158
Nikolic, D. ... 53
Osaragi, T. ... 141
Ozturk, O. ... 3
Pergl, R. ... 78
Petrin, N. ... 87
Pisoni, G. ... 136, 174
Podoynitsyna, K. ... 116
Pokorný, J. ... 78
Rybola, Z. ... 78
Sabani, R. ... 163
Sardinha-da Silva, V. ... 106
Sari, B. ... 147
Schrijen, M. ... 45, 116
Seddon, J. ... 193
Sedláková, D. ... 174
Skaftadottir, H. ... 174
Smit, D. ... 106
Smuts, H. ... 11, 106
Song, B. ... 21
Stefanovic, D. ... 169, 179
Taibi, D. ... 169, 179
Tupia, M. ... 61
Umel, A. ... 37
Valenta, M. ... 78
Van der Pas, M. ... 45, 116
Verástegui, F. ... 61
Vučetić, M. ... 174
Vuckovic, T. ... 53
Waechter, I. ... 106
Wang, M. ... 201
Yıldırım, S. ... 3, 131, 147
Zhou, Q. ... 21
Zikán, J. ... 78

International Association for Development of the Information Society (IADIS)
Rua Sao Sebastiao Da Pedreira
No. 100, 30, 1050-209
Lisbon, Portugal

ISBN 979-8-3313-0140-8

CURRAN ASSOCIATES INC.
proceedings.com

International Conferences ICT, Society, and Human Beings (ICT2020); Connected Smart Cities (CSC2020); and Web Based Communities and Social Media (WBC2020)

Held at MCCSIS 2020 (Held online due to COVID-19)

Lisbon, Portugal
21 - 25 July 2020

iadis